7/01

Teen

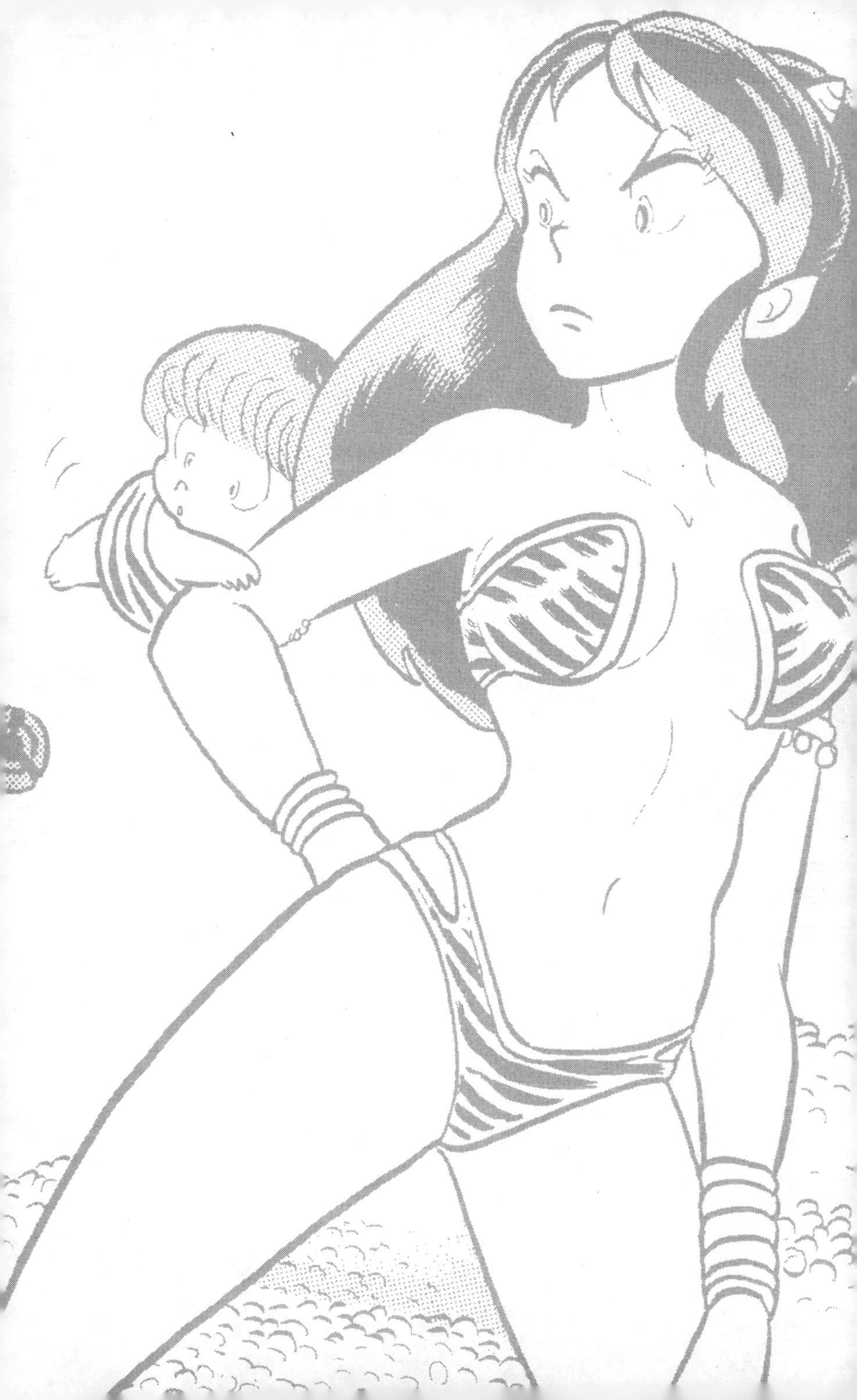

VIZ GRAPHIC NOVEL

THE RETURN OF
LUM * URUSEI YATSURA™
TROUBLE TIMES TEN

This volume contains THE RETURN OF LUM * URUSEI YATSURA PART TWO #6 through THE RETURN OF LUM * URUSEI YATSURA PART THREE #1 in their entirety.

**STORY AND ART BY
RUMIKO TAKAHASHI**

English Adaptation/Gerard Jones & Mari Morimoto
Touch-Up Art & Lettering/Mary Kelleher
Cover Design/Viz Graphics
Editor/Annette Roman
Assistant Editor/Toshifumi Yoshida

Senior Editor/Trish Ledoux
Editor-in-Chief/Satoru Fujii
Publisher/Seiji Horibuchi

Printed in Canada

Published by Viz Communications, Inc.
P.O. Box 77010 • San Francisco, CA 94107

10 9 8 7 6 5 4 3 2 1
First printing, February 1997

VIZ GRAPHIC NOVEL

THE RETURN OF LUM *
URUSEI YATSURA™

TROUBLE
TIMES TEN

STORY & ART BY
RUMIKO TAKAHASHI

CONTENTS

PART ONE
ATARU CALLS IT QUITS!

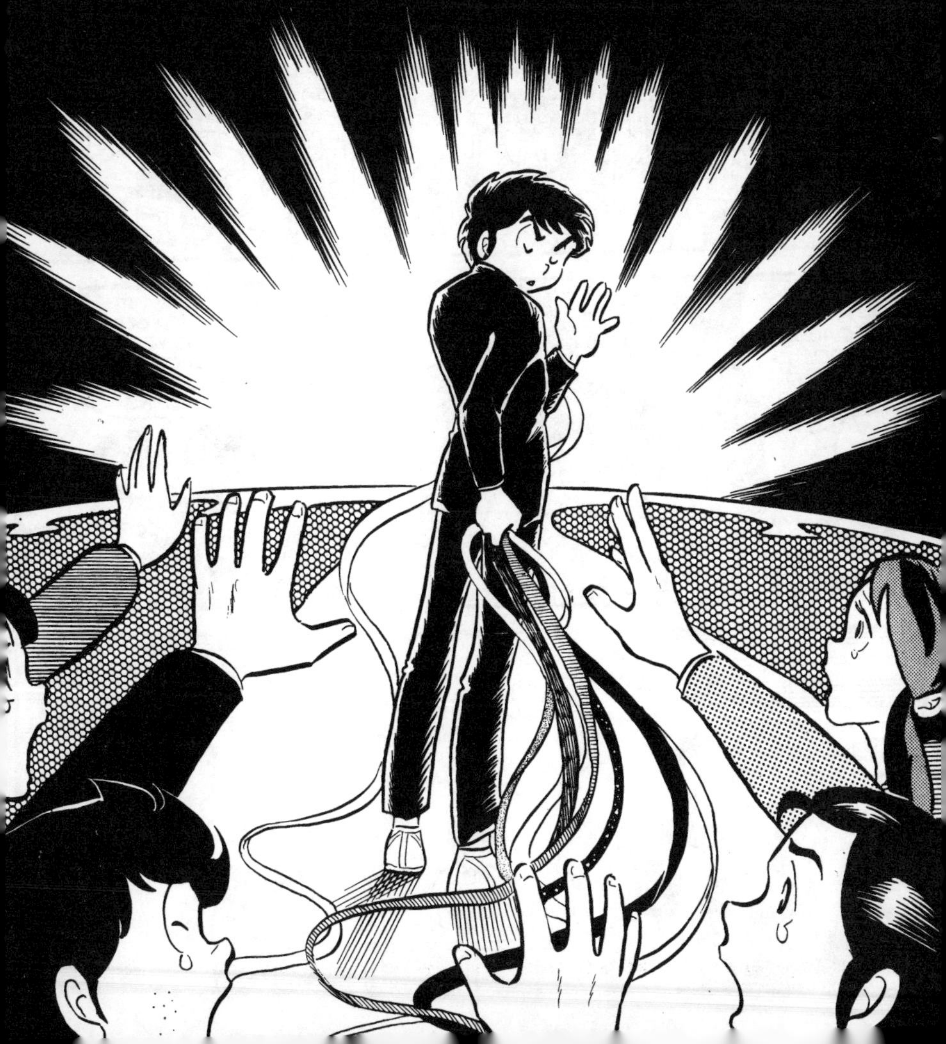

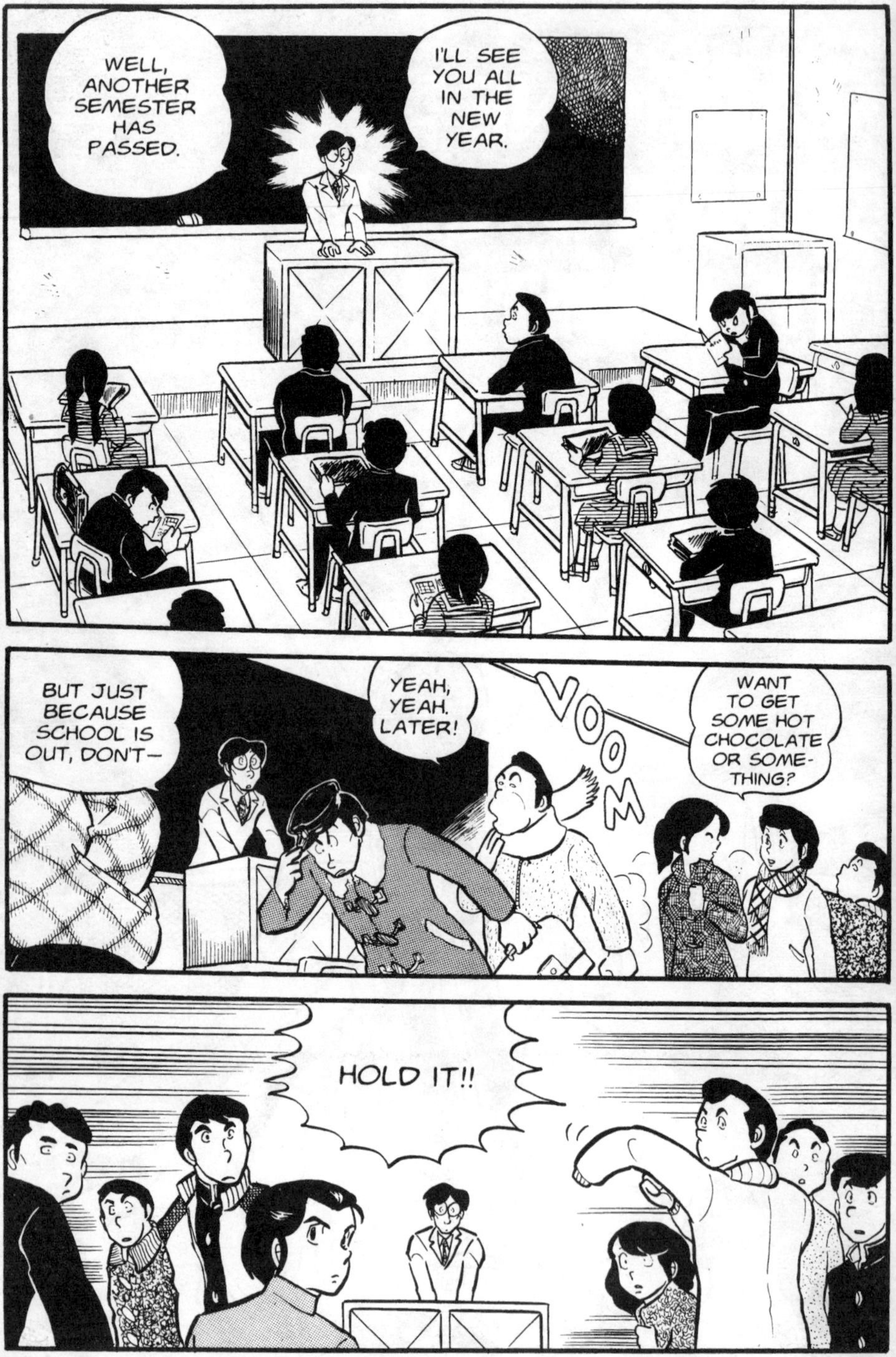
WELL, ANOTHER SEMESTER HAS PASSED.
I'LL SEE YOU ALL IN THE NEW YEAR.
BUT JUST BECAUSE SCHOOL IS OUT, DON'T—
YEAH, YEAH. LATER!
VOOOM
WANT TO GET SOME HOT CHOCOLATE OR SOME-THING?
HOLD IT!!

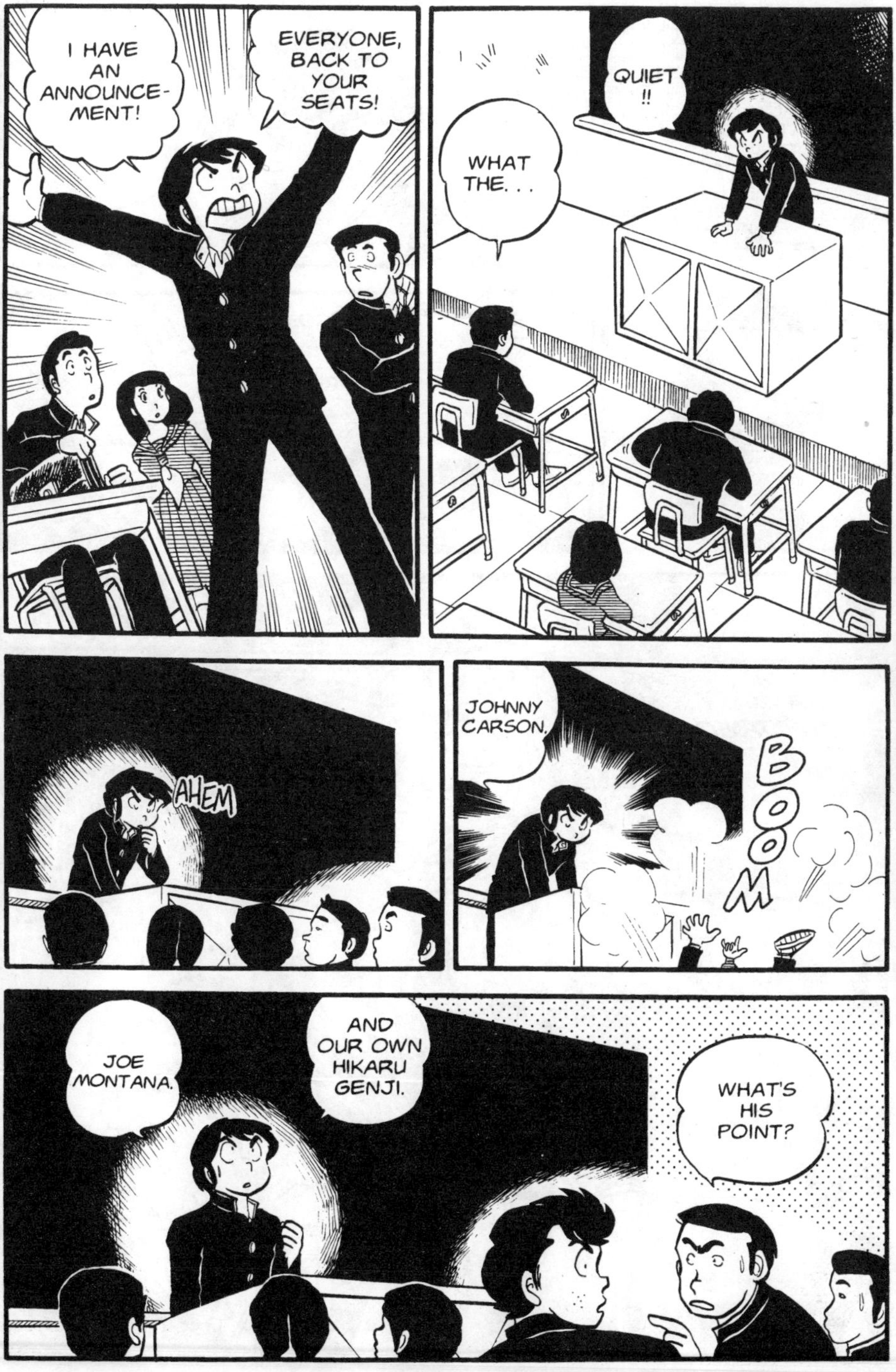
I HAVE AN ANNOUNCE-MENT!
EVERYONE, BACK TO YOUR SEATS!
WHAT THE. . .
QUIET !!
AHEM
JOHNNY CARSON.
BOOOM
JOE MONTANA.
AND OUR OWN HIKARU GENJI.
WHAT'S HIS POINT?

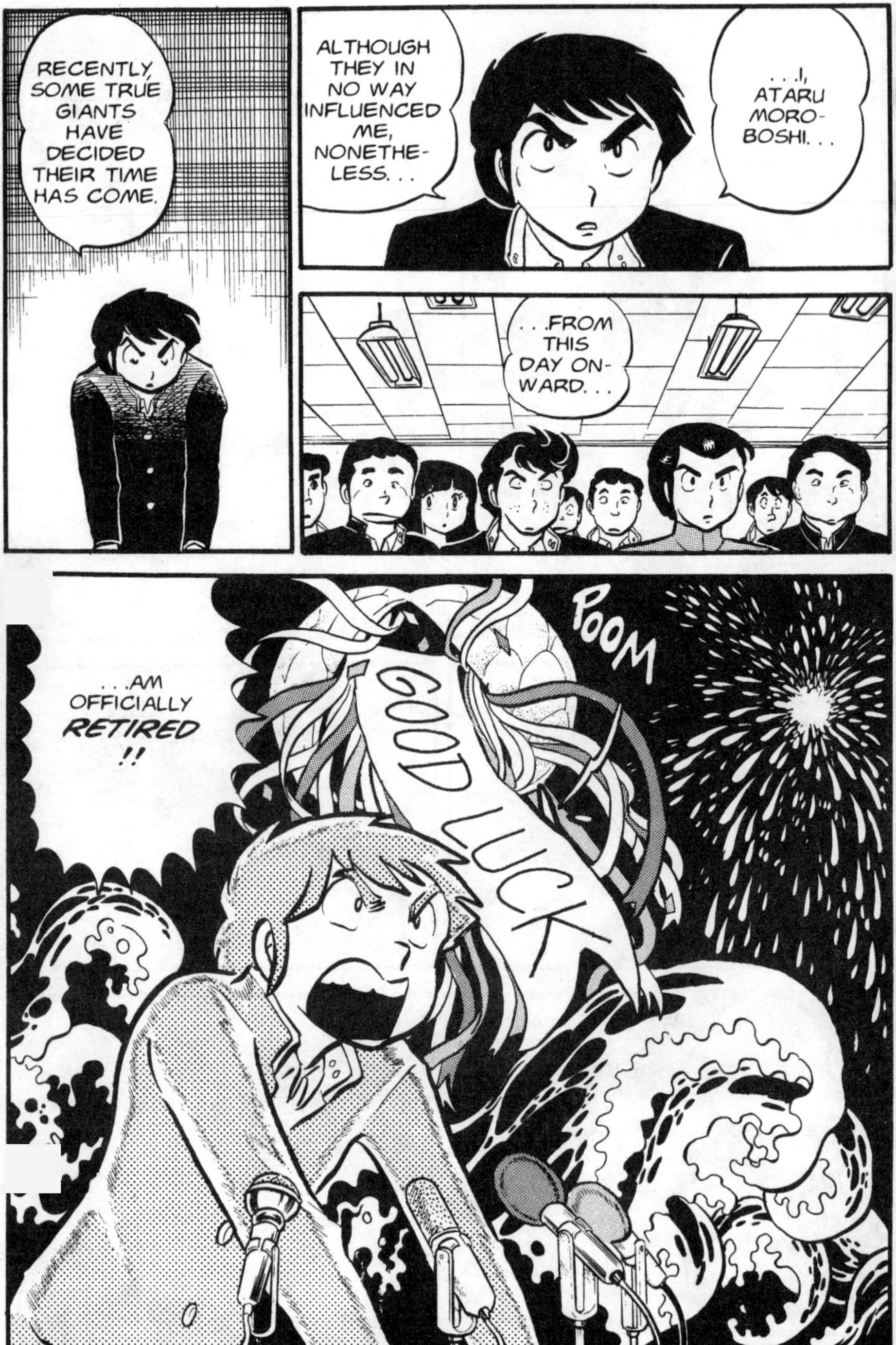
RECENTLY, SOME TRUE GIANTS HAVE DECIDED THEIR TIME HAS COME.
ALTHOUGH THEY IN NO WAY INFLUENCED ME, NONETHELESS. . .
. . .I, ATARU MOROBOSHI. . .
. . .FROM THIS DAY ONWARD. . .
. . .AM OFFICIALLY RETIRED !!
POOM
GOOD LUCK

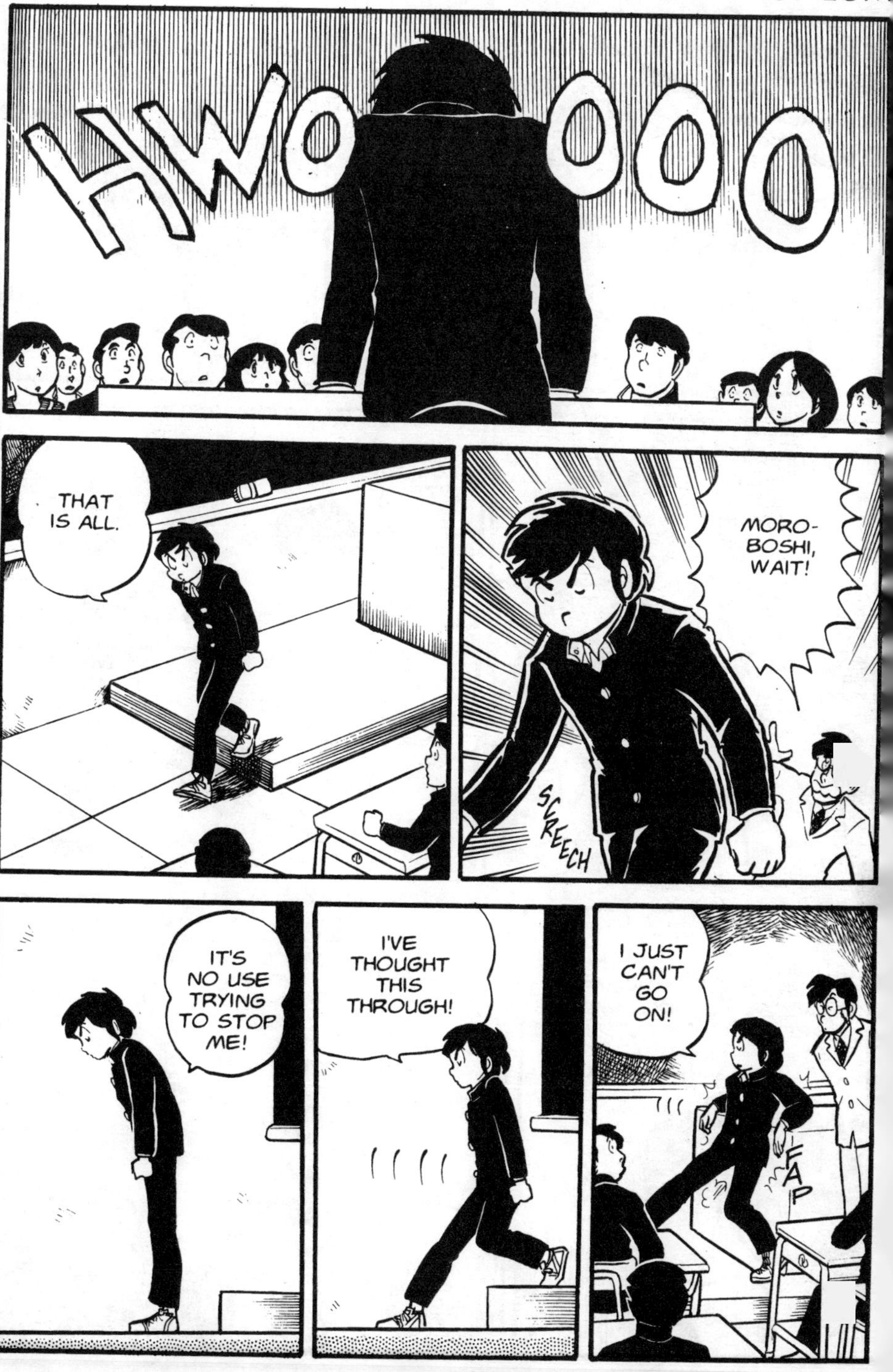
HWOOOOO
THAT IS ALL.
MORO-BOSHI, WAIT!
SCREECH
IT'S NO USE TRYING TO STOP ME!
I'VE THOUGHT THIS THROUGH!
I JUST CAN'T GO ON!
FAP

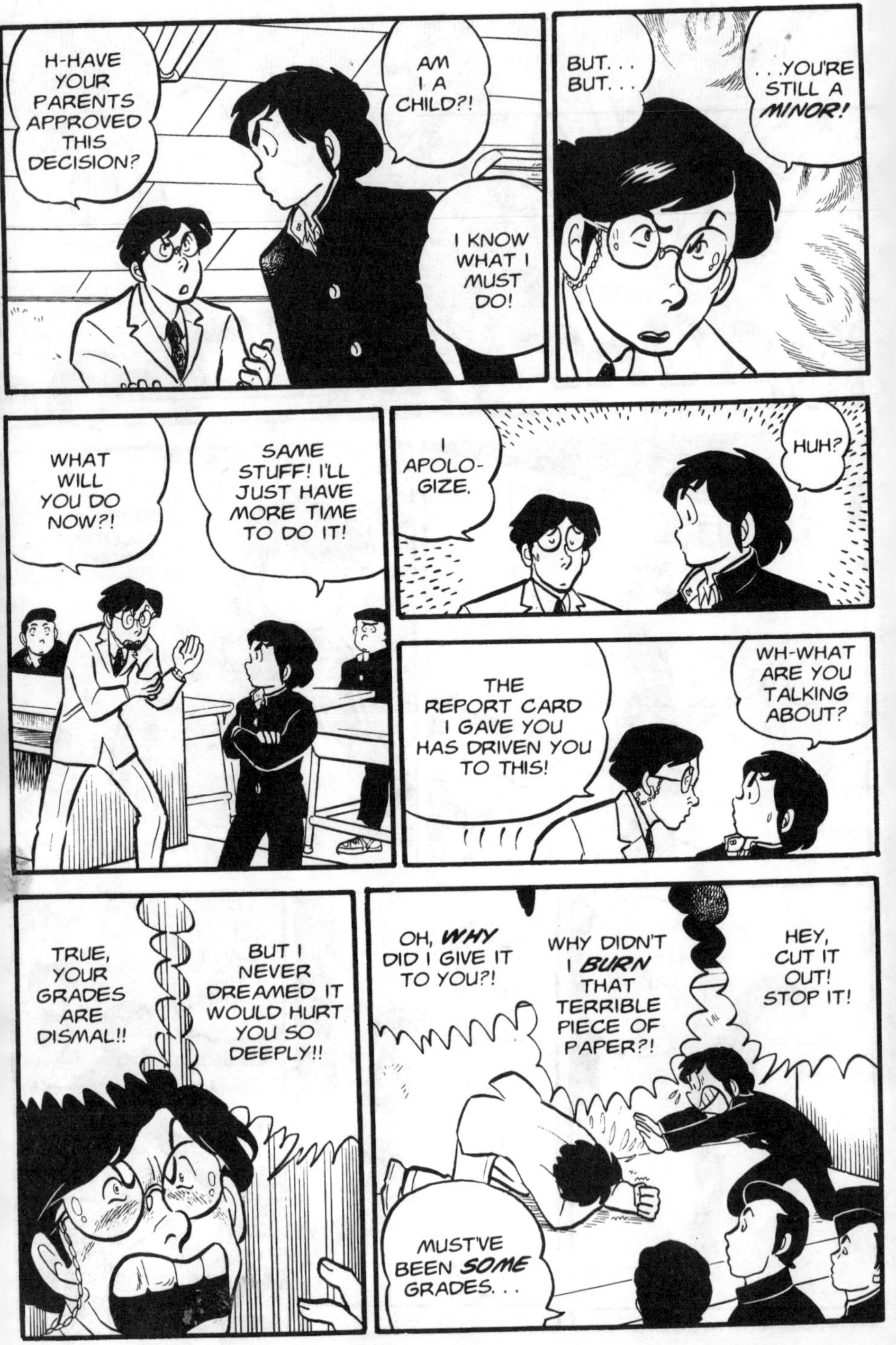
H-HAVE YOUR PARENTS APPROVED THIS DECISION?
AM I A CHILD?!
I KNOW WHAT I MUST DO!
BUT... BUT...
...YOU'RE STILL A *MINOR!*
WHAT WILL YOU DO NOW?!
SAME STUFF! I'LL JUST HAVE MORE TIME TO DO IT!
I APOLOGIZE.
HUH?
THE REPORT CARD I GAVE YOU HAS DRIVEN YOU TO THIS!
WH-WHAT ARE YOU TALKING ABOUT?
TRUE, YOUR GRADES ARE DISMAL!!
BUT I NEVER DREAMED IT WOULD HURT YOU SO DEEPLY!!
OH, *WHY* DID I GIVE IT TO YOU?!
WHY DIDN'T I *BURN* THAT TERRIBLE PIECE OF PAPER?!
HEY, CUT IT OUT! STOP IT!
MUST'VE BEEN *SOME* GRADES...

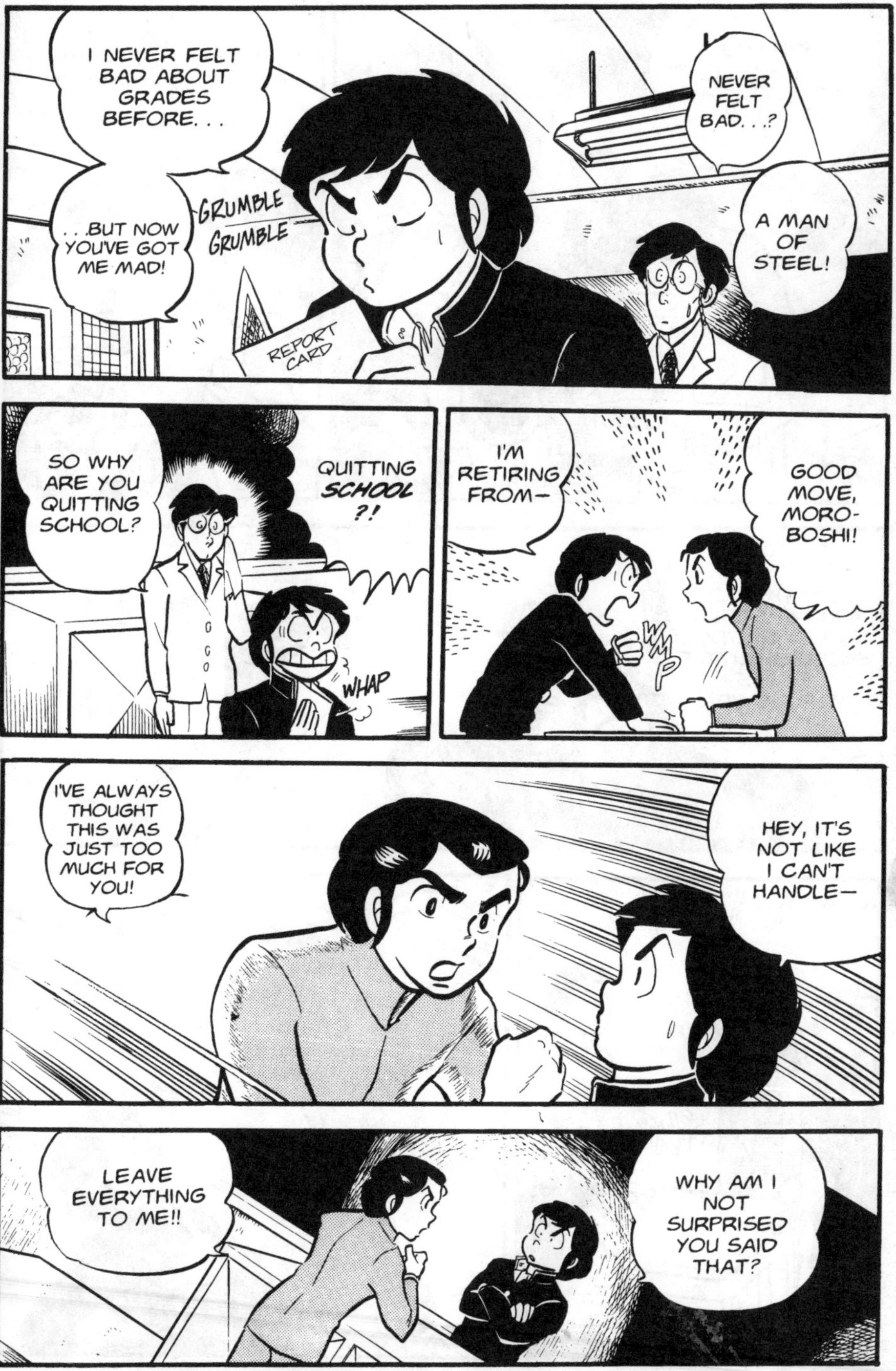
I NEVER FELT BAD ABOUT GRADES BEFORE. . .
. . .BUT NOW YOU'VE GOT ME MAD!
GRUMBLE GRUMBLE
REPORT CARD
NEVER FELT BAD. . .?
A MAN OF STEEL!
SO WHY ARE YOU QUITTING SCHOOL?
QUITTING SCHOOL ?!
WHAP
I'M RETIRING FROM—
WMP
GOOD MOVE, MORO-BOSHI!
I'VE ALWAYS THOUGHT THIS WAS JUST TOO MUCH FOR YOU!
HEY, IT'S NOT LIKE I CAN'T HANDLE—
LEAVE EVERYTHING TO ME!!
WHY AM I NOT SURPRISED YOU SAID THAT?

DID YOU HEAR HIM, LUM? NOW YOU CAN GO OUT WITH ME!!

WHAT?! ATARU'S BREAKING HIS ENGAGEMENT TO LUM?!

AS OF THIS MOMENT, SHE IS MINE!

YOURS? NEVER!

LUM! THINK OF YOUR CHILDREN! WHAT NASTY, SNOBBISH LITTLE BRATS THEY'LL BE!

BETTER THAT THAN THE FAT, CRUDE, AND STUPID OFFSPRING OF DORKS LIKE THESE!

GRRR

SUMP

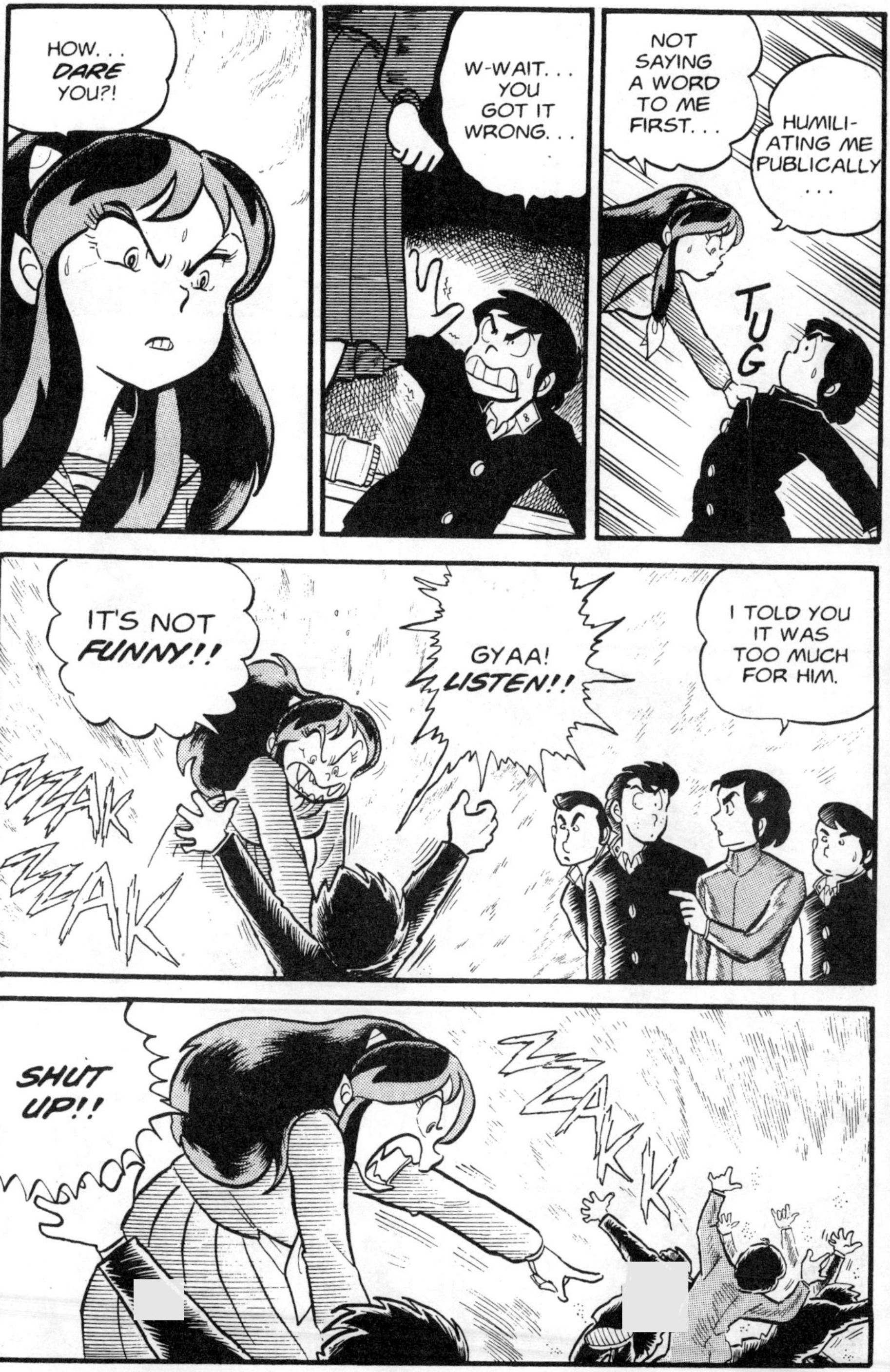
HOW... DARE YOU?!
W-WAIT... YOU GOT IT WRONG...
NOT SAYING A WORD TO ME FIRST...
HUMILI-ATING ME PUBLICALLY...
TUG
IT'S NOT FUNNY!!
GYAA! LISTEN!!
I TOLD YOU IT WAS TOO MUCH FOR HIM.
ZZAK
ZZAK
SHUT UP!!
ZZAKK

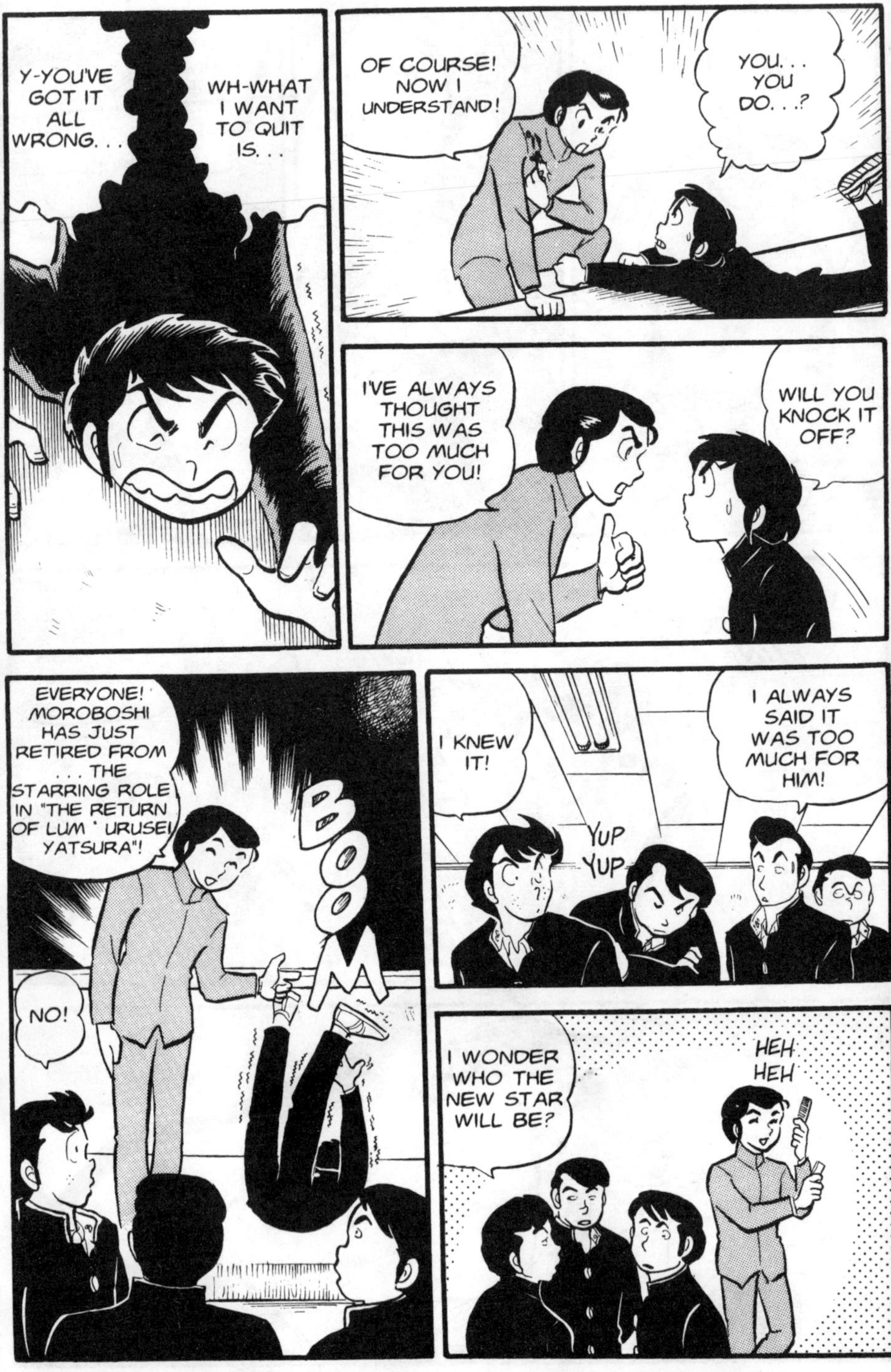
Y-YOU'VE GOT IT ALL WRONG. . .
WH-WHAT I WANT TO QUIT IS. . .
OF COURSE! NOW I UNDERSTAND!
YOU. . . YOU DO. . .?
I'VE ALWAYS THOUGHT THIS WAS TOO MUCH FOR YOU!
WILL YOU KNOCK IT OFF?
EVERYONE! MOROBOSHI HAS JUST RETIRED FROM . . . THE STARRING ROLE IN "THE RETURN OF LUM * URUSEI YATSURA"!
BOOOM
NO!
I KNEW IT!
I ALWAYS SAID IT WAS TOO MUCH FOR HIM!
YUP YUP
I WONDER WHO THE NEW STAR WILL BE?
HEH HEH

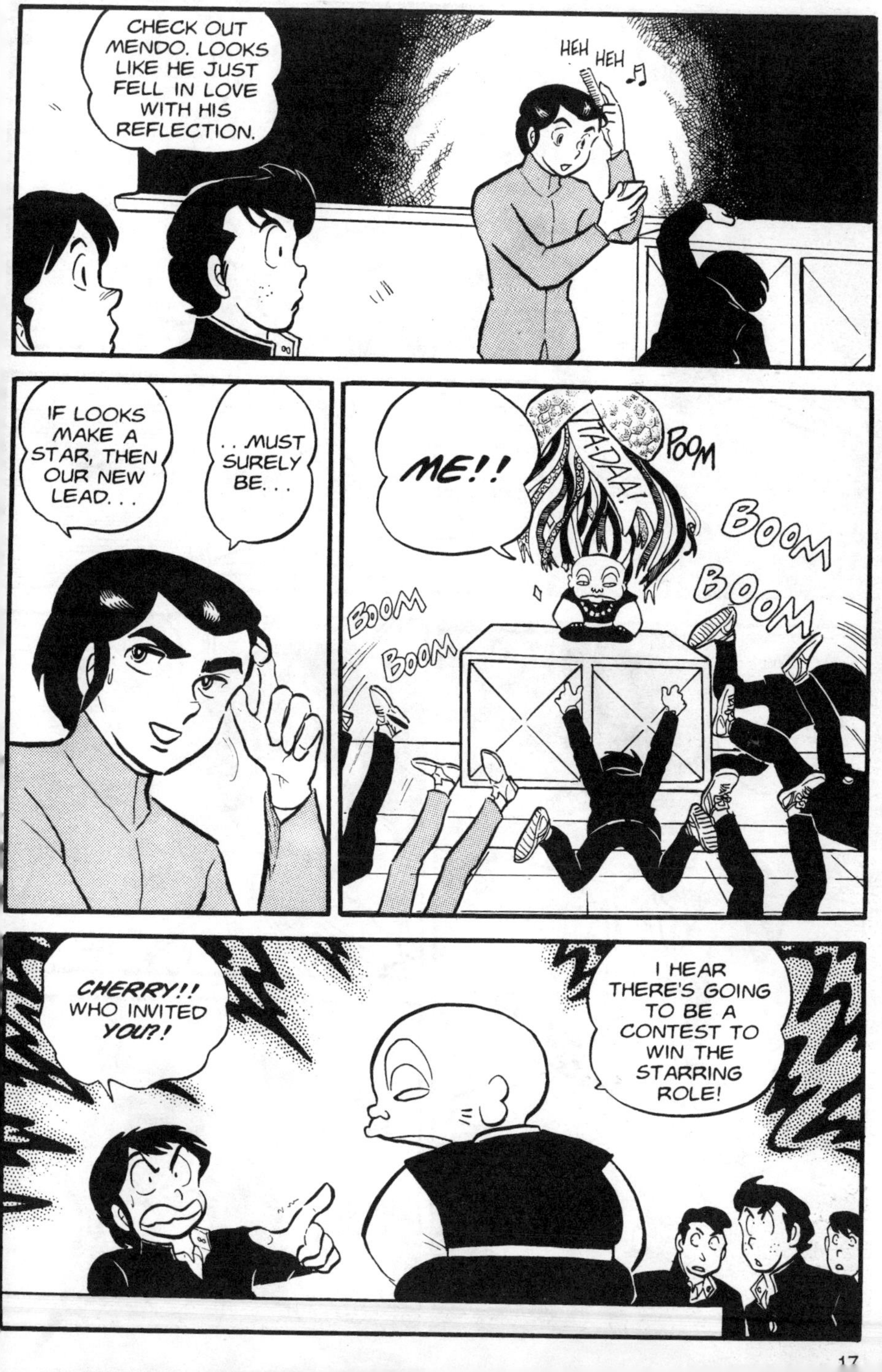
CHECK OUT MENDO. LOOKS LIKE HE JUST FELL IN LOVE WITH HIS REFLECTION.
HEH HEH ♪
IF LOOKS MAKE A STAR, THEN OUR NEW LEAD...
...MUST SURELY BE...
ME!!
TA-DAA!
POOM
BOOM BOOM
BOOM BOOM
CHERRY!! WHO INVITED YOU?!
I HEAR THERE'S GOING TO BE A CONTEST TO WIN THE STARRING ROLE!

AND WITH THIS PHYSIQUE . . .

THIS LOVELY FACE. . .

URK! GONNA HURRL!

BOP

HEY!

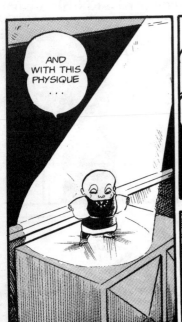

MY OWN UNCLE, EMBARRASSING ME LIKE THIS!

NURSE SAKURA! HOORAY!

"STARRING"? YOU SHOULDN'T EVEN BE IN THIS SCENE!

WHAT ARE YOU DOING HERE, SAKURA?

. . .

18

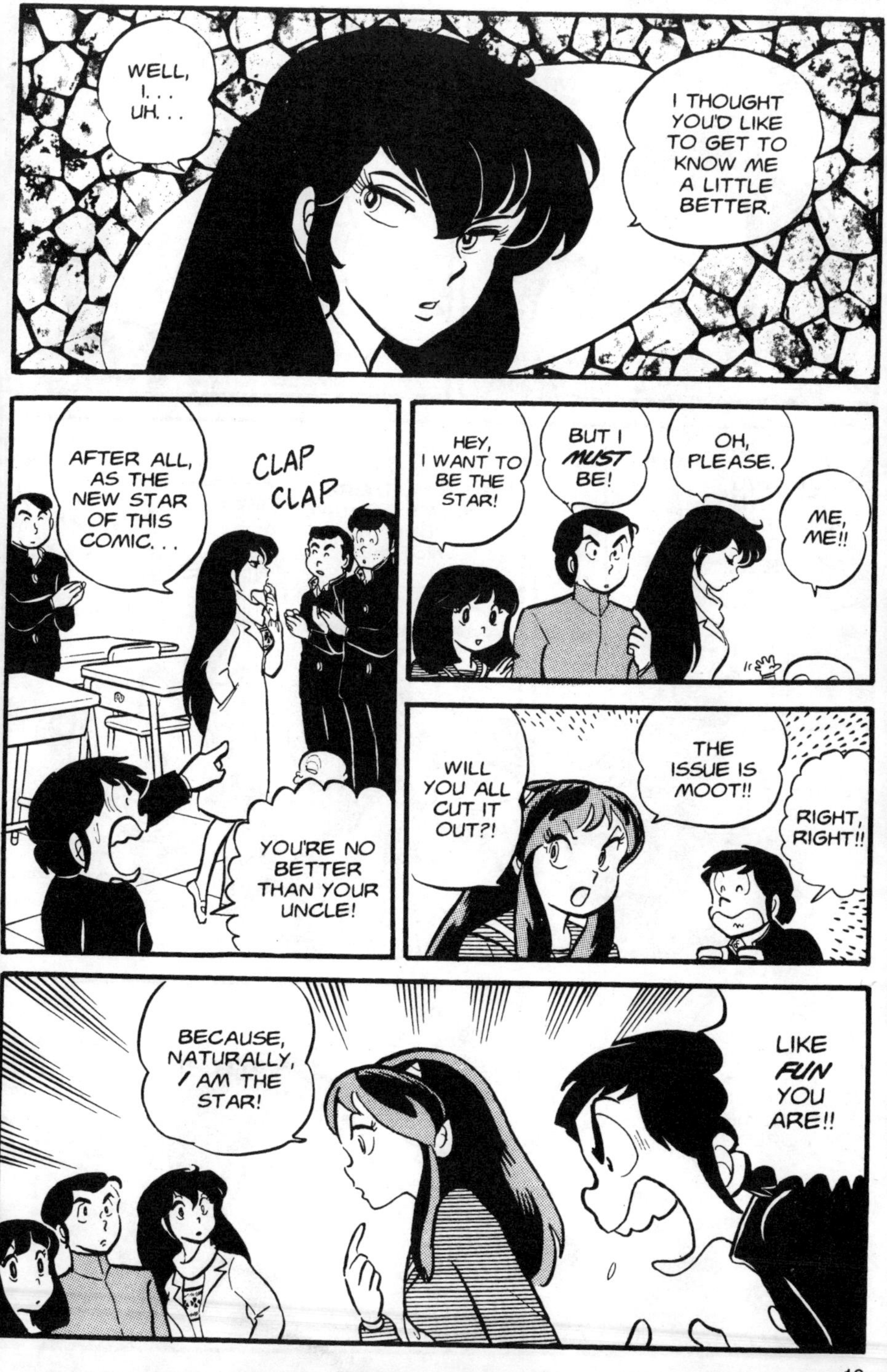
WELL, I. . . UH. . .
I THOUGHT YOU'D LIKE TO GET TO KNOW ME A LITTLE BETTER.
AFTER ALL, AS THE NEW STAR OF THIS COMIC. . .
CLAP CLAP
YOU'RE NO BETTER THAN YOUR UNCLE!
HEY, I WANT TO BE THE STAR!
BUT I *MUST* BE!
OH, PLEASE.
ME, ME!!
WILL YOU ALL CUT IT OUT?!
THE ISSUE IS MOOT!!
RIGHT, RIGHT!!
BECAUSE, NATURALLY, *I* AM THE STAR!
LIKE *FUN* YOU ARE!!

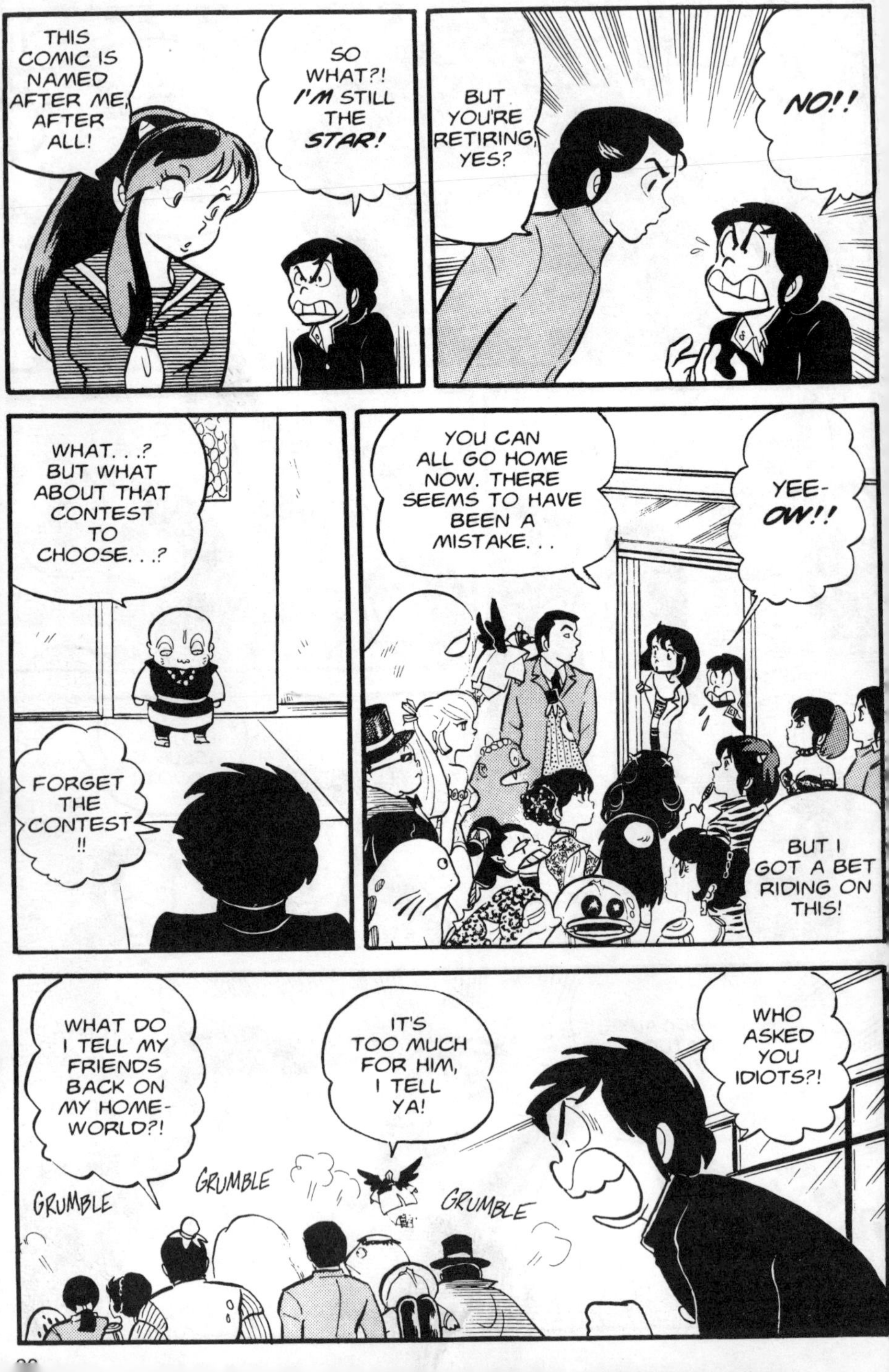
THIS COMIC IS NAMED AFTER ME, AFTER ALL!
SO WHAT?! I'M STILL THE STAR!
BUT YOU'RE RETIRING, YES?
NO!!
WHAT...? BUT WHAT ABOUT THAT CONTEST TO CHOOSE...?
FORGET THE CONTEST!!
YOU CAN ALL GO HOME NOW. THERE SEEMS TO HAVE BEEN A MISTAKE...
YEE-OW!!
BUT I GOT A BET RIDING ON THIS!
WHAT DO I TELL MY FRIENDS BACK ON MY HOME-WORLD?!
GRUMBLE
GRUMBLE
IT'S TOO MUCH FOR HIM, I TELL YA!
GRUMBLE
WHO ASKED YOU IDIOTS?!

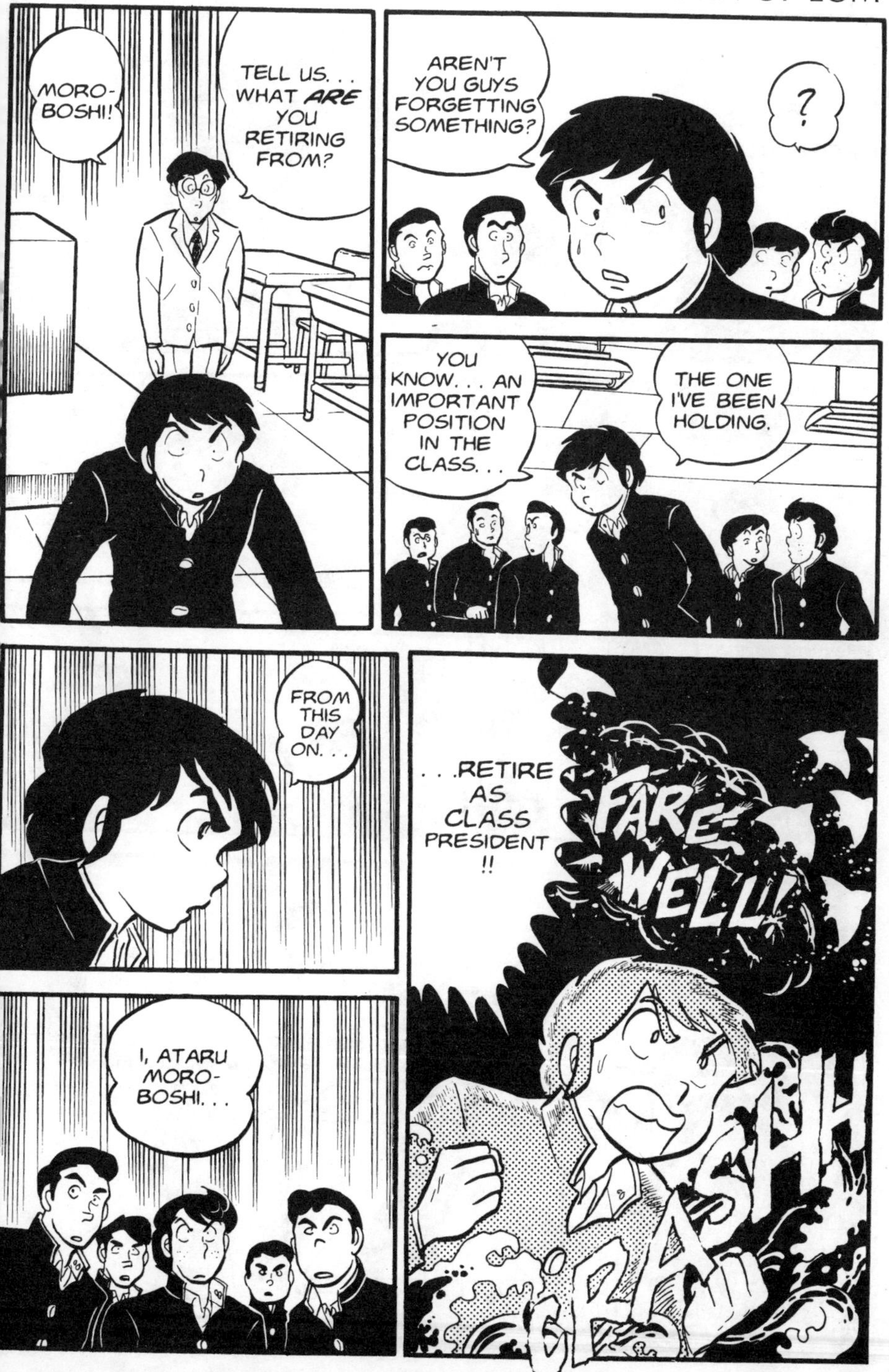
MORO-BOSHI!
TELL US. . . WHAT *ARE* YOU RETIRING FROM?
AREN'T YOU GUYS FORGETTING SOMETHING?
?
YOU KNOW. . . AN IMPORTANT POSITION IN THE CLASS. . .
THE ONE I'VE BEEN HOLDING.
FROM THIS DAY ON. . .
I, ATARU MORO-BOSHI. . .
. . .RETIRE AS CLASS PRESIDENT !!
FARE-WELL!!
CRASHH

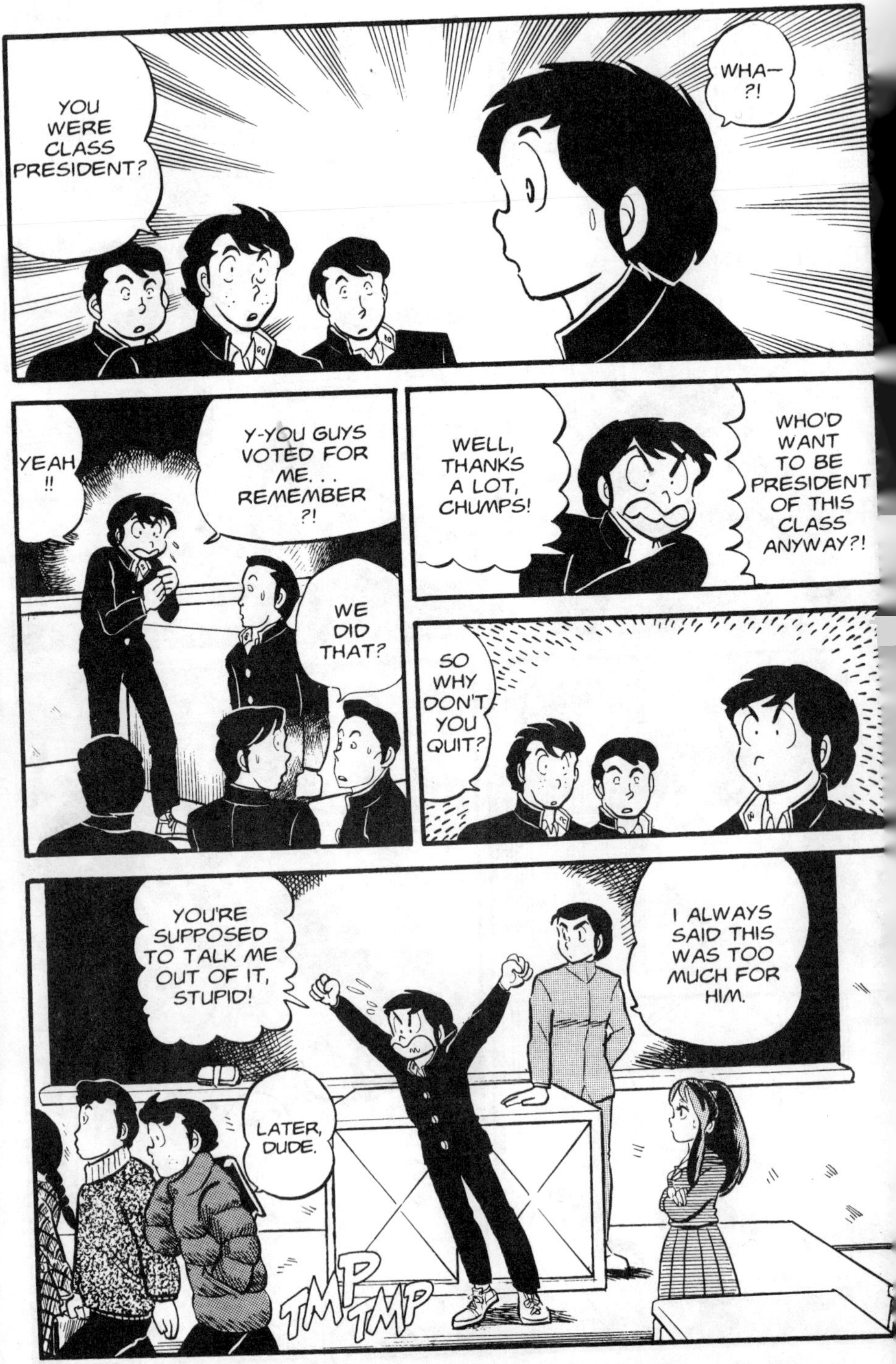
YOU WERE CLASS PRESIDENT?
WHA— ?!
YEAH !!
Y-YOU GUYS VOTED FOR ME. . . REMEMBER ?!
WE DID THAT?
WELL, THANKS A LOT, CHUMPS!
WHO'D WANT TO BE PRESIDENT OF THIS CLASS ANYWAY?!
SO WHY DON'T YOU QUIT?
YOU'RE SUPPOSED TO TALK ME OUT OF IT, STUPID!
I ALWAYS SAID THIS WAS TOO MUCH FOR HIM.
LATER, DUDE.
TMP TMP

PART TWO
FORTUNE KOOKIE

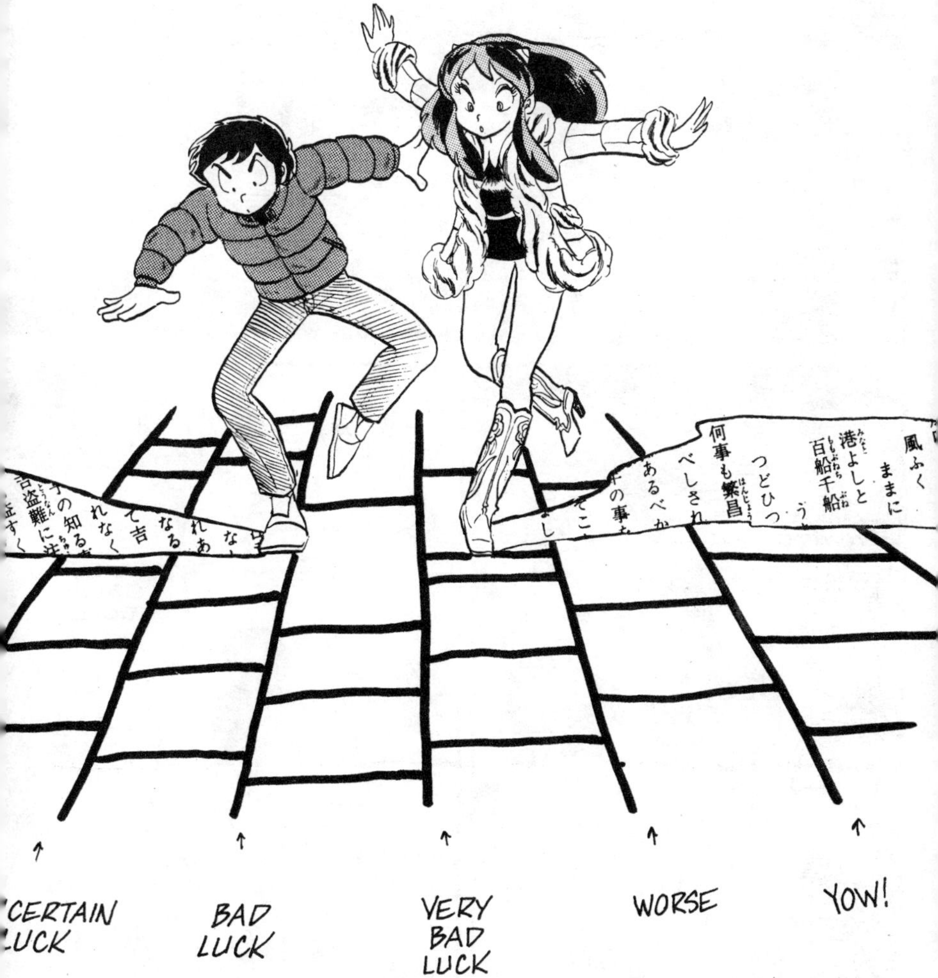
CERTAIN LUCK
BAD LUCK
VERY BAD LUCK
WORSE
YOW!

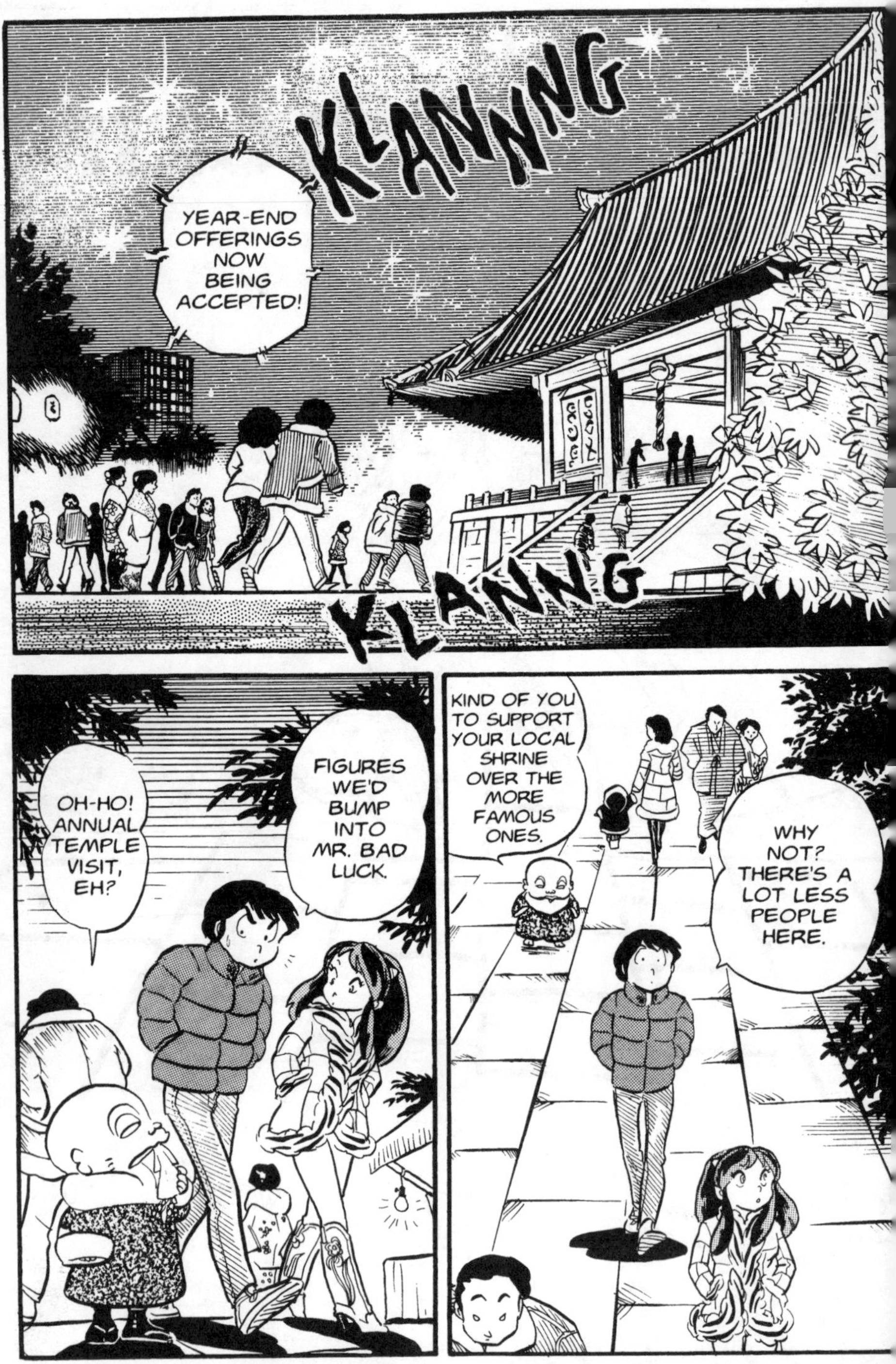
YEAR-END OFFERINGS NOW BEING ACCEPTED!
KLANNNG
KLANNG
OH-HO! ANNUAL TEMPLE VISIT, EH?
FIGURES WE'D BUMP INTO MR. BAD LUCK.
KIND OF YOU TO SUPPORT YOUR LOCAL SHRINE OVER THE MORE FAMOUS ONES.
WHY NOT? THERE'S A LOT LESS PEOPLE HERE.

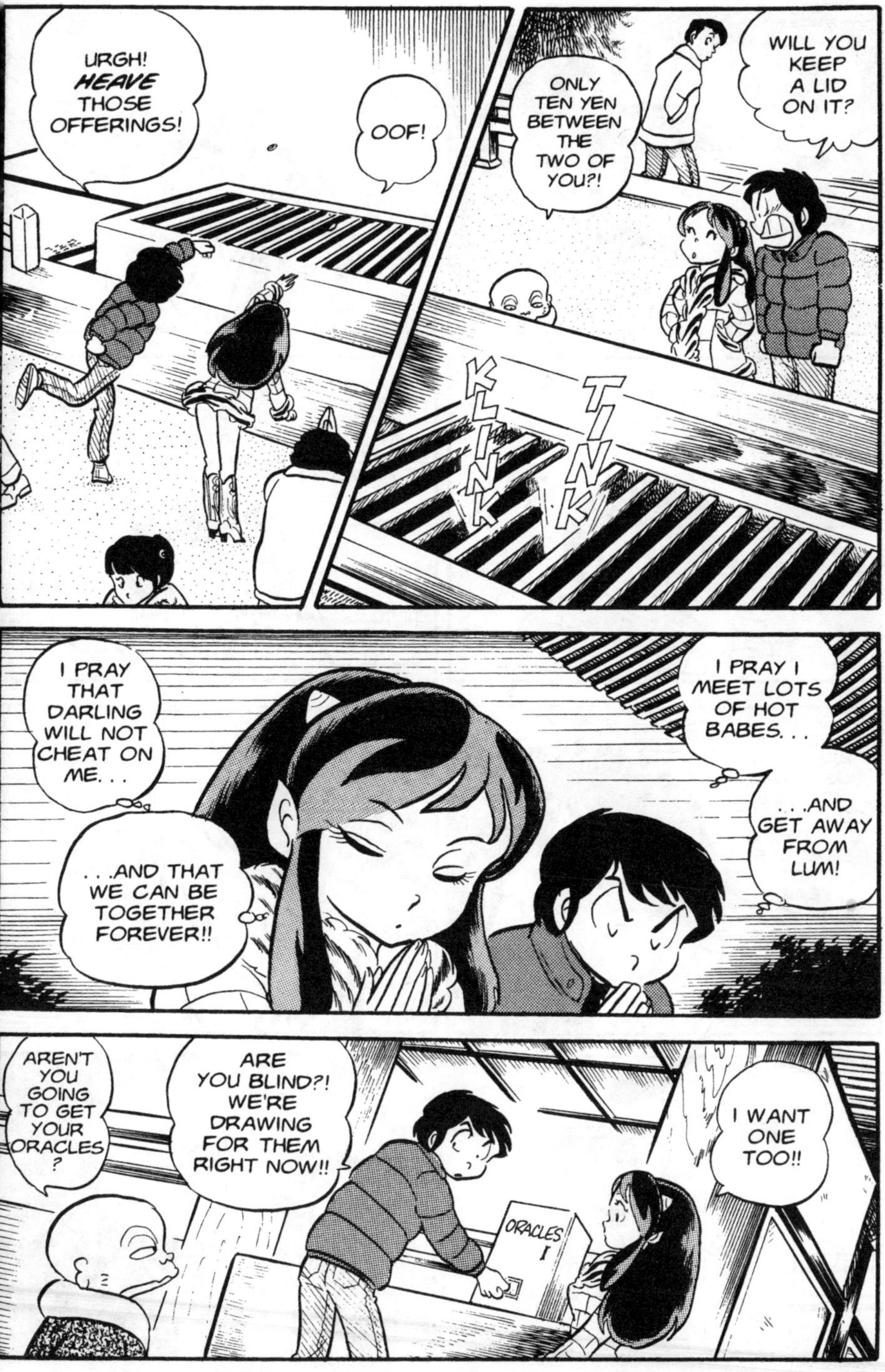
URGH! HEAVE THOSE OFFERINGS!
OOF!
ONLY TEN YEN BETWEEN THE TWO OF YOU?!
WILL YOU KEEP A LID ON IT?
KLINK
TINK
I PRAY THAT DARLING WILL NOT CHEAT ON ME. . .
. . .AND THAT WE CAN BE TOGETHER FOREVER!!
I PRAY I MEET LOTS OF HOT BABES. . .
. . .AND GET AWAY FROM LUM!
AREN'T YOU GOING TO GET YOUR ORACLES?
ARE YOU BLIND?! WE'RE DRAWING FOR THEM RIGHT NOW!!
I WANT ONE TOO!!
ORACLES

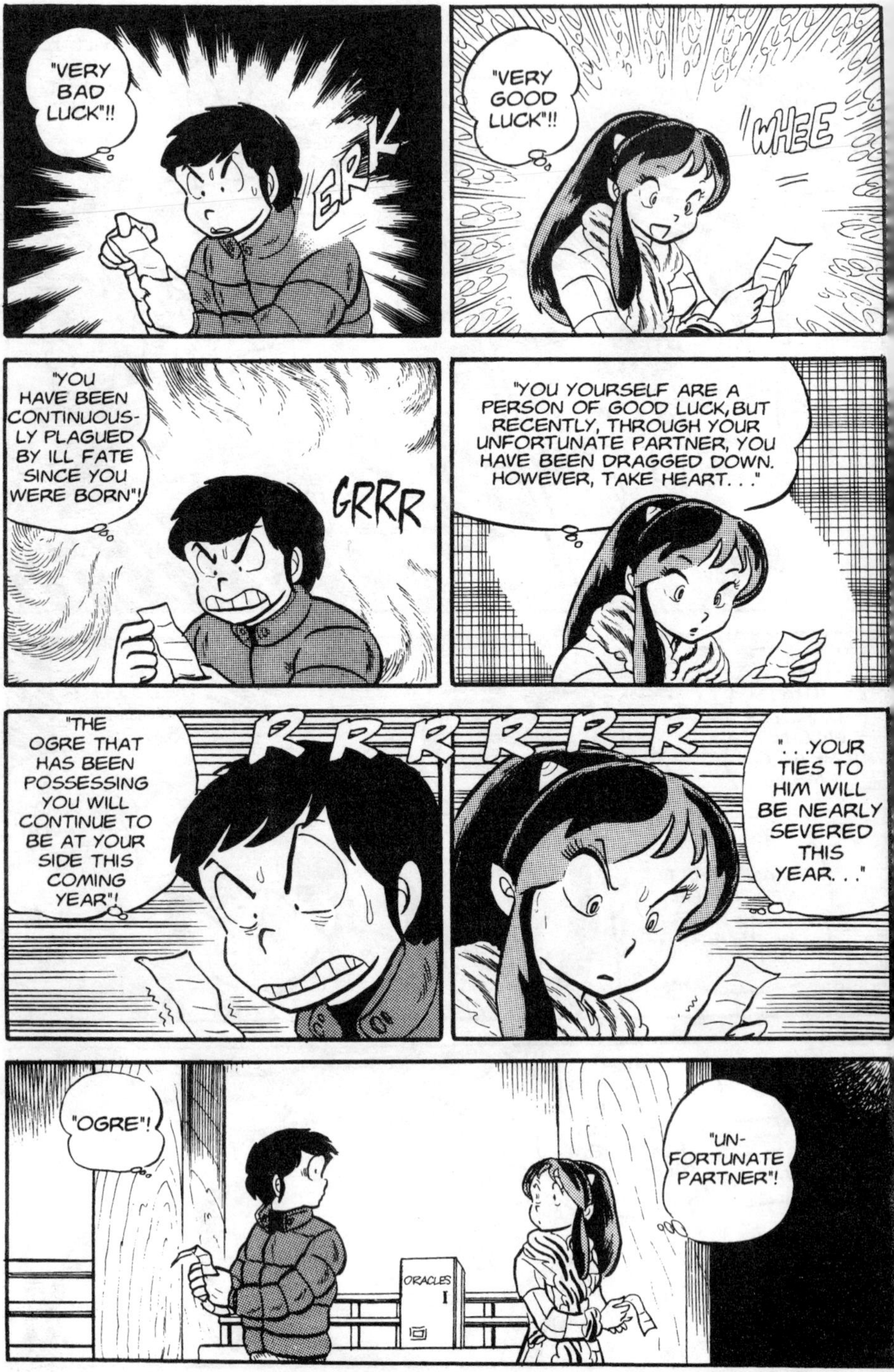

"VERY BAD LUCK"!!
ERK
"VERY GOOD LUCK"!!
WHEE
"YOU HAVE BEEN CONTINUOUSLY PLAGUED BY ILL FATE SINCE YOU WERE BORN"!
GRRR
"YOU YOURSELF ARE A PERSON OF GOOD LUCK, BUT RECENTLY, THROUGH YOUR UNFORTUNATE PARTNER, YOU HAVE BEEN DRAGGED DOWN. HOWEVER, TAKE HEART. . ."
"THE OGRE THAT HAS BEEN POSSESSING YOU WILL CONTINUE TO BE AT YOUR SIDE THIS COMING YEAR"!
RRRRRRR
". . .YOUR TIES TO HIM WILL BE NEARLY SEVERED THIS YEAR. . ."
"OGRE"!
"UN-FORTUNATE PARTNER"!
ORACLES

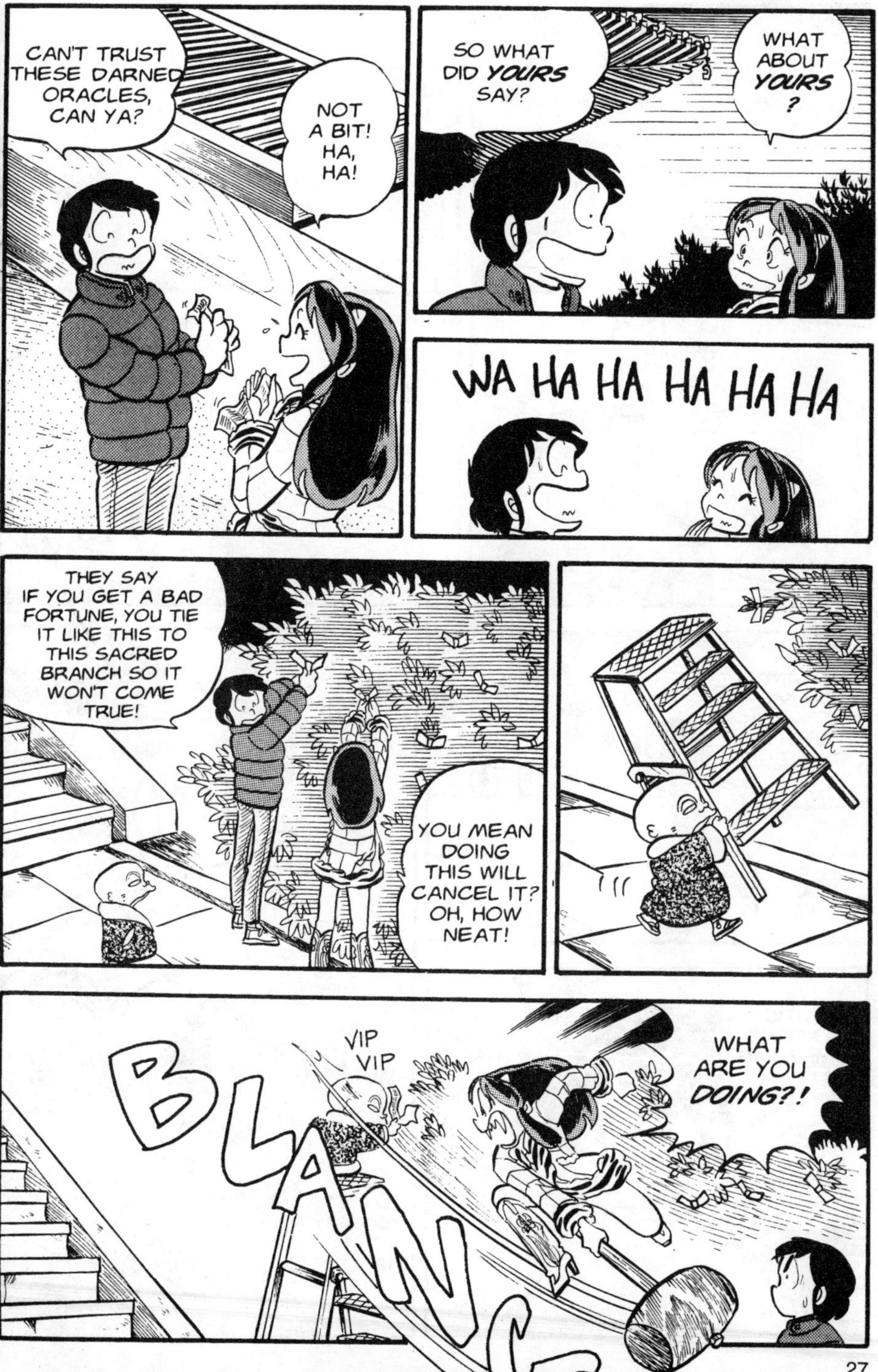
CAN'T TRUST THESE DARNED ORACLES, CAN YA?
NOT A BIT! HA, HA!
SO WHAT DID YOURS SAY?
WHAT ABOUT YOURS?
WA HA HA HA HA HA
THEY SAY IF YOU GET A BAD FORTUNE, YOU TIE IT LIKE THIS TO THIS SACRED BRANCH SO IT WON'T COME TRUE!
YOU MEAN DOING THIS WILL CANCEL IT? OH, HOW NEAT!
VIP VIP
BLAM
WHAT ARE YOU DOING?!

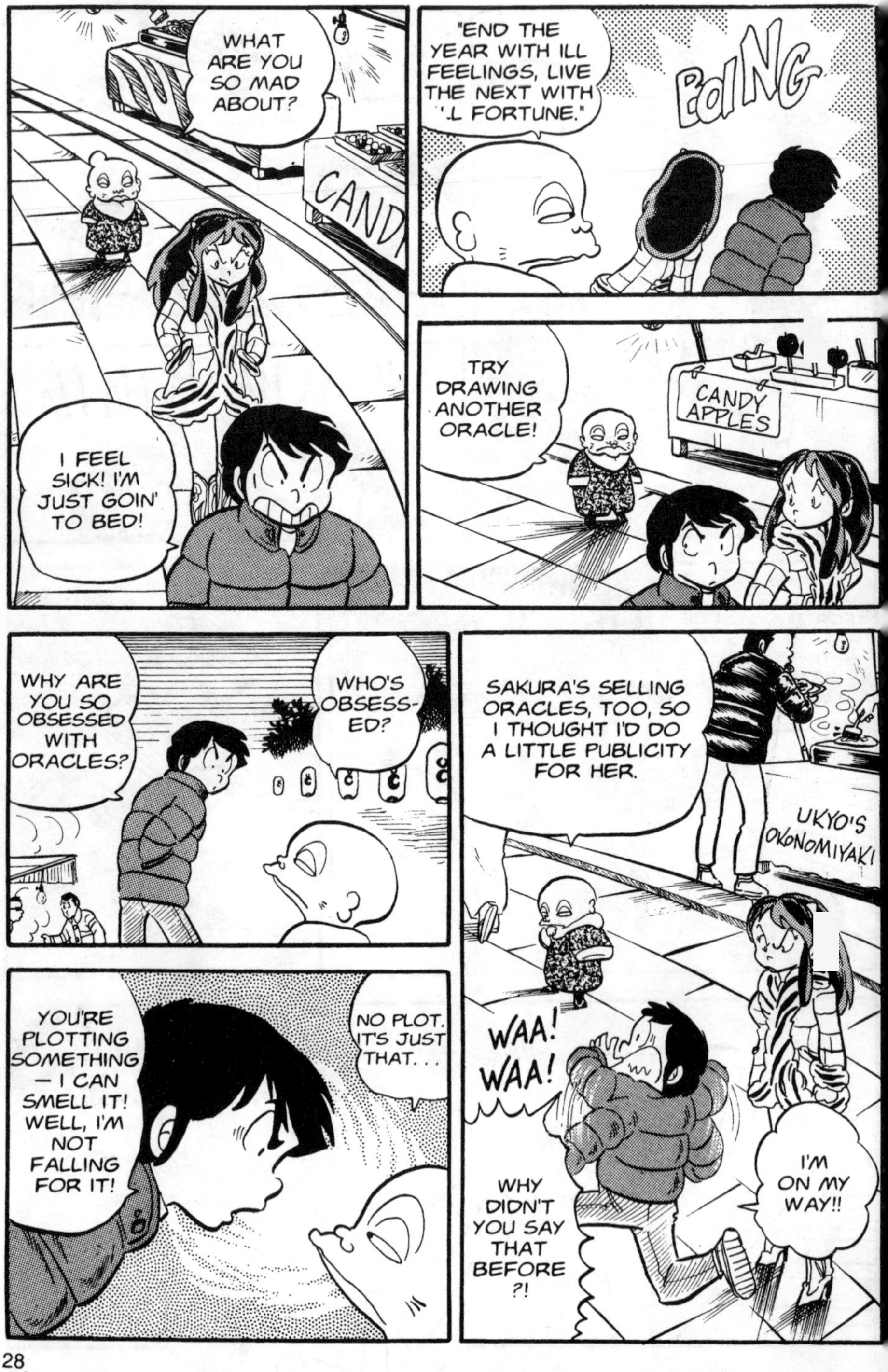

CANDY
WHAT ARE YOU SO MAD ABOUT?
I FEEL SICK! I'M JUST GOIN' TO BED!
"END THE YEAR WITH ILL FEELINGS, LIVE THE NEXT WITH '.L FORTUNE."
BOING
TRY DRAWING ANOTHER ORACLE!
CANDY APPLES
WHY ARE YOU SO OBSESSED WITH ORACLES?
WHO'S OBSESSED?
YOU'RE PLOTTING SOMETHING — I CAN SMELL IT! WELL, I'M NOT FALLING FOR IT!
NO PLOT. IT'S JUST THAT. . .
SAKURA'S SELLING ORACLES, TOO, SO I THOUGHT I'D DO A LITTLE PUBLICITY FOR HER.
UKYO'S OKONOMIYAKI
WAA! WAA!
WHY DIDN'T YOU SAY THAT BEFORE ?!
I'M ON MY WAY!!

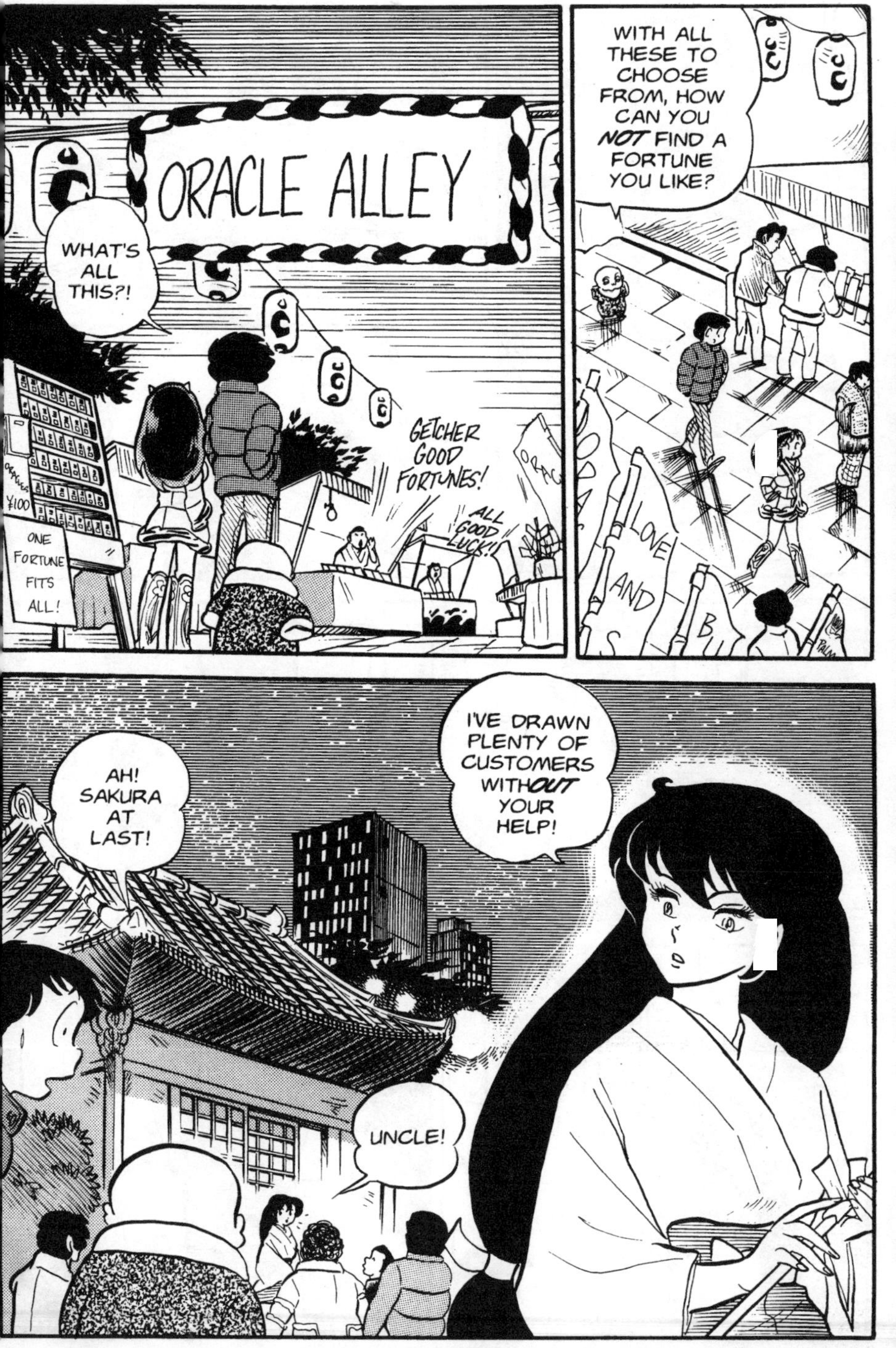
ORACLE ALLEY
WHAT'S ALL THIS?!
ORACLES ¥100
ONE FORTUNE FITS ALL!
GETCHER GOOD FORTUNES!
ALL GOOD LUCK!
WITH ALL THESE TO CHOOSE FROM, HOW CAN YOU NOT FIND A FORTUNE YOU LIKE?
AH! SAKURA AT LAST!
I'VE DRAWN PLENTY OF CUSTOMERS WITHOUT YOUR HELP!
UNCLE!

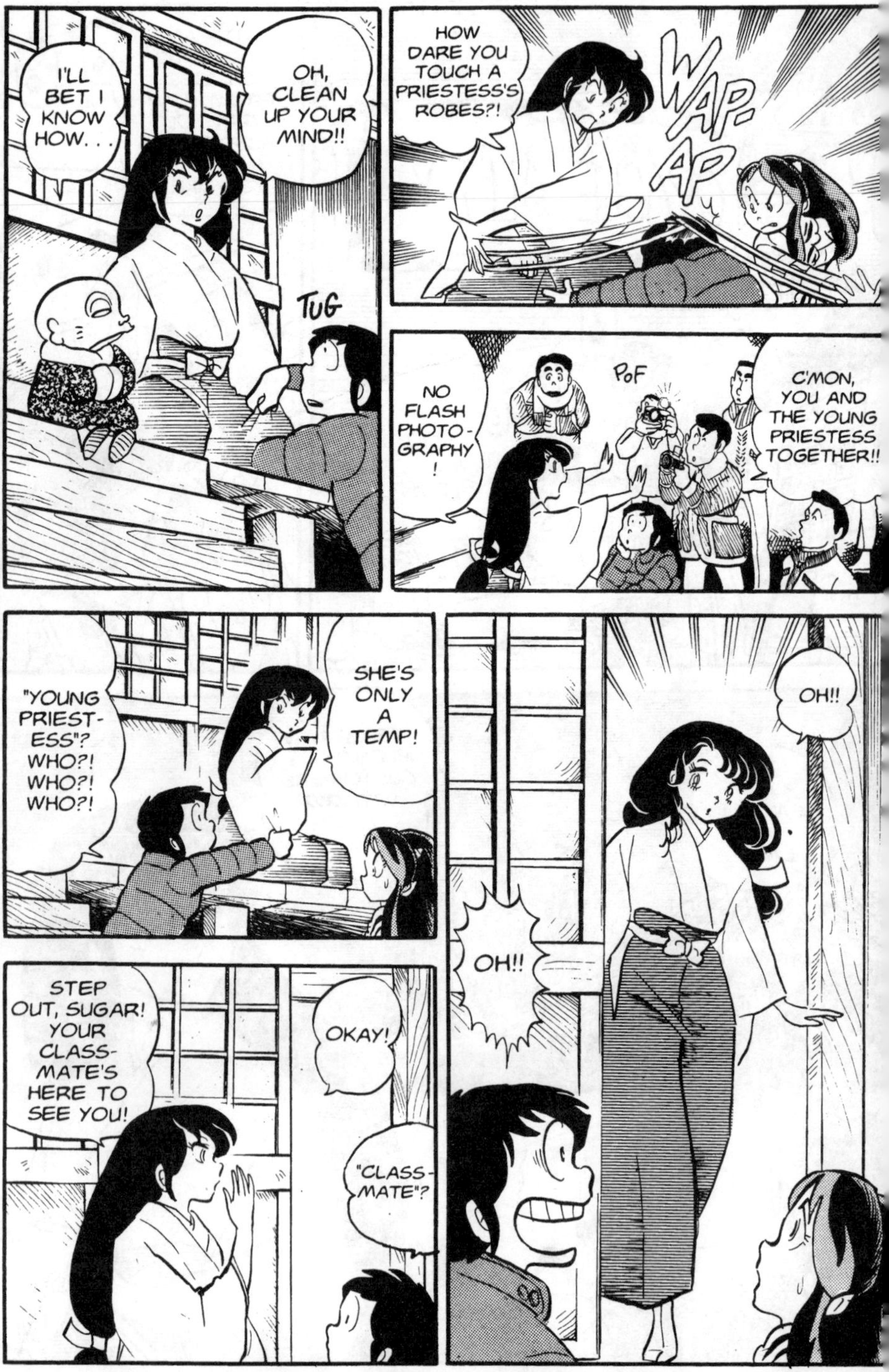
I'LL BET I KNOW HOW. . .
OH, CLEAN UP YOUR MIND!!
TUG
HOW DARE YOU TOUCH A PRIESTESS'S ROBES?!
WAP-AP
NO FLASH PHOTOGRAPHY!
POF
C'MON, YOU AND THE YOUNG PRIESTESS TOGETHER!!
"YOUNG PRIESTESS"? WHO?! WHO?! WHO?!
SHE'S ONLY A TEMP!
STEP OUT, SUGAR! YOUR CLASSMATE'S HERE TO SEE YOU!
OKAY!
"CLASSMATE"?
OH!!
OH!!

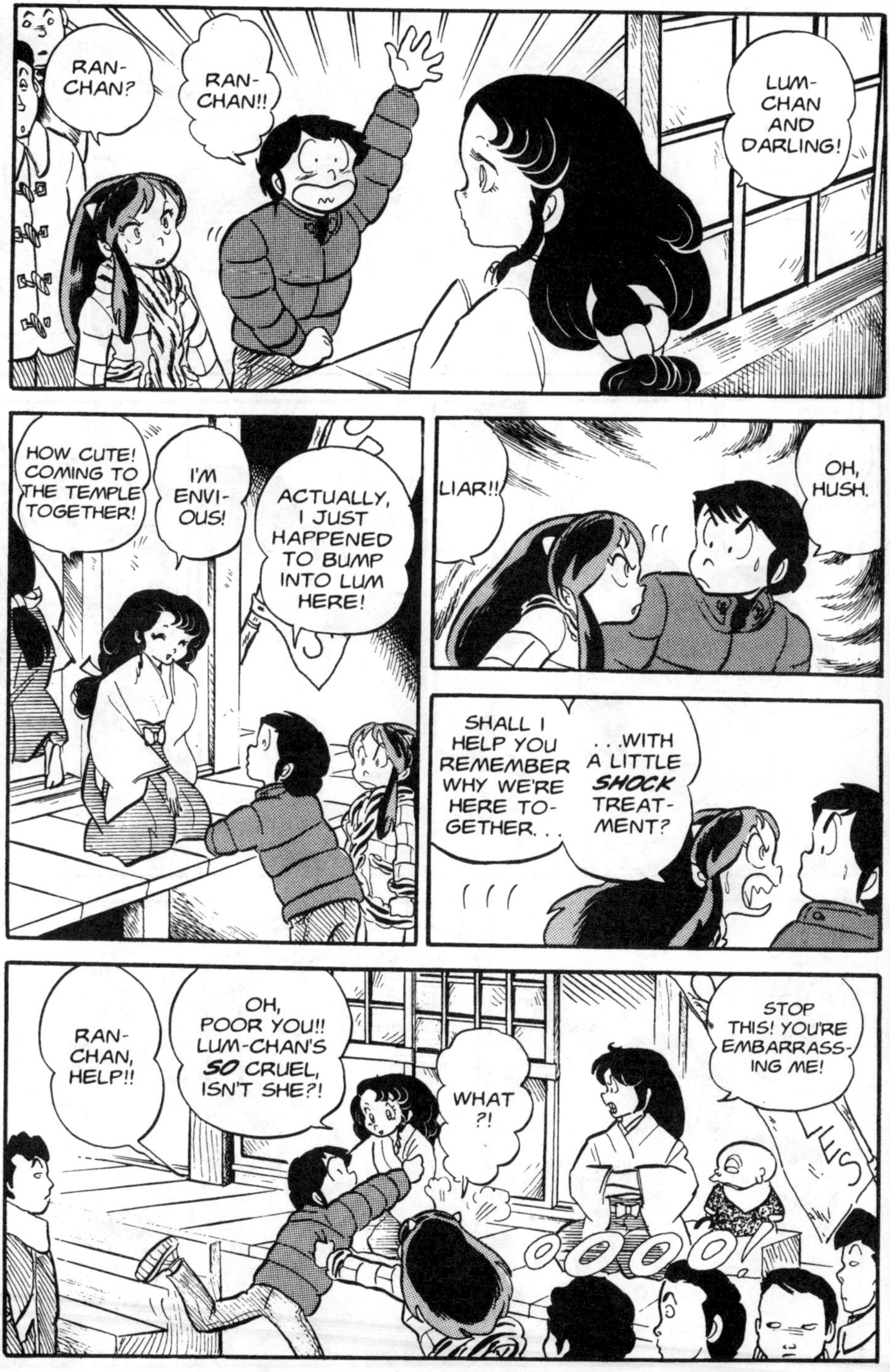
RAN-
CHAN?
RAN-
CHAN!!
LUM-
CHAN
AND
DARLING!
HOW CUTE! COMING TO THE TEMPLE TOGETHER!
I'M ENVI-OUS!
ACTUALLY, I JUST HAPPENED TO BUMP INTO LUM HERE!
LIAR!!
OH, HUSH.
SHALL I HELP YOU REMEMBER WHY WE'RE HERE TO-GETHER. . .
. . .WITH A LITTLE *SHOCK* TREAT-MENT?
RAN-CHAN, HELP!!
OH, POOR YOU!! LUM-CHAN'S *SO* CRUEL, ISN'T SHE?!
WHAT ?!
STOP THIS! YOU'RE EMBARRASS-ING ME!

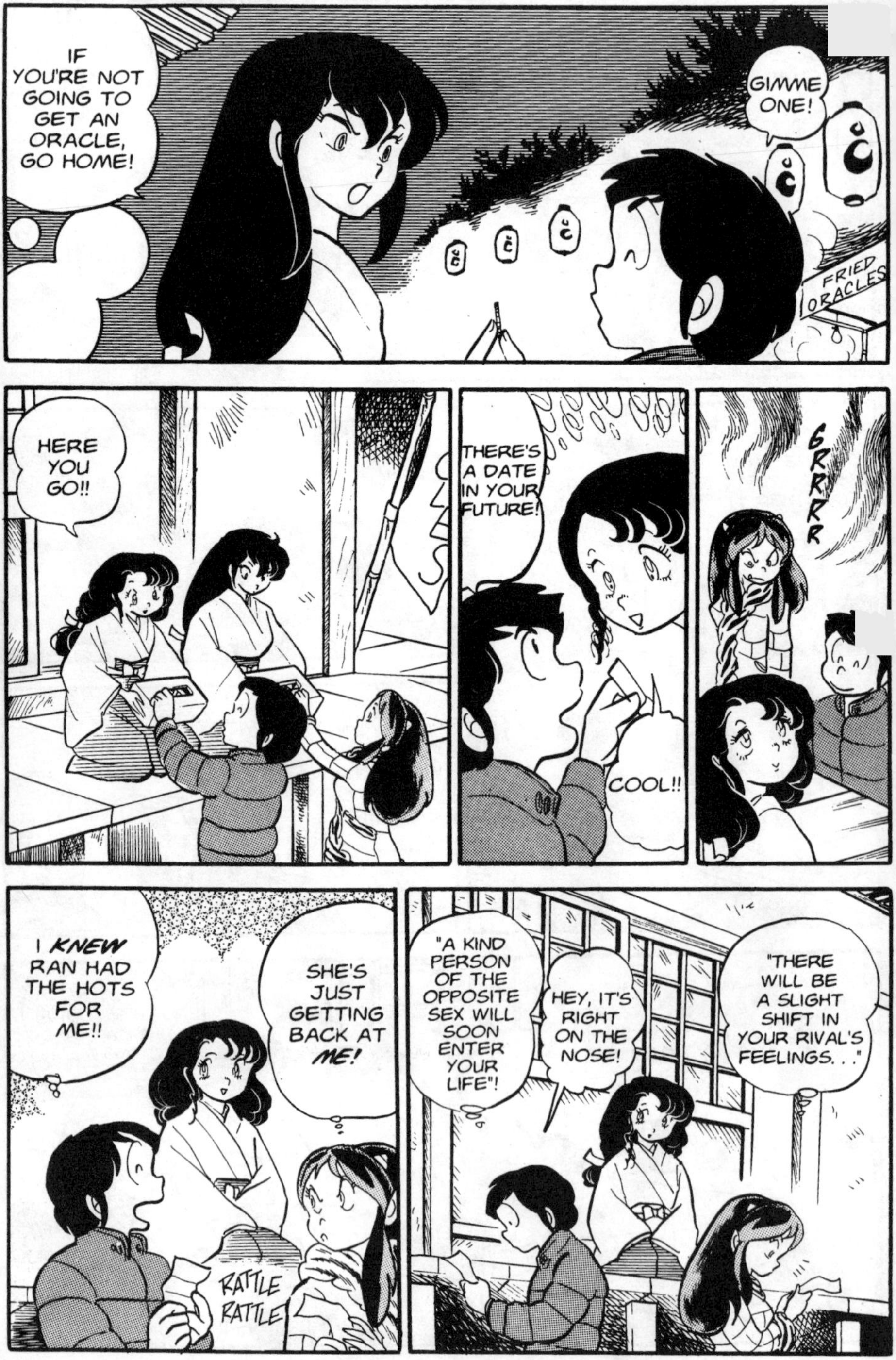
IF YOU'RE NOT GOING TO GET AN ORACLE, GO HOME!
GIMME ONE!
FRIED ORACLES
HERE YOU GO!!
THERE'S A DATE IN YOUR FUTURE!
COOL!!
GRRRR
I *KNEW* RAN HAD THE HOTS FOR ME!!
SHE'S JUST GETTING BACK AT *ME!*
RATTLE RATTLE
"A KIND PERSON OF THE OPPOSITE SEX WILL SOON ENTER YOUR LIFE"!
HEY, IT'S RIGHT ON THE NOSE!
"THERE WILL BE A SLIGHT SHIFT IN YOUR RIVAL'S FEELINGS. . ."

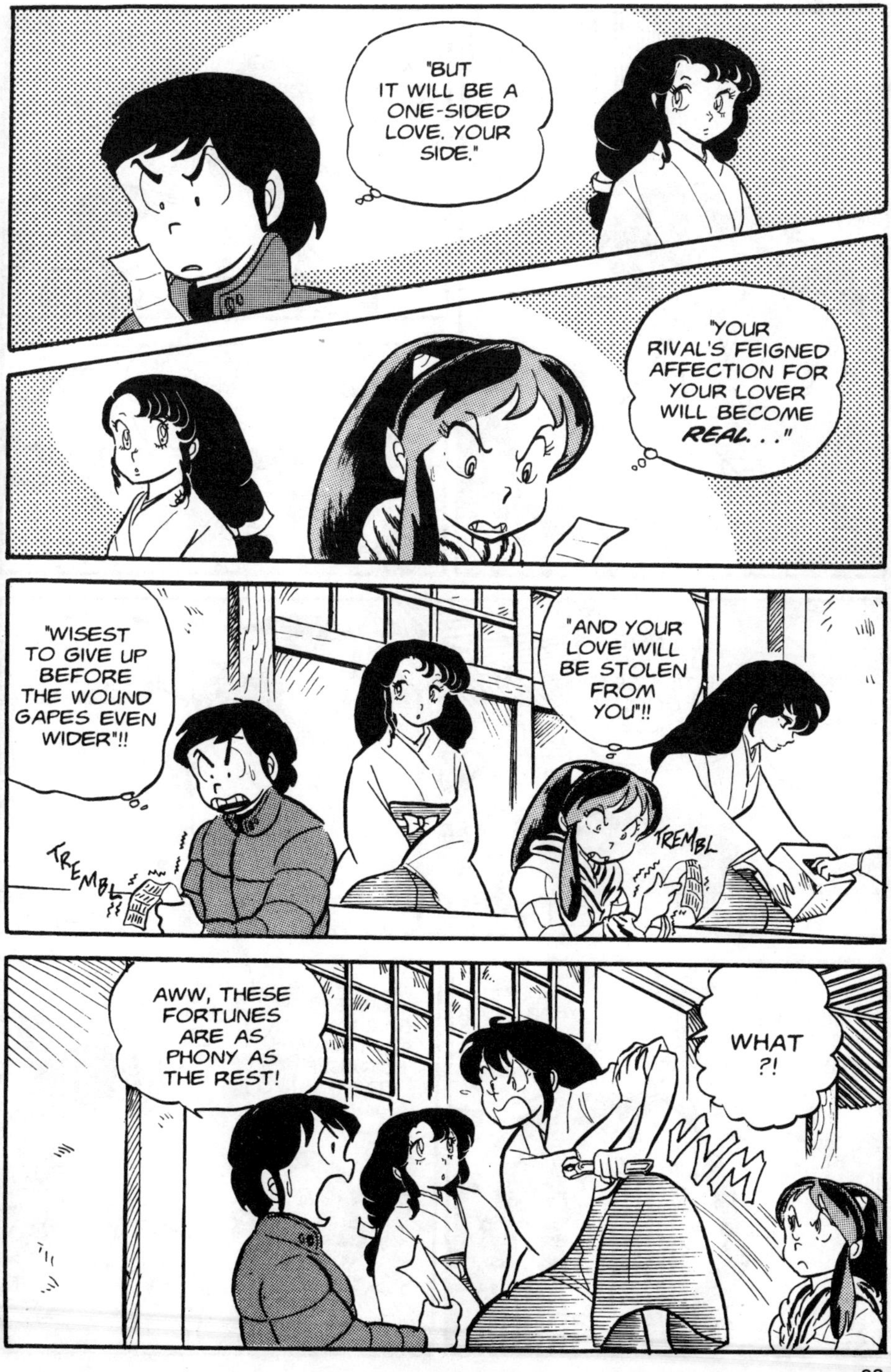
"BUT IT WILL BE A ONE-SIDED LOVE. YOUR SIDE."
"YOUR RIVAL'S FEIGNED AFFECTION FOR YOUR LOVER WILL BECOME REAL. . ."
"WISEST TO GIVE UP BEFORE THE WOUND GAPES EVEN WIDER"!!
TREMBL
"AND YOUR LOVE WILL BE STOLEN FROM YOU"!!
TREMBL
AWW, THESE FORTUNES ARE AS PHONY AS THE REST!
WHAT ?!
VVM

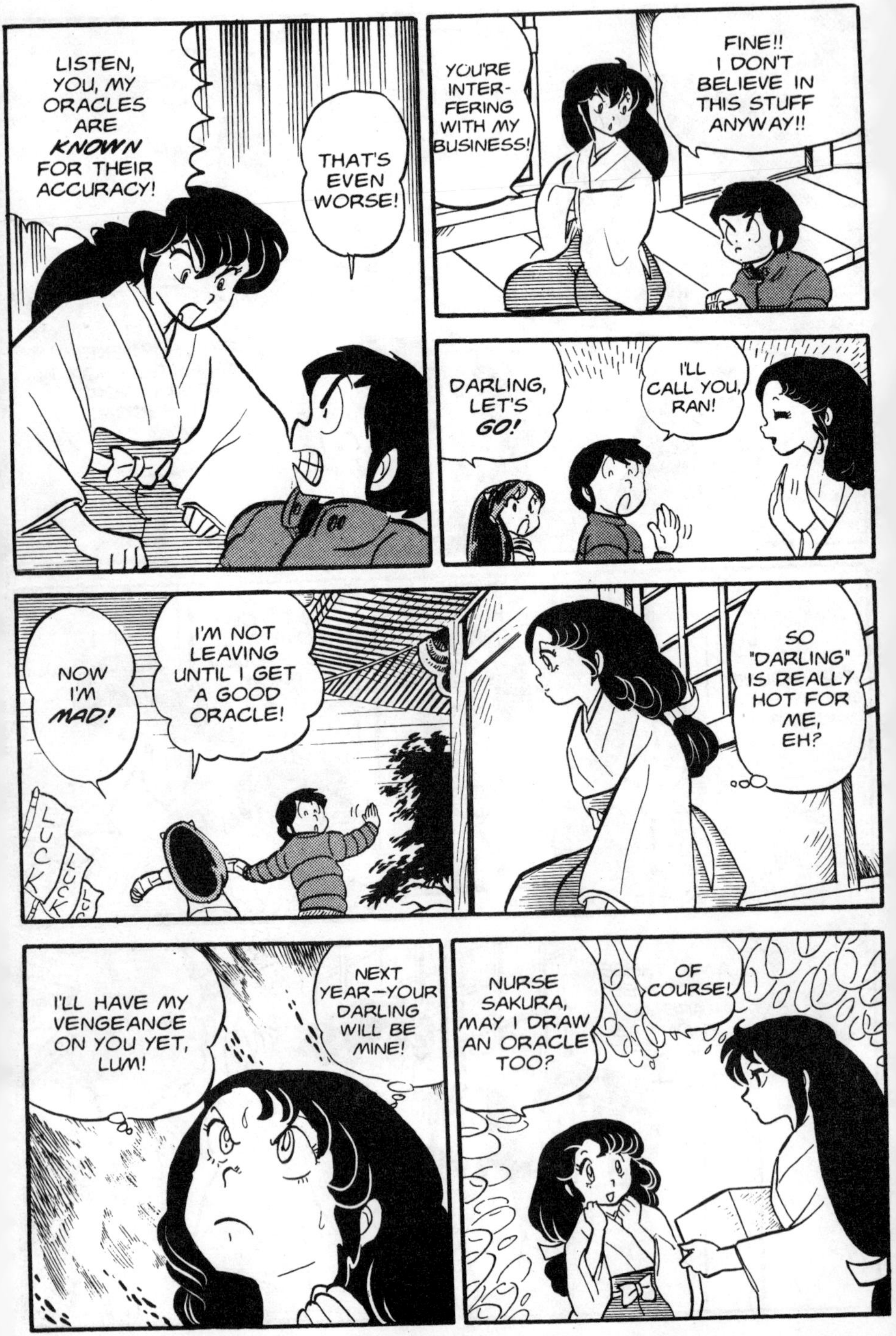
LISTEN, YOU, MY ORACLES ARE *KNOWN* FOR THEIR ACCURACY!
THAT'S EVEN WORSE!
YOU'RE INTER-FERING WITH MY BUSINESS!
FINE!! I DON'T BELIEVE IN THIS STUFF ANYWAY!!
DARLING, LET'S *GO!*
I'LL CALL YOU, RAN!
NOW I'M *MAD!*
I'M NOT LEAVING UNTIL I GET A GOOD ORACLE!
LUCK
LUCK
SO "DARLING" IS REALLY HOT FOR ME, EH?
I'LL HAVE MY VENGEANCE ON YOU YET, LUM!
NEXT YEAR—YOUR DARLING WILL BE MINE!
NURSE SAKURA, MAY I DRAW AN ORACLE TOO?
OF COURSE!

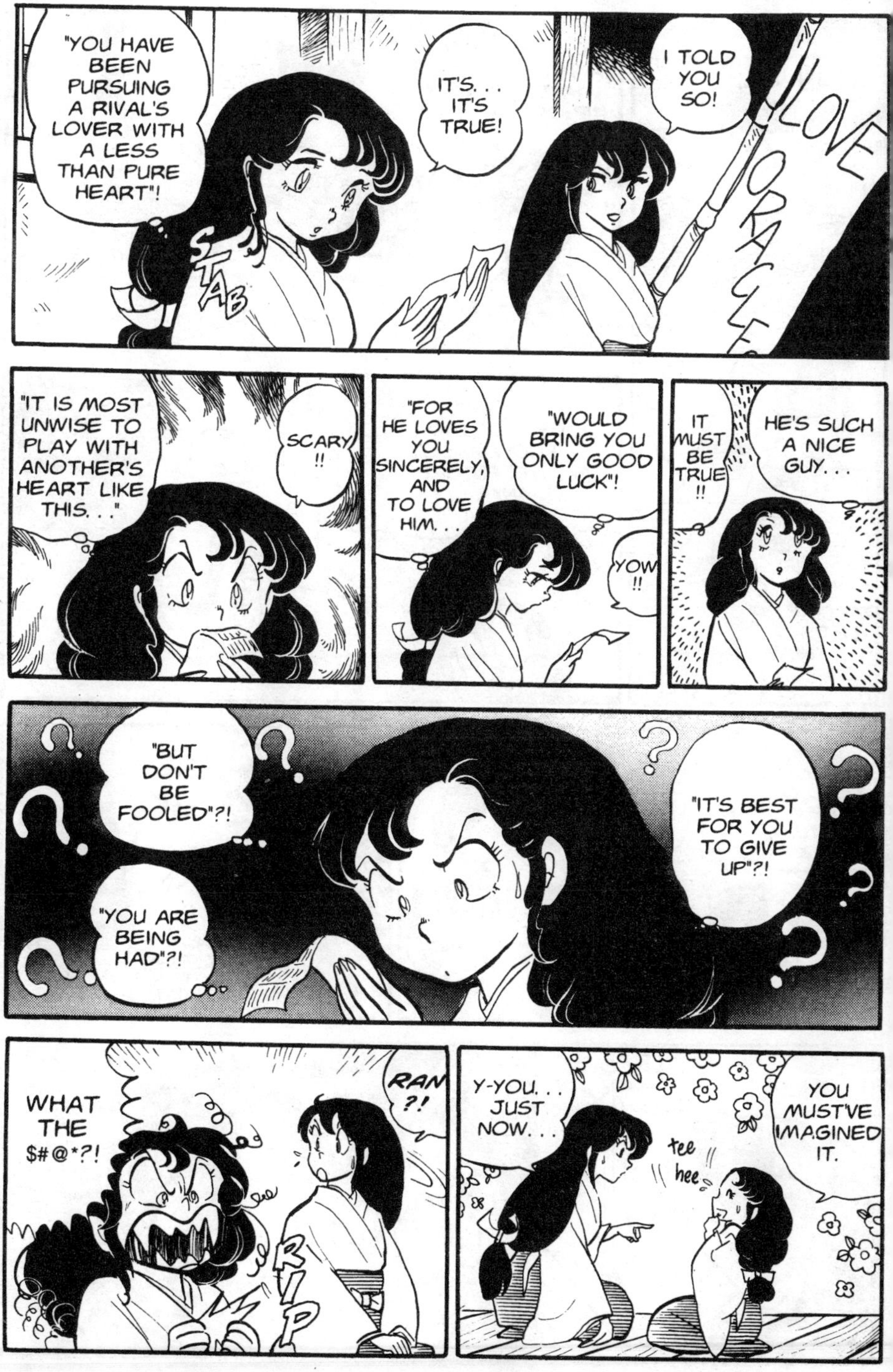
"YOU HAVE BEEN PURSUING A RIVAL'S LOVER WITH A LESS THAN PURE HEART"!
STAB
IT'S... IT'S TRUE!
I TOLD YOU SO!
LOVE ORACLE
"IT IS MOST UNWISE TO PLAY WITH ANOTHER'S HEART LIKE THIS..."
SCARY!!
"FOR HE LOVES YOU SINCERELY, AND TO LOVE HIM...
"WOULD BRING YOU ONLY GOOD LUCK"!
YOW!!
IT MUST BE TRUE!!
HE'S SUCH A NICE GUY...
"BUT DON'T BE FOOLED"?!
"YOU ARE BEING HAD"?!
"IT'S BEST FOR YOU TO GIVE UP"?!
WHAT THE $#@*?!
RAN?!
RIP
Y-YOU... JUST NOW...
tee hee
YOU MUST'VE IMAGINED IT.

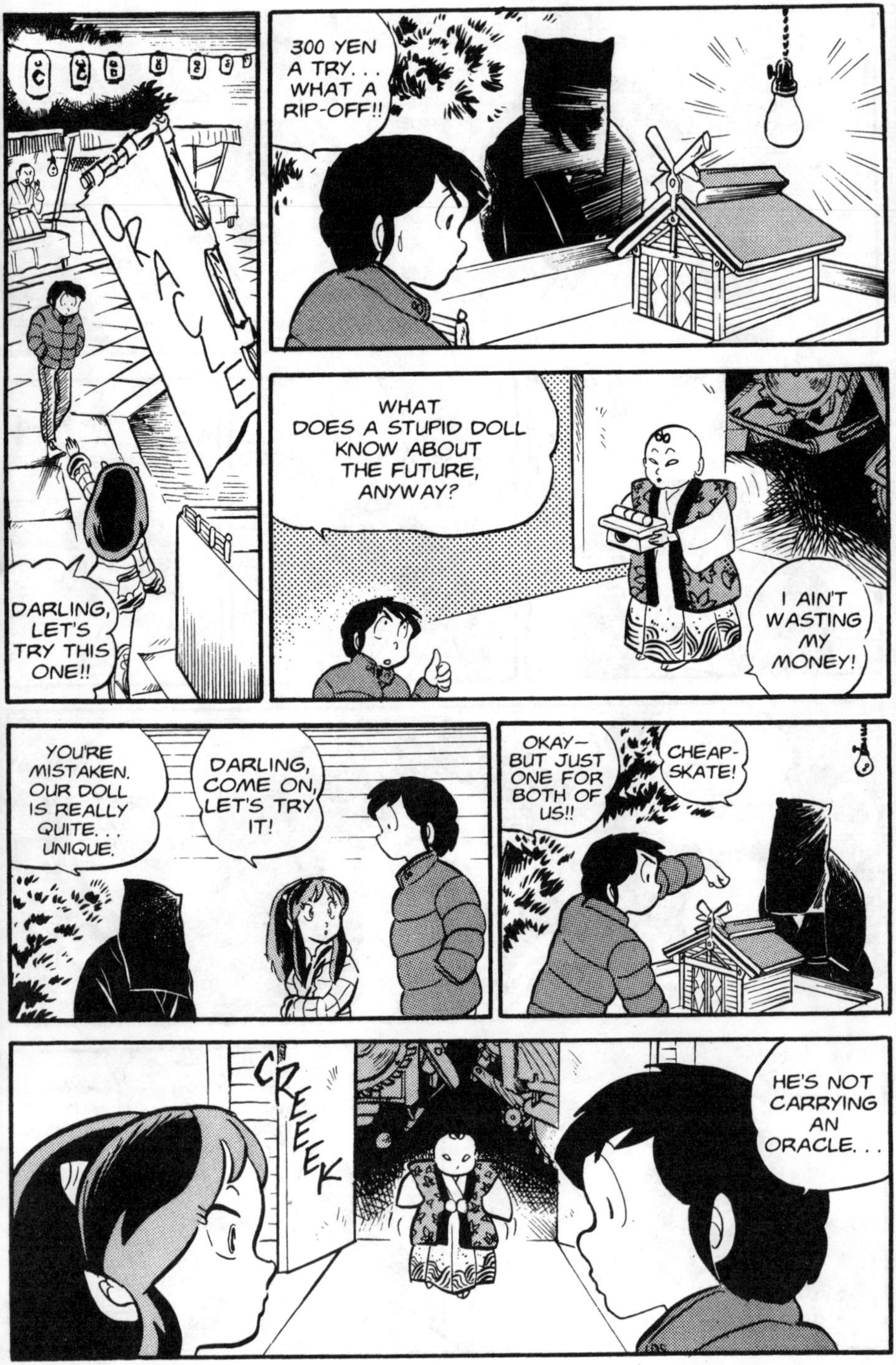
ORACLE
DARLING, LET'S TRY THIS ONE!!
300 YEN A TRY. . . WHAT A RIP-OFF!!
WHAT DOES A STUPID DOLL KNOW ABOUT THE FUTURE, ANYWAY?
I AIN'T WASTING MY MONEY!
YOU'RE MISTAKEN. OUR DOLL IS REALLY QUITE. . . UNIQUE.
DARLING, COME ON, LET'S TRY IT!
OKAY— BUT JUST ONE FOR BOTH OF US!!
CHEAP-SKATE!
CREEEK
HE'S NOT CARRYING AN ORACLE. . .

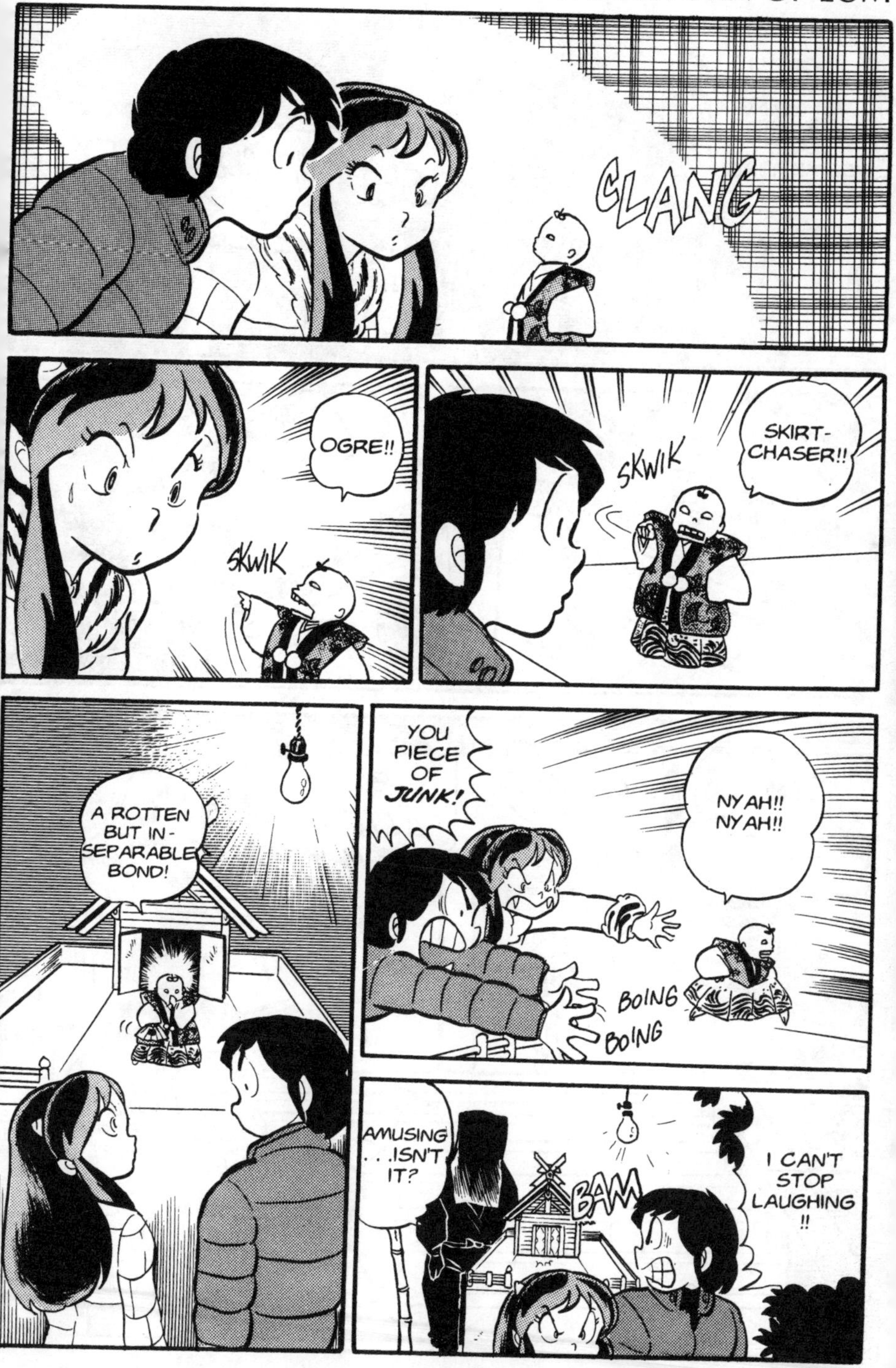
CLANG
OGRE!!
SKWIK
SKWIK
SKIRT-CHASER!!
A ROTTEN BUT IN-SEPARABLE BOND!
YOU PIECE OF JUNK!
NYAH!! NYAH!!
BOING
BOING
AMUSING . . .ISN'T IT?
BAM
I CAN'T STOP LAUGHING !!

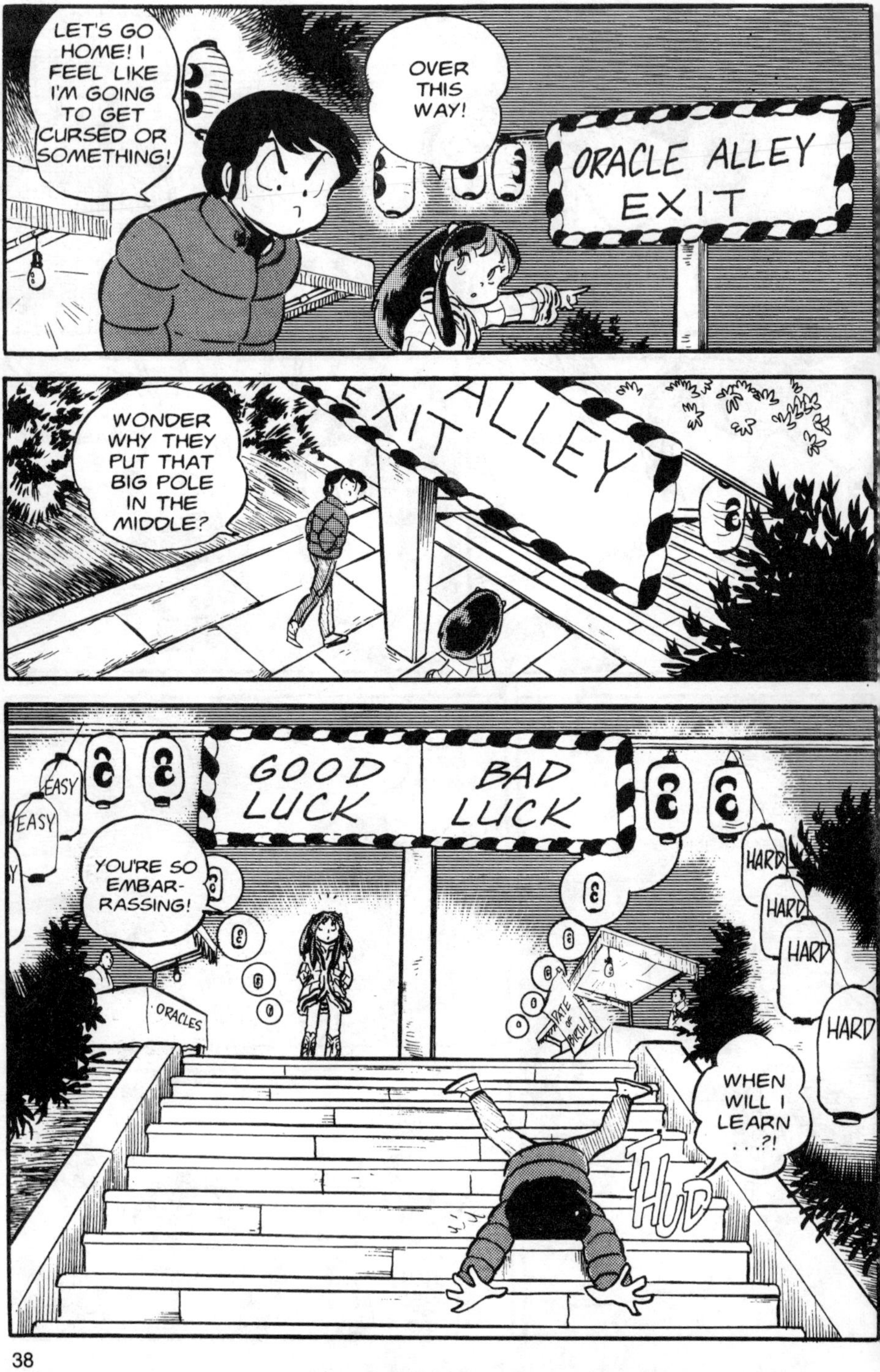
LET'S GO HOME! I FEEL LIKE I'M GOING TO GET CURSED OR SOMETHING!
OVER THIS WAY!
ORACLE ALLEY EXIT
WONDER WHY THEY PUT THAT BIG POLE IN THE MIDDLE?
ALLEY
EXIT
GOOD LUCK
BAD LUCK
EASY
EASY
YOU'RE SO EMBARRASSING!
ORACLES
DATE OF BIRTH
HARD
HARD
HARD
HARD
WHEN WILL I LEARN . . .?!
THUD

PART THREE
ARRIVAL OF TEN-CHAN

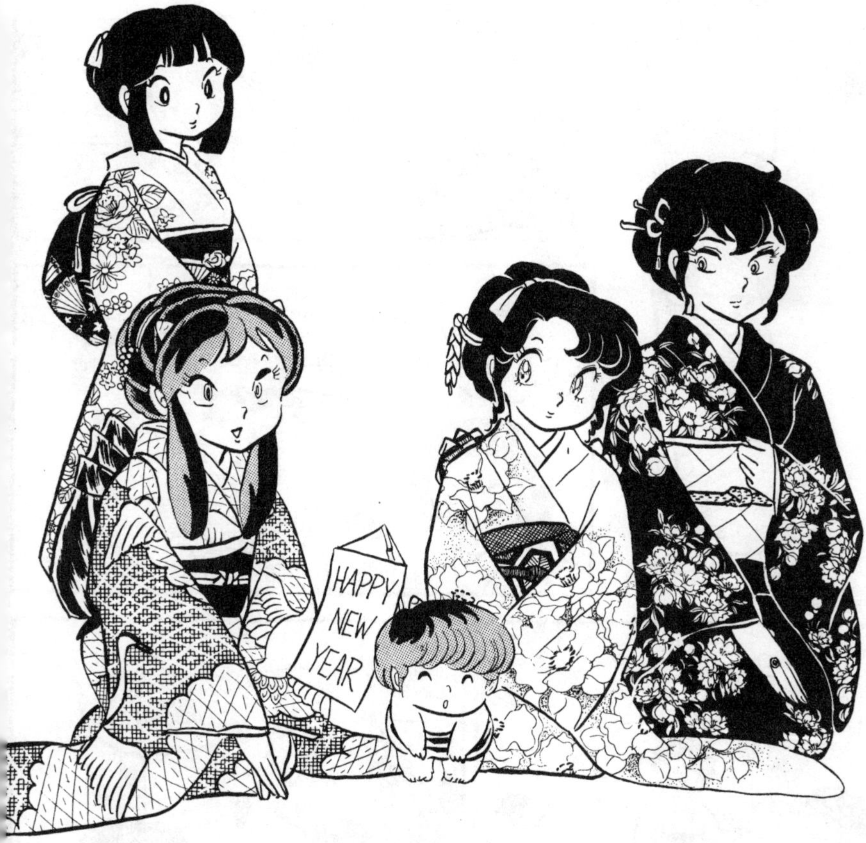
HAPPY NEW YEAR

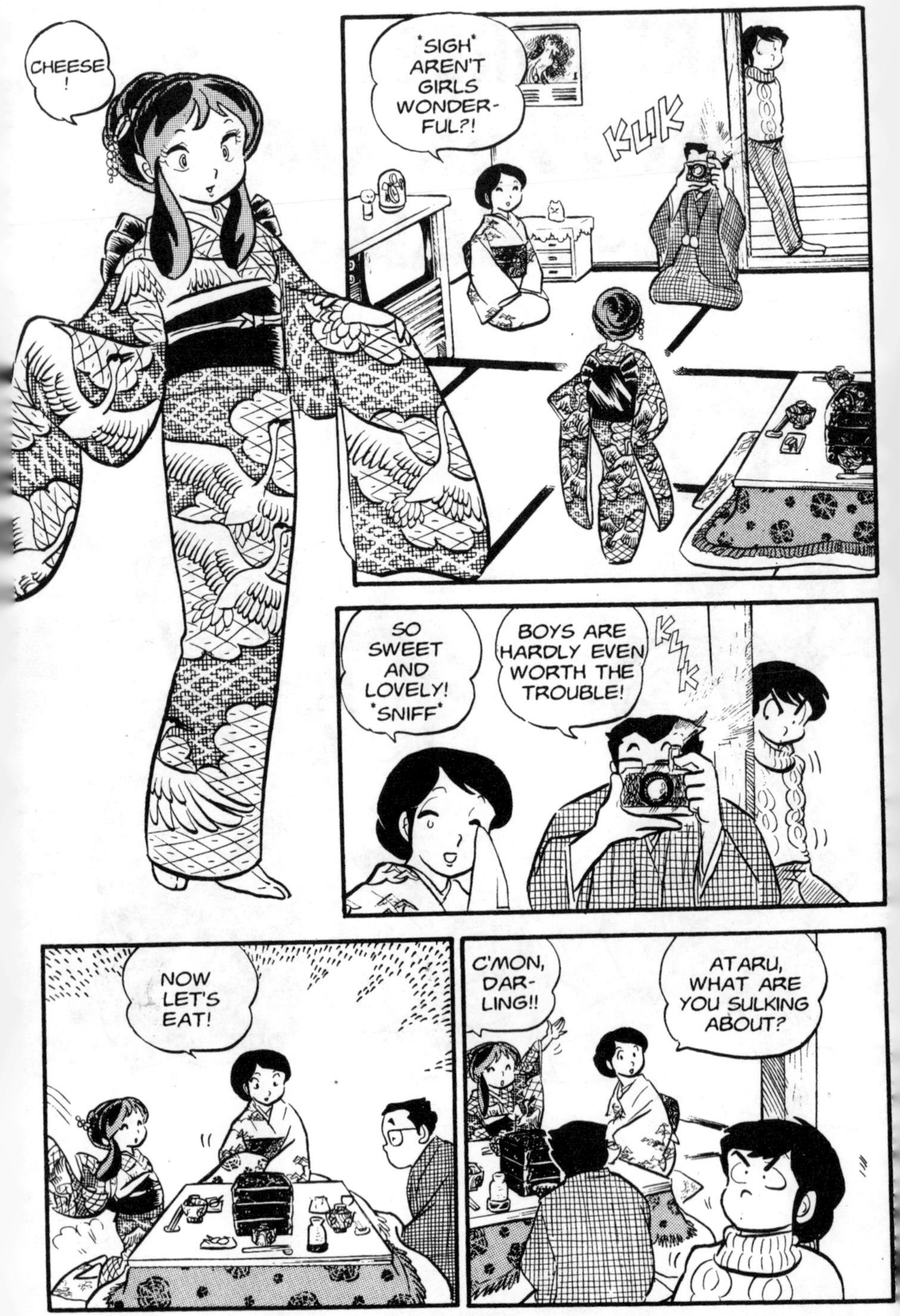
CHEESE!
SIGH AREN'T GIRLS WONDERFUL?!
KLIK
SO SWEET AND LOVELY! *SNIFF*
BOYS ARE HARDLY EVEN WORTH THE TROUBLE!
KLIK
NOW LET'S EAT!
C'MON, DARLING!!
ATARU, WHAT ARE YOU SULKING ABOUT?

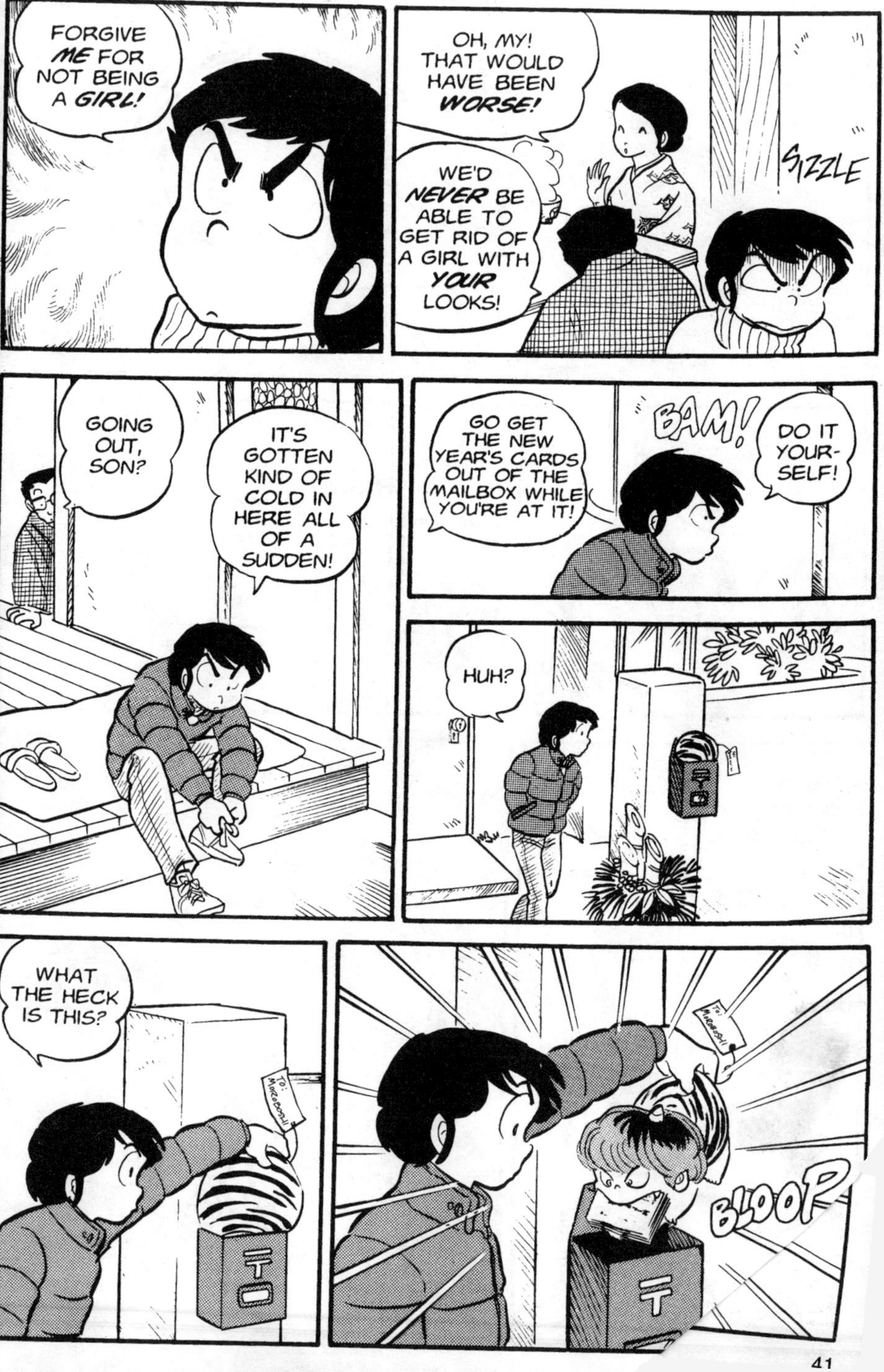
FORGIVE *ME* FOR NOT BEING A *GIRL!*
OH, MY! THAT WOULD HAVE BEEN *WORSE!*
WE'D *NEVER* BE ABLE TO GET RID OF A GIRL WITH *YOUR* LOOKS!
SIZZLE
GOING OUT, SON?
IT'S GOTTEN KIND OF COLD IN HERE ALL OF A SUDDEN!
GO GET THE NEW YEAR'S CARDS OUT OF THE MAILBOX WHILE YOU'RE AT IT!
BAM!
DO IT YOURSELF!
HUH?
WHAT THE HECK IS THIS?
BLOOP

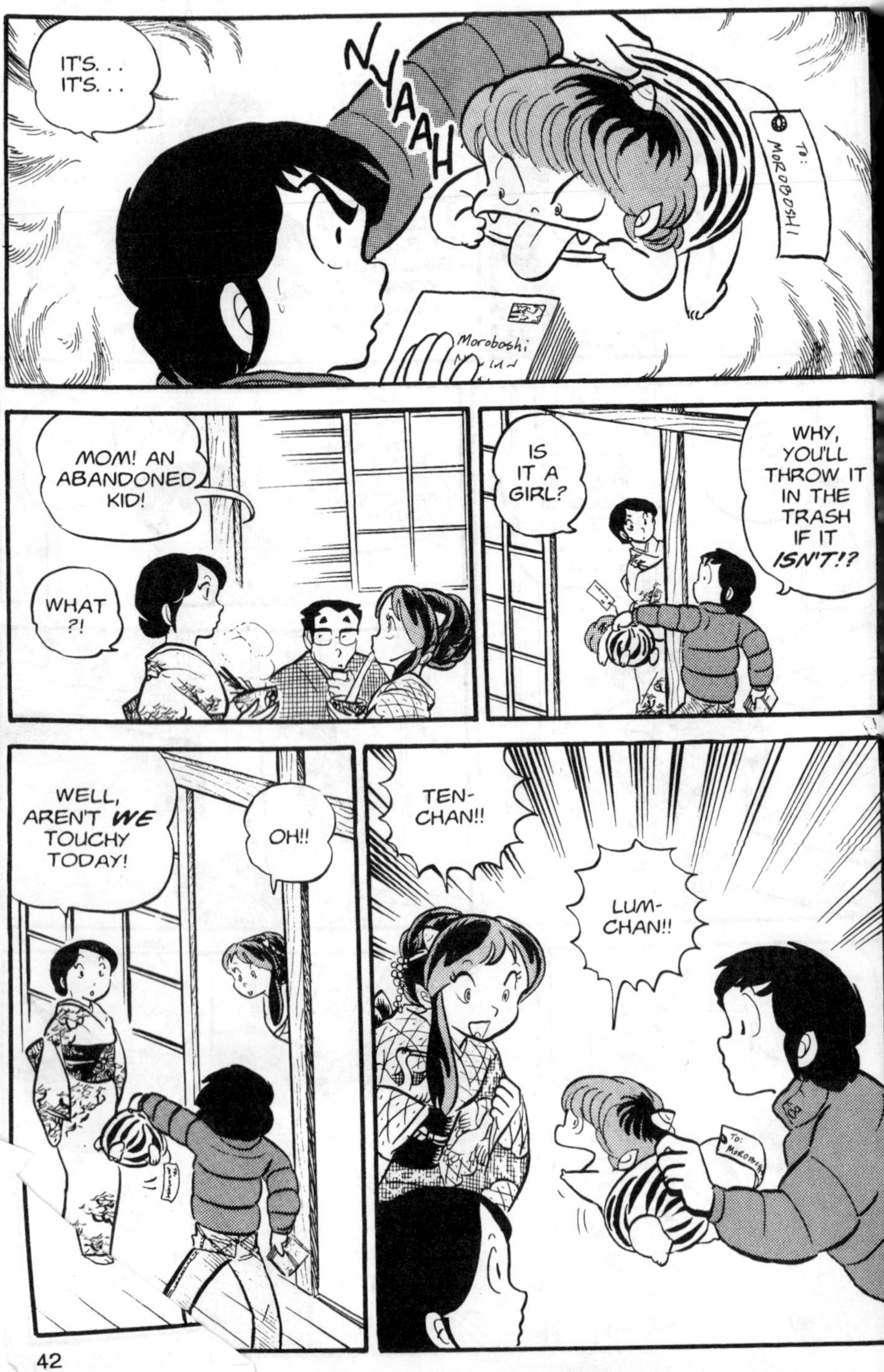
IT'S. . .
IT'S. . .
NYAAAH
TO:
MOROBOSHI
Moroboshi
MOM! AN ABANDONED KID!
WHAT ?!
IS IT A GIRL?
WHY, YOU'LL THROW IT IN THE TRASH IF IT *ISN'T!?*
WELL, AREN'T ***WE*** TOUCHY TODAY!
OH!!
TEN-CHAN!!
LUM-CHAN!!
TO:

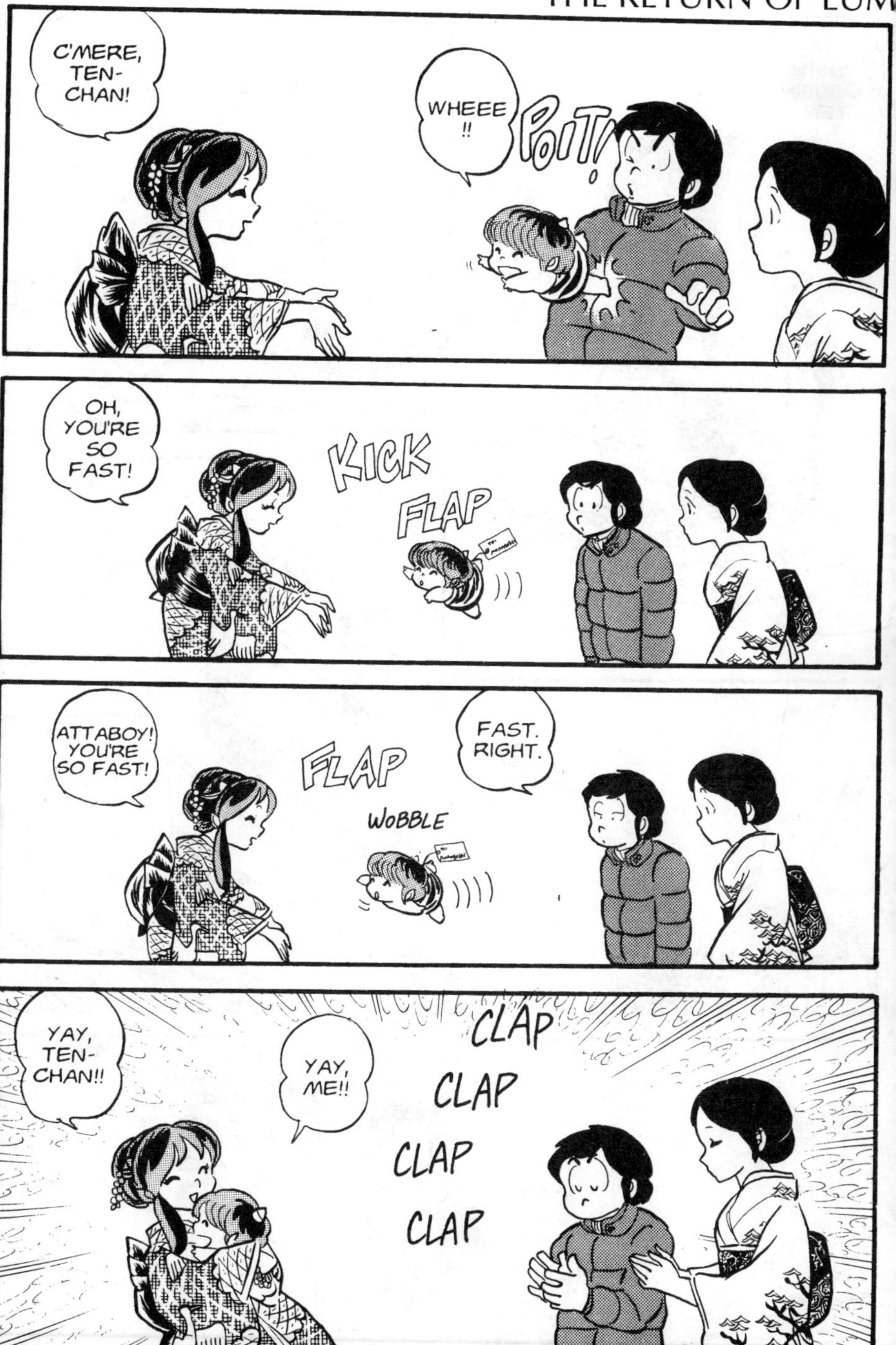
C'MERE, TEN-CHAN!
WHEEE !!
POIT!
OH, YOU'RE SO FAST!
KICK
FLAP
ATTABOY! YOU'RE SO FAST!
FLAP
WOBBLE
FAST. RIGHT.
YAY, TEN-CHAN!!
YAY, ME!!
CLAP
CLAP
CLAP
CLAP

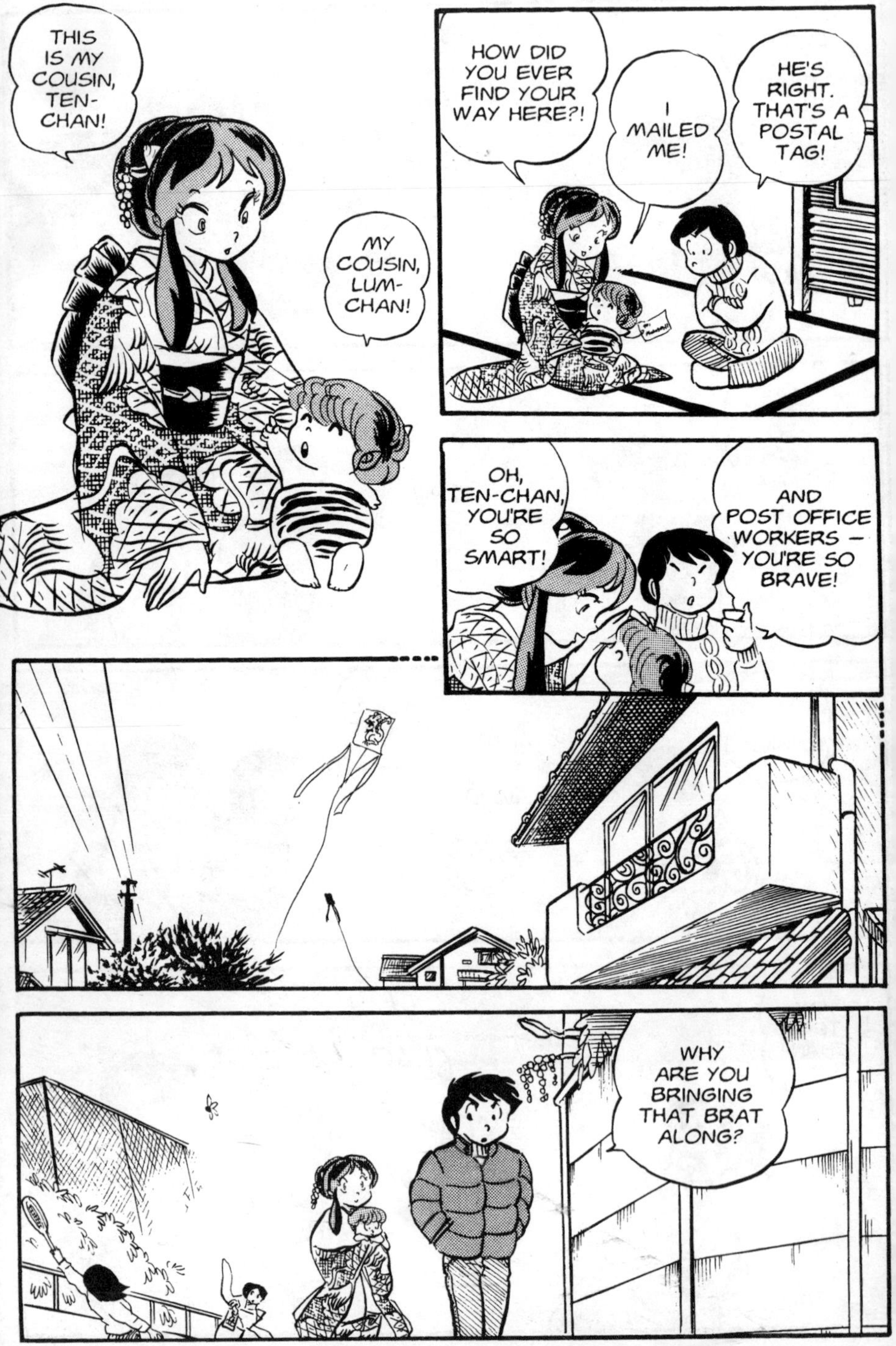

THIS IS MY COUSIN, TEN-CHAN!
MY COUSIN, LUM-CHAN!
HOW DID YOU EVER FIND YOUR WAY HERE?!
I MAILED ME!
HE'S RIGHT. THAT'S A POSTAL TAG!
OH, TEN-CHAN, YOU'RE SO SMART!
AND POST OFFICE WORKERS — YOU'RE SO BRAVE!
WHY ARE YOU BRINGING THAT BRAT ALONG?

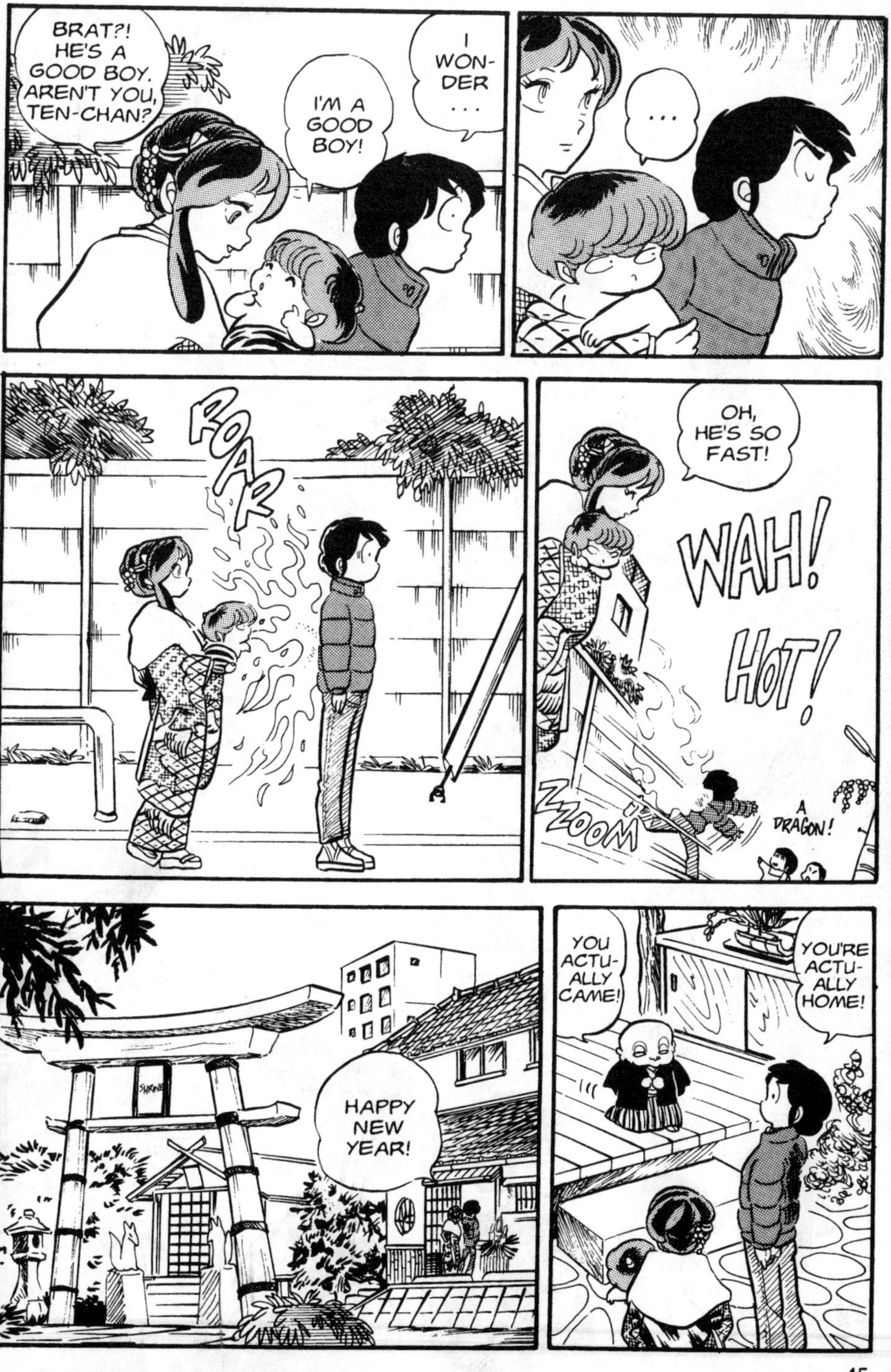
BRAT?! HE'S A GOOD BOY. AREN'T YOU, TEN-CHAN?
I'M A GOOD BOY!
I WON-DER . . .
. . .
ROAR
OH, HE'S SO FAST!
WAH!
HOT!
ZZOOM
A DRAGON!
SHRINE
HAPPY NEW YEAR!
YOU ACTU-ALLY CAME!
YOU'RE ACTU-ALLY HOME!

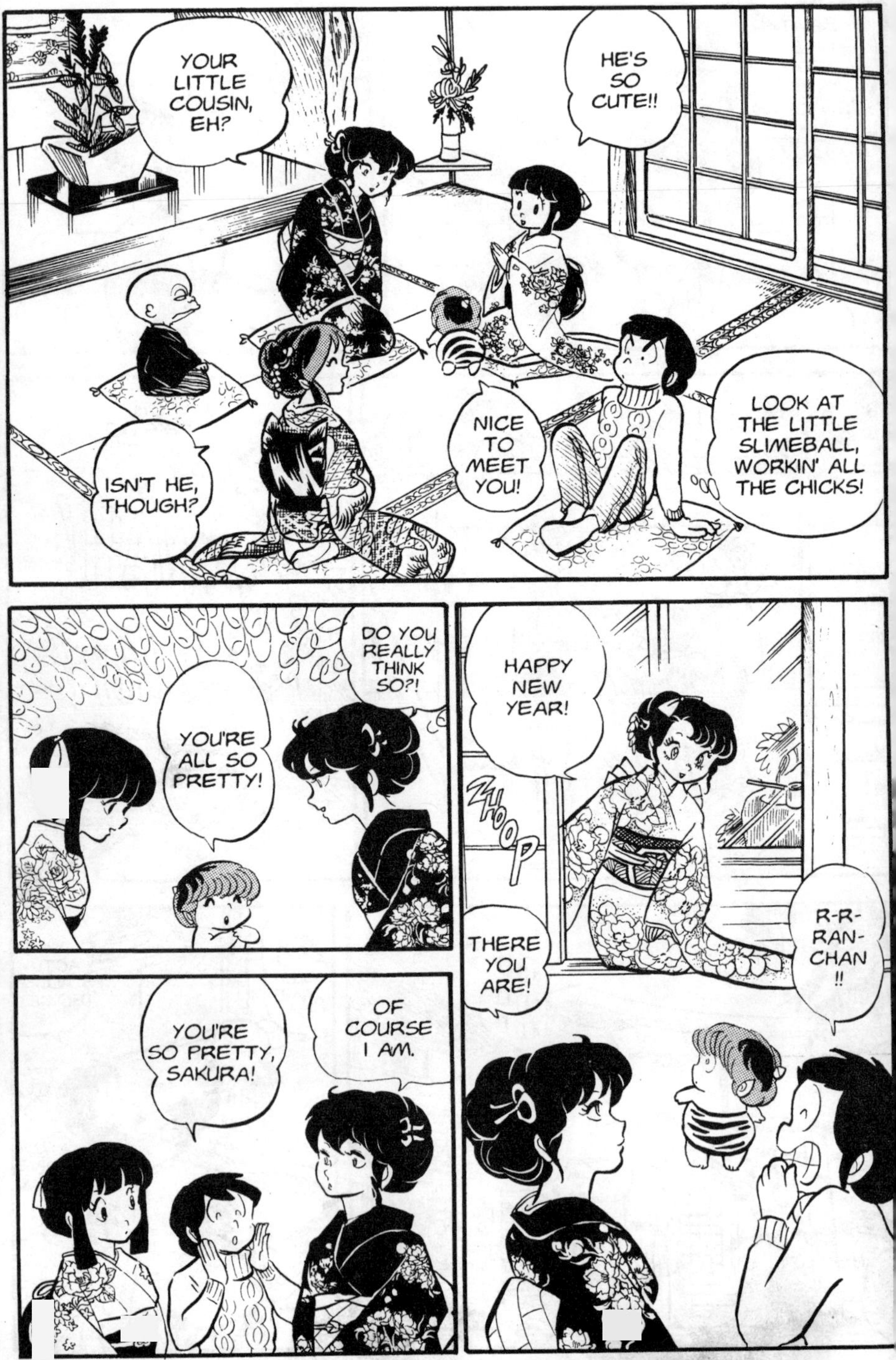
YOUR LITTLE COUSIN, EH?
HE'S SO CUTE!!
ISN'T HE, THOUGH?
NICE TO MEET YOU!
LOOK AT THE LITTLE SLIMEBALL, WORKIN' ALL THE CHICKS!
YOU'RE ALL SO PRETTY!
DO YOU REALLY THINK SO?!
YOU'RE SO PRETTY, SAKURA!
OF COURSE I AM.
HAPPY NEW YEAR!
ZHOOP
THERE YOU ARE!
R-R-RAN-CHAN!!

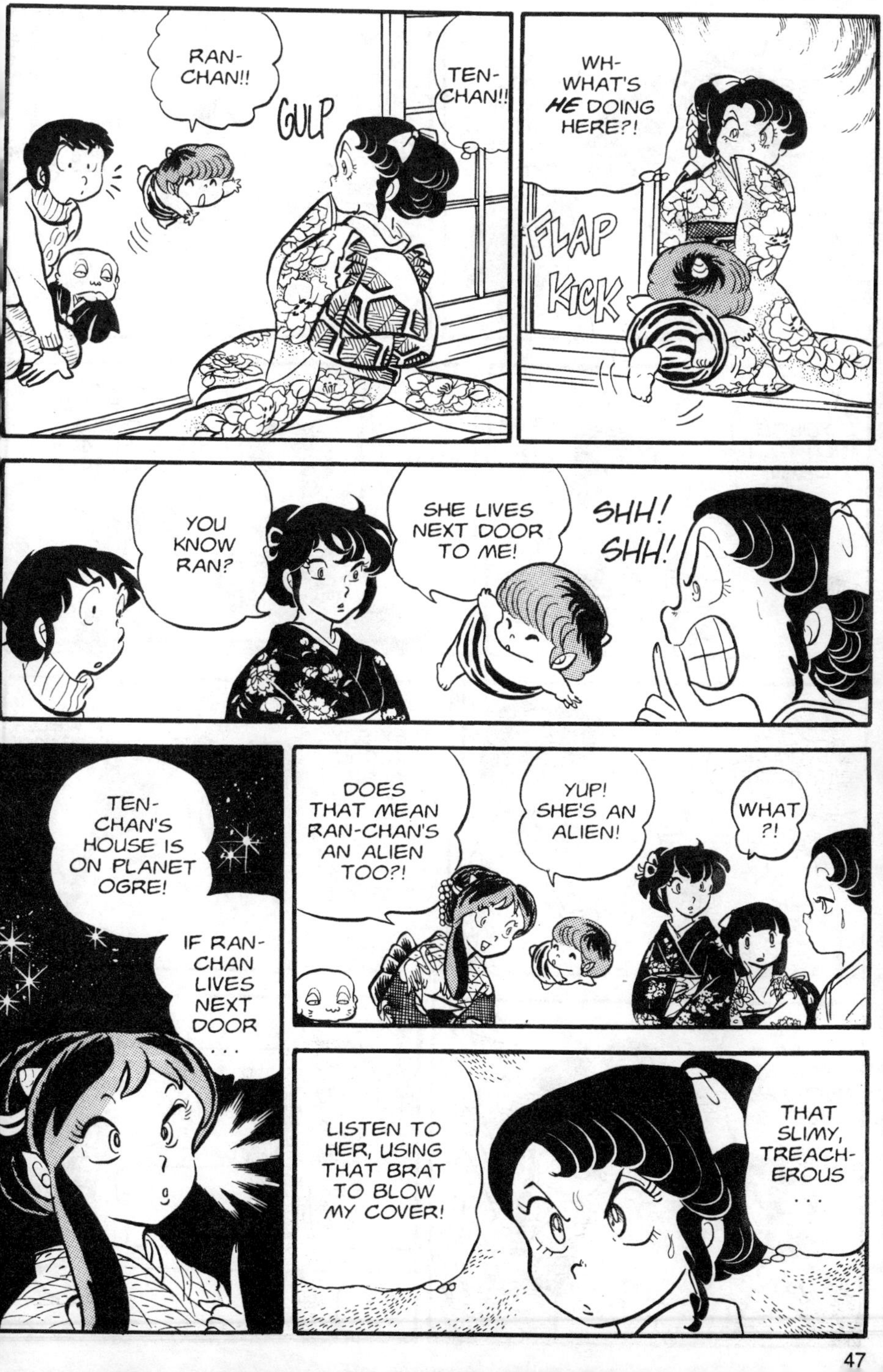
RAN-CHAN!!
GULP
TEN-CHAN!!
WH-WHAT'S HE DOING HERE?!
FLAP
KICK
YOU KNOW RAN?
SHE LIVES NEXT DOOR TO ME!
SHH! SHH!
TEN-CHAN'S HOUSE IS ON PLANET OGRE!
IF RAN-CHAN LIVES NEXT DOOR . . .
DOES THAT MEAN RAN-CHAN'S AN ALIEN TOO?!
YUP! SHE'S AN ALIEN!
WHAT?!
LISTEN TO HER, USING THAT BRAT TO BLOW MY COVER!
THAT SLIMY, TREACH-EROUS . . .

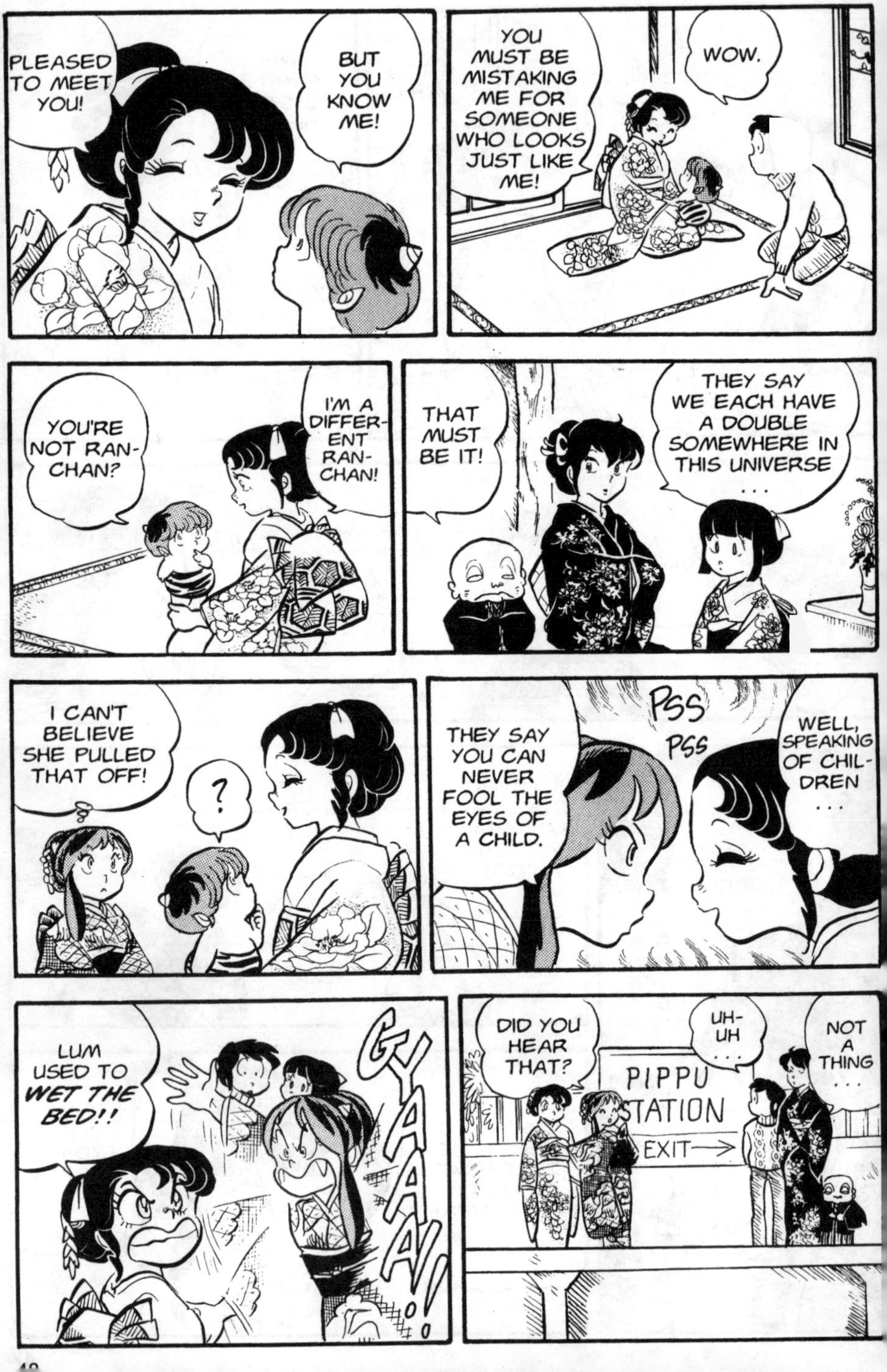
PLEASED TO MEET YOU!
BUT YOU KNOW ME!
YOU MUST BE MISTAKING ME FOR SOMEONE WHO LOOKS JUST LIKE ME!
WOW.
YOU'RE NOT RAN-CHAN?
I'M A DIFFERENT RAN-CHAN!
THAT MUST BE IT!
THEY SAY WE EACH HAVE A DOUBLE SOMEWHERE IN THIS UNIVERSE . . .
I CAN'T BELIEVE SHE PULLED THAT OFF!
?
PSS
PSS
THEY SAY YOU CAN NEVER FOOL THE EYES OF A CHILD.
WELL, SPEAKING OF CHILDREN . . .
LUM USED TO WET THE BED!!
GYAAAA!!
DID YOU HEAR THAT?
UH-UH . . .
NOT A THING . . .
PIPPU STATION
EXIT→

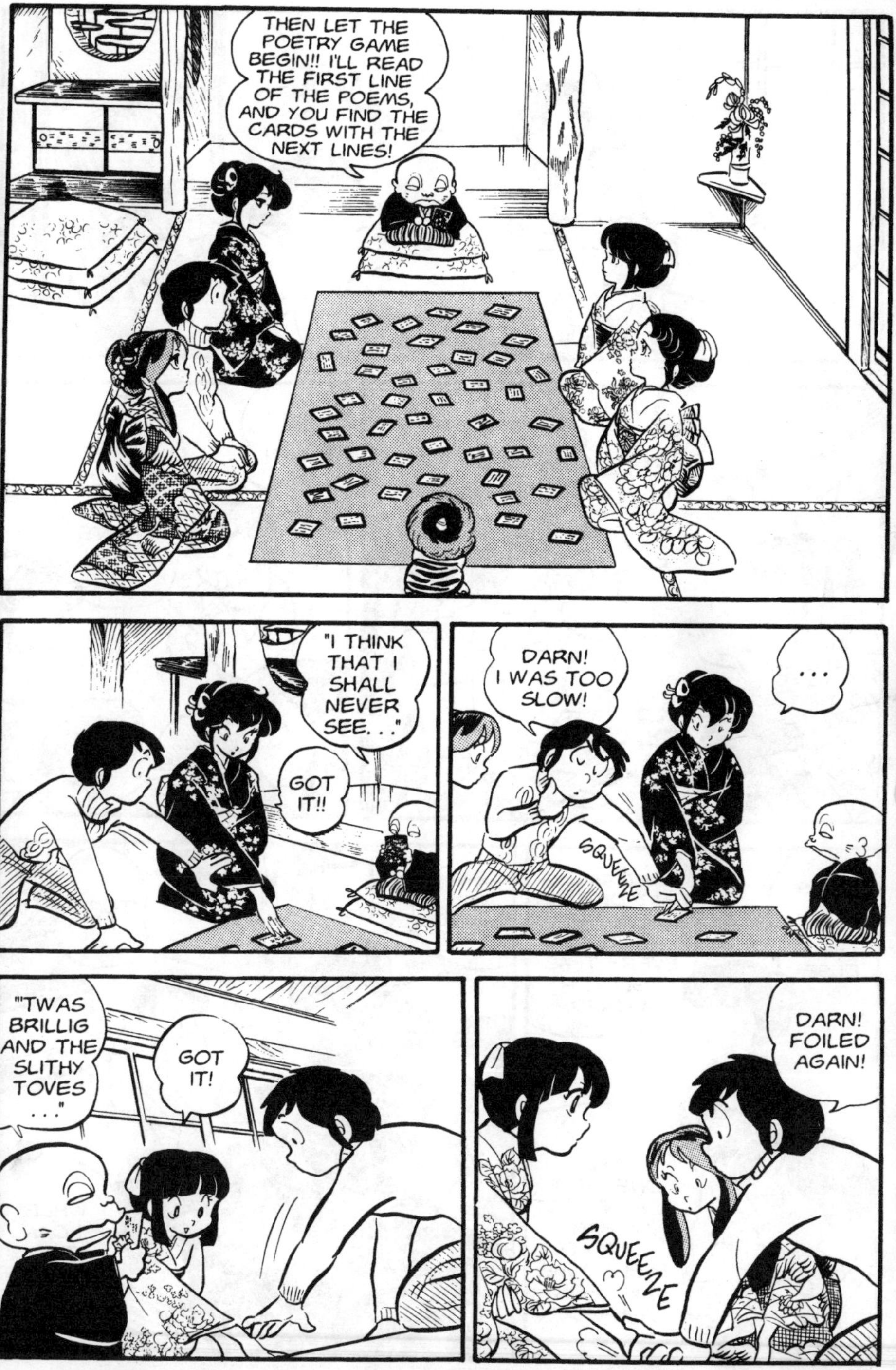
THEN LET THE POETRY GAME BEGIN!! I'LL READ THE FIRST LINE OF THE POEMS, AND YOU FIND THE CARDS WITH THE NEXT LINES!
"I THINK THAT I SHALL NEVER SEE. . ."
GOT IT!!
DARN! I WAS TOO SLOW!
. . .
SQUEEZE
"TWAS BRILLIG AND THE SLITHY TOVES . . ."
GOT IT!
DARN! FOILED AGAIN!
SQUEEZE

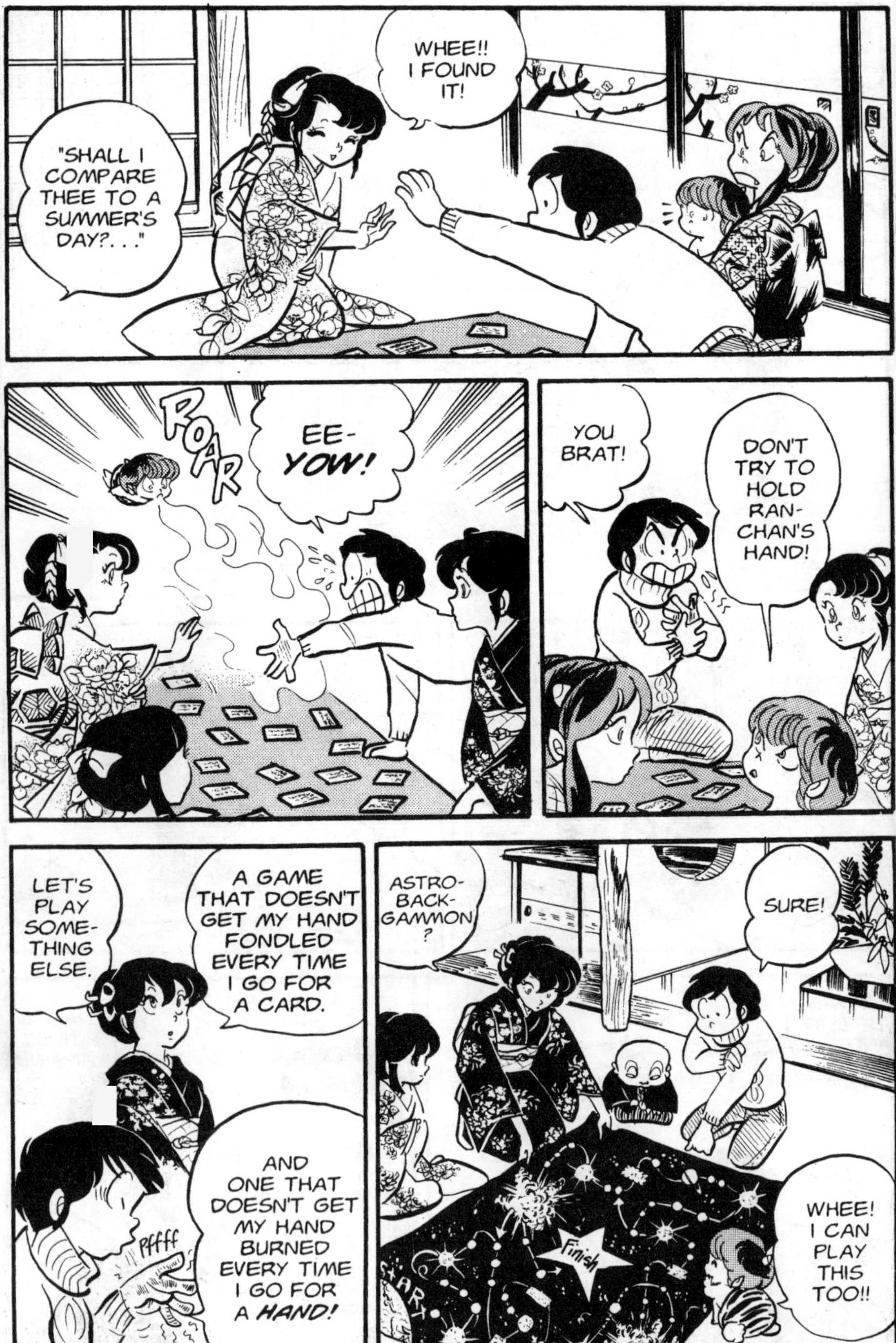
"SHALL I COMPARE THEE TO A SUMMER'S DAY?. . ."
WHEE!! I FOUND IT!
ROAR
EE-YOW!
YOU BRAT!
DON'T TRY TO HOLD RAN-CHAN'S HAND!
LET'S PLAY SOMETHING ELSE.
A GAME THAT DOESN'T GET MY HAND FONDLED EVERY TIME I GO FOR A CARD.
AND ONE THAT DOESN'T GET MY HAND BURNED EVERY TIME I GO FOR A HAND!
Pffff
ASTRO-BACKGAMMON?
SURE!
Finish
START
WHEE! I CAN PLAY THIS TOO!!

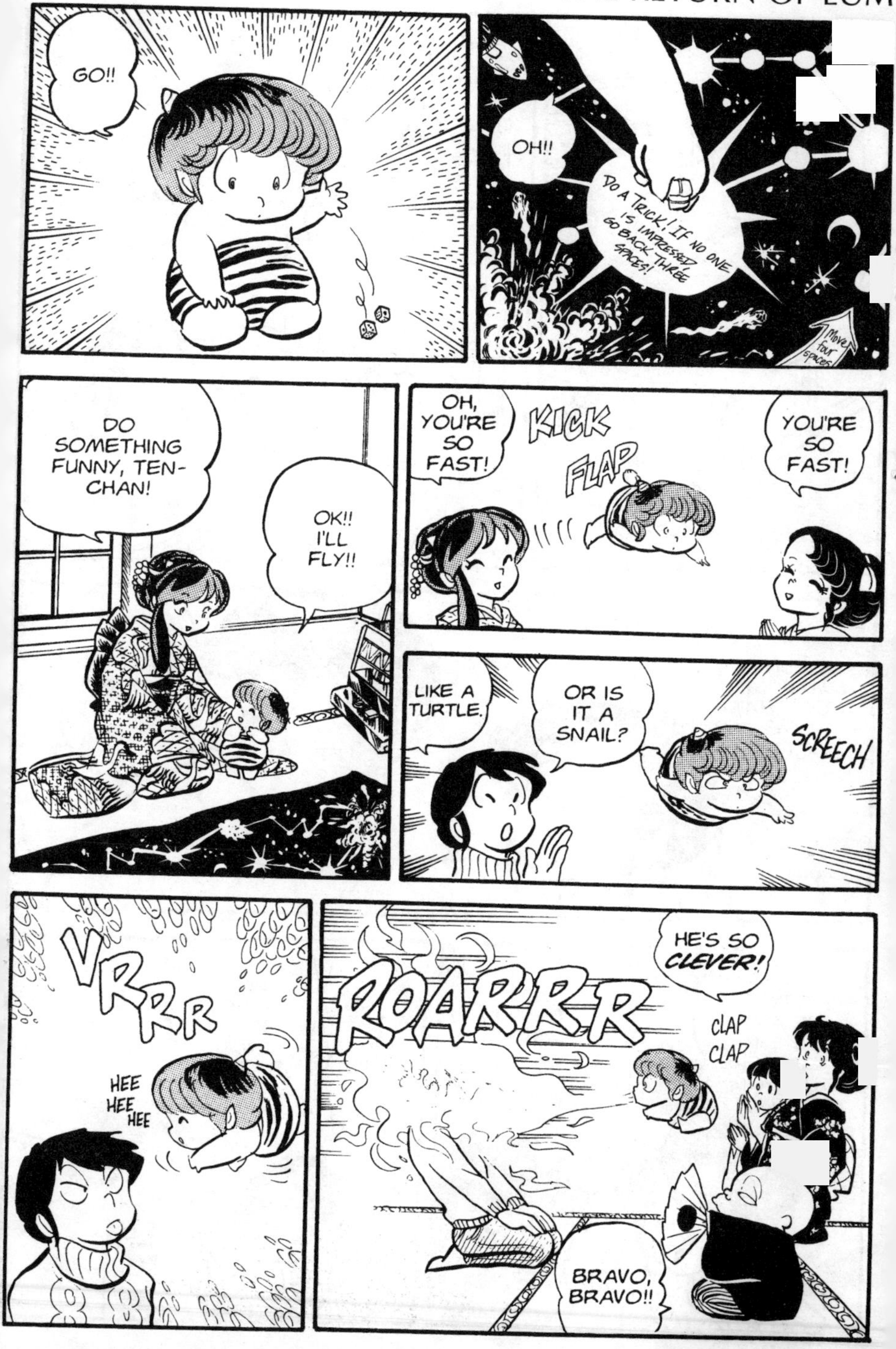
GO!!
OH!!
DO A TRICK! IF NO ONE IS IMPRESSED, GO BACK THREE SPACES!
Move four spaces
DO SOMETHING FUNNY, TEN-CHAN!
OK!! I'LL FLY!!
OH, YOU'RE SO FAST!
KICK
FLAP
YOU'RE SO FAST!
LIKE A TURTLE.
OR IS IT A SNAIL?
SCREECH
VRRR
HEE HEE HEE
ROARRR
HE'S SO CLEVER!
CLAP CLAP
BRAVO, BRAVO!!

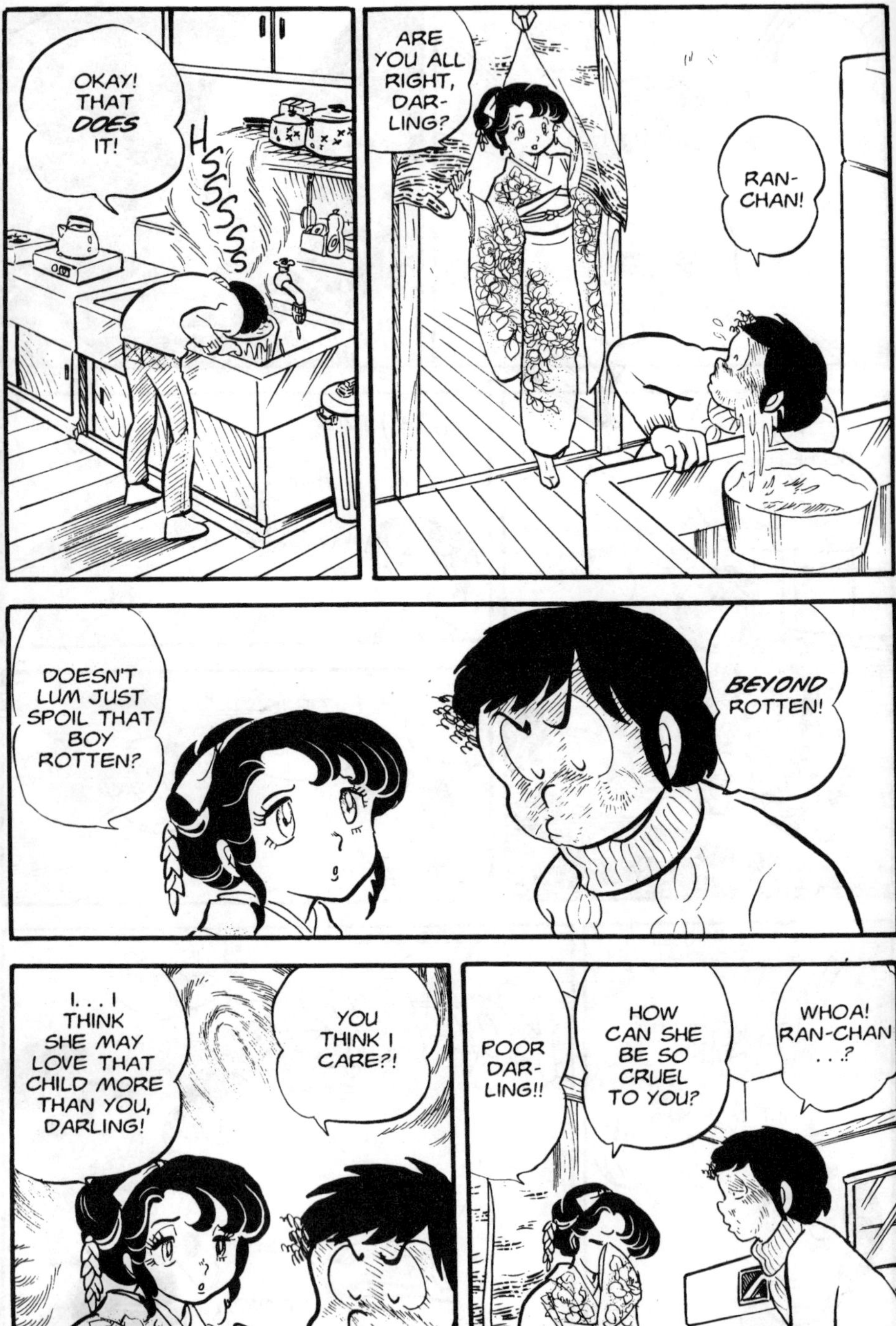
OKAY! THAT DOES IT!
HSSSSS
ARE YOU ALL RIGHT, DAR-LING?
RAN-CHAN!
DOESN'T LUM JUST SPOIL THAT BOY ROTTEN?
BEYOND ROTTEN!
I. . . I THINK SHE MAY LOVE THAT CHILD MORE THAN YOU, DARLING!
YOU THINK I CARE?!
POOR DAR-LING!!
HOW CAN SHE BE SO CRUEL TO YOU?
WHOA! RAN-CHAN . . .?

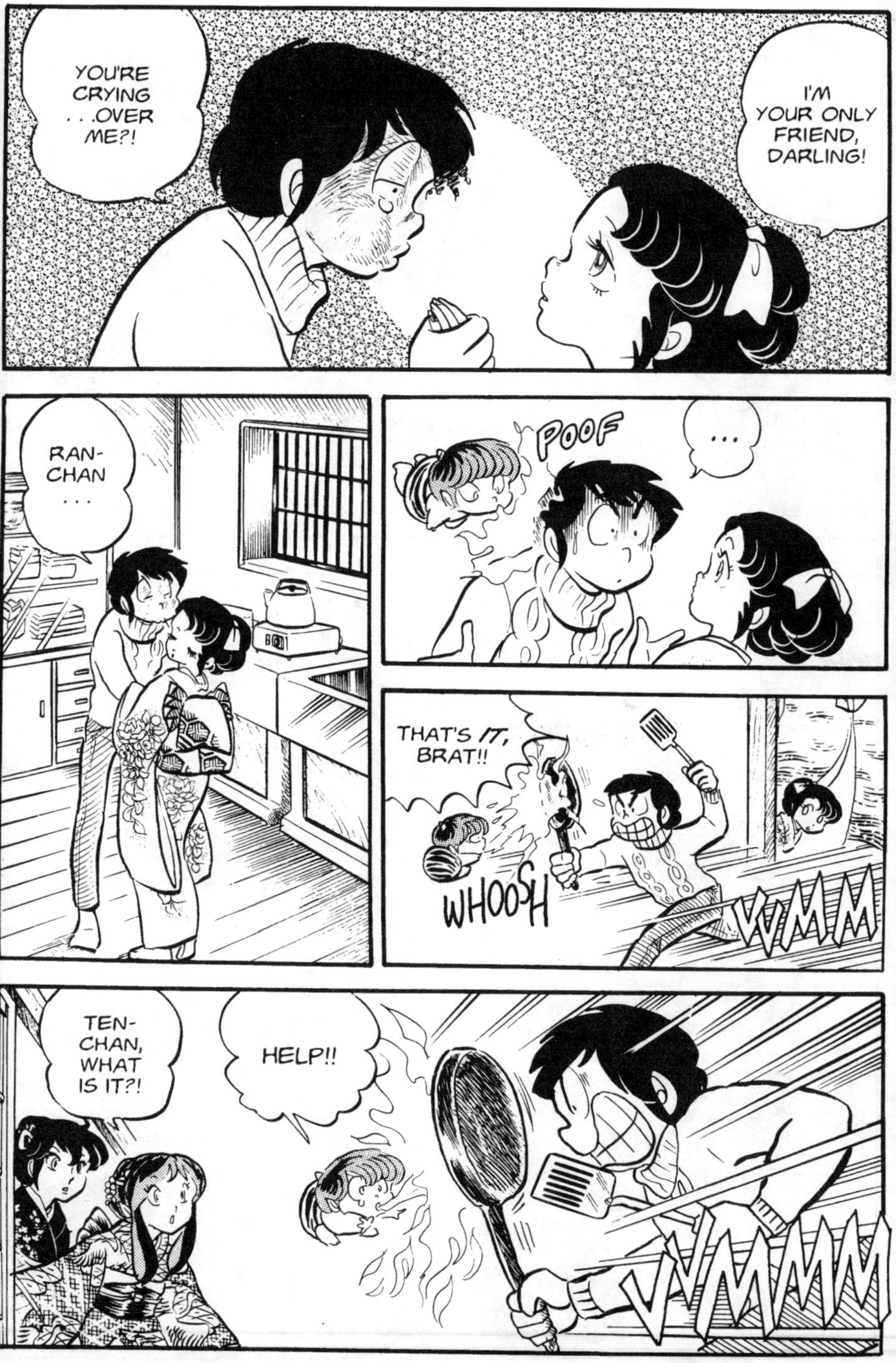
YOU'RE CRYING . . .OVER ME?!
I'M YOUR ONLY FRIEND, DARLING!
RAN-CHAN . . .
POOF
. . .
THAT'S IT, BRAT!!
WHOOSH
VMMM
TEN-CHAN, WHAT IS IT?!
HELP!!
VMMM

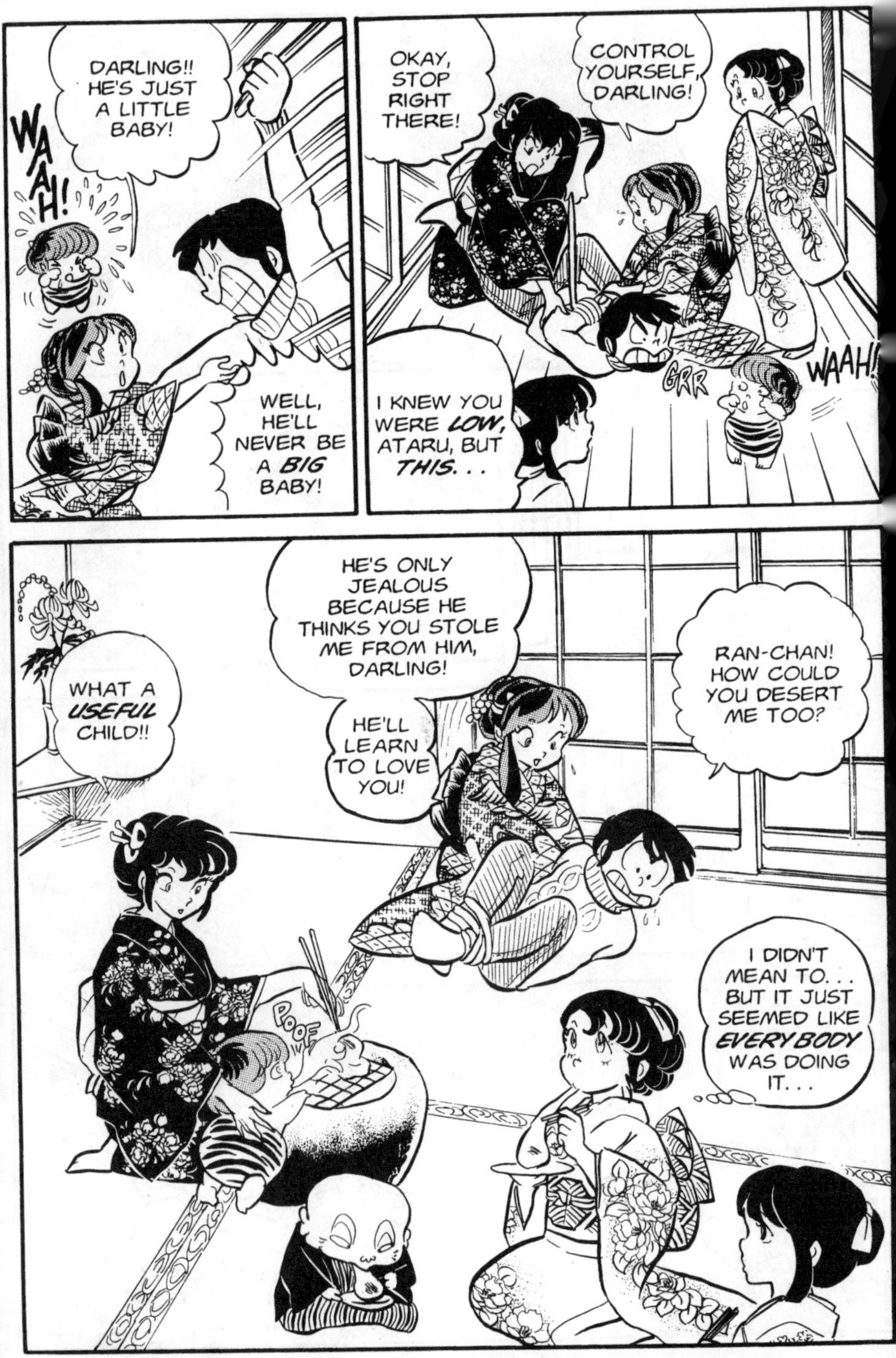
WAAH!
DARLING!! HE'S JUST A LITTLE BABY!
WELL, HE'LL NEVER BE A BIG BABY!
OKAY, STOP RIGHT THERE!
CONTROL YOURSELF, DARLING!
I KNEW YOU WERE LOW, ATARU, BUT THIS. . .
GRR
WAAH!
WHAT A USEFUL CHILD!!
HE'S ONLY JEALOUS BECAUSE HE THINKS YOU STOLE ME FROM HIM, DARLING!
HE'LL LEARN TO LOVE YOU!
RAN-CHAN! HOW COULD YOU DESERT ME TOO?
POOF
I DIDN'T MEAN TO. . . BUT IT JUST SEEMED LIKE EVERYBODY WAS DOING IT. . .

PART FOUR
TEN-CHAN IN LOVE

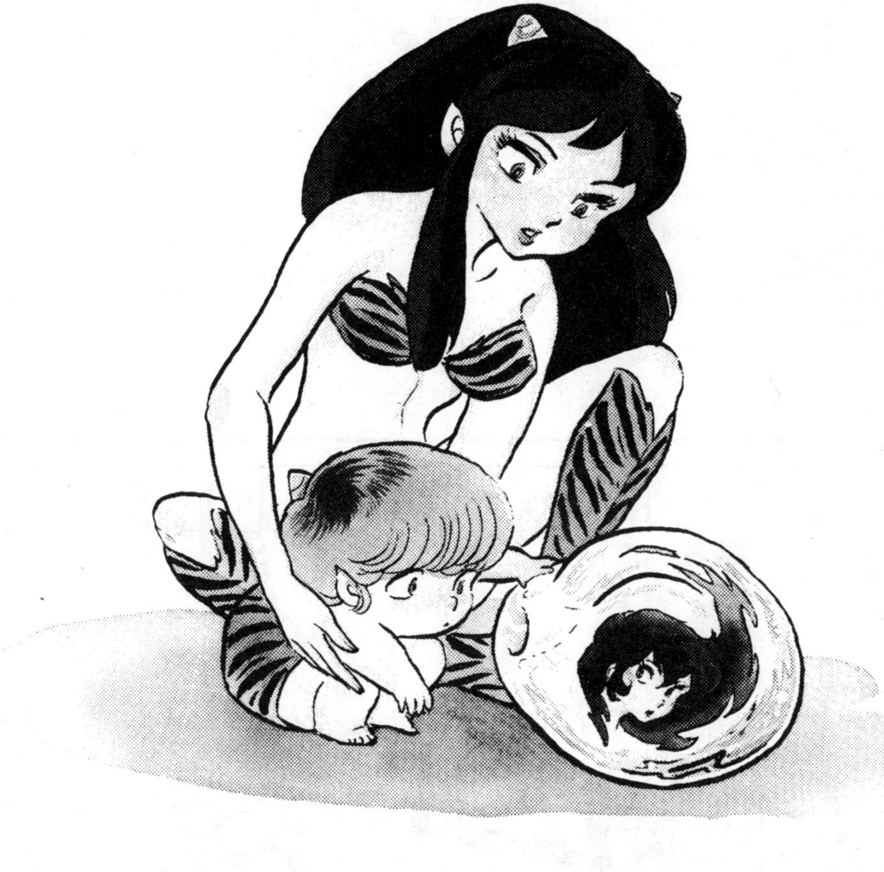

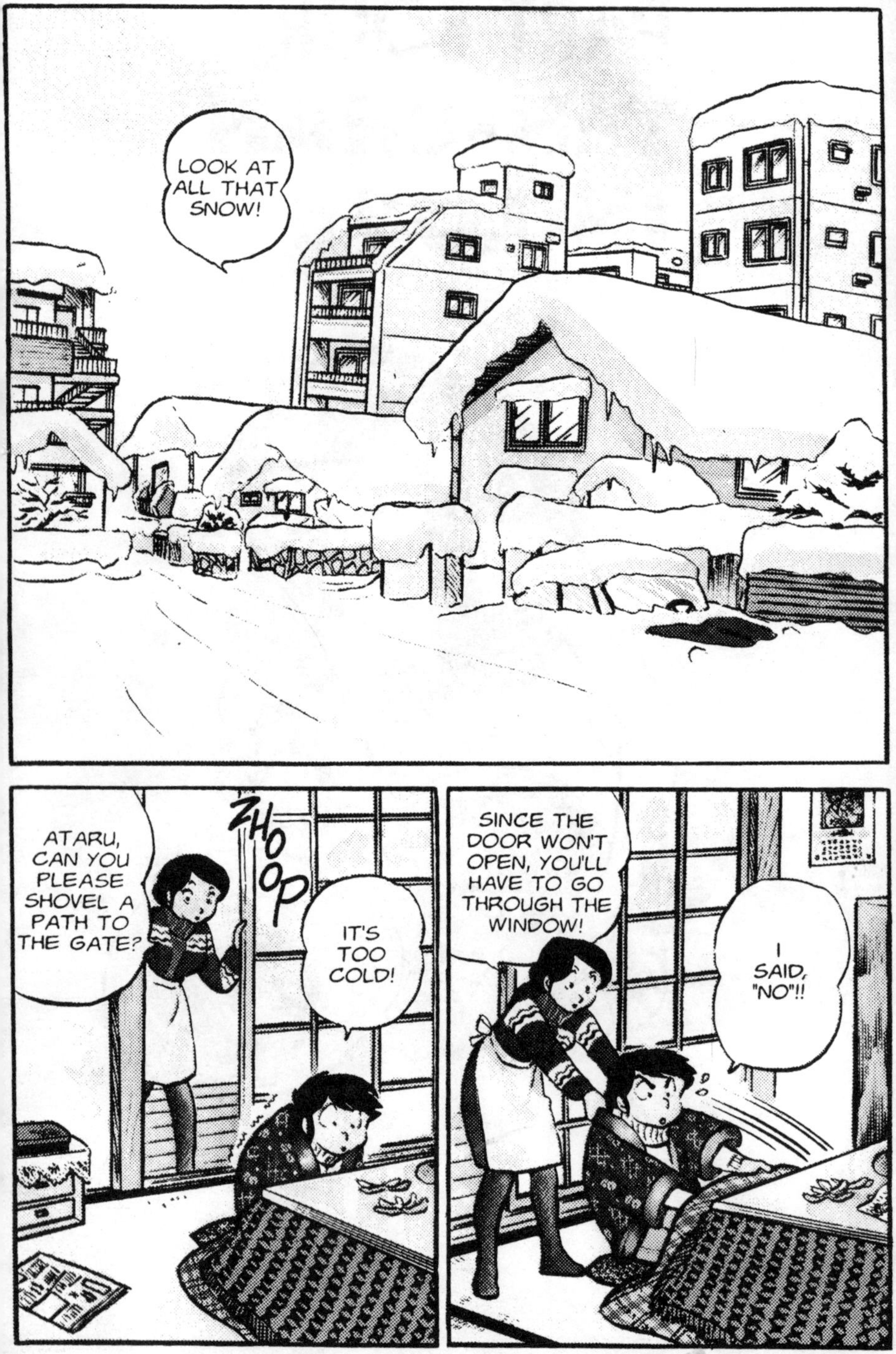
LOOK AT ALL THAT SNOW!
ATARU, CAN YOU PLEASE SHOVEL A PATH TO THE GATE?
ZHOOP
IT'S TOO COLD!
SINCE THE DOOR WON'T OPEN, YOU'LL HAVE TO GO THROUGH THE WINDOW!
I SAID, "NO"!!

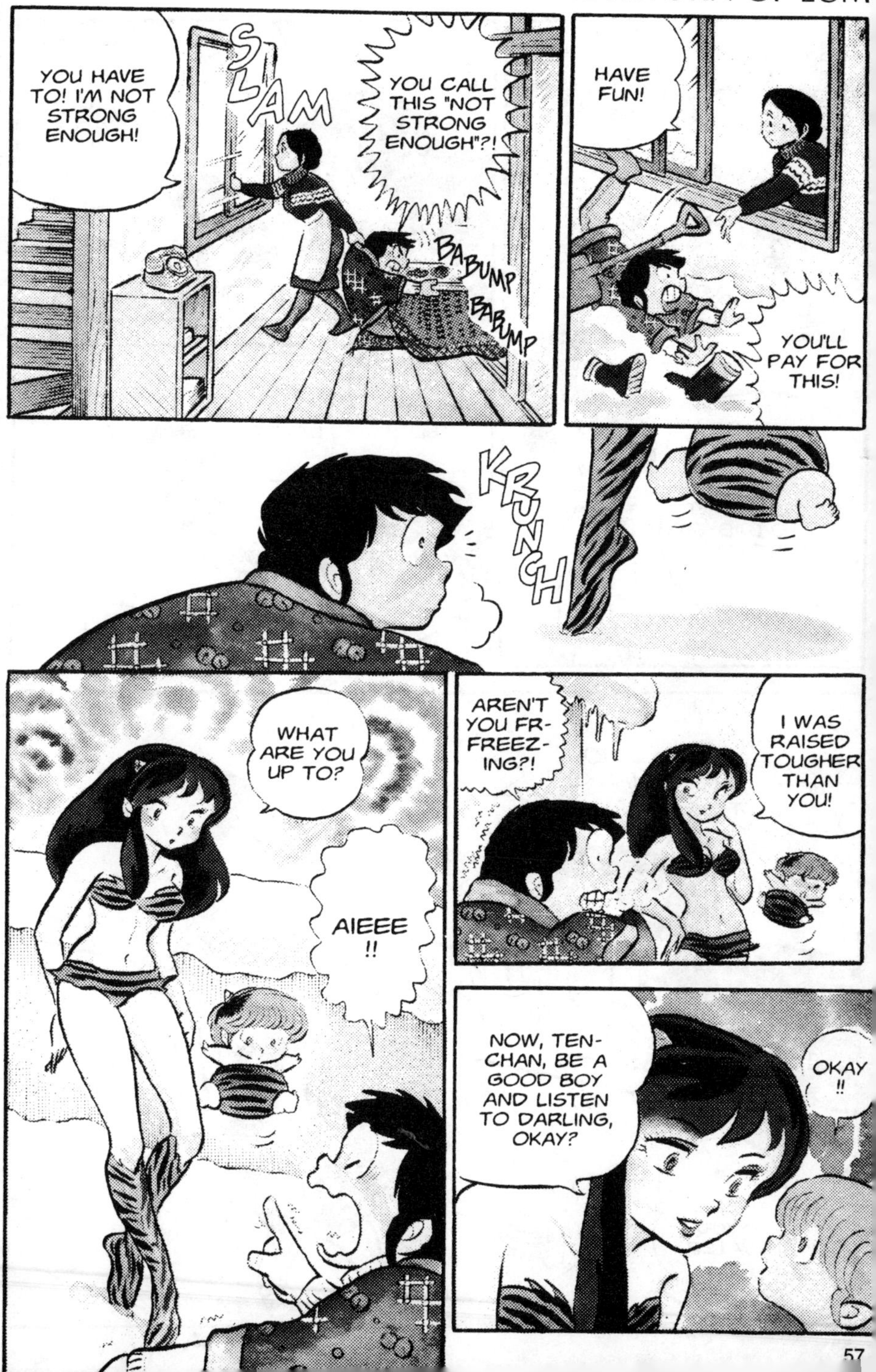
YOU HAVE TO! I'M NOT STRONG ENOUGH!
SLAM
YOU CALL THIS "NOT STRONG ENOUGH"?!
BABUMP
BABUMP
HAVE FUN!
YOU'LL PAY FOR THIS!
KRUNCH
WHAT ARE YOU UP TO?
AIEEE !!
AREN'T YOU FR-FREEZ-ING?!
I WAS RAISED TOUGHER THAN YOU!
NOW, TEN-CHAN, BE A GOOD BOY AND LISTEN TO DARLING, OKAY?
OKAY !!

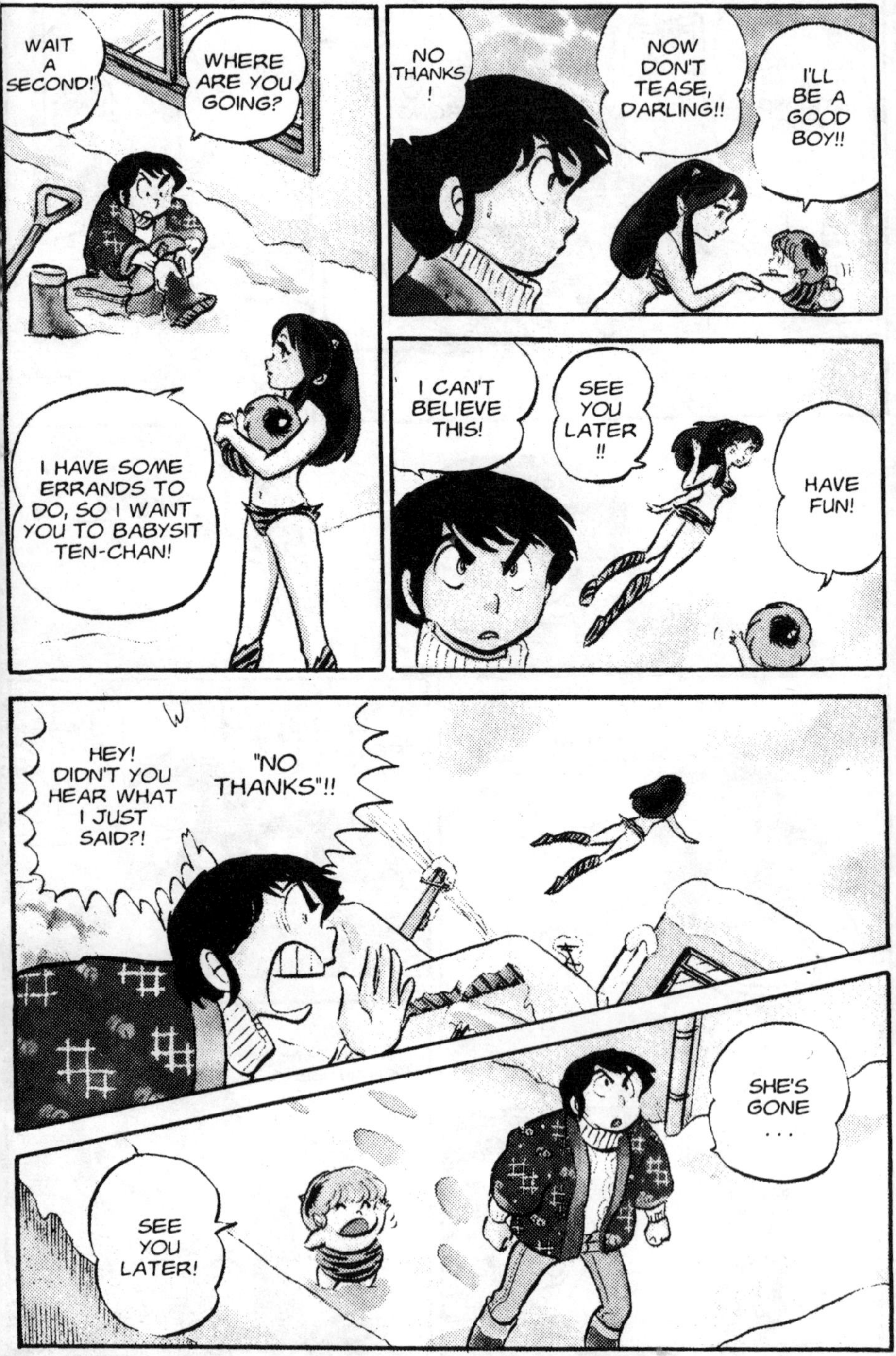
WAIT A SECOND!
WHERE ARE YOU GOING?
I HAVE SOME ERRANDS TO DO, SO I WANT YOU TO BABYSIT TEN-CHAN!
NO THANKS!
NOW DON'T TEASE, DARLING!!
I'LL BE A GOOD BOY!!
I CAN'T BELIEVE THIS!
SEE YOU LATER!!
HAVE FUN!
HEY! DIDN'T YOU HEAR WHAT I JUST SAID?!
"NO THANKS"!!
SEE YOU LATER!
SHE'S GONE . . .

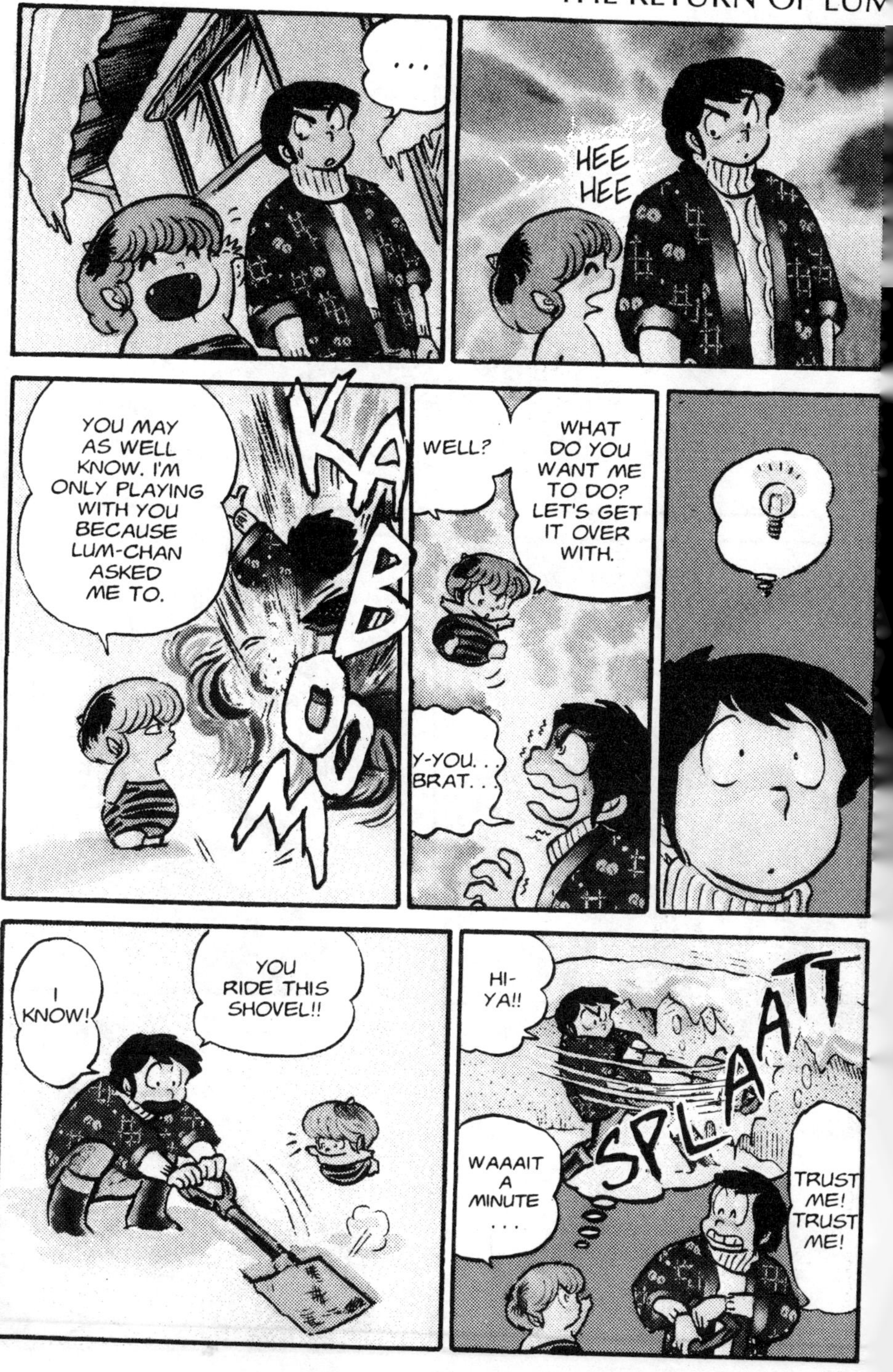
. . .
HEE HEE
YOU MAY AS WELL KNOW. I'M ONLY PLAYING WITH YOU BECAUSE LUM-CHAN ASKED ME TO.
KABOOOM
WELL?
WHAT DO YOU WANT ME TO DO? LET'S GET IT OVER WITH.
Y-YOU. . . BRAT. . .
I KNOW!
YOU RIDE THIS SHOVEL!!
HI-YA!!
SPLAATT
WAAAIT A MINUTE . . .
TRUST ME! TRUST ME!

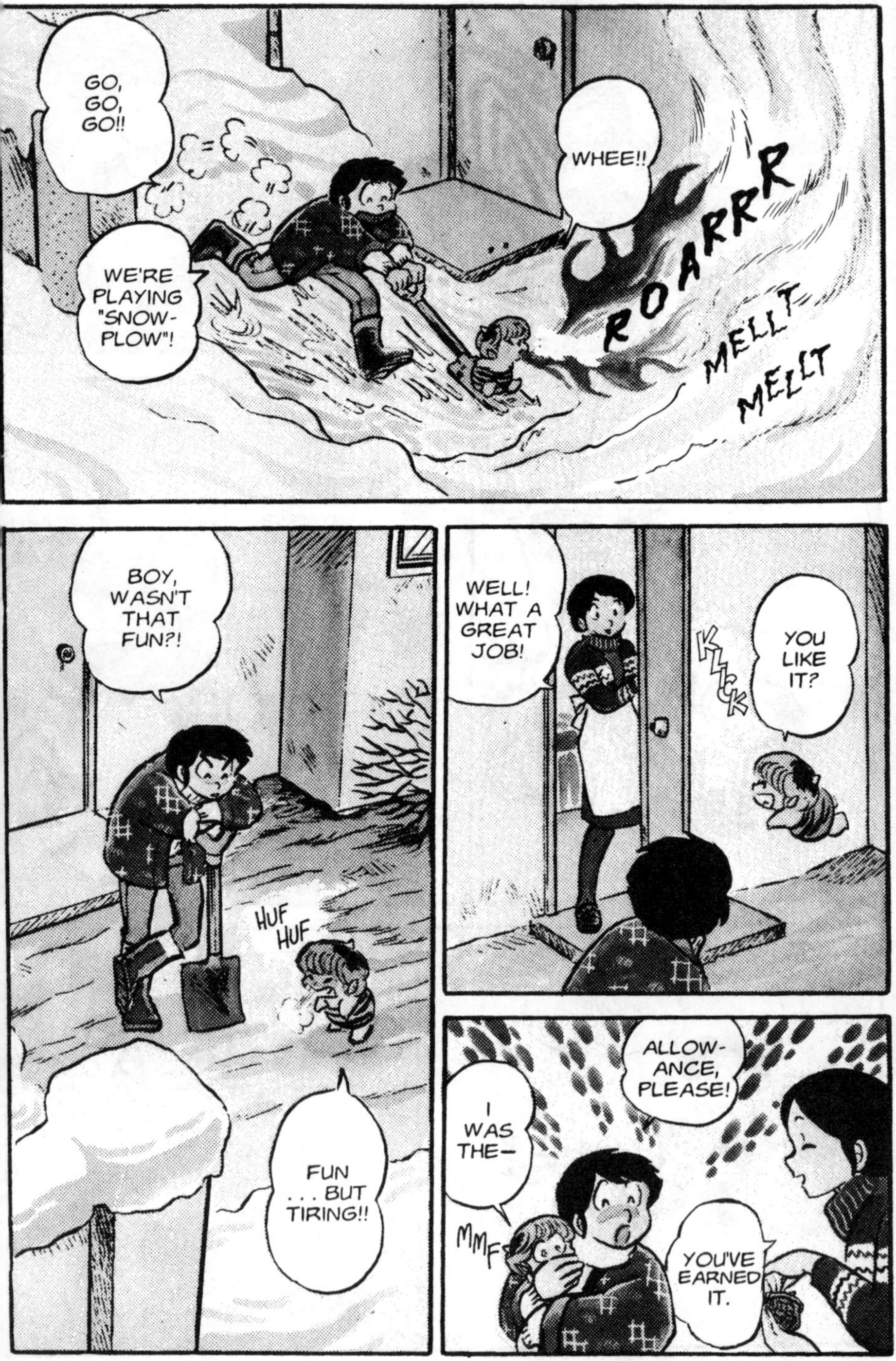
GO, GO, GO!!
WE'RE PLAYING "SNOW-PLOW"!
WHEE!!
ROARRR
MELLT
MELLT
BOY, WASN'T THAT FUN?!
HUF HUF
FUN . . . BUT TIRING!!
WELL! WHAT A GREAT JOB!
KLICK
YOU LIKE IT?
ALLOWANCE, PLEASE!
I WAS THE–
MMF
YOU'VE EARNED IT.

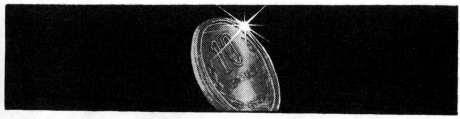

WHAT'S THIS?!

IT'S A 10 YEN COIN! REMEMBER?

WHEN YOU WERE LITTLE, YOU WERE SO HAPPY WHEN I GAVE YOU A SHINY 10 YEN!

UH, HELLO ...

YOU WERE SO SWEET!

IT SEEMS LIKE YESTERDAY!

"GIMME 10 YEN," YOU'D SAY! *SIGH*

TUMP TUMP

HEY!!

KRUNCH

KRUNCH

I JUST HOPE IT'S NOT HEREDITARY!

HEY, I WAS THINKING ...

WHAT?

SNOW SHOVELING ¥1000

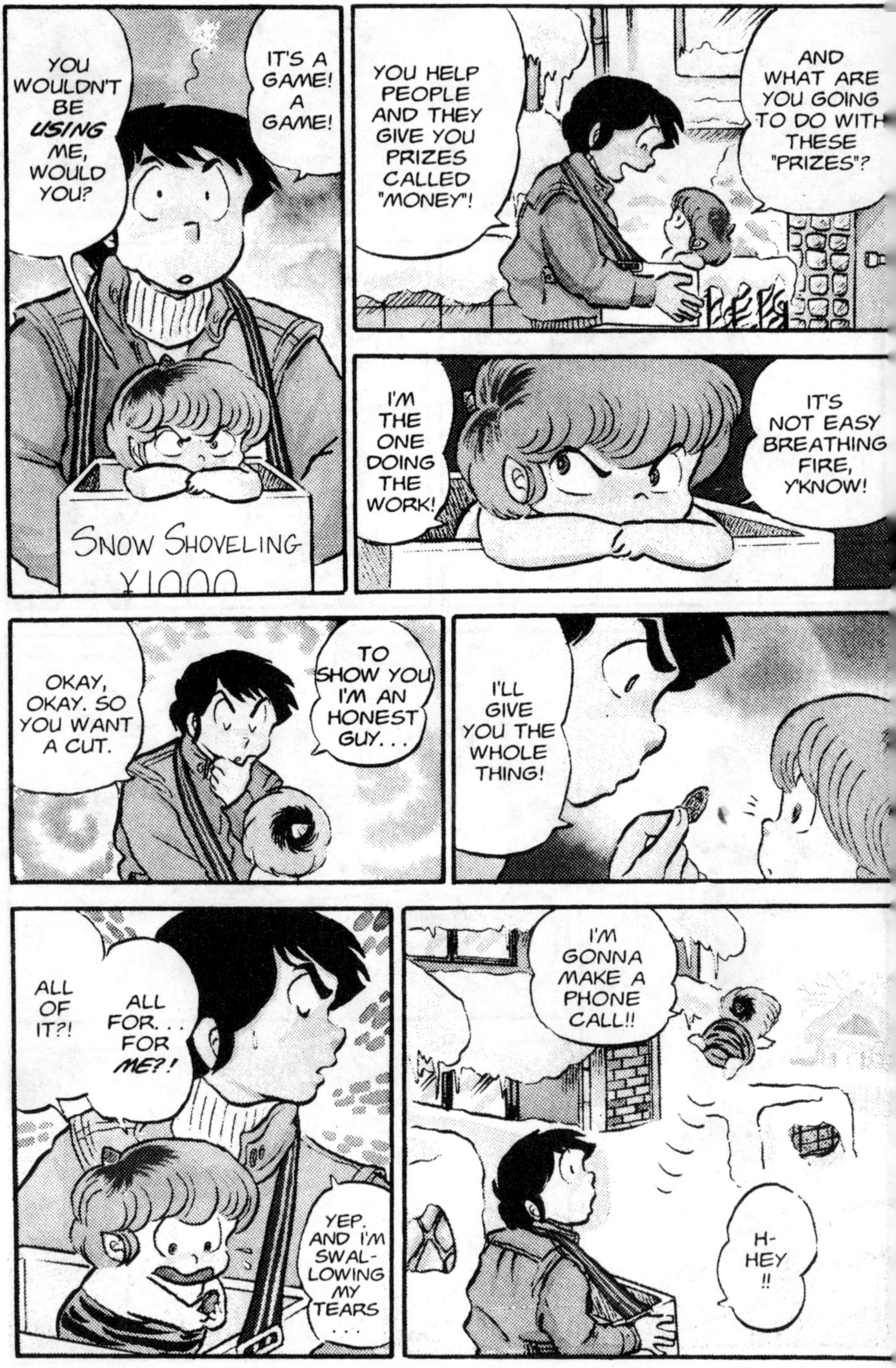
YOU WOULDN'T BE *USING* ME, WOULD YOU?
IT'S A GAME! A GAME!
SNOW SHOVELING
¥1000
YOU HELP PEOPLE AND THEY GIVE YOU PRIZES CALLED "MONEY"!
AND WHAT ARE YOU GOING TO DO WITH THESE "PRIZES"?
I'M THE ONE DOING THE WORK!
IT'S NOT EASY BREATHING FIRE, Y'KNOW!
OKAY, OKAY. SO YOU WANT A CUT.
TO SHOW YOU I'M AN HONEST GUY...
I'LL GIVE YOU THE WHOLE THING!
ALL OF IT?!
ALL FOR... FOR *ME?!*
YEP. AND I'M SWAL-LOWING MY TEARS...
I'M GONNA MAKE A PHONE CALL!!
H-HEY!!

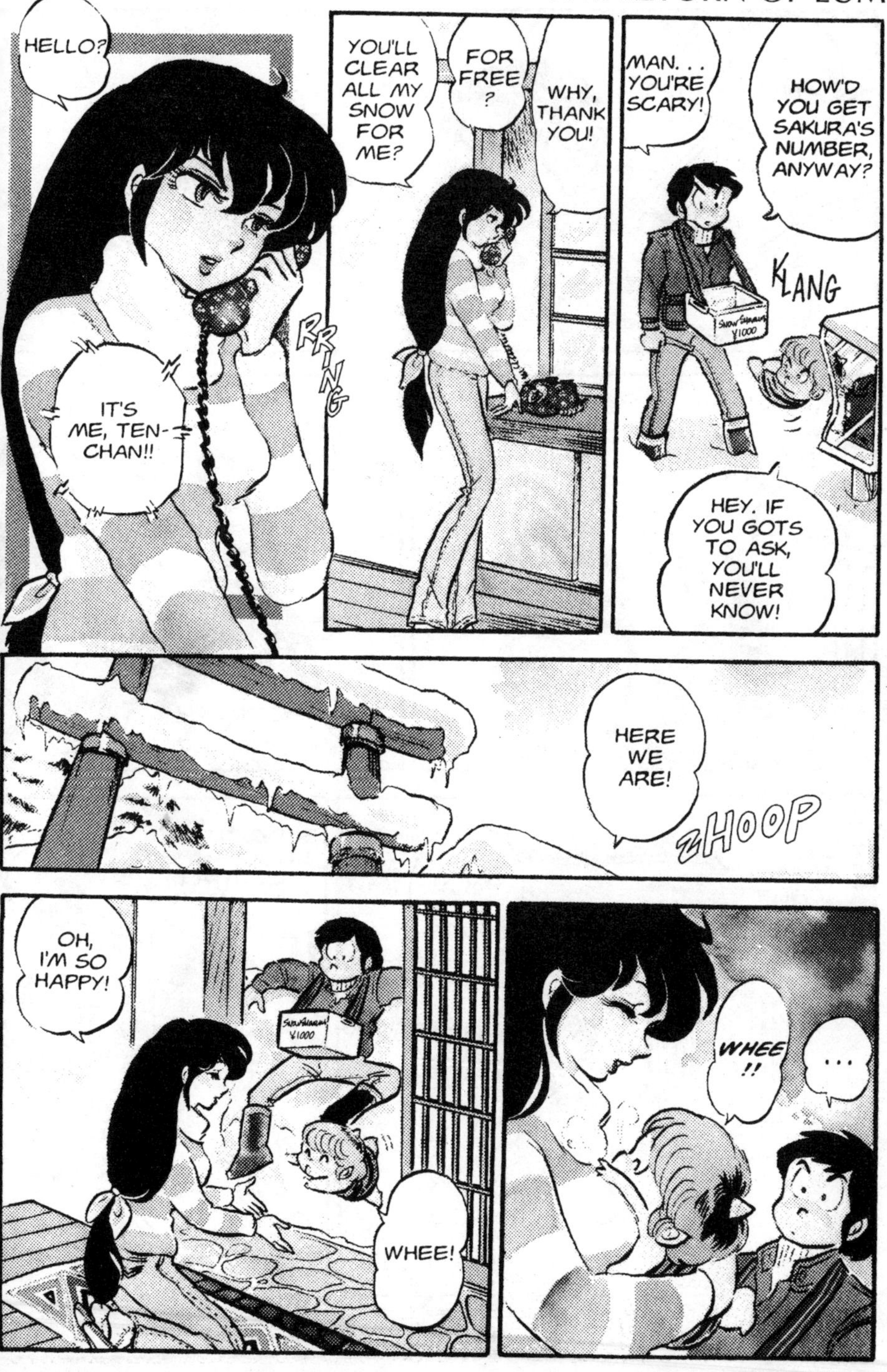
HELLO?
IT'S ME, TEN-CHAN!!
RRING
YOU'LL CLEAR ALL MY SNOW FOR ME?
FOR FREE?
WHY, THANK YOU!
MAN. . . YOU'RE SCARY!
HOW'D YOU GET SAKURA'S NUMBER, ANYWAY?
KLANG
HEY. IF YOU GOTS TO ASK, YOU'LL NEVER KNOW!
HERE WE ARE!
ZHOOP
OH, I'M SO HAPPY!
WHEE!
WHEE!!
. . .

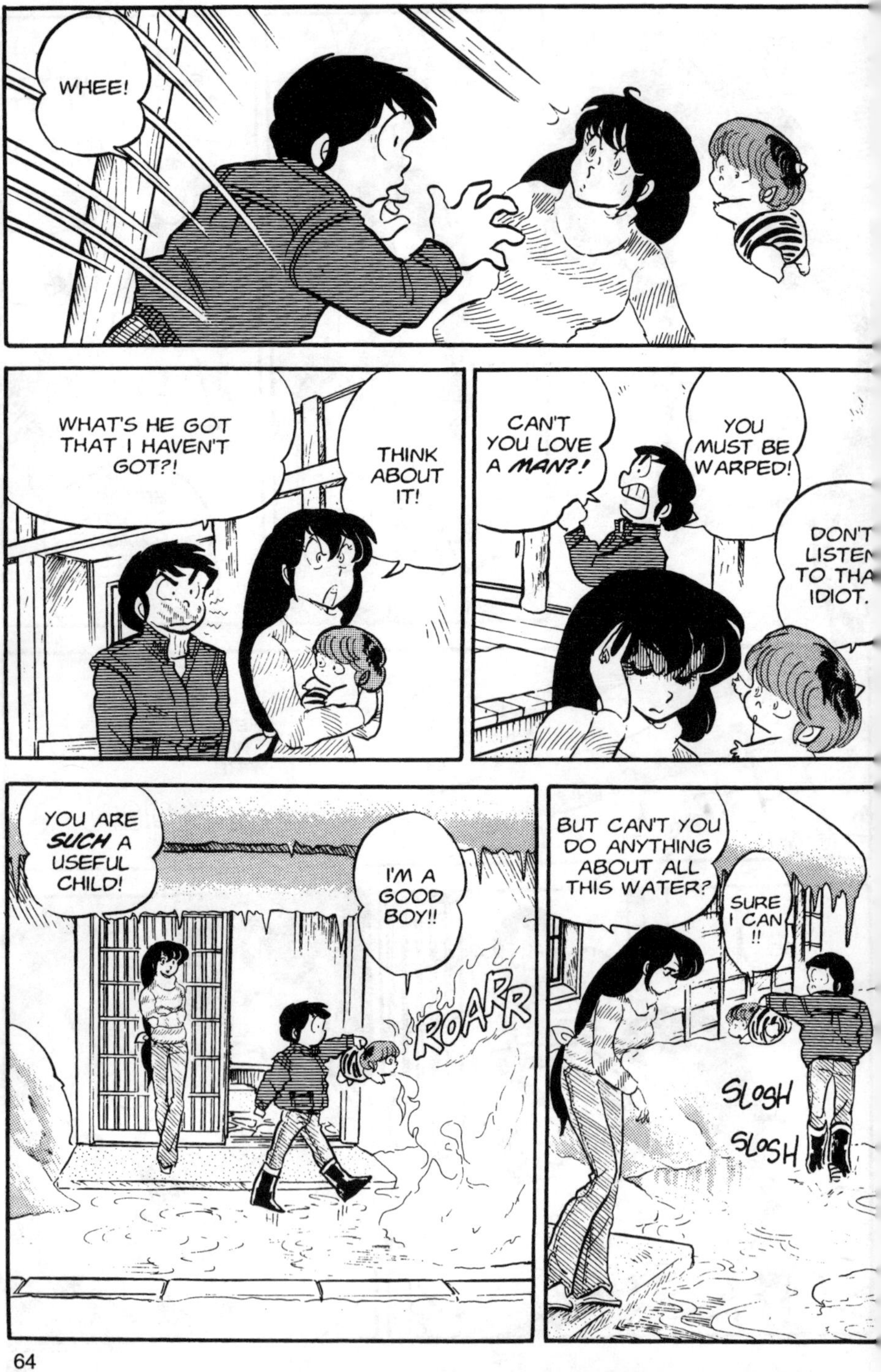
WHEE!
WHAT'S HE GOT THAT I HAVEN'T GOT?!
THINK ABOUT IT!
CAN'T YOU LOVE A *MAN?!*
YOU MUST BE WARPED!
DON'T LISTEN TO THAT IDIOT.
YOU ARE *SUCH* A USEFUL CHILD!
I'M A GOOD BOY!!
ROARR
BUT CAN'T YOU DO ANYTHING ABOUT ALL THIS WATER?
SURE I CAN !!
SLOSH
SLOSH

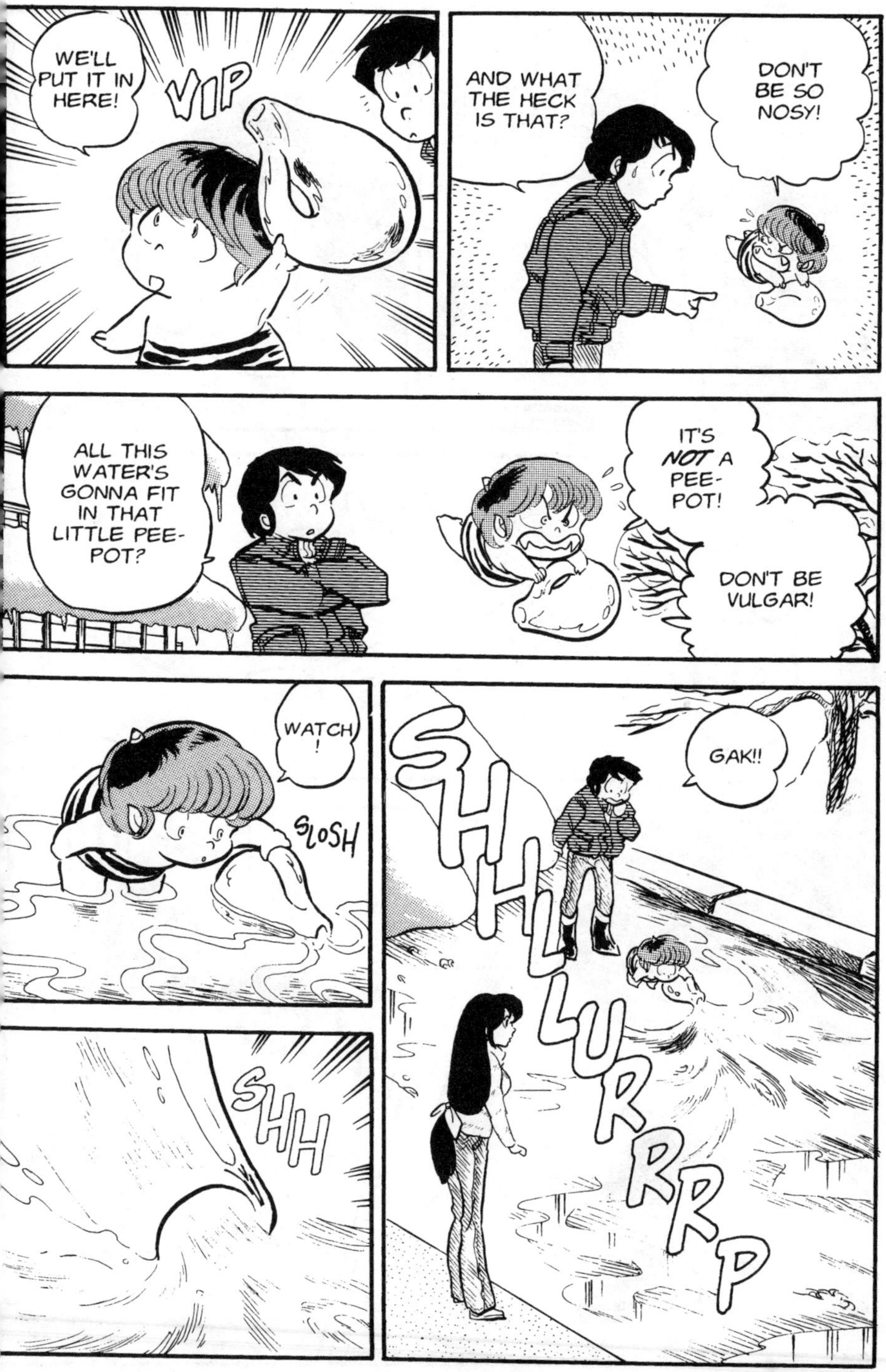
WE'LL PUT IT IN HERE!
VIP
AND WHAT THE HECK IS THAT?
DON'T BE SO NOSY!
ALL THIS WATER'S GONNA FIT IN THAT LITTLE PEE-POT?
IT'S *NOT* A PEE-POT!
DON'T BE VULGAR!
WATCH!
SLOSH
SHH
SHHLLURRRP
GAK!!

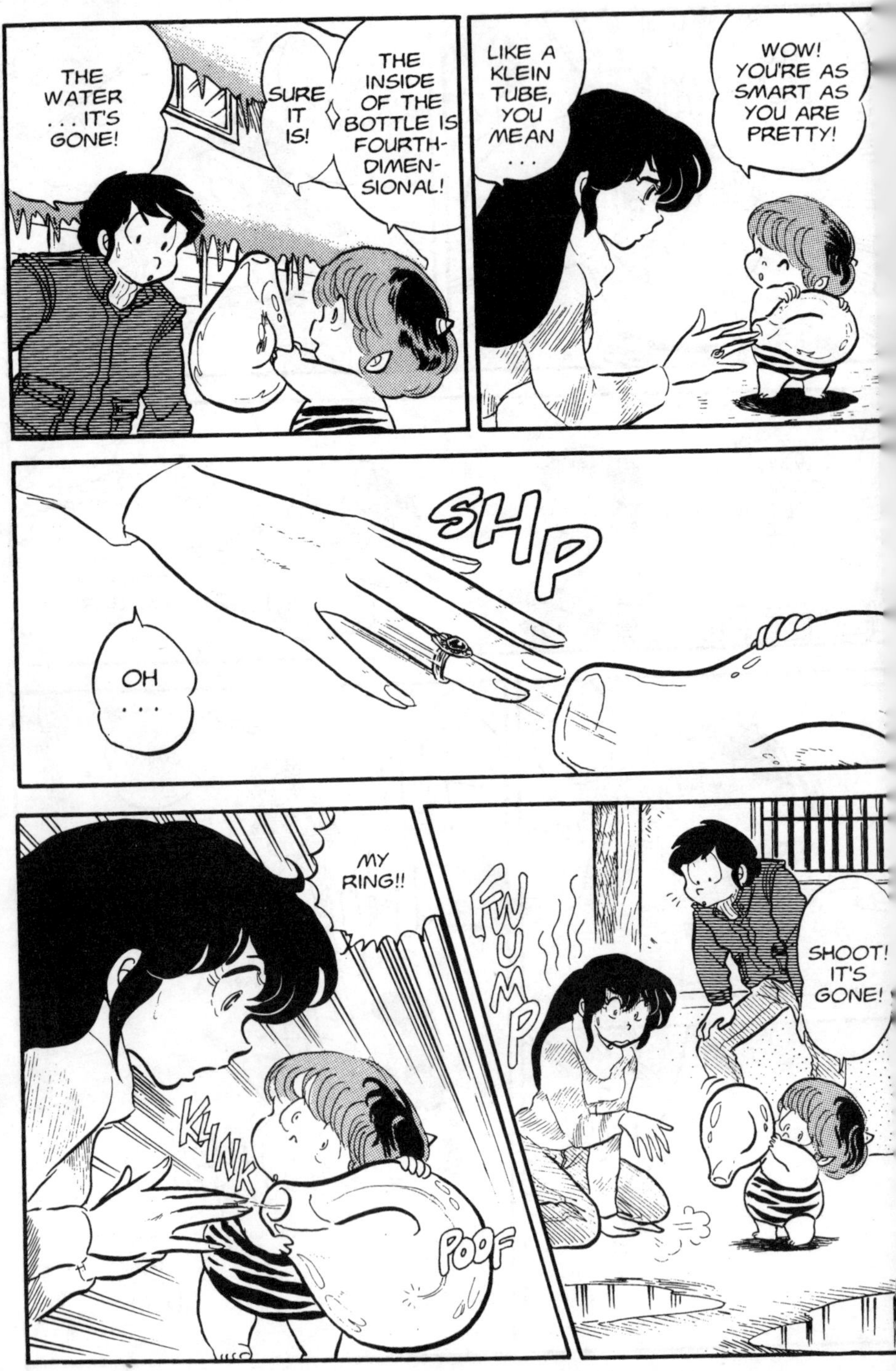
THE WATER . . . IT'S GONE!
SURE IT IS!
THE INSIDE OF THE BOTTLE IS FOURTH-DIMENSIONAL!
LIKE A KLEIN TUBE, YOU MEAN . . .
WOW! YOU'RE AS SMART AS YOU ARE PRETTY!
SHP
OH . . .
MY RING!!
KLINK
POOF
FWUMP
SHOOT! IT'S GONE!

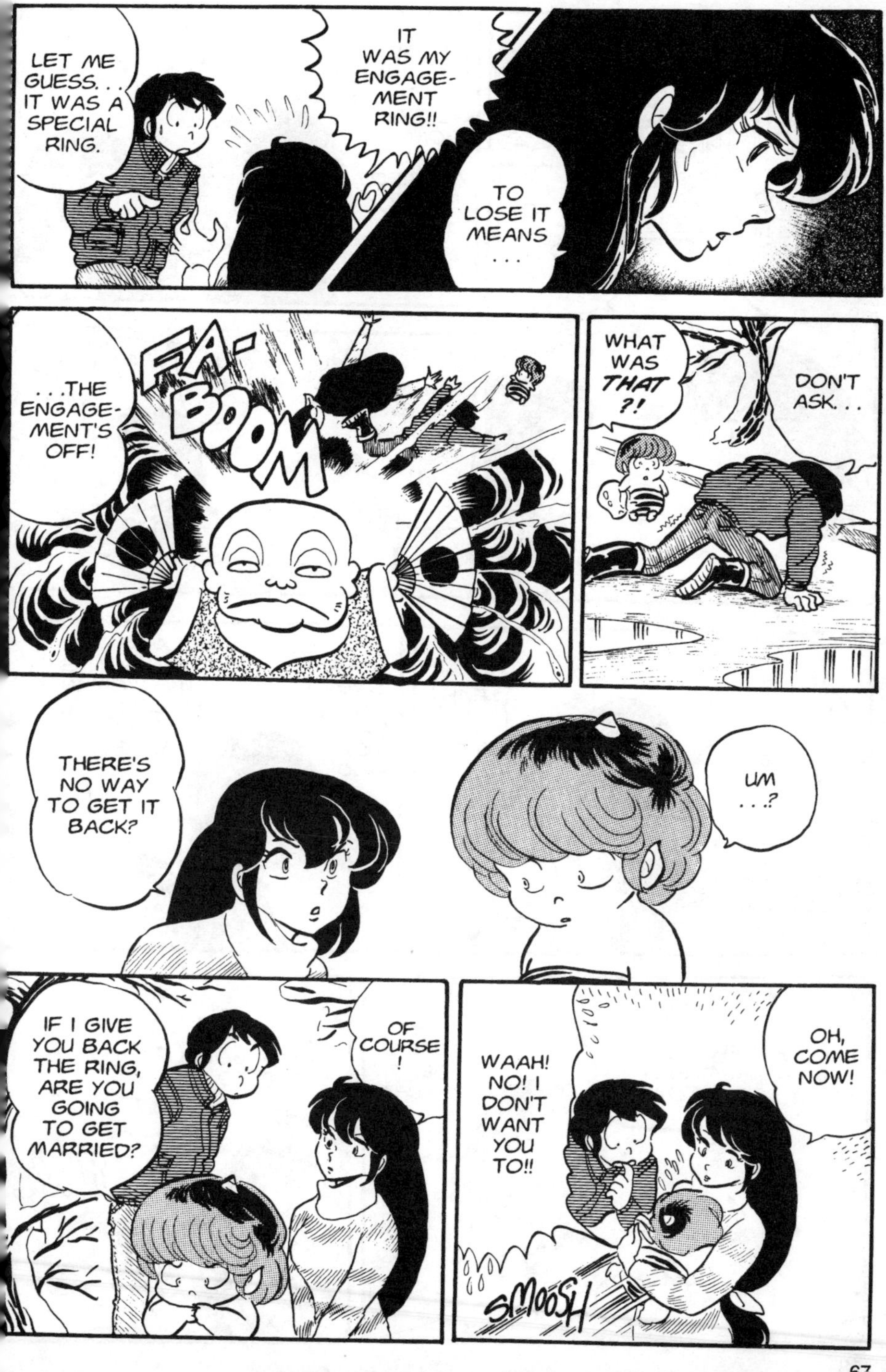
LET ME GUESS. . . IT WAS A SPECIAL RING.
IT WAS MY ENGAGE-MENT RING!!
TO LOSE IT MEANS . . .
. . .THE ENGAGE-MENT'S OFF!
FA-BOOOM
WHAT WAS THAT ?!
DON'T ASK. . .
THERE'S NO WAY TO GET IT BACK?
UM . . .?
IF I GIVE YOU BACK THE RING, ARE YOU GOING TO GET MARRIED?
OF COURSE !
WAAH! NO! I DON'T WANT YOU TO!!
OH, COME NOW!
SMOOSH

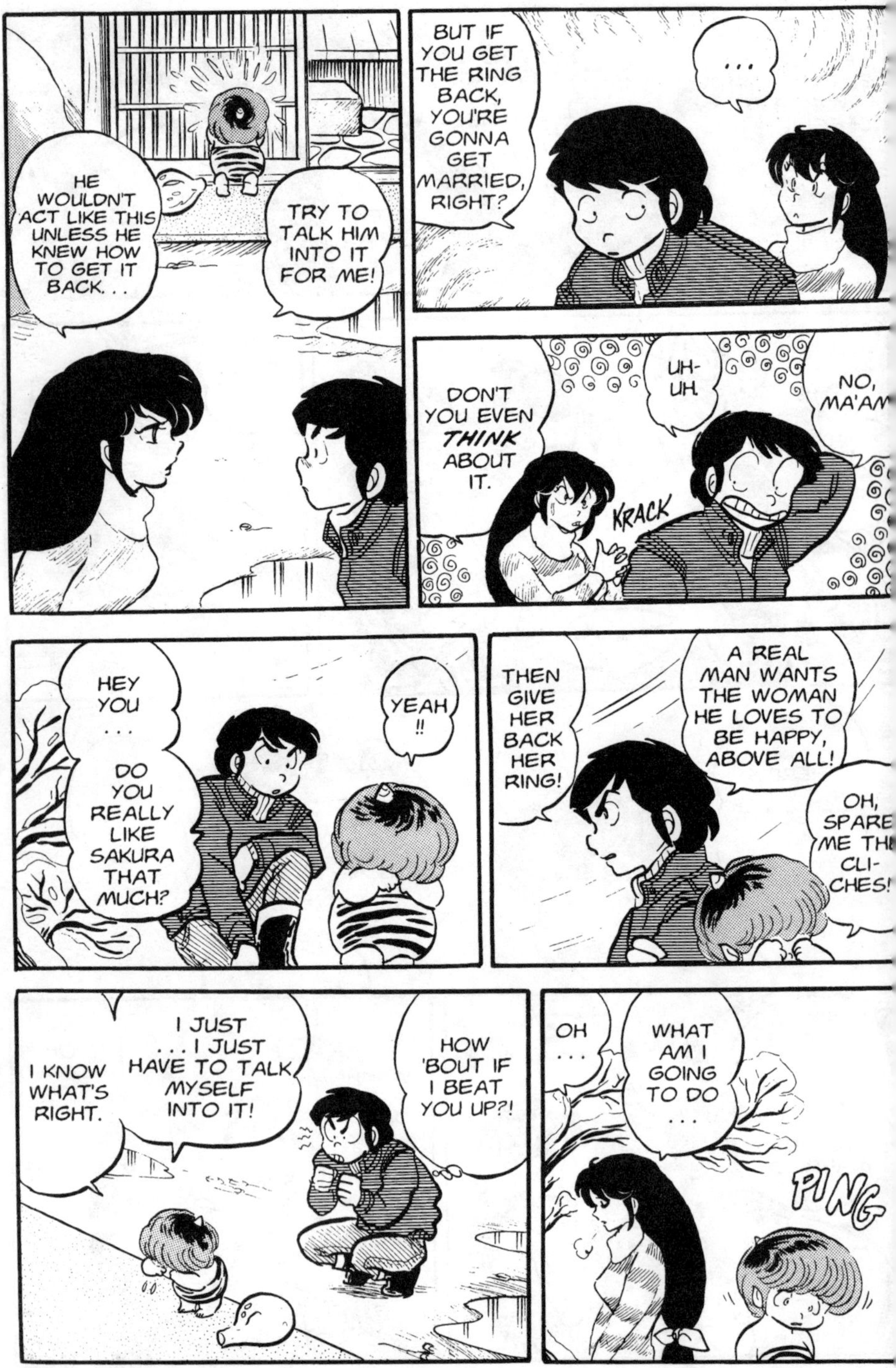
HE WOULDN'T ACT LIKE THIS UNLESS HE KNEW HOW TO GET IT BACK. . .
TRY TO TALK HIM INTO IT FOR ME!
BUT IF YOU GET THE RING BACK, YOU'RE GONNA GET MARRIED, RIGHT?
. . .
DON'T YOU EVEN THINK ABOUT IT.
UH-UH.
NO, MA'AM
KRACK
HEY YOU . . .
DO YOU REALLY LIKE SAKURA THAT MUCH?
YEAH !!
THEN GIVE HER BACK HER RING!
A REAL MAN WANTS THE WOMAN HE LOVES TO BE HAPPY, ABOVE ALL!
OH, SPARE ME THE CLI-CHES!
I KNOW WHAT'S RIGHT.
I JUST . . . I JUST HAVE TO TALK MYSELF INTO IT!
HOW 'BOUT IF I BEAT YOU UP?!
OH . . .
WHAT AM I GOING TO DO . . .
PING

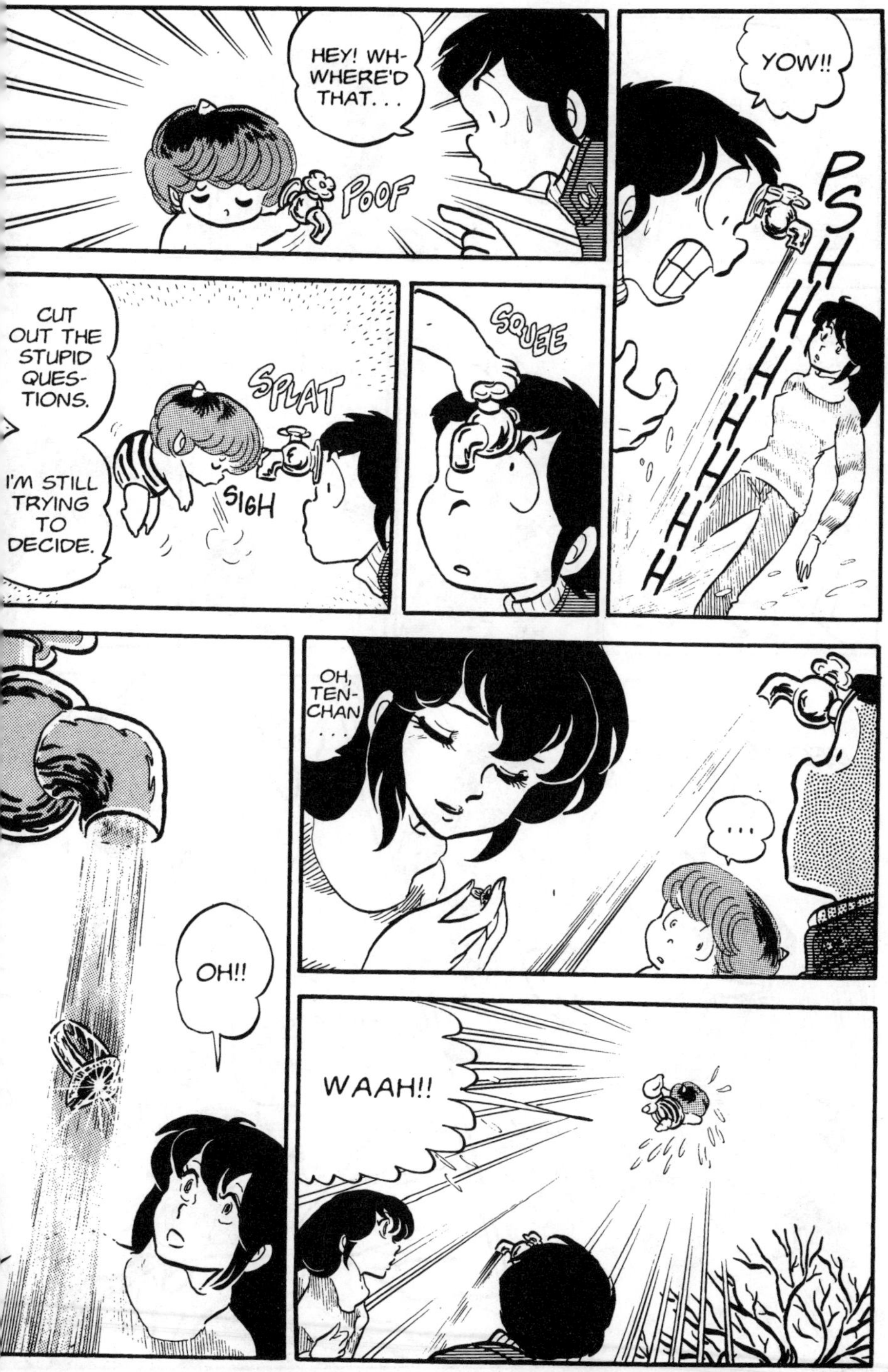
HEY! WH- WHERE'D THAT. . .
POOF
CUT OUT THE STUPID QUES- TIONS.
SPLAT
SIGH
I'M STILL TRYING TO DECIDE.
SQUEE
YOW!!
PSHHHHHHHHHH
OH!!
OH, TEN- CHAN . . .
. . .
WAAH!!

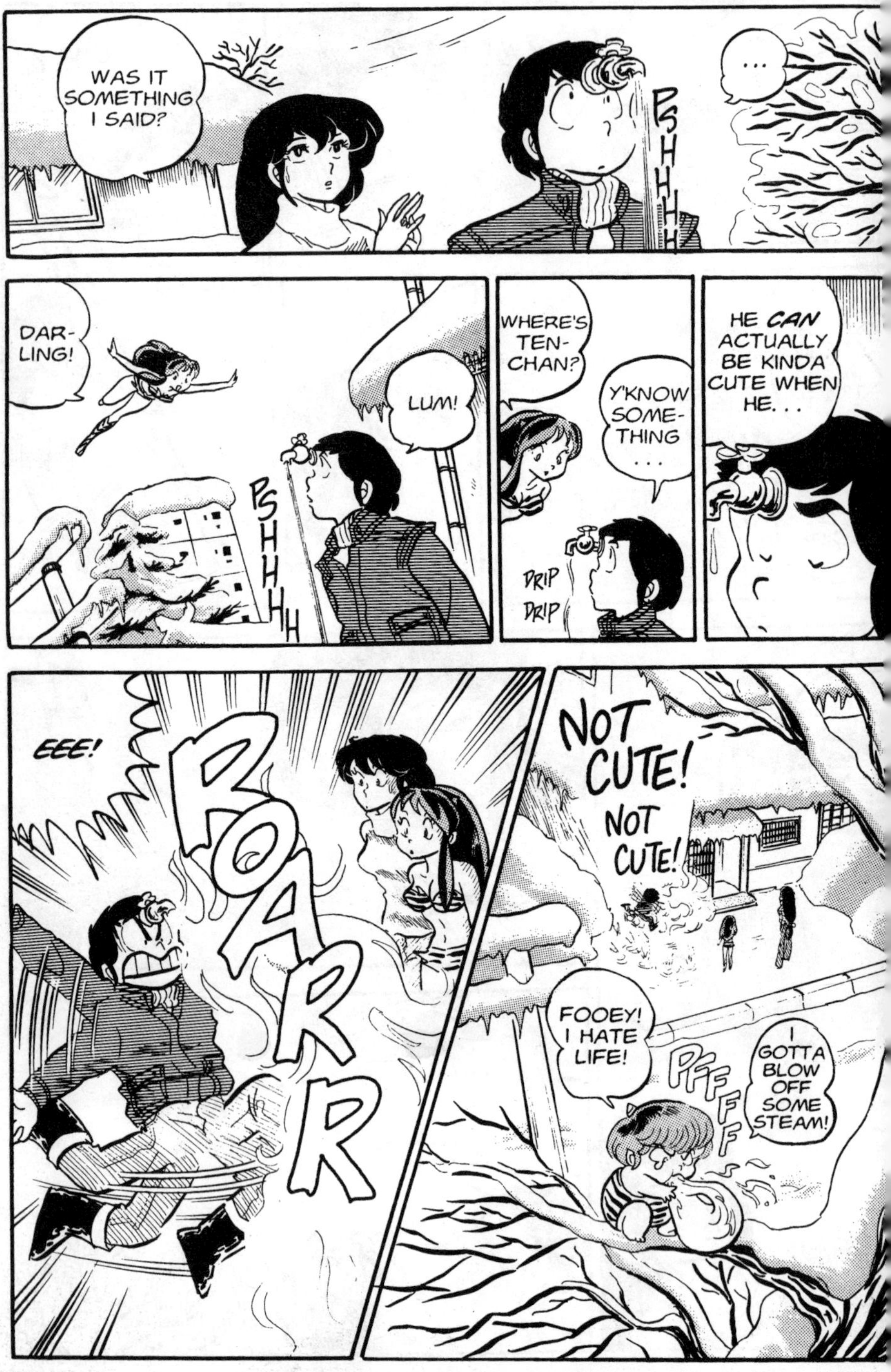
WAS IT SOMETHING I SAID?
PSHHHH
...
DAR-LING!
LUM!
PSHHHHH
WHERE'S TEN-CHAN?
Y'KNOW SOME-THING . . .
DRIP DRIP
HE CAN ACTUALLY BE KINDA CUTE WHEN HE. . .
EEE!
ROARR
NOT CUTE!
NOT CUTE!
FOOEY! I HATE LIFE!
PFFFFF
I GOTTA BLOW OFF SOME STEAM!

PART FIVE
BABES IN ARMS

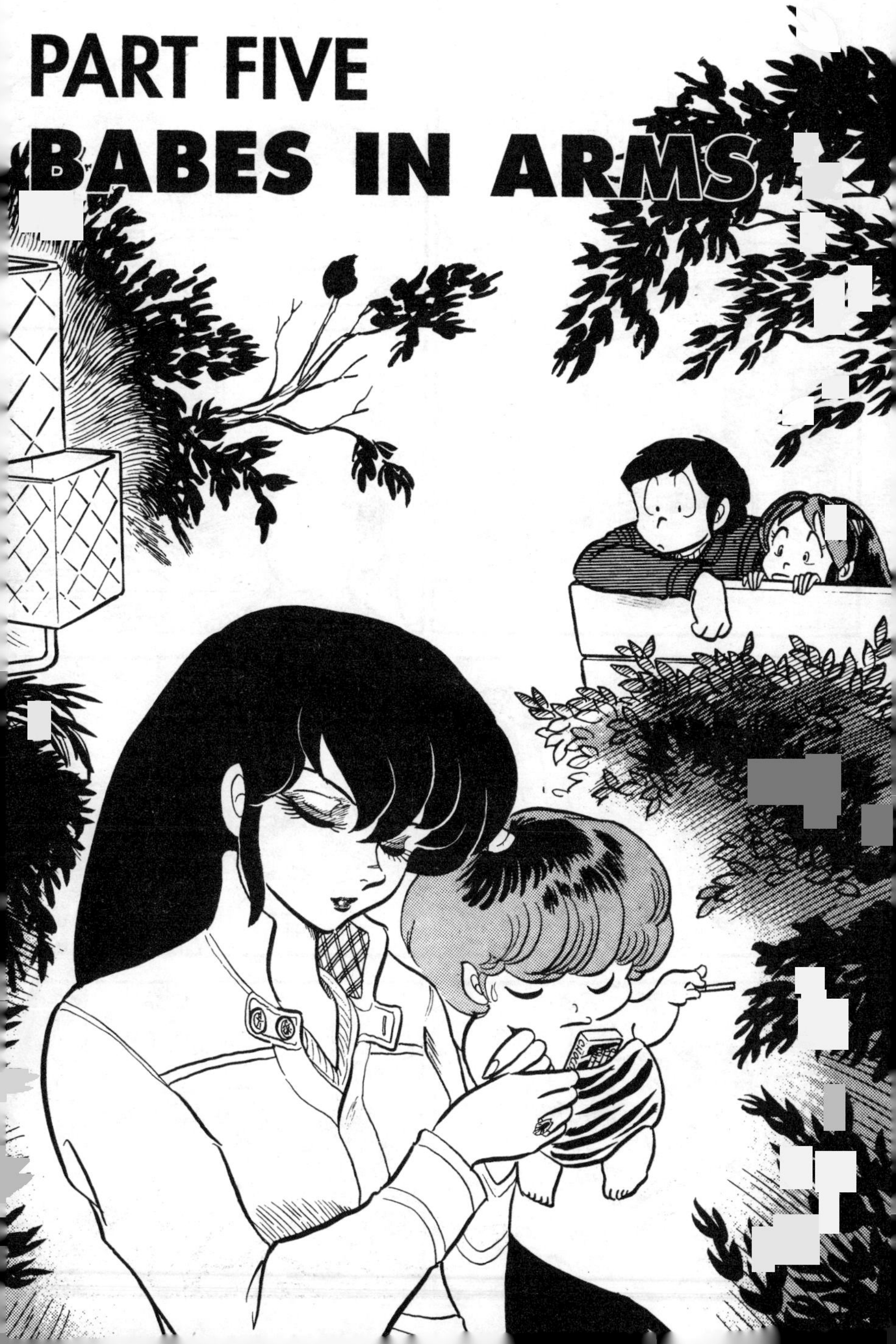

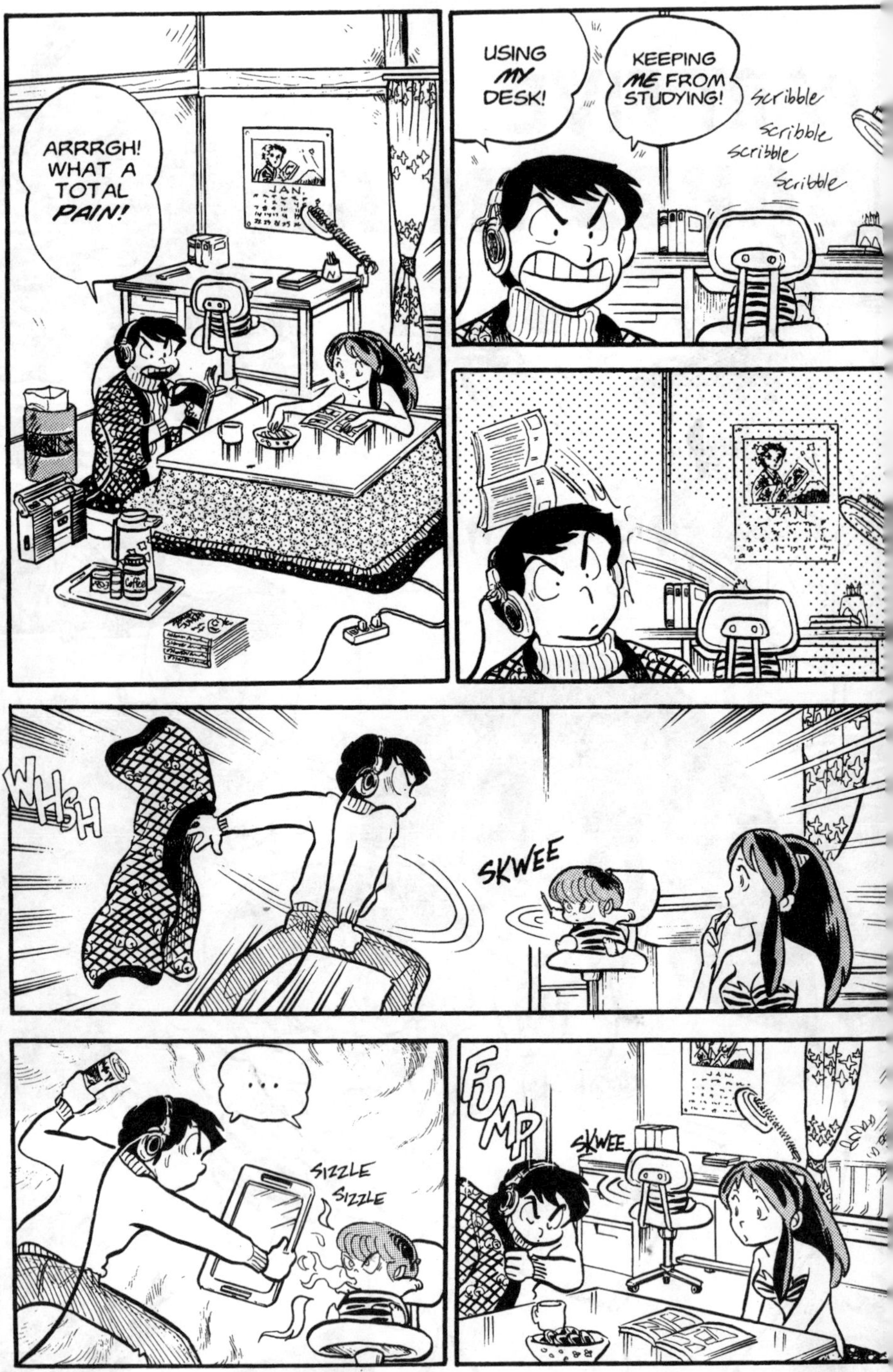
ARRRGH! WHAT A TOTAL PAIN!
JAN.
COFFEE
USING MY DESK!
KEEPING ME FROM STUDYING!
Scribble
Scribble
Scribble
Scribble
JAN
WHSH
SKWEE
. . .
SIZZLE
SIZZLE
FUMP
SKWEE
JAN.

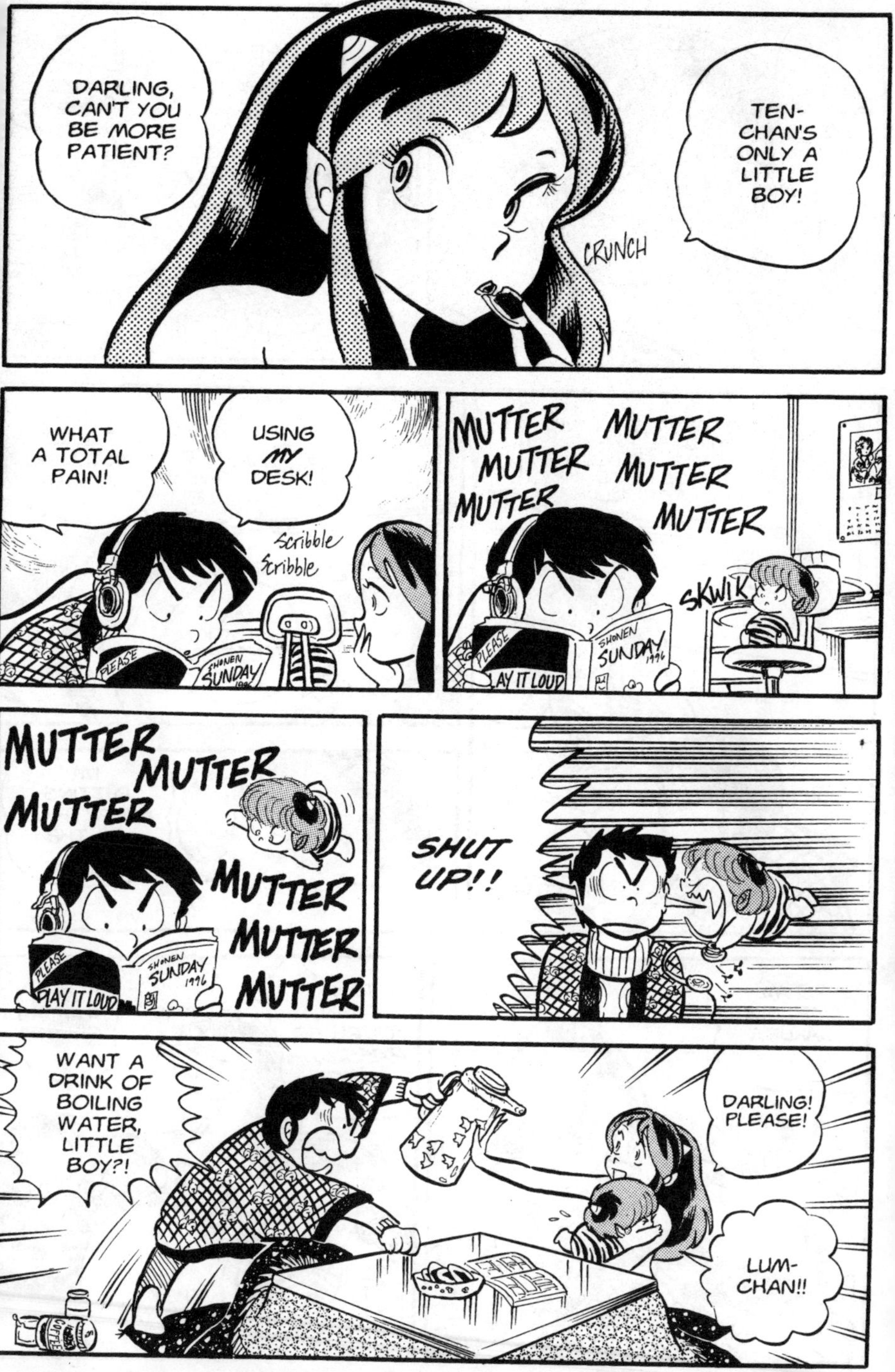
DARLING, CAN'T YOU BE MORE PATIENT?
CRUNCH
TEN-CHAN'S ONLY A LITTLE BOY!
WHAT A TOTAL PAIN!
USING MY DESK!
Scribble
Scribble
PLEASE
SHONEN SUNDAY 1996
MUTTER MUTTER MUTTER MUTTER MUTTER MUTTER
SKWIK
PLEASE PLAY IT LOUD
SHONEN SUNDAY 1996
MUTTER MUTTER MUTTER
MUTTER MUTTER MUTTER
PLEASE PLAY IT LOUD
SHONEN SUNDAY 1996
SHUT UP!!
WANT A DRINK OF BOILING WATER, LITTLE BOY?!
DARLING! PLEASE!
LUM-CHAN!!
COFFEE

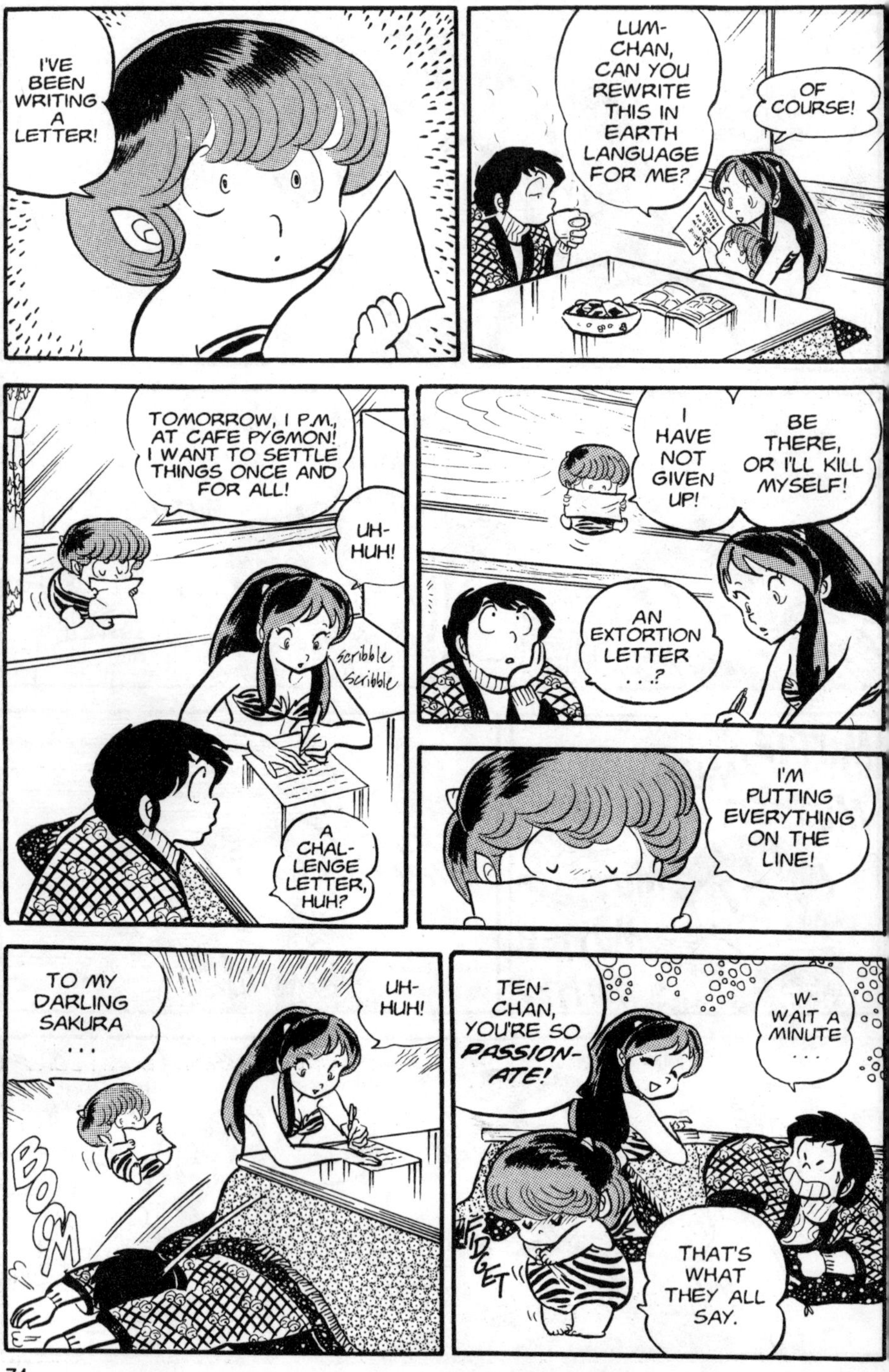

I'VE BEEN WRITING A LETTER!
LUM-CHAN, CAN YOU REWRITE THIS IN EARTH LANGUAGE FOR ME?
OF COURSE!
TOMORROW, 1 P.M., AT CAFE PYGMON! I WANT TO SETTLE THINGS ONCE AND FOR ALL!
UH-HUH!
scribble scribble
A CHAL-LENGE LETTER, HUH?
I HAVE NOT GIVEN UP!
BE THERE, OR I'LL KILL MYSELF!
AN EXTORTION LETTER . . .?
I'M PUTTING EVERYTHING ON THE LINE!
TO MY DARLING SAKURA . . .
UH-HUH!
BOOM
TEN-CHAN, YOU'RE SO PASSION-ATE!
W-WAIT A MINUTE . . .
FIDGET
THAT'S WHAT THEY ALL SAY.

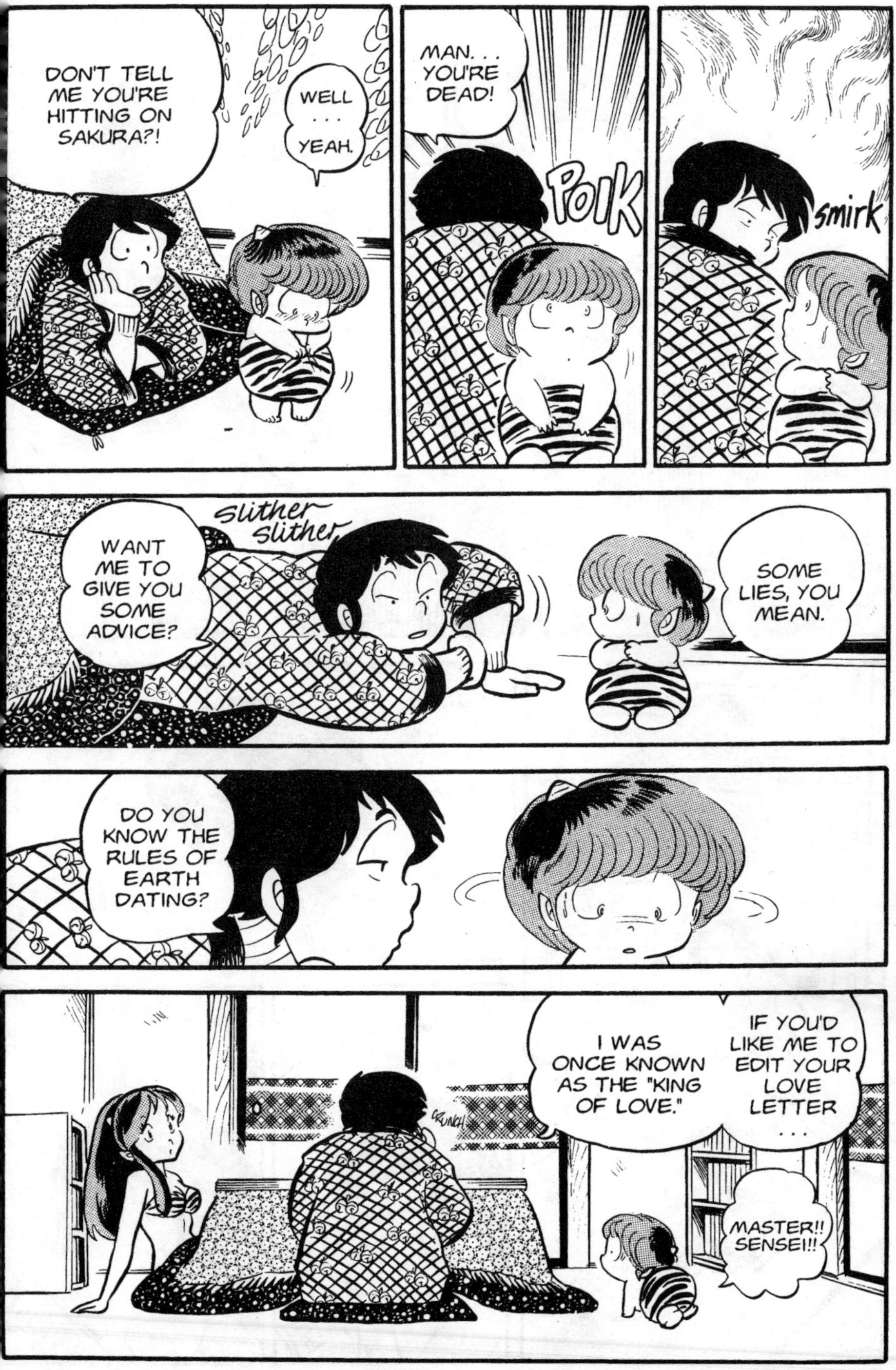
DON'T TELL ME YOU'RE HITTING ON SAKURA?!
WELL . . . YEAH.
MAN. . . YOU'RE DEAD!
POIK
smirk
Slither slither
WANT ME TO GIVE YOU SOME ADVICE?
SOME LIES, YOU MEAN.
DO YOU KNOW THE RULES OF EARTH DATING?
CRUNCH
I WAS ONCE KNOWN AS THE "KING OF LOVE."
IF YOU'D LIKE ME TO EDIT YOUR LOVE LETTER . . .
MASTER!! SENSEI!!!

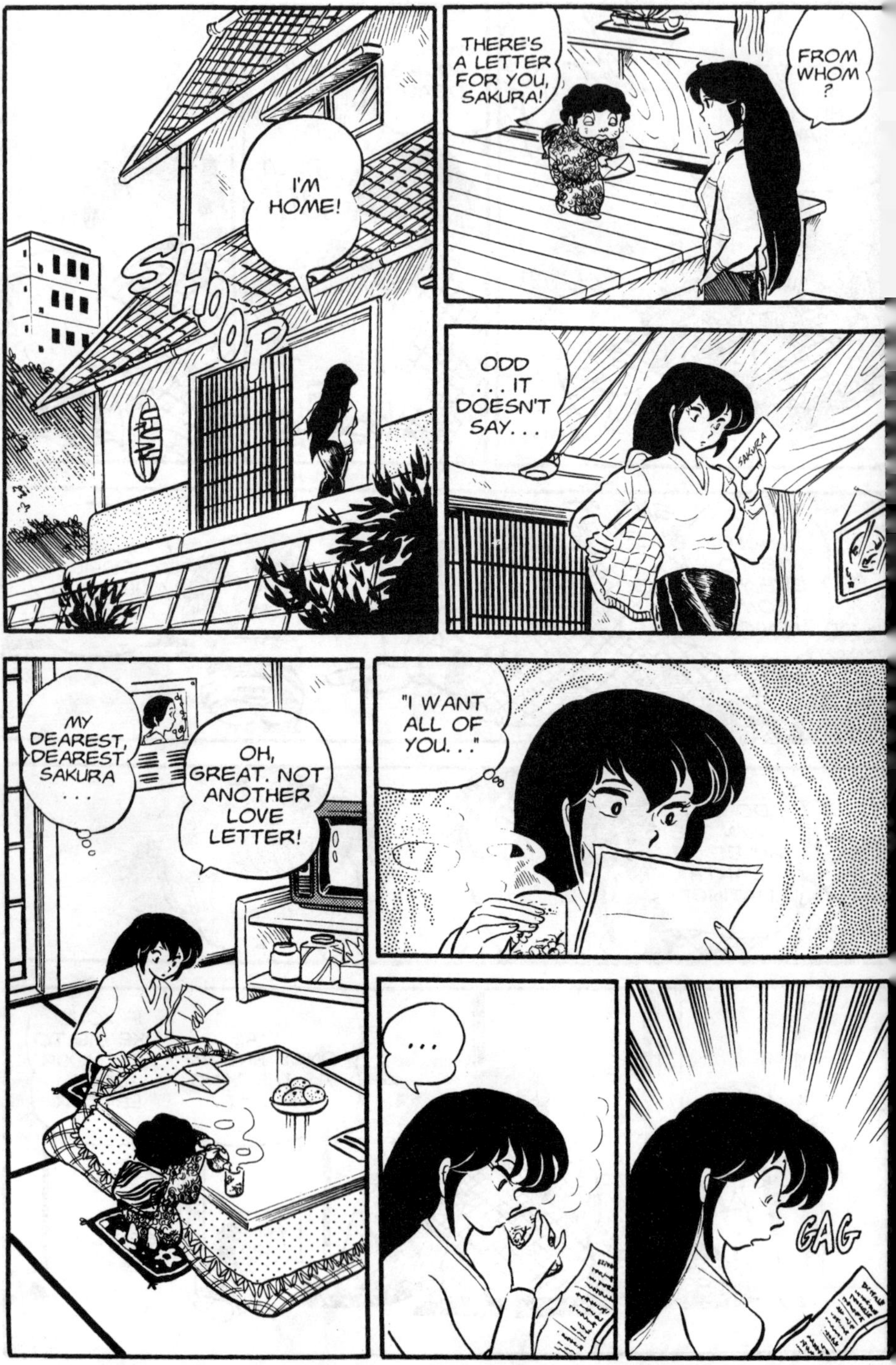
I'M HOME!
SHOOP
THERE'S A LETTER FOR YOU, SAKURA!
FROM WHOM?
ODD . . . IT DOESN'T SAY. . .
SAKURA
MY DEAREST, DEAREST SAKURA . . .
OH, GREAT. NOT ANOTHER LOVE LETTER!
"I WANT ALL OF YOU. . ."
. . .
GAG

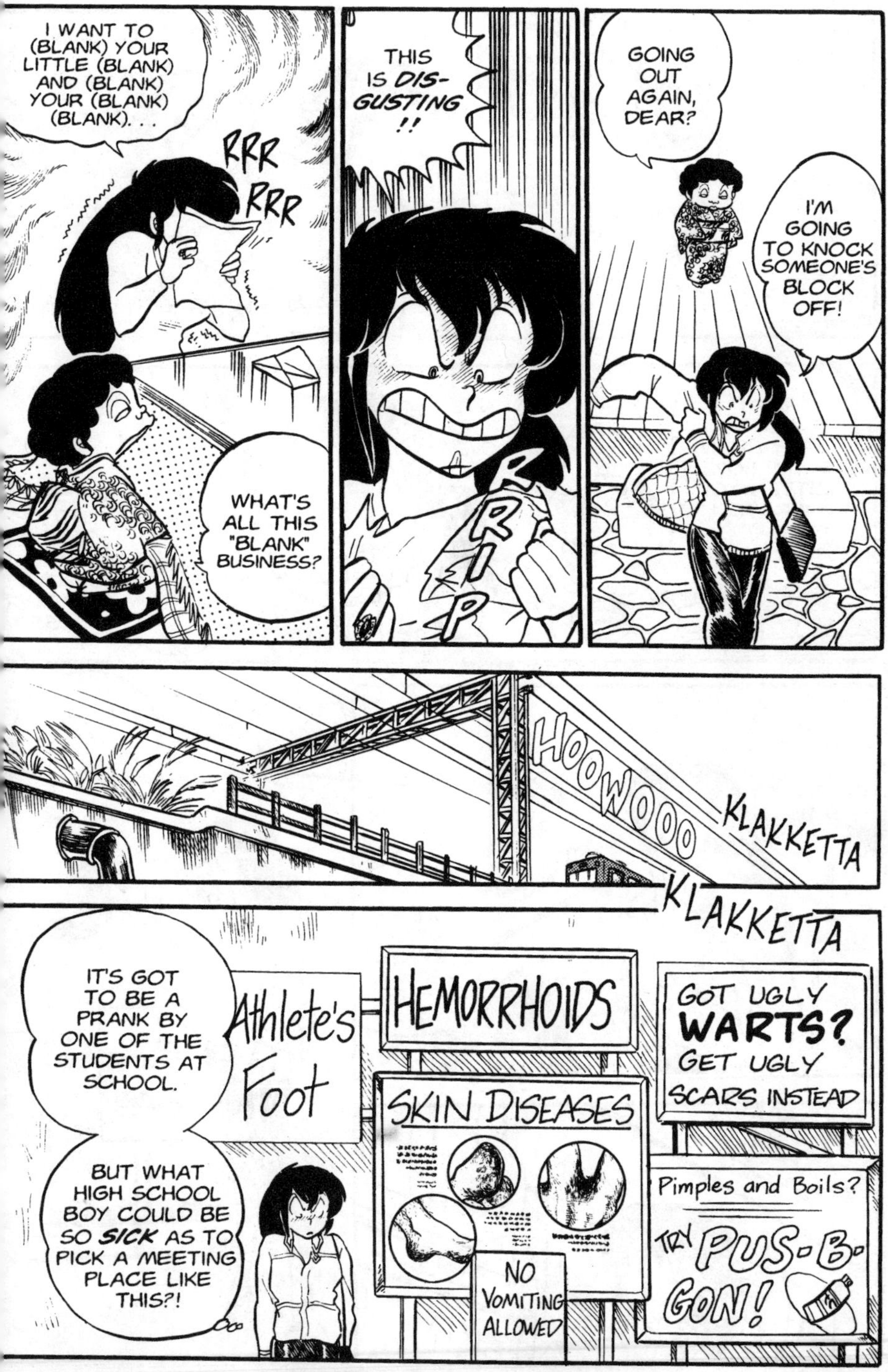
I WANT TO (BLANK) YOUR LITTLE (BLANK) AND (BLANK) YOUR (BLANK) (BLANK). . .
RRR RRR
WHAT'S ALL THIS "BLANK" BUSINESS?
THIS IS DIS-GUSTING !!
RRIP
GOING OUT AGAIN, DEAR?
I'M GOING TO KNOCK SOMEONE'S BLOCK OFF!
HOOWOOO
KLAKKETTA
KLAKKETTA
IT'S GOT TO BE A PRANK BY ONE OF THE STUDENTS AT SCHOOL.
BUT WHAT HIGH SCHOOL BOY COULD BE SO SICK AS TO PICK A MEETING PLACE LIKE THIS?!
Athlete's Foot
HEMORRHOIDS
GOT UGLY WARTS? GET UGLY SCARS INSTEAD
SKIN DISEASES
NO VOMITING ALLOWED
Pimples and Boils?
TRY PUS-B-GON!

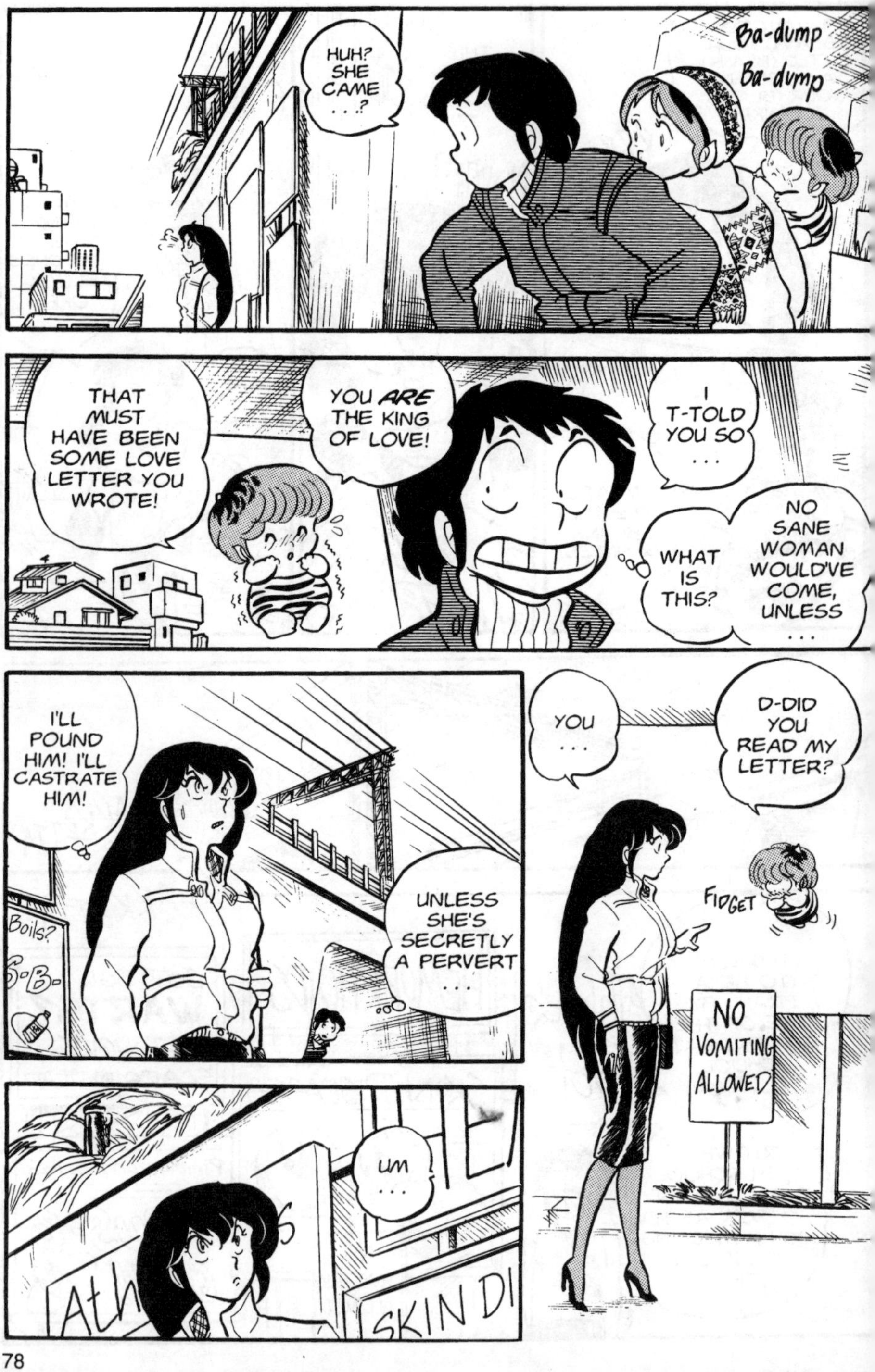
HUH? SHE CAME . . .?
Ba-dump Ba-dump
THAT MUST HAVE BEEN SOME LOVE LETTER YOU WROTE!
YOU *ARE* THE KING OF LOVE!
I T-TOLD YOU SO . . .
WHAT IS THIS?
NO SANE WOMAN WOULD'VE COME, UNLESS . . .
I'LL POUND HIM! I'LL CASTRATE HIM!
UNLESS SHE'S SECRETLY A PERVERT . . .
Boils?
UM . . .
SKIN DI
YOU . . .
D-DID YOU READ MY LETTER?
FIDGET
NO VOMITING ALLOWED

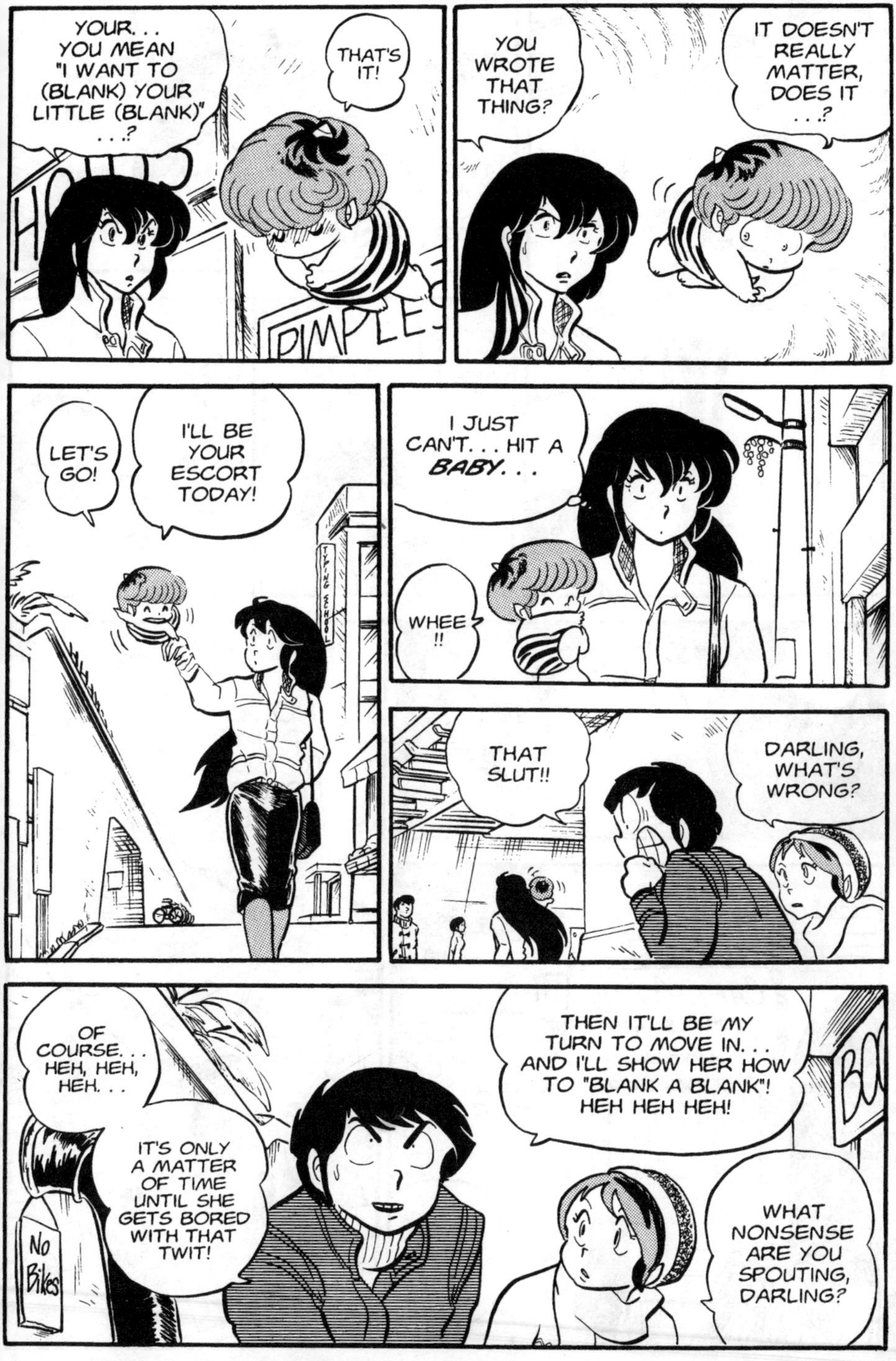
YOUR. . . YOU MEAN "I WANT TO (BLANK) YOUR LITTLE (BLANK)" . . .?
THAT'S IT!
YOU WROTE THAT THING?
IT DOESN'T REALLY MATTER, DOES IT . . .?
LET'S GO!
I'LL BE YOUR ESCORT TODAY!
TYPING SCHOOL
I JUST CAN'T. . . HIT A *BABY*. . .
WHEE !!
THAT SLUT!!
DARLING, WHAT'S WRONG?
OF COURSE. . . HEH, HEH, HEH. . .
IT'S ONLY A MATTER OF TIME UNTIL SHE GETS BORED WITH THAT TWIT!
THEN IT'LL BE MY TURN TO MOVE IN. . . AND I'LL SHOW HER HOW TO "BLANK A BLANK"! HEH HEH HEH!
WHAT NONSENSE ARE YOU SPOUTING, DARLING?
No Bikes

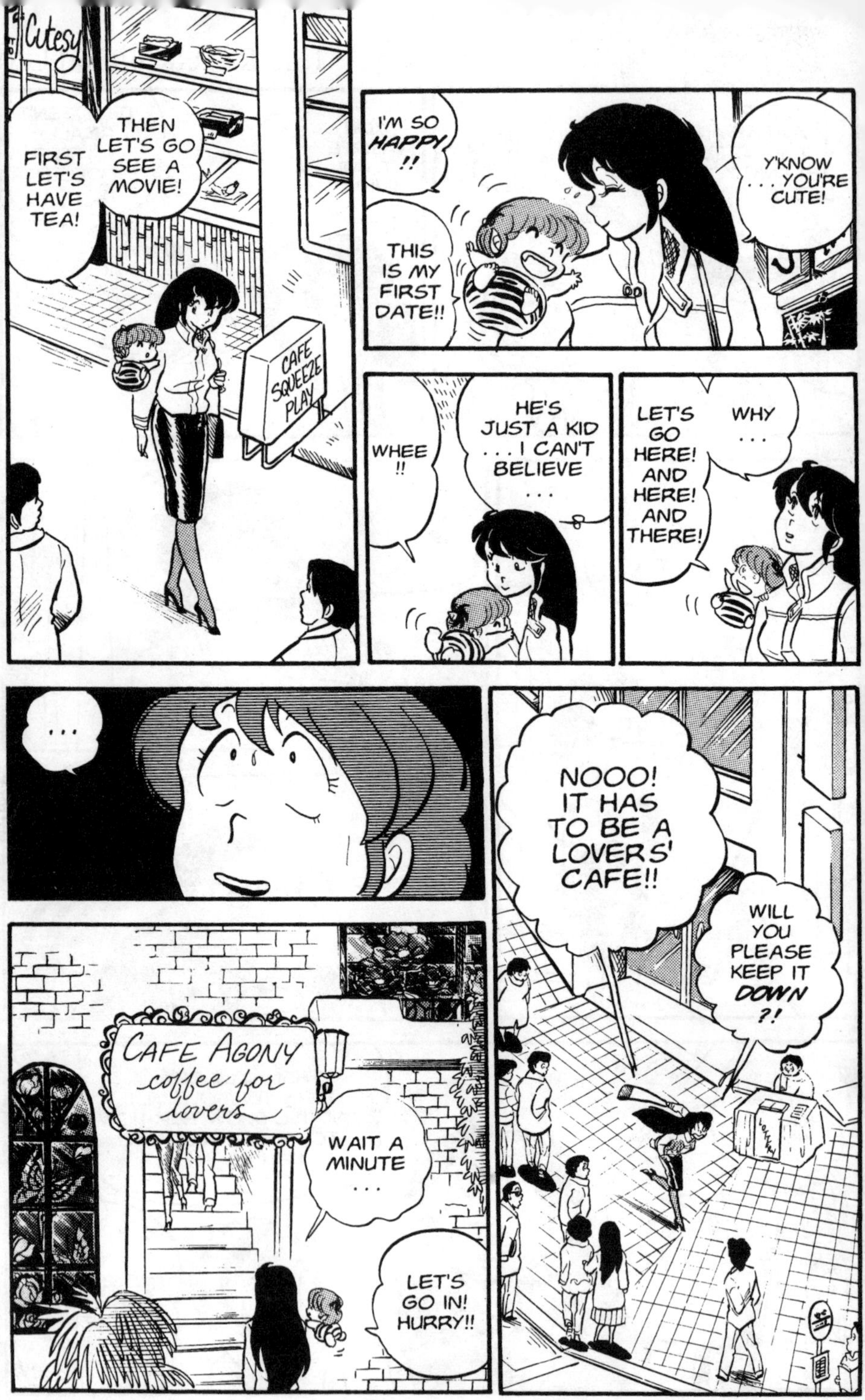
Cutesy
FIRST LET'S HAVE TEA!
THEN LET'S GO SEE A MOVIE!
CAFE SQUEEZE PLAY
I'M SO HAPPY!!
THIS IS MY FIRST DATE!!
Y'KNOW . . . YOU'RE CUTE!
WHEE!!
HE'S JUST A KID . . . I CAN'T BELIEVE . . .
LET'S GO HERE! AND HERE! AND THERE!
WHY . . .
. . .
NOOO! IT HAS TO BE A LOVERS' CAFE!!
WILL YOU PLEASE KEEP IT DOWN?!
CAFE AGONY coffee for lovers
WAIT A MINUTE . . .
LET'S GO IN! HURRY!!

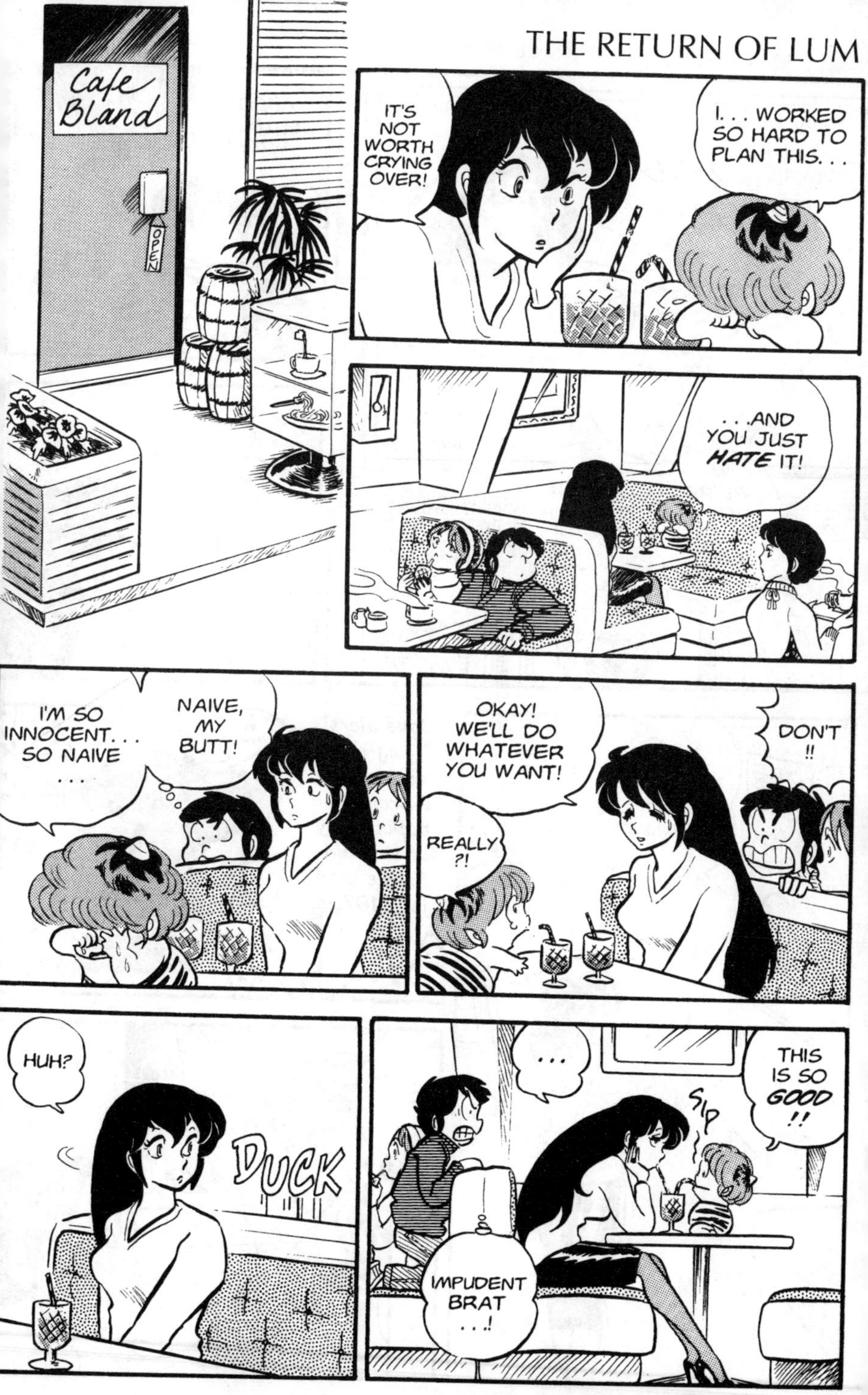
Cafe Bland
OPEN
IT'S NOT WORTH CRYING OVER!
I. . . WORKED SO HARD TO PLAN THIS. . .
. . .AND YOU JUST HATE IT!
I'M SO INNOCENT. . . SO NAIVE . . .
NAIVE, MY BUTT!
OKAY! WE'LL DO WHATEVER YOU WANT!
DON'T !!
REALLY ?!
HUH?
DUCK
. . .
THIS IS SO GOOD !!
SIP
IMPUDENT BRAT . . .!

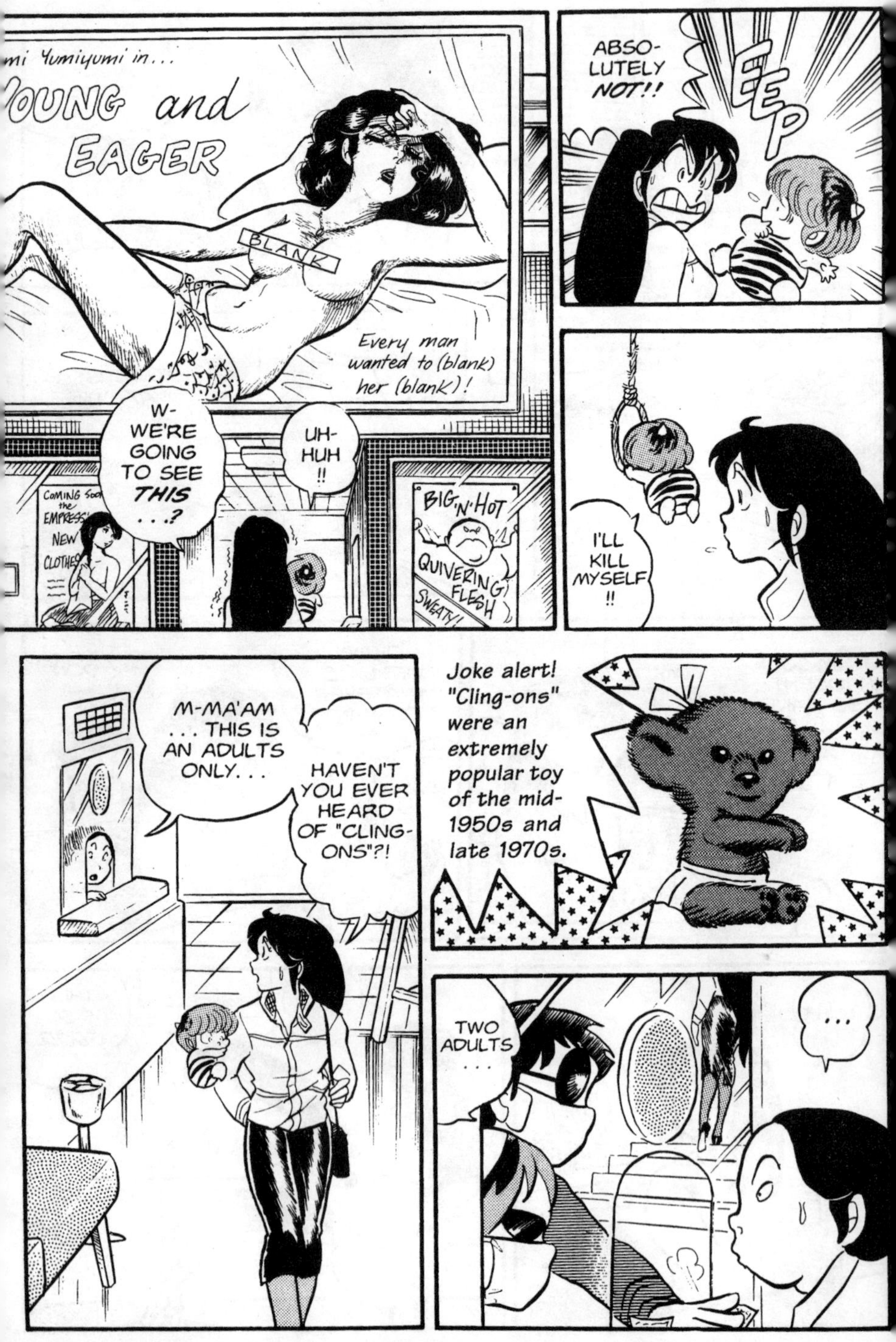
mi Yumiyumi in...
YOUNG and EAGER
BLANK
Every man wanted to (blank) her (blank)!
W-WE'RE GOING TO SEE THIS . . .?
UH-HUH !!
COMING SOON the EMPRESS' NEW CLOTHES
BIG 'N' HOT
QUIVERING FLESH
SWEATY!
ABSO-LUTELY NOT!!
EEEP
I'LL KILL MYSELF !!
M-MA'AM . . . THIS IS AN ADULTS ONLY. . .
HAVEN'T YOU EVER HEARD OF "CLING-ONS"?!
Joke alert! "Cling-ons" were an extremely popular toy of the mid-1950s and late 1970s.
TWO ADULTS . . .
. . .

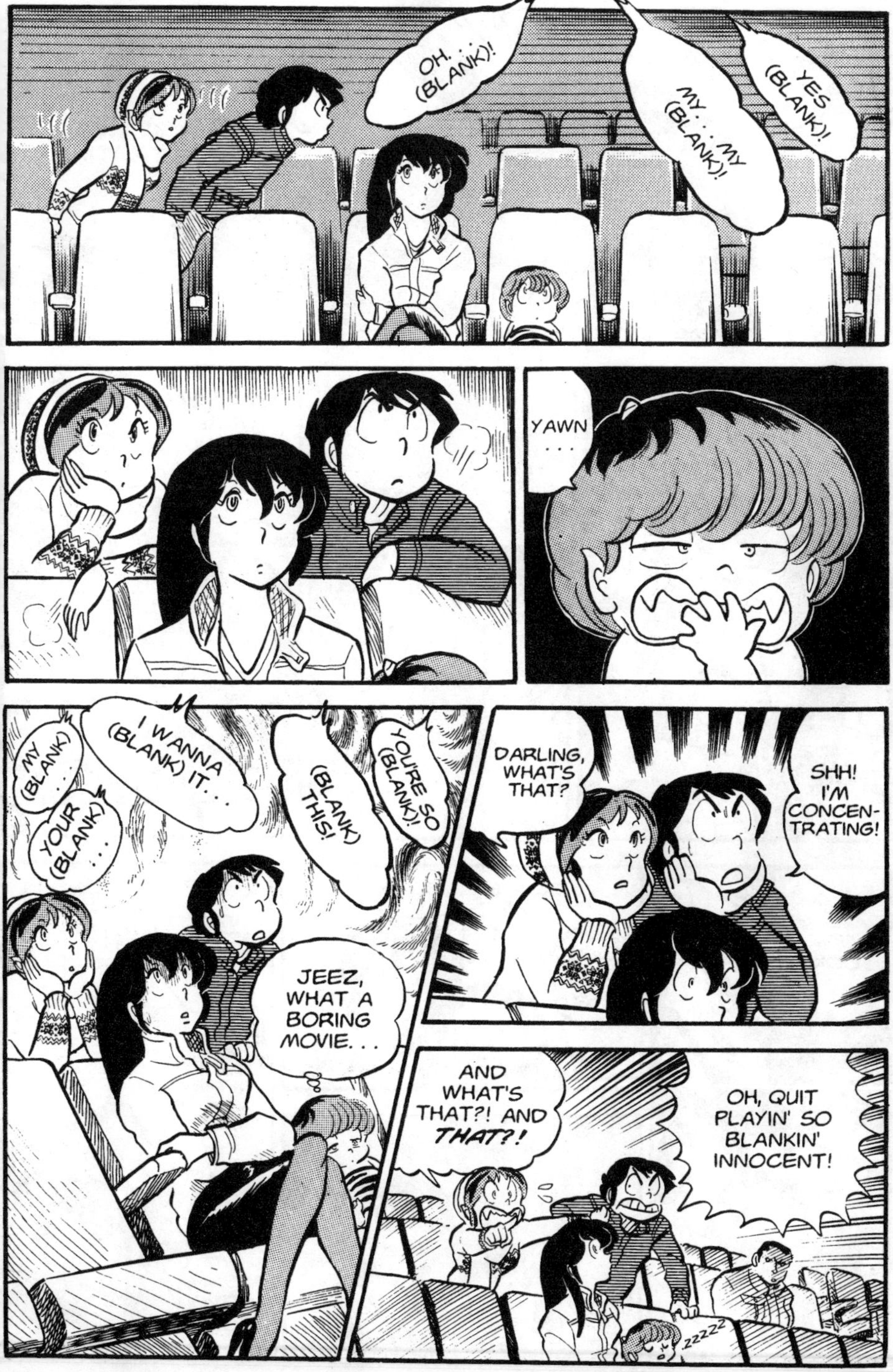

OH. . . (BLANK)!
MY. . . MY (BLANK)!
YES (BLANK)!
YAWN . . .
MY (BLANK) . . .
I WANNA (BLANK) IT. . .
YOUR (BLANK) . . .
(BLANK) THIS!
YOU'RE SO (BLANK)!
JEEZ, WHAT A BORING MOVIE. . .
DARLING, WHAT'S THAT?
SHH! I'M CONCEN-TRATING!
AND WHAT'S THAT?! AND ***THAT?!***
OH, QUIT PLAYIN' SO BLANKIN' INNOCENT!
ZZZZZ

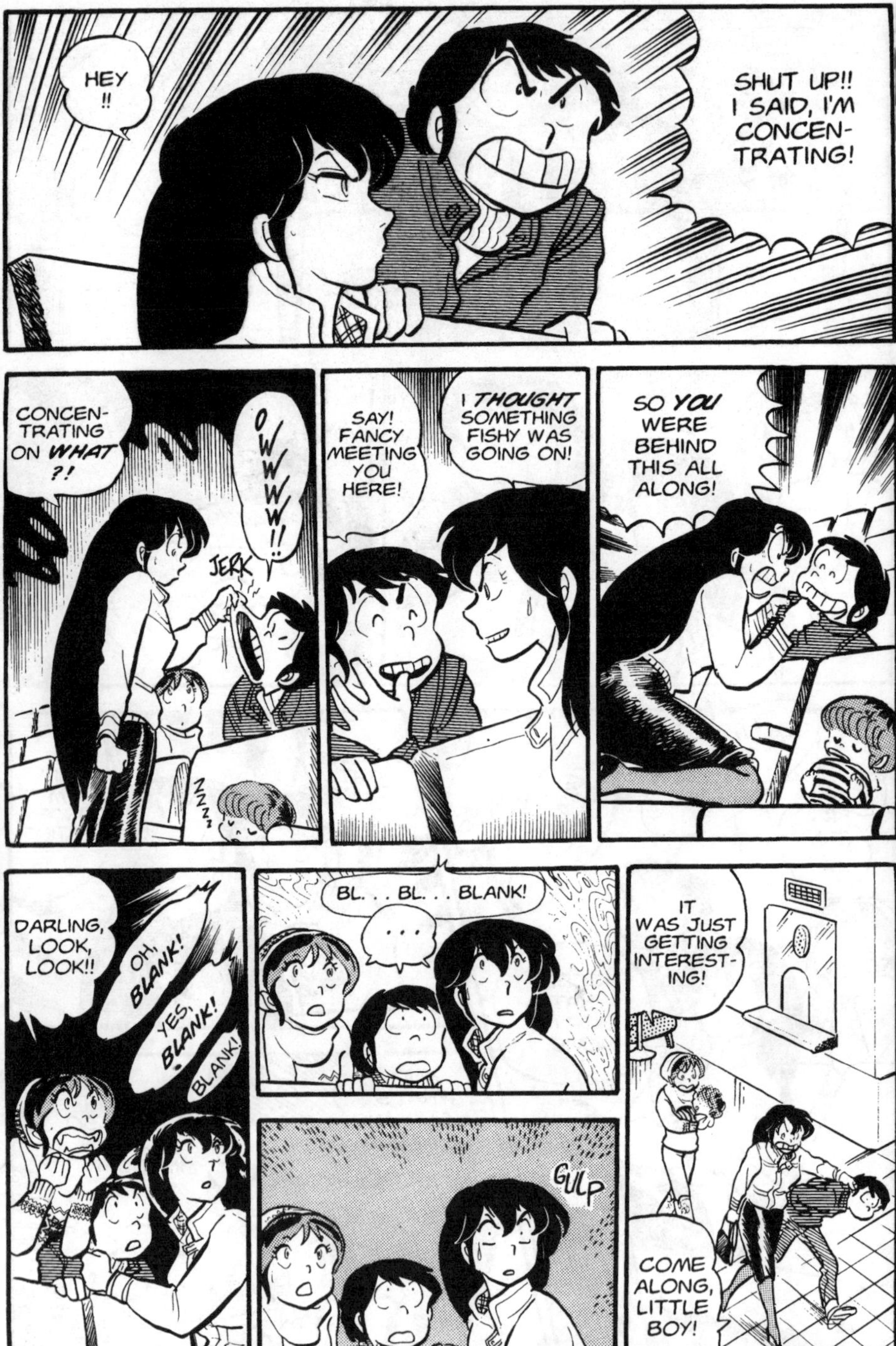
HEY !!
SHUT UP!! I SAID, I'M CONCEN-TRATING!
CONCEN-TRATING ON WHAT ?!
OWWWWW!!
JERK
SAY! FANCY MEETING YOU HERE!
I THOUGHT SOMETHING FISHY WAS GOING ON!
SO YOU WERE BEHIND THIS ALL ALONG!
DARLING, LOOK, LOOK!!
OH, BLANK!
YES, BLANK!
BLANK!
BL. . . BL. . . BLANK!
. . .
GULP
IT WAS JUST GETTING INTEREST-ING!
COME ALONG, LITTLE BOY!

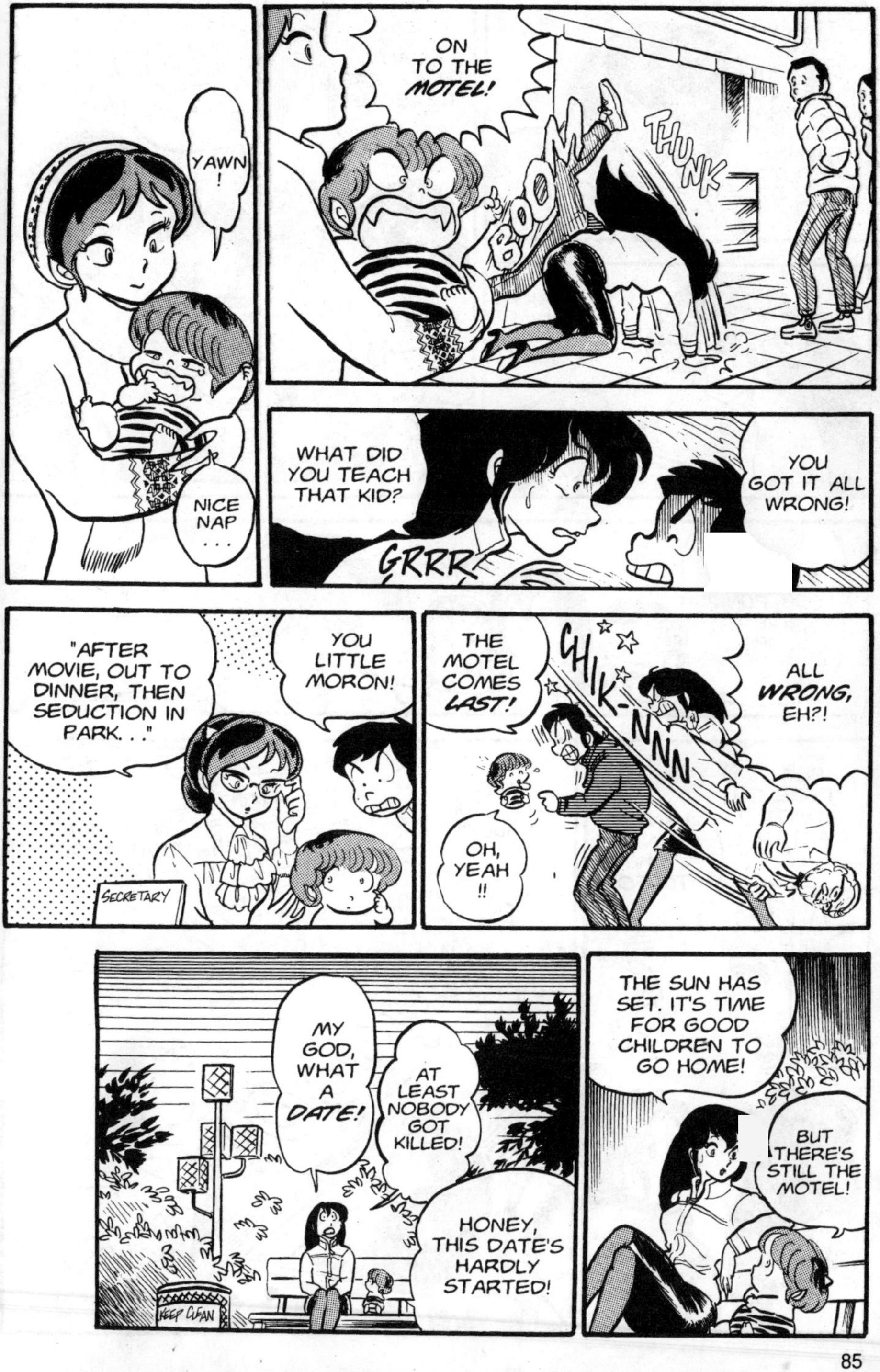
YAWN!
NICE NAP . . .
ON TO THE MOTEL!
BOOM
THUNK
WHAT DID YOU TEACH THAT KID?
GRRR
YOU GOT IT ALL WRONG!
"AFTER MOVIE, OUT TO DINNER, THEN SEDUCTION IN PARK. . ."
YOU LITTLE MORON!
SECRETARY
THE MOTEL COMES LAST!
CHIK-NNN
ALL WRONG, EH?!
OH, YEAH !!
MY GOD, WHAT A DATE!
AT LEAST NOBODY GOT KILLED!
HONEY, THIS DATE'S HARDLY STARTED!
KEEP CLEAN
THE SUN HAS SET. IT'S TIME FOR GOOD CHILDREN TO GO HOME!
BUT THERE'S STILL THE MOTEL!

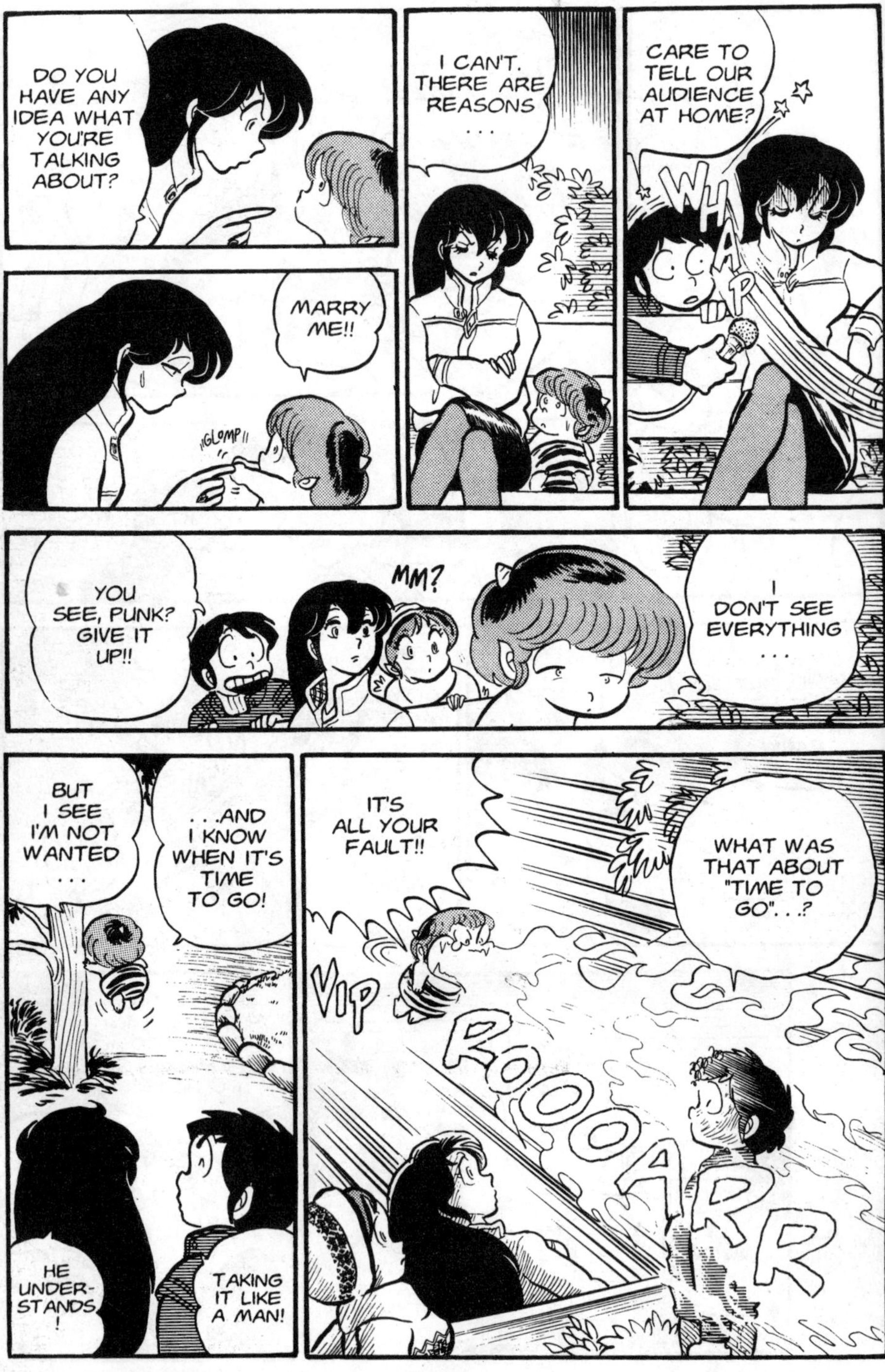
DO YOU HAVE ANY IDEA WHAT YOU'RE TALKING ABOUT?
I CAN'T. THERE ARE REASONS . . .
CARE TO TELL OUR AUDIENCE AT HOME?
WHAP
MARRY ME!!
GLOMP
YOU SEE, PUNK? GIVE IT UP!!
MM?
I DON'T SEE EVERYTHING . . .
BUT I SEE I'M NOT WANTED . . .
. . .AND I KNOW WHEN IT'S TIME TO GO!
HE UNDER-STANDS!
TAKING IT LIKE A MAN!
IT'S ALL YOUR FAULT!!
WHAT WAS THAT ABOUT "TIME TO GO". . .?
VIP
ROOOARRR

PART SIX
FROM FLOWER TO FLOWER

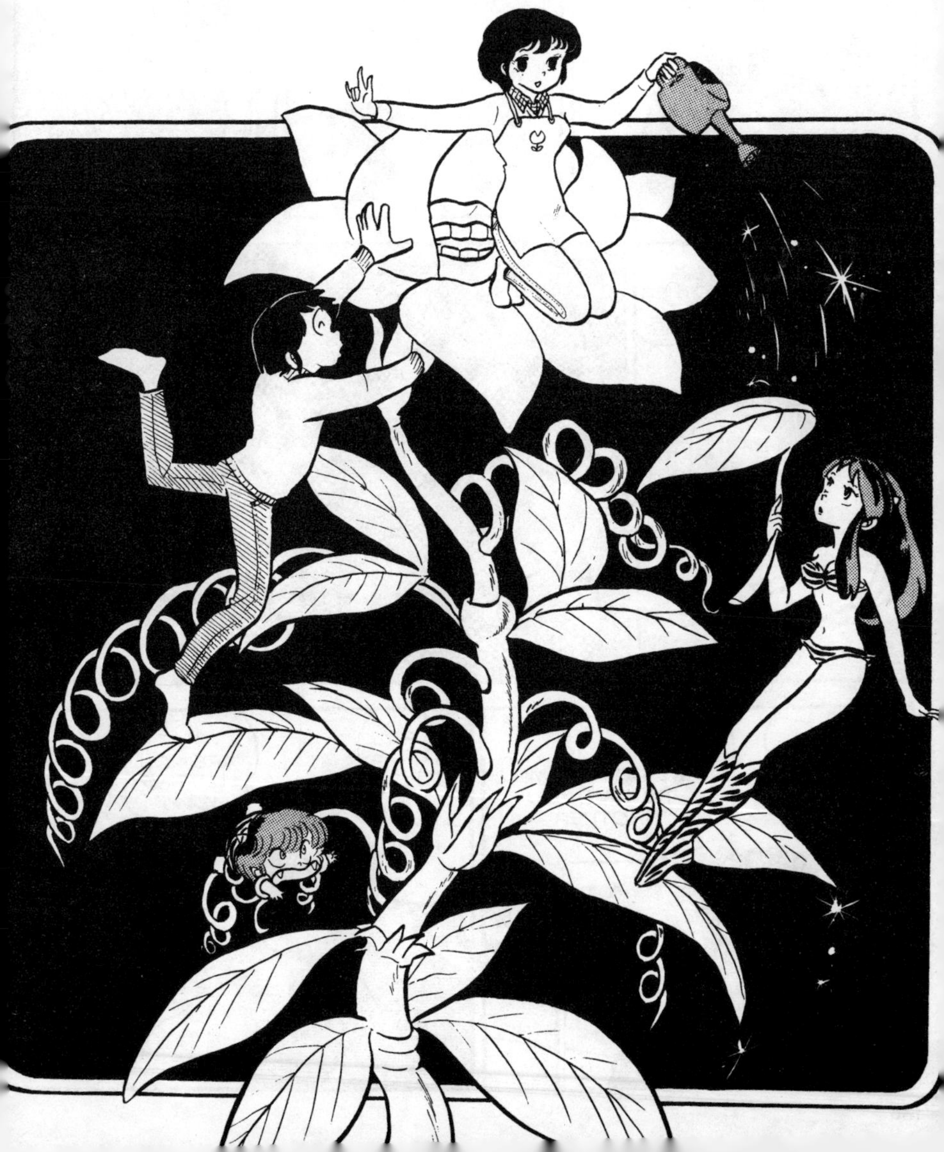

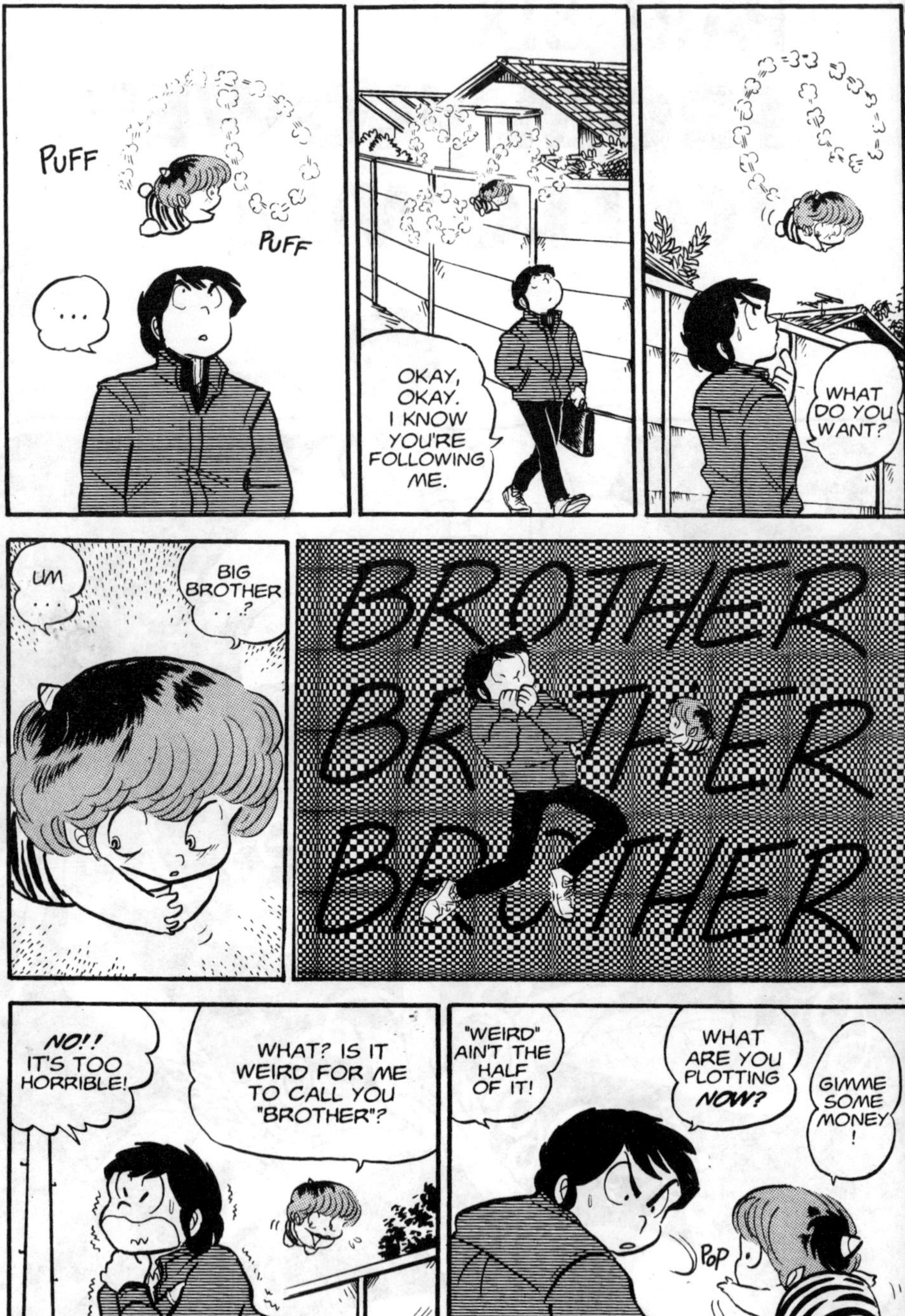
PUFF
PUFF
...
OKAY, OKAY. I KNOW YOU'RE FOLLOWING ME.
WHAT DO YOU WANT?
UM ...
BIG BROTHER ...?
BROTHER BROTHER BROTHER
NO!! IT'S TOO HORRIBLE!
WHAT? IS IT WEIRD FOR ME TO CALL YOU "BROTHER"?
"WEIRD" AIN'T THE HALF OF IT!
WHAT ARE YOU PLOTTING NOW?
GIMME SOME MONEY!
POP

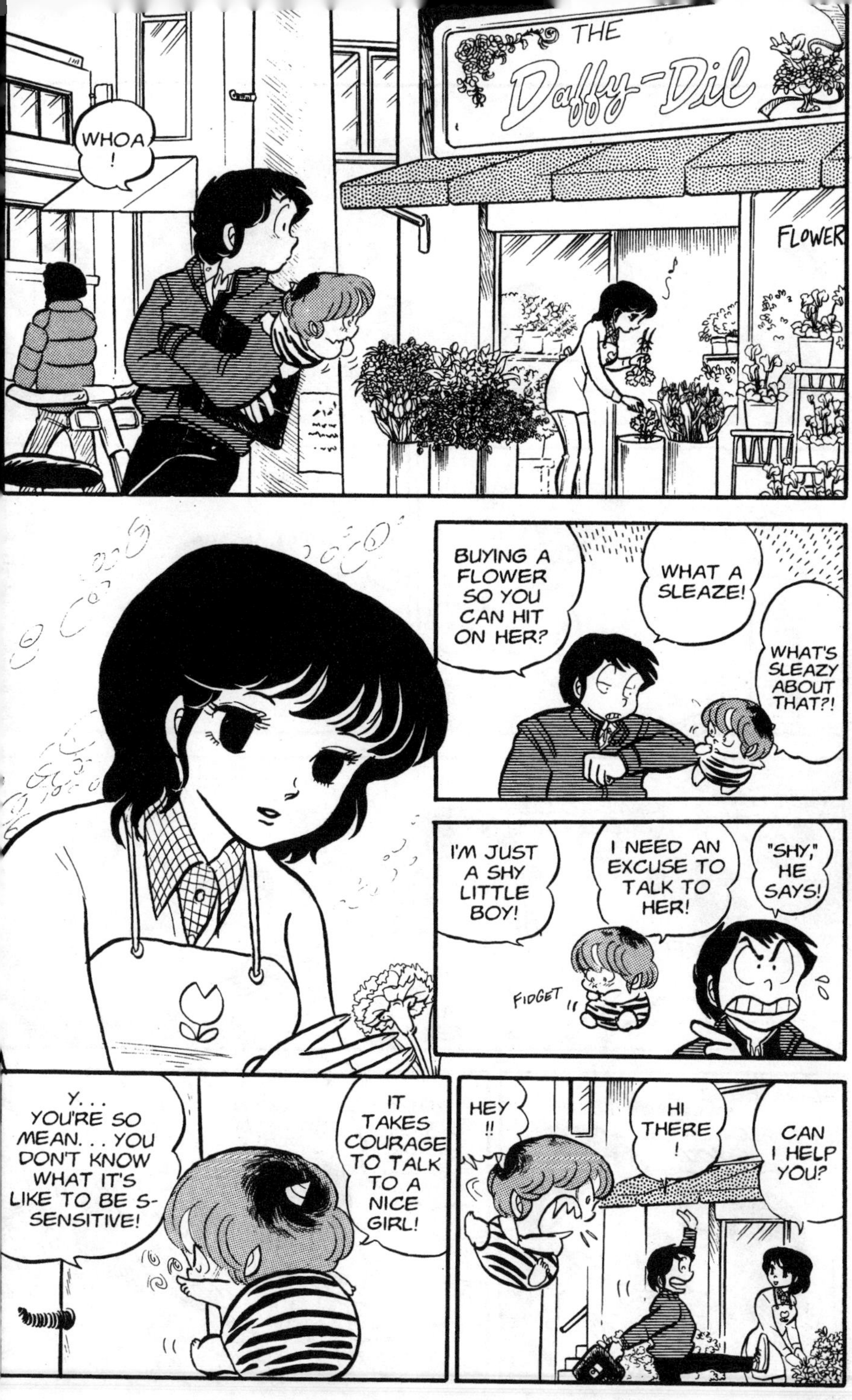
WHOA !
THE Daffy-Dil
FLOWER
BUYING A FLOWER SO YOU CAN HIT ON HER?
WHAT A SLEAZE!
WHAT'S SLEAZY ABOUT THAT?!
I'M JUST A SHY LITTLE BOY!
I NEED AN EXCUSE TO TALK TO HER!
"SHY," HE SAYS!
FIDGET
Y. . . YOU'RE SO MEAN. . . YOU DON'T KNOW WHAT IT'S LIKE TO BE S-SENSITIVE!
IT TAKES COURAGE TO TALK TO A NICE GIRL!
HEY !!
HI THERE !
CAN I HELP YOU?

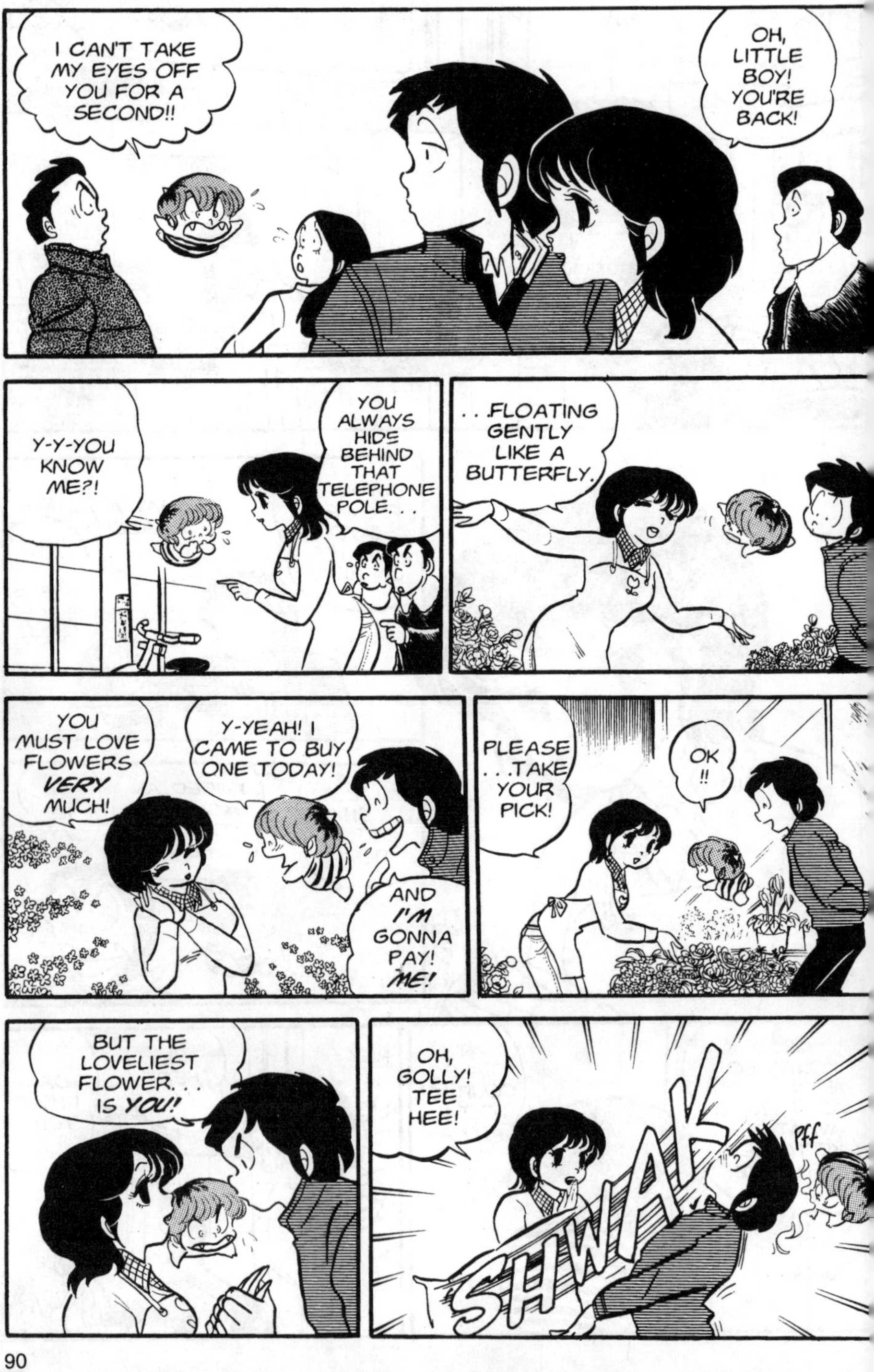
I CAN'T TAKE MY EYES OFF YOU FOR A SECOND!!
OH, LITTLE BOY! YOU'RE BACK!
Y-Y-YOU KNOW ME?!
YOU ALWAYS HIDE BEHIND THAT TELEPHONE POLE. . .
. . .FLOATING GENTLY LIKE A BUTTERFLY.
YOU MUST LOVE FLOWERS VERY MUCH!
Y-YEAH! I CAME TO BUY ONE TODAY!
AND I'M GONNA PAY! ME!
PLEASE . . .TAKE YOUR PICK!
OK !!
BUT THE LOVELIEST FLOWER. . . IS YOU!
OH, GOLLY! TEE HEE!
SHWAK
Pff

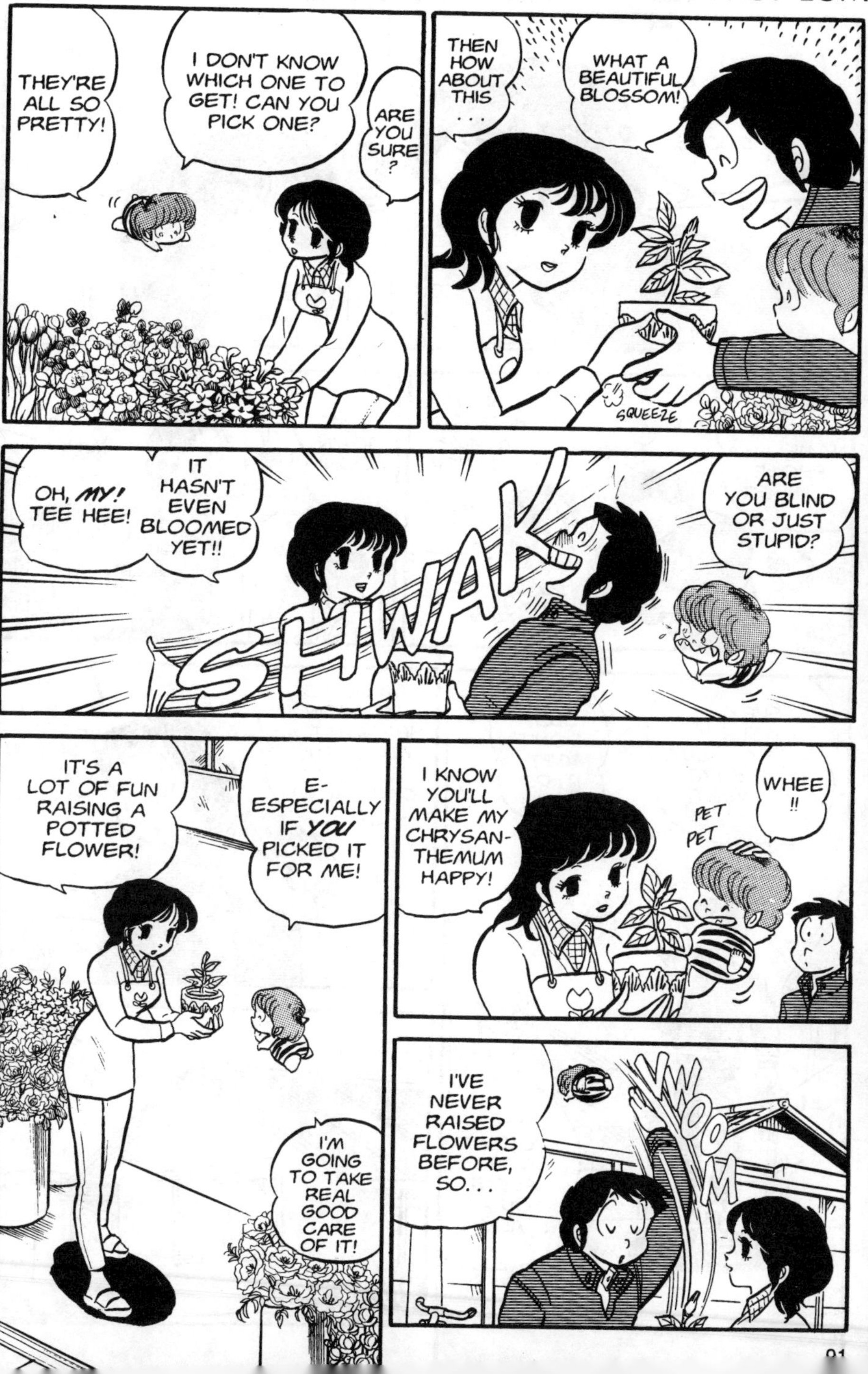
THEY'RE ALL SO PRETTY!
I DON'T KNOW WHICH ONE TO GET! CAN YOU PICK ONE?
ARE YOU SURE?
THEN HOW ABOUT THIS . . .
WHAT A BEAUTIFUL BLOSSOM!
SQUEEZE
OH, MY! TEE HEE!
IT HASN'T EVEN BLOOMED YET!!
SHWAK!
ARE YOU BLIND OR JUST STUPID?
IT'S A LOT OF FUN RAISING A POTTED FLOWER!
E-ESPECIALLY IF YOU PICKED IT FOR ME!
I'M GOING TO TAKE REAL GOOD CARE OF IT!
I KNOW YOU'LL MAKE MY CHRYSANTHEMUM HAPPY!
PET PET
WHEE!!
I'VE NEVER RAISED FLOWERS BEFORE, SO. . .
VWOOOM

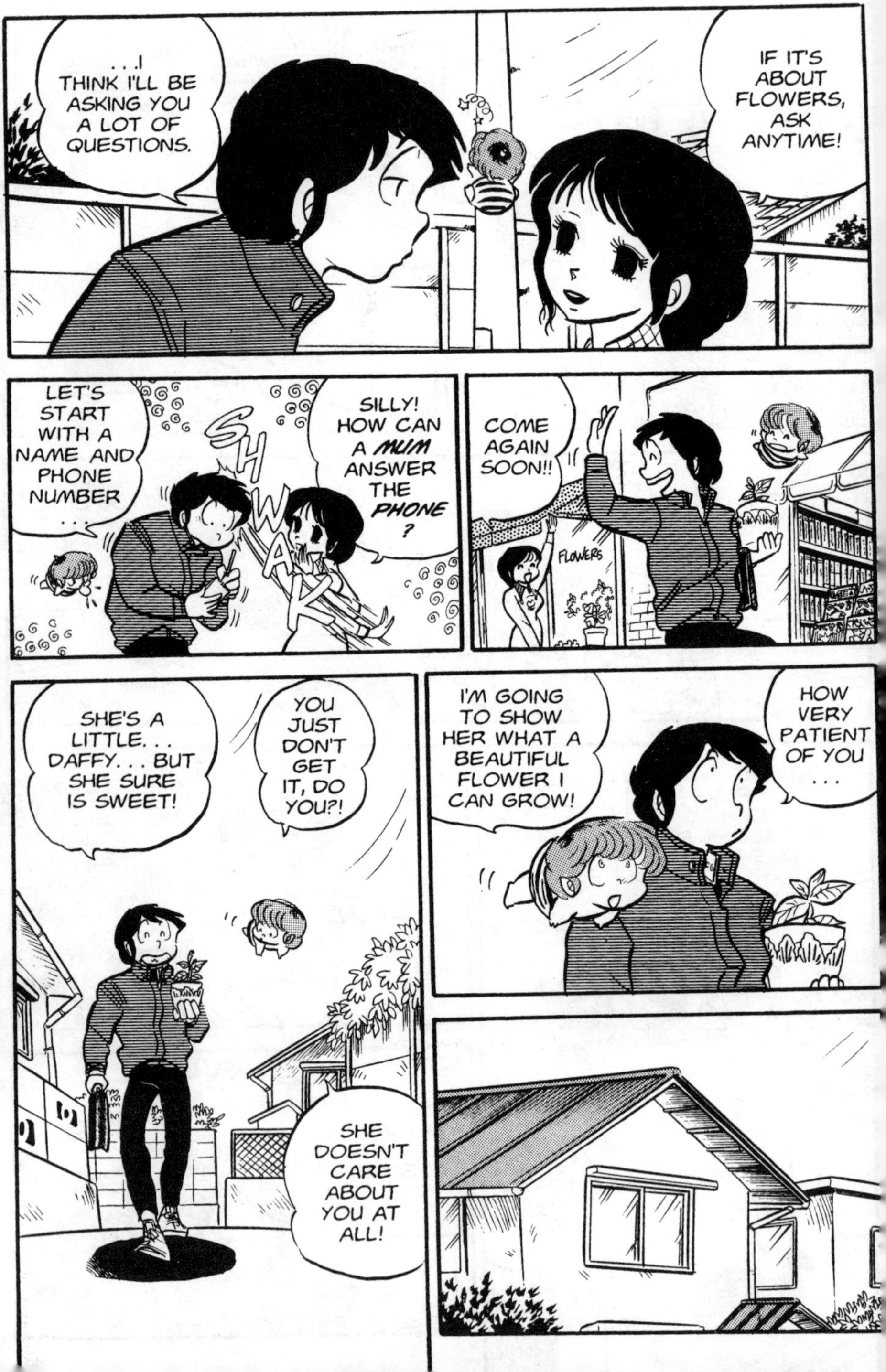
. . .I THINK I'LL BE ASKING YOU A LOT OF QUESTIONS.
IF IT'S ABOUT FLOWERS, ASK ANYTIME!
LET'S START WITH A NAME AND PHONE NUMBER . . .
SHWAK
SILLY! HOW CAN A MUM ANSWER THE PHONE?
COME AGAIN SOON!!
FLOWERS
SHE'S A LITTLE. . . DAFFY. . . BUT SHE SURE IS SWEET!
YOU JUST DON'T GET IT, DO YOU?!
SHE DOESN'T CARE ABOUT YOU AT ALL!
I'M GOING TO SHOW HER WHAT A BEAUTIFUL FLOWER I CAN GROW!
HOW VERY PATIENT OF YOU . . .

For Our Petaled Friends

50 Things NOT to Do

friends of the flowers

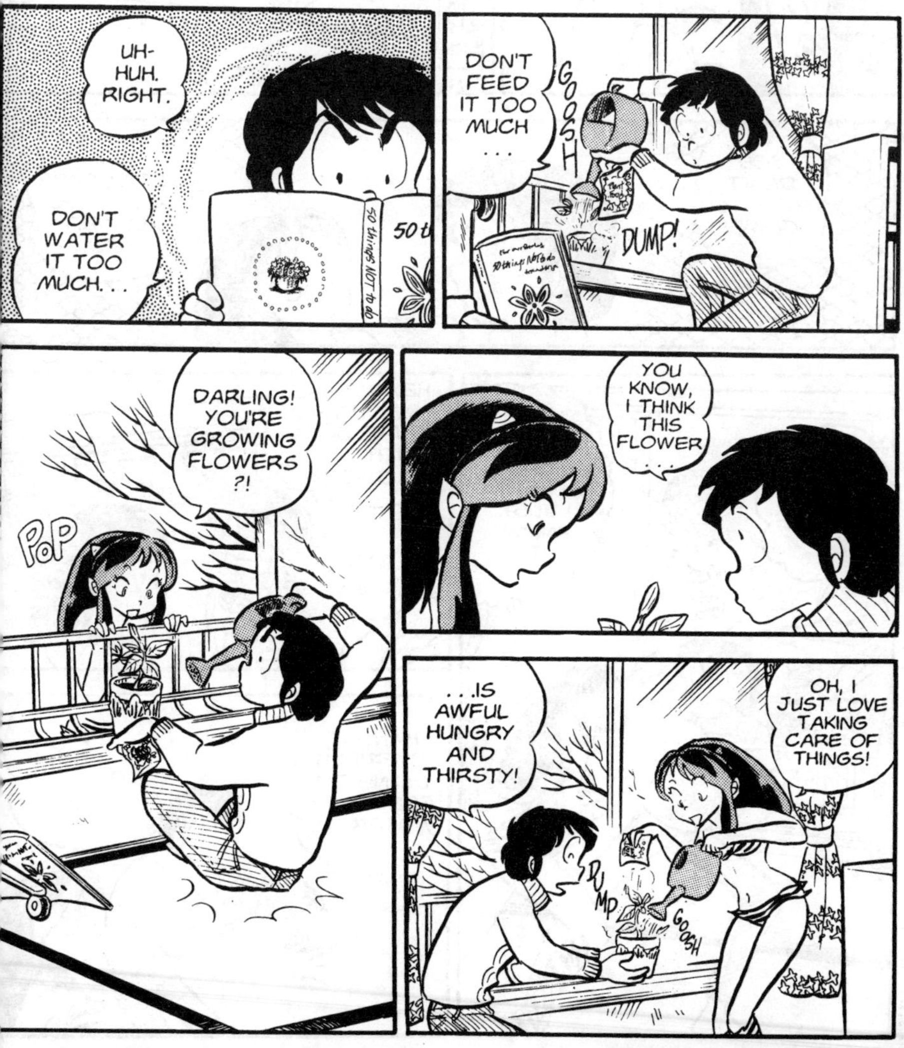
UH-HUH. RIGHT.
DON'T WATER IT TOO MUCH. . .
50 things NOT to do
DON'T FEED IT TOO MUCH . . .
GOOSH
DUMP!
DARLING! YOU'RE GROWING FLOWERS ?!
POP
YOU KNOW, I THINK THIS FLOWER . . .
. . .IS AWFUL HUNGRY AND THIRSTY!
OH, I JUST LOVE TAKING CARE OF THINGS!
DUMP
GOOSH

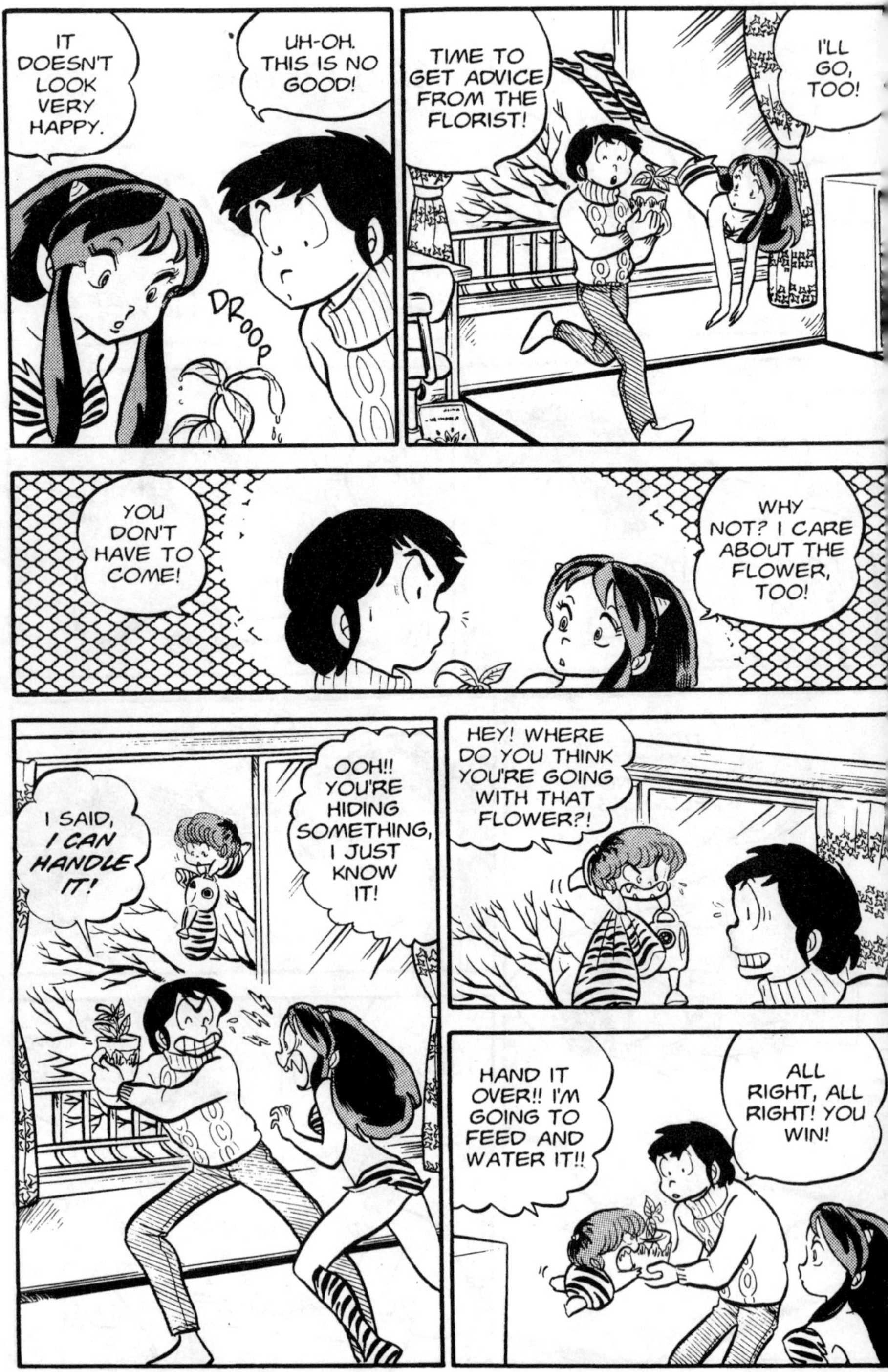
IT DOESN'T LOOK VERY HAPPY.
UH-OH. THIS IS NO GOOD!
DROOP
TIME TO GET ADVICE FROM THE FLORIST!
I'LL GO, TOO!
YOU DON'T HAVE TO COME!
WHY NOT? I CARE ABOUT THE FLOWER, TOO!
I SAID, *I CAN HANDLE IT!*
OOH!! YOU'RE HIDING SOMETHING, I JUST KNOW IT!
HEY! WHERE DO YOU THINK YOU'RE GOING WITH THAT FLOWER?!
HAND IT OVER!! I'M GOING TO FEED AND WATER IT!!
ALL RIGHT, ALL RIGHT! YOU WIN!

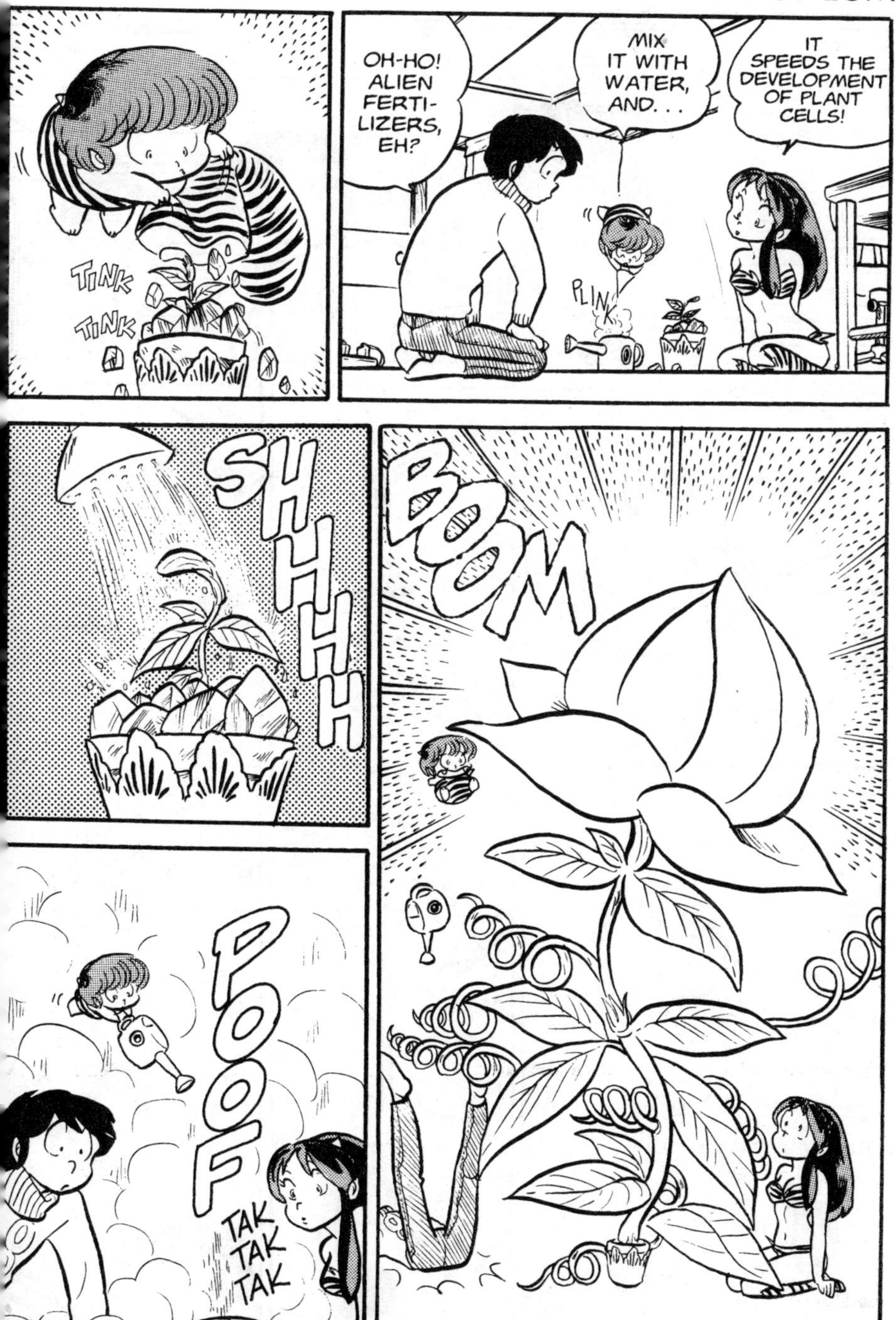
TINK
TINK
OH-HO! ALIEN FERTI-LIZERS, EH?
MIX IT WITH WATER, AND. . .
IT SPEEDS THE DEVELOPMENT OF PLANT CELLS!
PLINK
SHHHHHH
BOOM
POOF
TAK TAK TAK

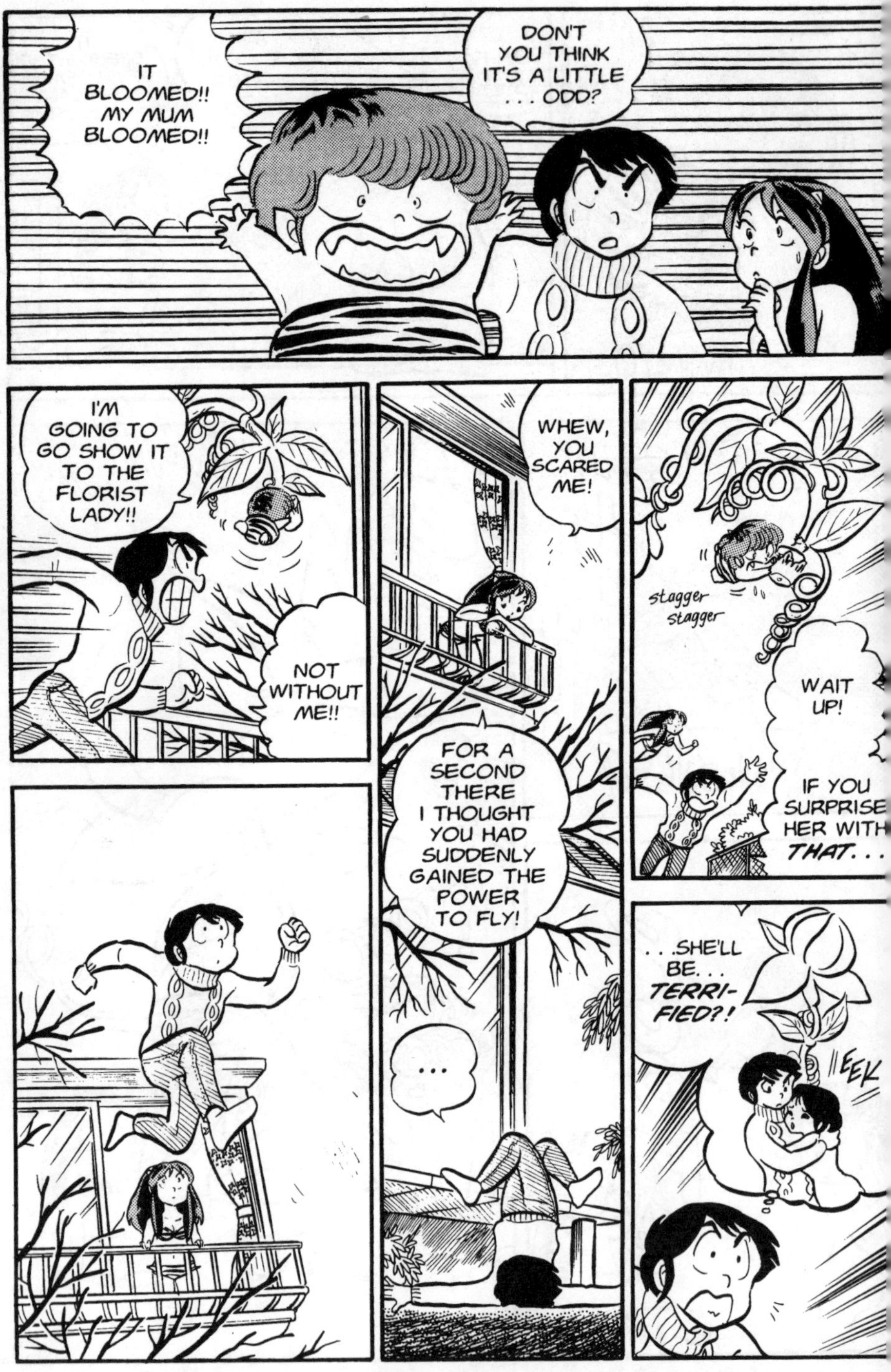
IT BLOOMED!! MY MUM BLOOMED!!
DON'T YOU THINK IT'S A LITTLE . . . ODD?
I'M GOING TO GO SHOW IT TO THE FLORIST LADY!!
NOT WITHOUT ME!!
WHEW, YOU SCARED ME!
FOR A SECOND THERE I THOUGHT YOU HAD SUDDENLY GAINED THE POWER TO FLY!
stagger stagger
WAIT UP!
IF YOU SURPRISE HER WITH *THAT*. . .
. . .
. . .SHE'LL BE. . . *TERRI-FIED?!*
EEK

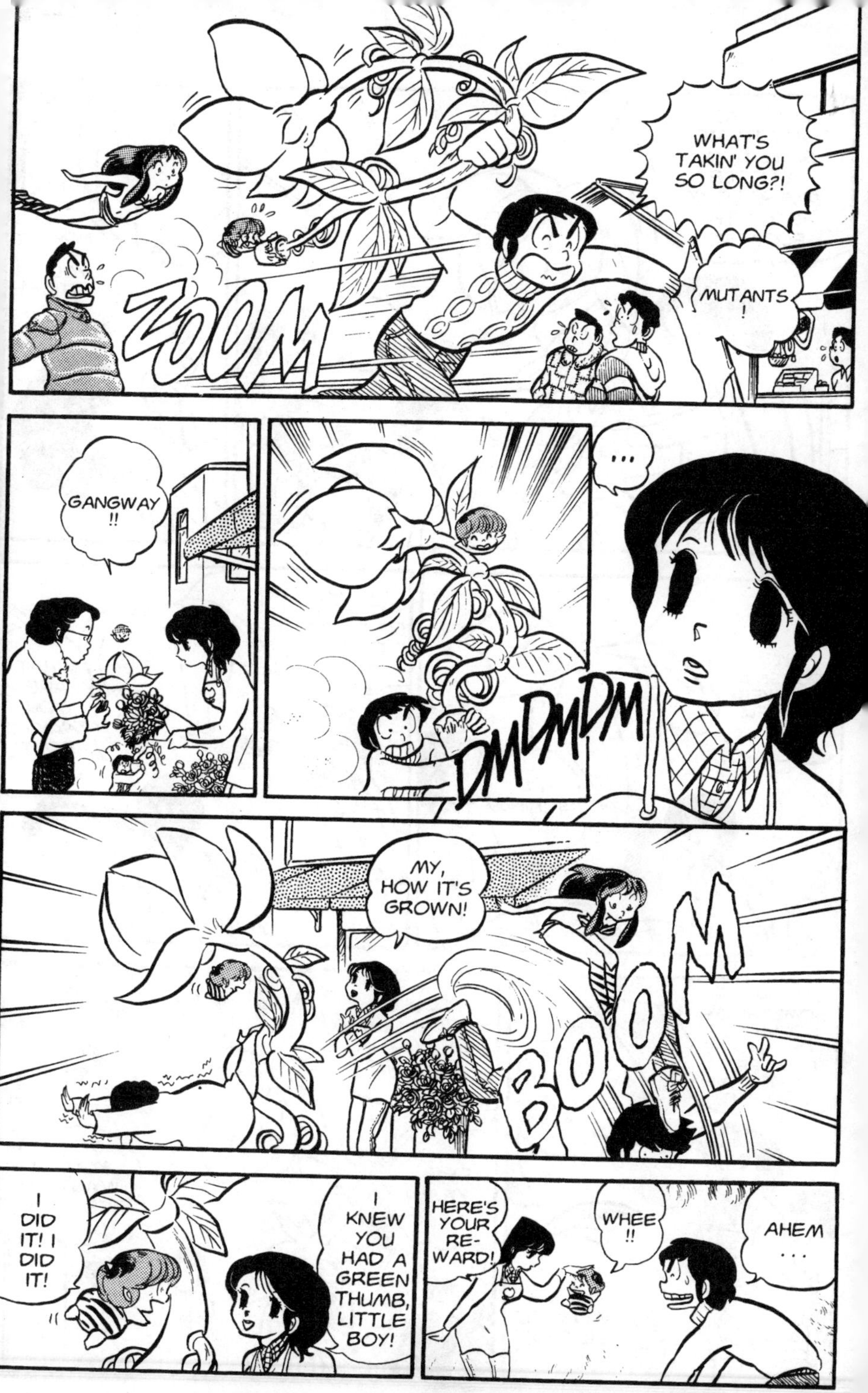
WHAT'S TAKIN' YOU SO LONG?!
ZOOM
MUTANTS!
GANGWAY!!
DMDMDM
...
MY, HOW IT'S GROWN!
BOOOM
I DID IT! I DID IT!
I KNEW YOU HAD A GREEN THUMB, LITTLE BOY!
HERE'S YOUR RE-WARD!
WHEE!!
AHEM...

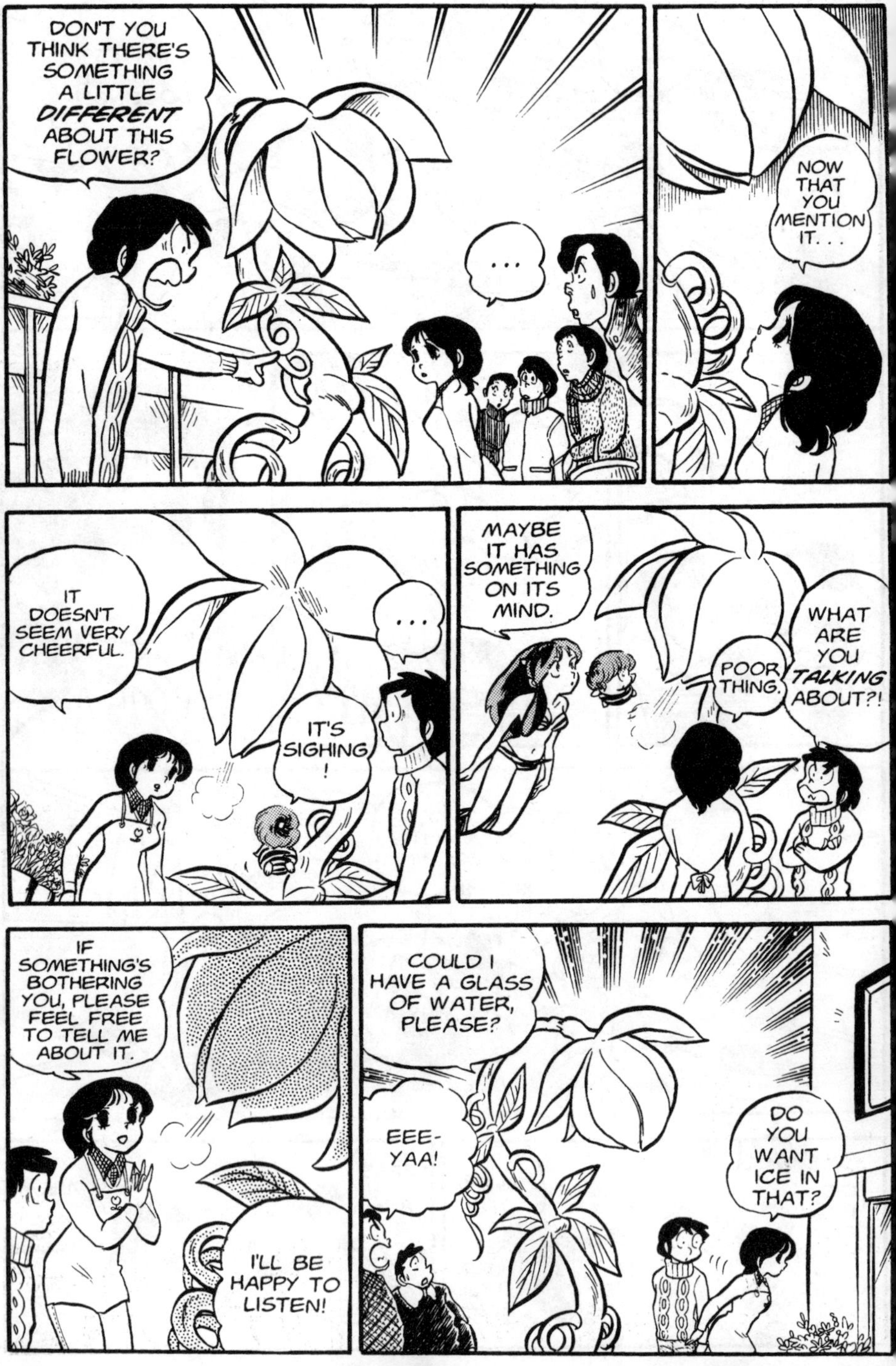
DON'T YOU THINK THERE'S SOMETHING A LITTLE DIFFERENT ABOUT THIS FLOWER?
...
NOW THAT YOU MENTION IT...
IT DOESN'T SEEM VERY CHEERFUL.
...
IT'S SIGHING!
MAYBE IT HAS SOMETHING ON ITS MIND.
POOR THING.
WHAT ARE YOU TALKING ABOUT?!
IF SOMETHING'S BOTHERING YOU, PLEASE FEEL FREE TO TELL ME ABOUT IT.
I'LL BE HAPPY TO LISTEN!
COULD I HAVE A GLASS OF WATER, PLEASE?
EEE-YAA!
DO YOU WANT ICE IN THAT?

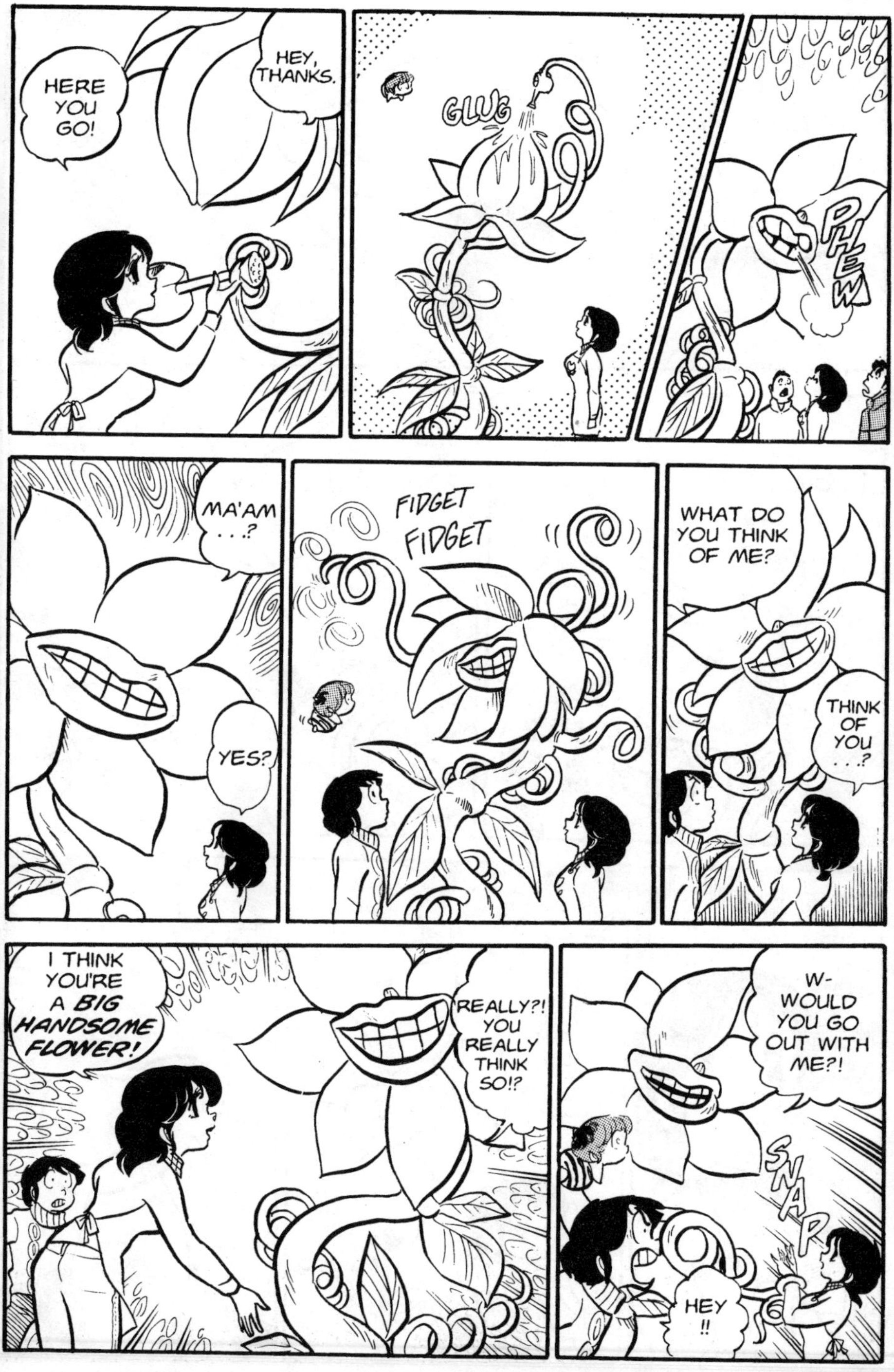
HERE YOU GO!
HEY, THANKS.
GLUG
PHEW
MA'AM . . .?
YES?
FIDGET FIDGET
WHAT DO YOU THINK OF ME?
THINK OF YOU . . .?
I THINK YOU'RE A BIG HANDSOME FLOWER!
REALLY?! YOU REALLY THINK SO!?
W- WOULD YOU GO OUT WITH ME?!
SNAP
HEY !!

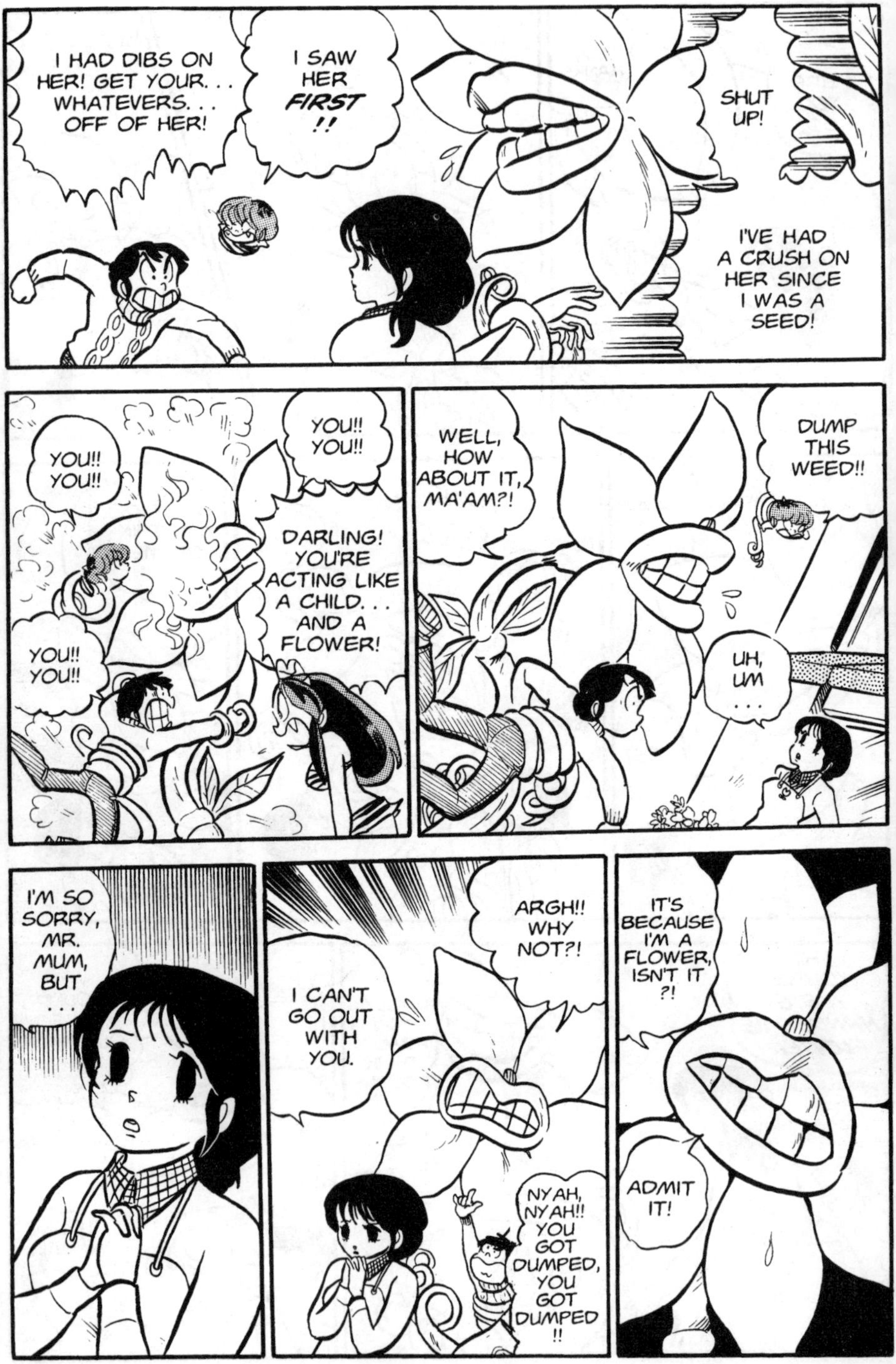
I HAD DIBS ON HER! GET YOUR. . . WHATEVERS. . . OFF OF HER!
I SAW HER *FIRST* !!
SHUT UP!
I'VE HAD A CRUSH ON HER SINCE I WAS A SEED!
YOU!! YOU!!
YOU!! YOU!!
DARLING! YOU'RE ACTING LIKE A CHILD. . . AND A FLOWER!
YOU!! YOU!!
WELL, HOW ABOUT IT, MA'AM?!
DUMP THIS WEED!!
UH, UM . . .
I'M SO SORRY, MR. MUM, BUT . . .
ARGH!! WHY NOT?!
I CAN'T GO OUT WITH YOU.
NYAH, NYAH!! YOU GOT DUMPED, YOU GOT DUMPED !!
IT'S BECAUSE I'M A FLOWER, ISN'T IT ?!
ADMIT IT!

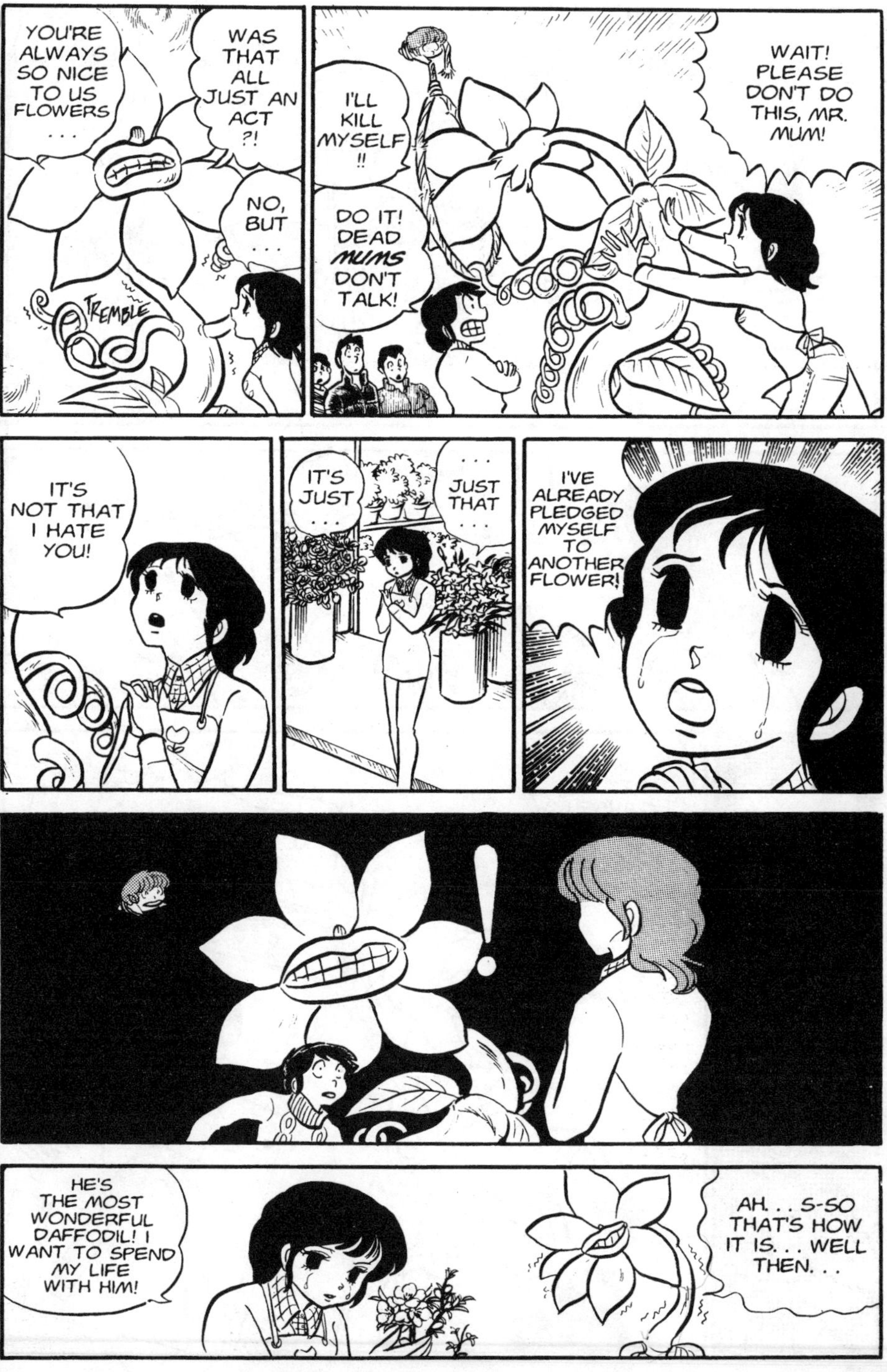
YOU'RE ALWAYS SO NICE TO US FLOWERS . . .
WAS THAT ALL JUST AN ACT ?!
NO, BUT . . .
TREMBLE
I'LL KILL MYSELF !!
DO IT! DEAD MUMS DON'T TALK!
WAIT! PLEASE DON'T DO THIS, MR. MUM!
IT'S NOT THAT I HATE YOU!
IT'S JUST . . .
. . . JUST THAT . . .
I'VE ALREADY PLEDGED MYSELF TO ANOTHER FLOWER!
!
HE'S THE MOST WONDERFUL DAFFODIL! I WANT TO SPEND MY LIFE WITH HIM!
AH. . . S-SO THAT'S HOW IT IS. . . WELL THEN. . .

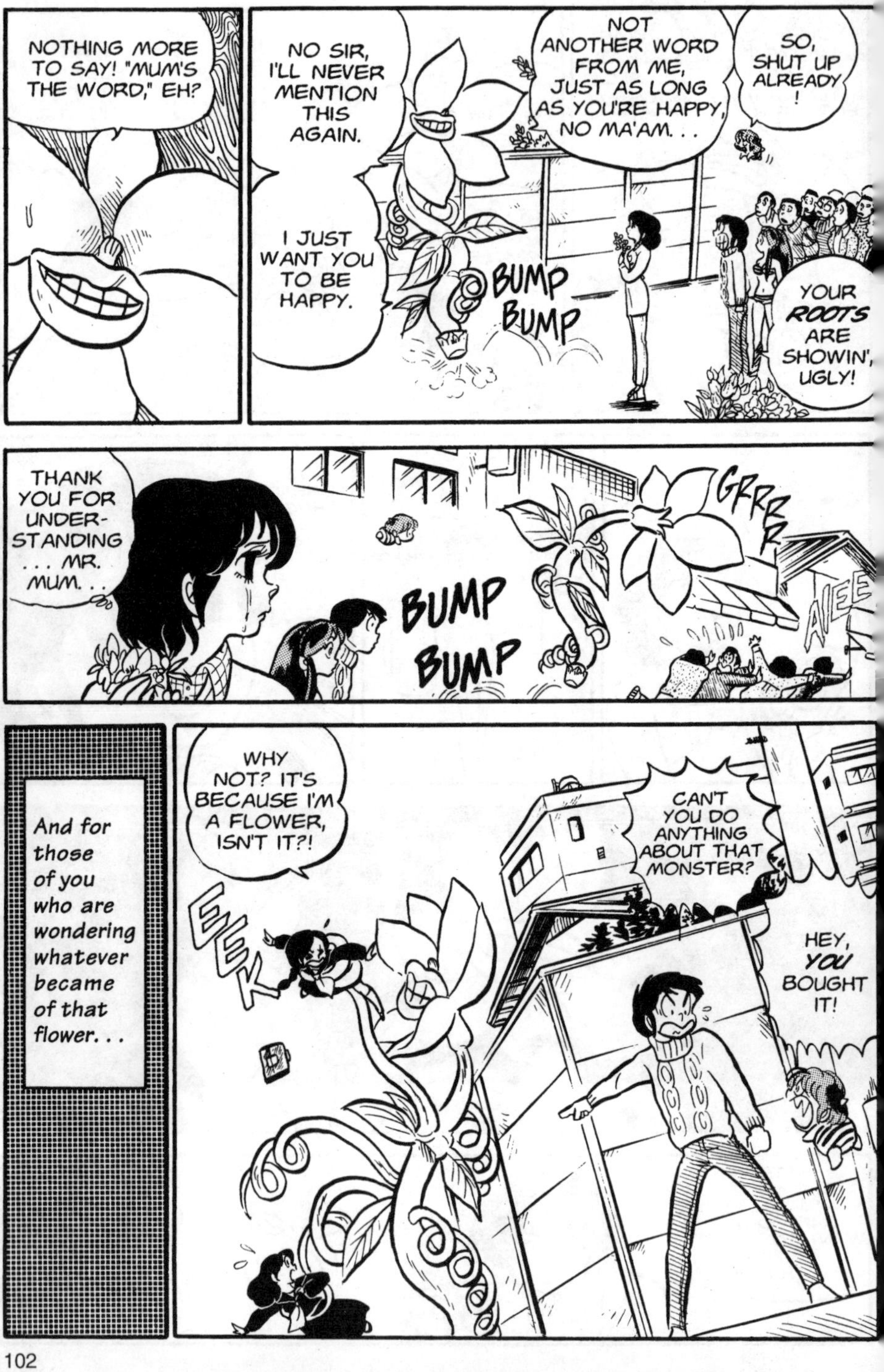
NOTHING MORE TO SAY! "MUM'S THE WORD," EH?
NO SIR, I'LL NEVER MENTION THIS AGAIN.
I JUST WANT YOU TO BE HAPPY.
BUMP BUMP
NOT ANOTHER WORD FROM ME, JUST AS LONG AS YOU'RE HAPPY, NO MA'AM. . .
SO, SHUT UP ALREADY!
YOUR ROOTS ARE SHOWIN', UGLY!
THANK YOU FOR UNDER-STANDING . . . MR. MUM. . .
BUMP BUMP
GRRRR
AIEE
And for those of you who are wondering whatever became of that flower. . .
WHY NOT? IT'S BECAUSE I'M A FLOWER, ISN'T IT?!
EEK
CAN'T YOU DO ANYTHING ABOUT THAT MONSTER?
HEY, YOU BOUGHT IT!

PART SEVEN
HUNTING DEMONS WITH A BEAN SHOOTER

Special Guest Star:
Benten!

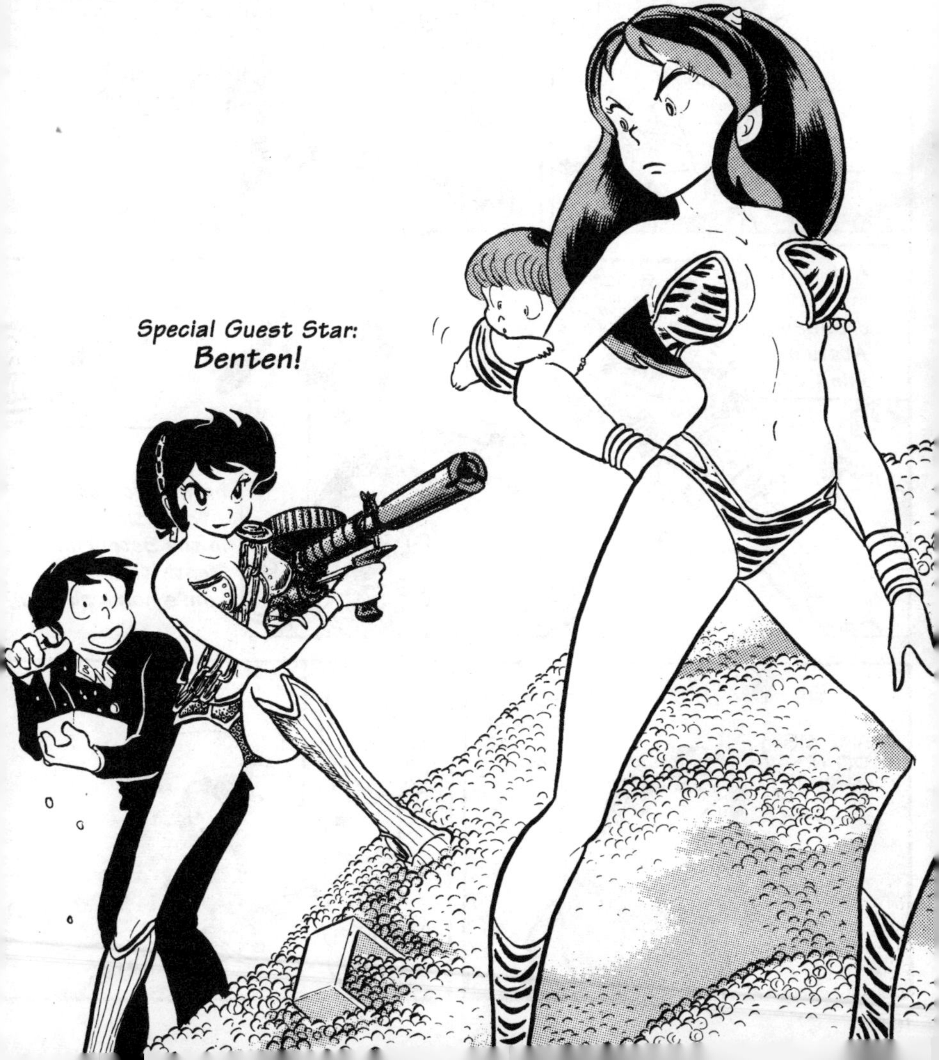

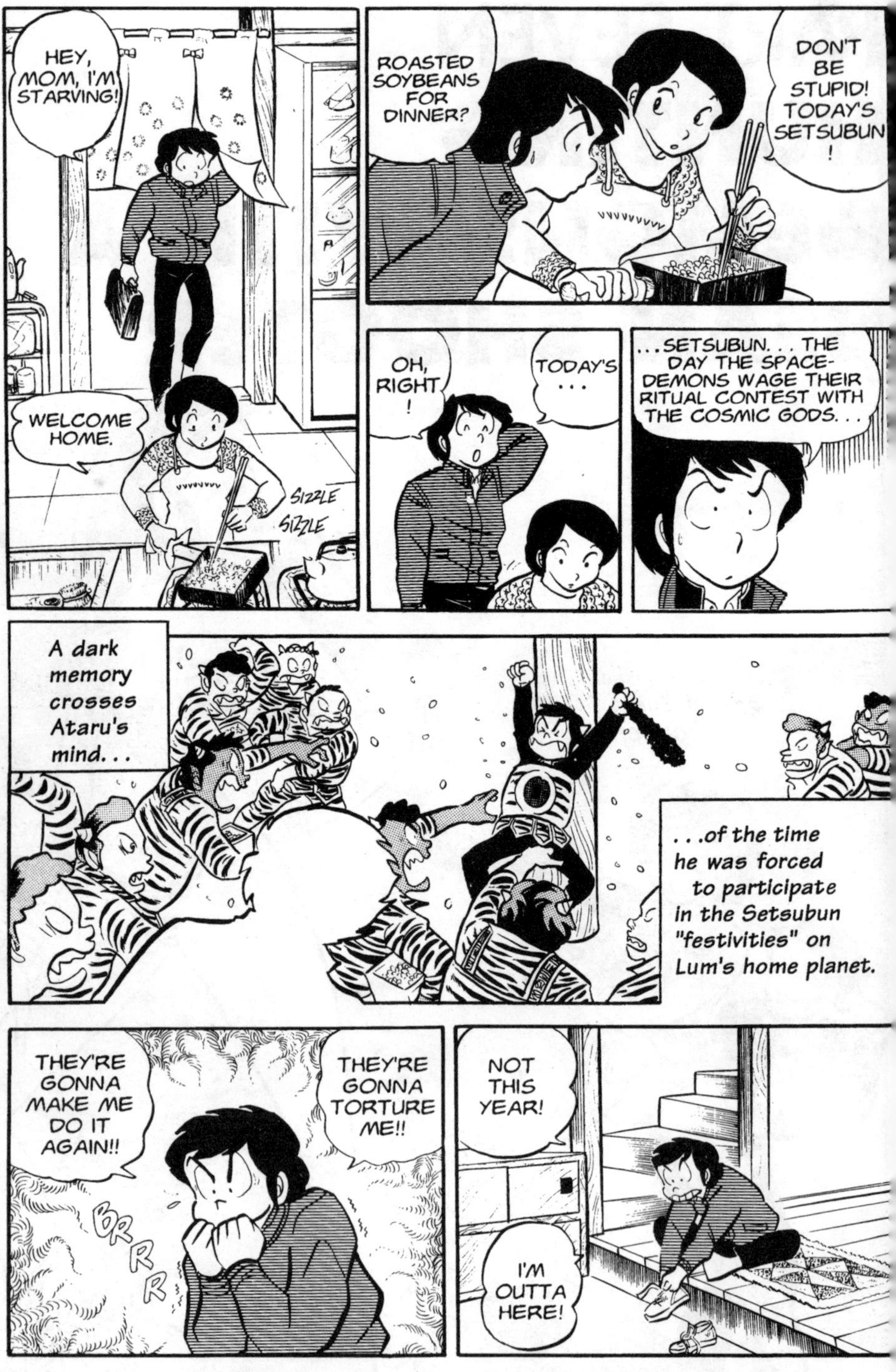
HEY, MOM, I'M STARVING!
WELCOME HOME.
SIZZLE
SIZZLE
ROASTED SOYBEANS FOR DINNER?
DON'T BE STUPID! TODAY'S SETSUBUN!
OH, RIGHT!
TODAY'S . . .
. . . SETSUBUN. . . THE DAY THE SPACE-DEMONS WAGE THEIR RITUAL CONTEST WITH THE COSMIC GODS. . .
A dark memory crosses Ataru's mind. . .
. . .of the time he was forced to participate in the Setsubun "festivities" on Lum's home planet.
THEY'RE GONNA MAKE ME DO IT AGAIN!!
THEY'RE GONNA TORTURE ME!!
BRRR
NOT THIS YEAR!
I'M OUTTA HERE!

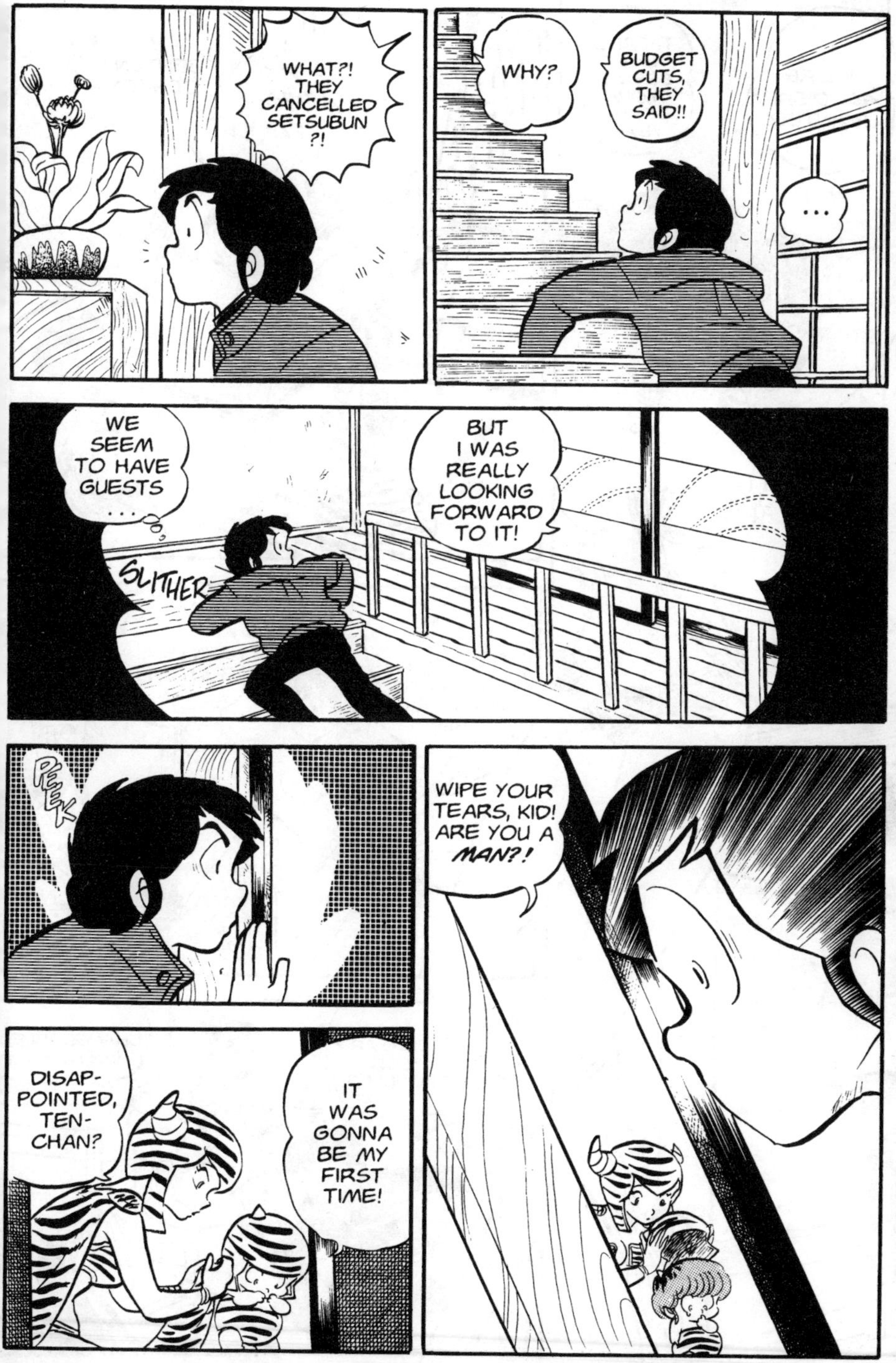
WHAT?! THEY CANCELLED SETSUBUN ?!
WHY?
BUDGET CUTS, THEY SAID!!
...
WE SEEM TO HAVE GUESTS ...
BUT I WAS REALLY LOOKING FORWARD TO IT!
SLITHER
PEEK
WIPE YOUR TEARS, KID! ARE YOU A *MAN?!*
DISAP-POINTED, TEN-CHAN?
IT WAS GONNA BE MY FIRST TIME!

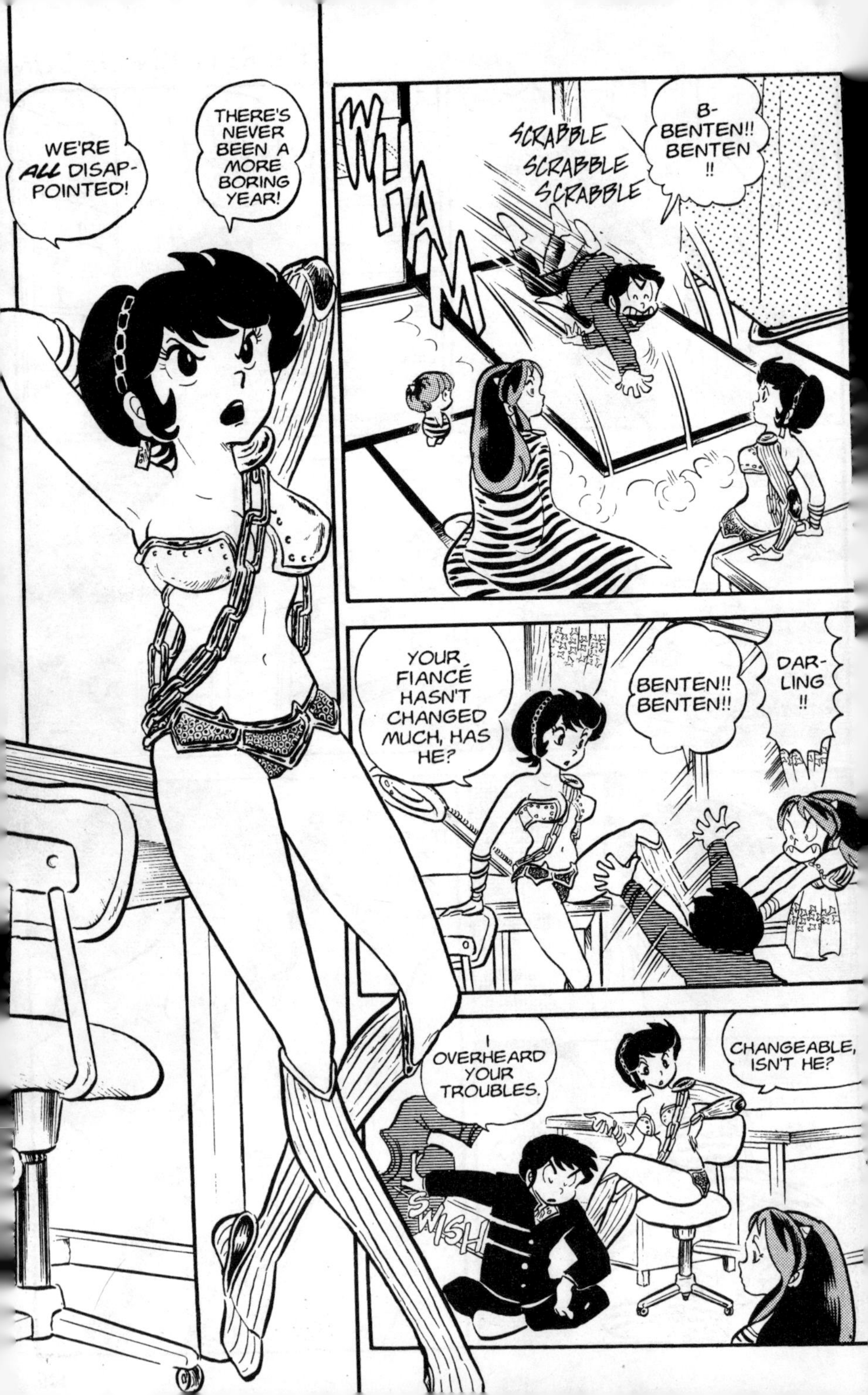
WE'RE ALL DISAP-POINTED!
THERE'S NEVER BEEN A MORE BORING YEAR!
WHAM
SCRABBLE SCRABBLE SCRABBLE
B-BENTEN!! BENTEN !!
YOUR FIANCÉ HASN'T CHANGED MUCH, HAS HE?
BENTEN!! BENTEN!!
DAR-LING !!
I OVERHEARD YOUR TROUBLES.
CHANGEABLE, ISN'T HE?
SWISH

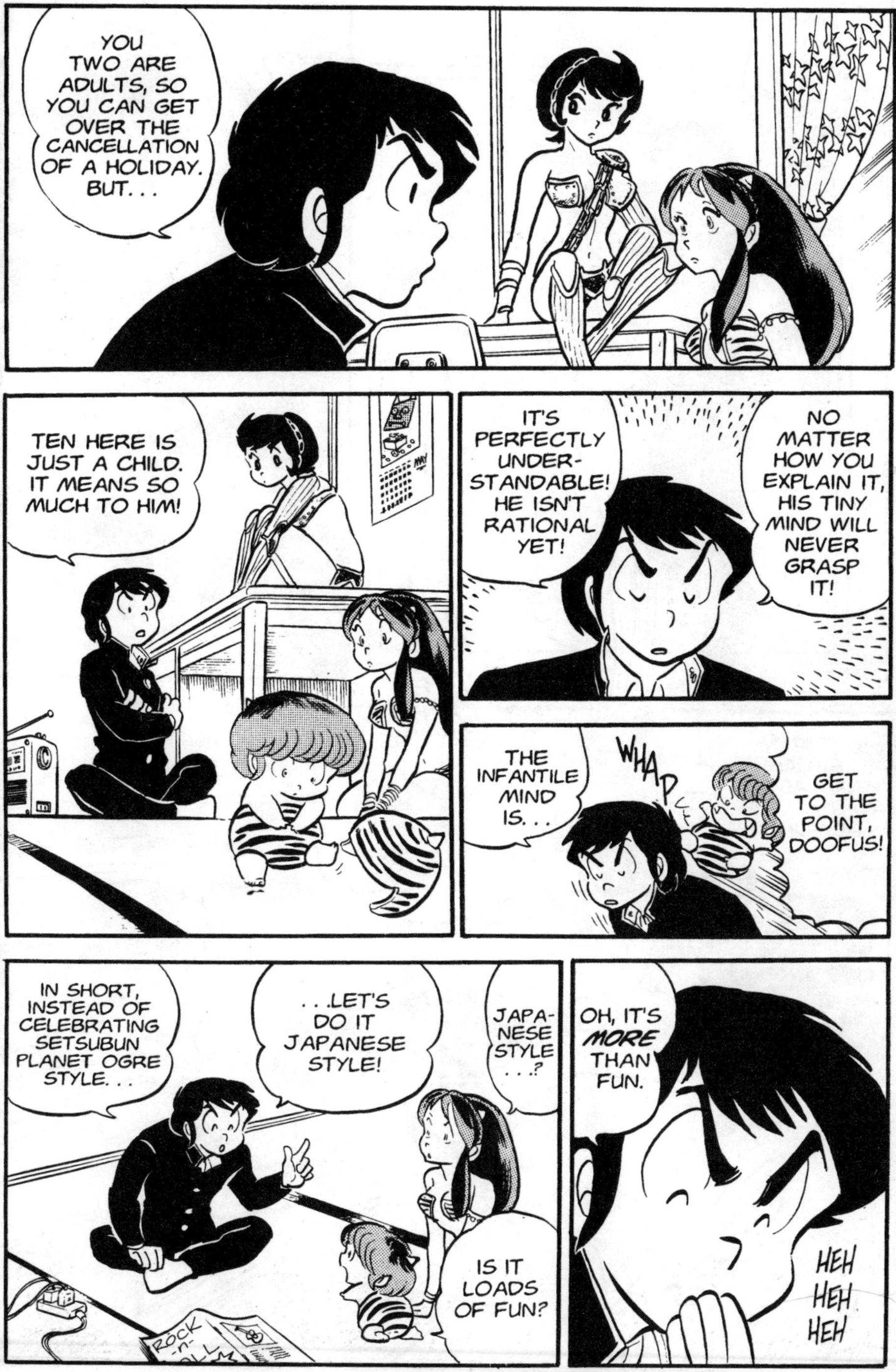
YOU TWO ARE ADULTS, SO YOU CAN GET OVER THE CANCELLATION OF A HOLIDAY. BUT. . .
TEN HERE IS JUST A CHILD. IT MEANS SO MUCH TO HIM!
IT'S PERFECTLY UNDER-STANDABLE! HE ISN'T RATIONAL YET!
NO MATTER HOW YOU EXPLAIN IT, HIS TINY MIND WILL NEVER GRASP IT!
THE INFANTILE MIND IS. . .
WHAP
GET TO THE POINT, DOOFUS!
IN SHORT, INSTEAD OF CELEBRATING SETSUBUN PLANET OGRE STYLE. . .
. . .LET'S DO IT JAPANESE STYLE!
JAPA-NESE STYLE . . .?
IS IT LOADS OF FUN?
OH, IT'S MORE THAN FUN.
HEH HEH HEH

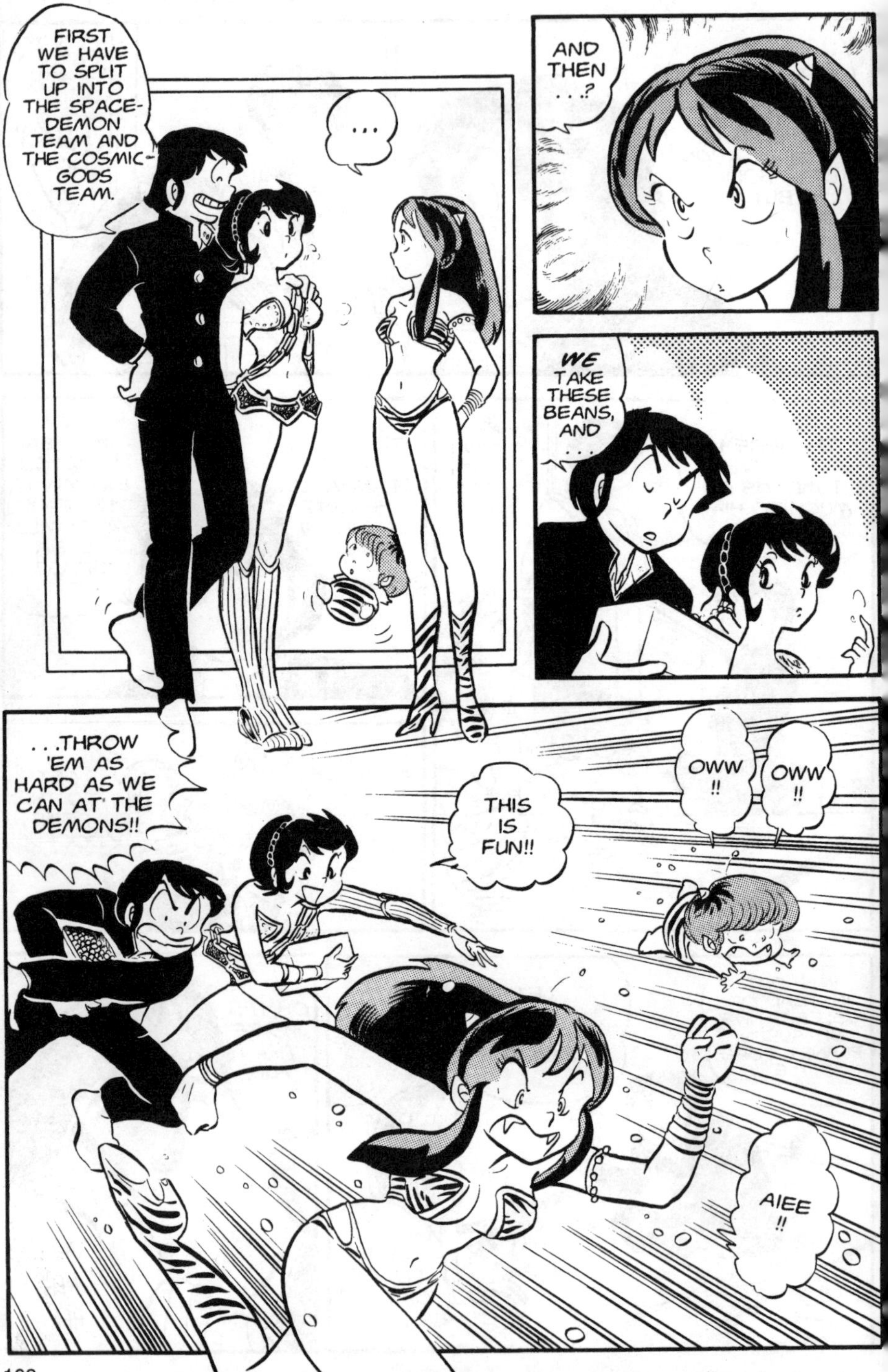
FIRST WE HAVE TO SPLIT UP INTO THE SPACE-DEMON TEAM AND THE COSMIC-GODS TEAM.
...
AND THEN . . .?
WE TAKE THESE BEANS, AND . . .
. . .THROW 'EM AS HARD AS WE CAN AT THE DEMONS!!
THIS IS FUN!!
OWW !!
OWW !!
AIEE !!

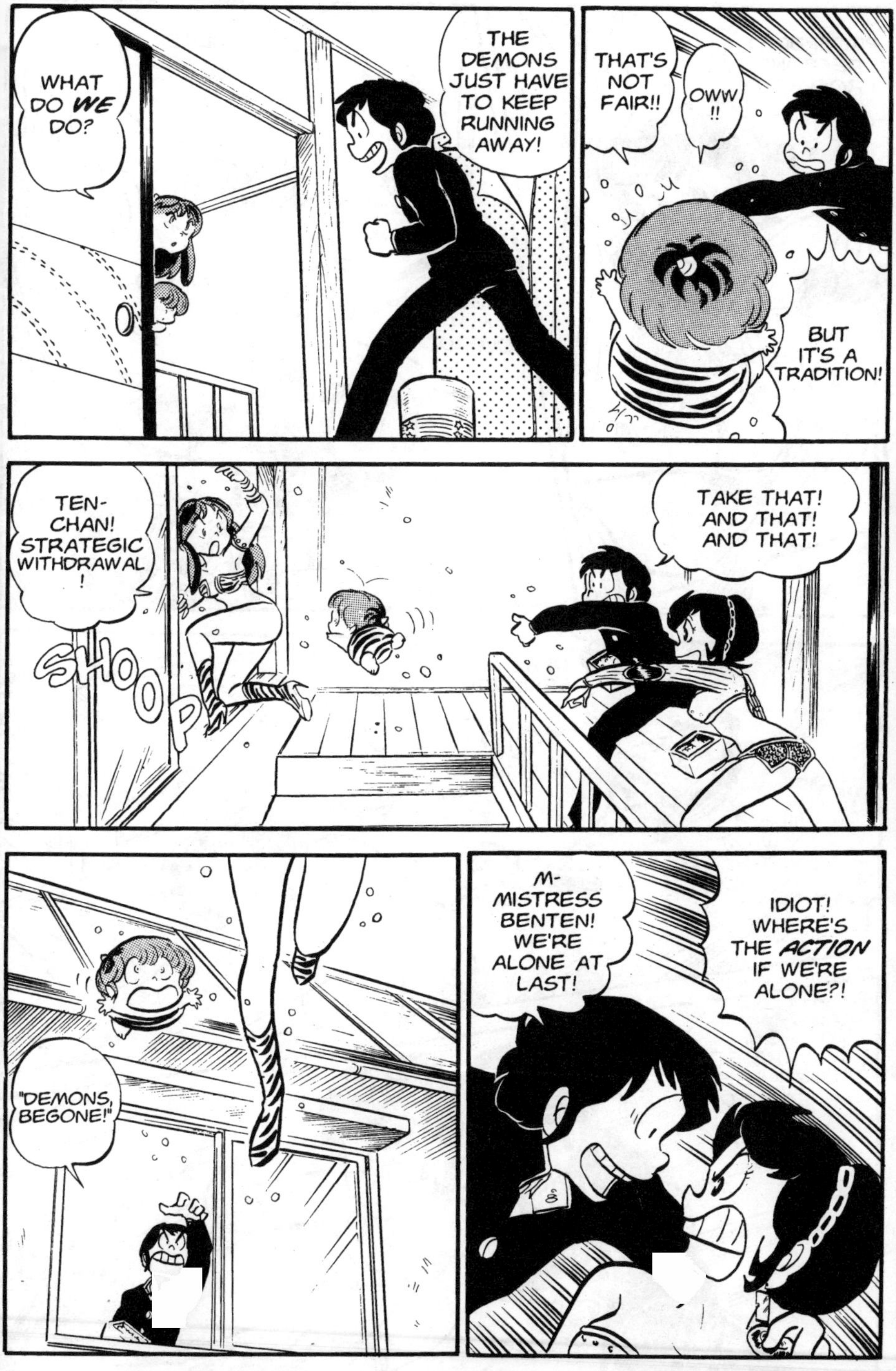
WHAT DO *WE* DO?
THE DEMONS JUST HAVE TO KEEP RUNNING AWAY!
THAT'S NOT FAIR!!
OWW!!
BUT IT'S A TRADITION!
TEN-CHAN! STRATEGIC WITHDRAWAL!
SHOOOP
TAKE THAT! AND THAT! AND THAT!
"DEMONS, BEGONE!"
M-MISTRESS BENTEN! WE'RE ALONE AT LAST!
IDIOT! WHERE'S THE *ACTION* IF WE'RE ALONE?!

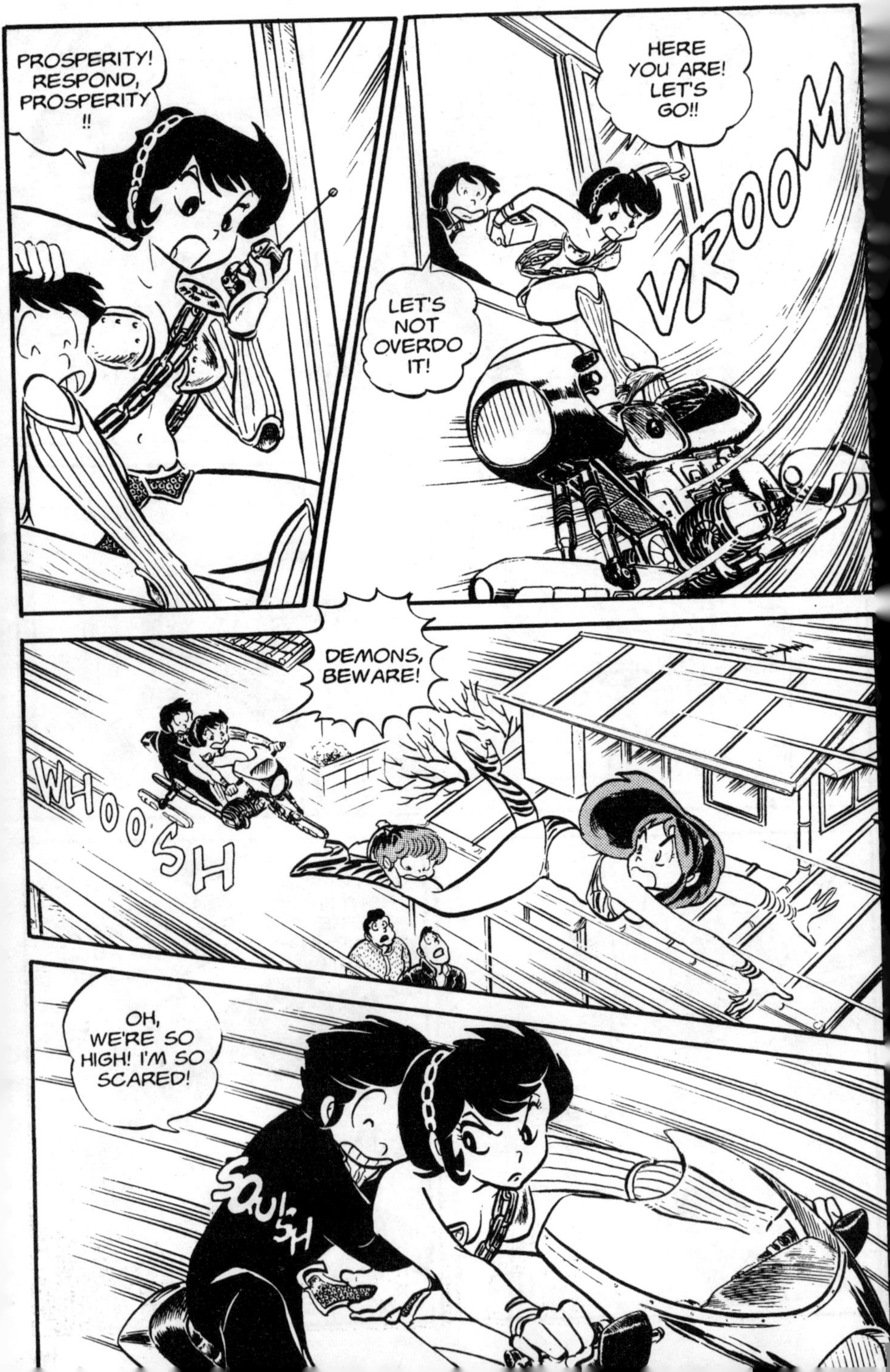
PROSPERITY! RESPOND, PROSPERITY !!
HERE YOU ARE! LET'S GO!!
LET'S NOT OVERDO IT!
VROOM
DEMONS, BEWARE!
WHOOSH
OH, WE'RE SO HIGH! I'M SO SCARED!
SQUISH

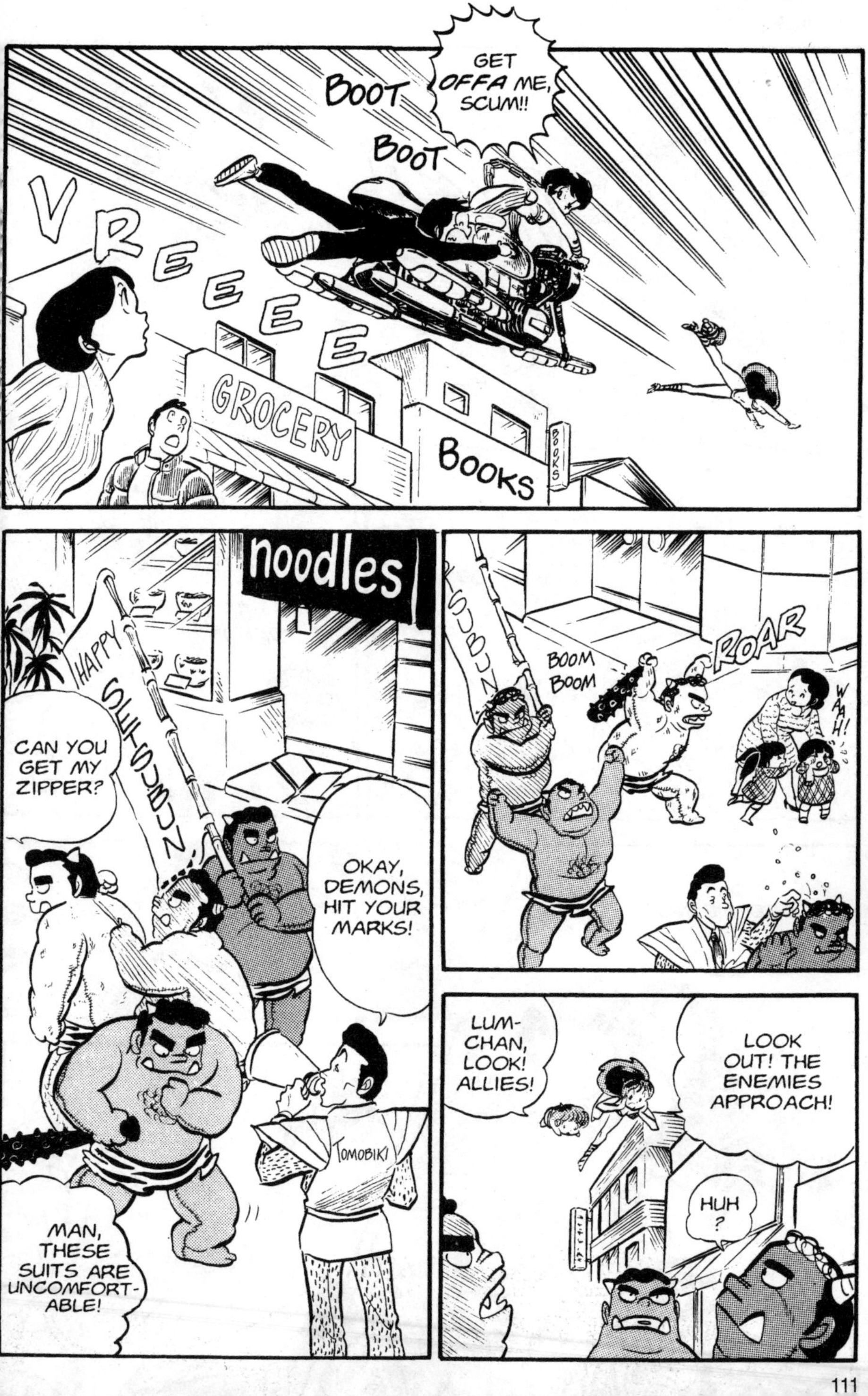
BOOT
GET OFFA ME, SCUM!!
BOOT
VREEEEE
GROCERY
BOOKS
BOOKS
noodles
HAPPY
SETSUBUN
CAN YOU GET MY ZIPPER?
OKAY, DEMONS, HIT YOUR MARKS!
TOMOBIKI
MAN, THESE SUITS ARE UNCOMFORT-ABLE!
SUBUN
BOOM BOOM
ROAR
WAAAH!
LUM-CHAN, LOOK! ALLIES!
LOOK OUT! THE ENEMIES APPROACH!
HUH?

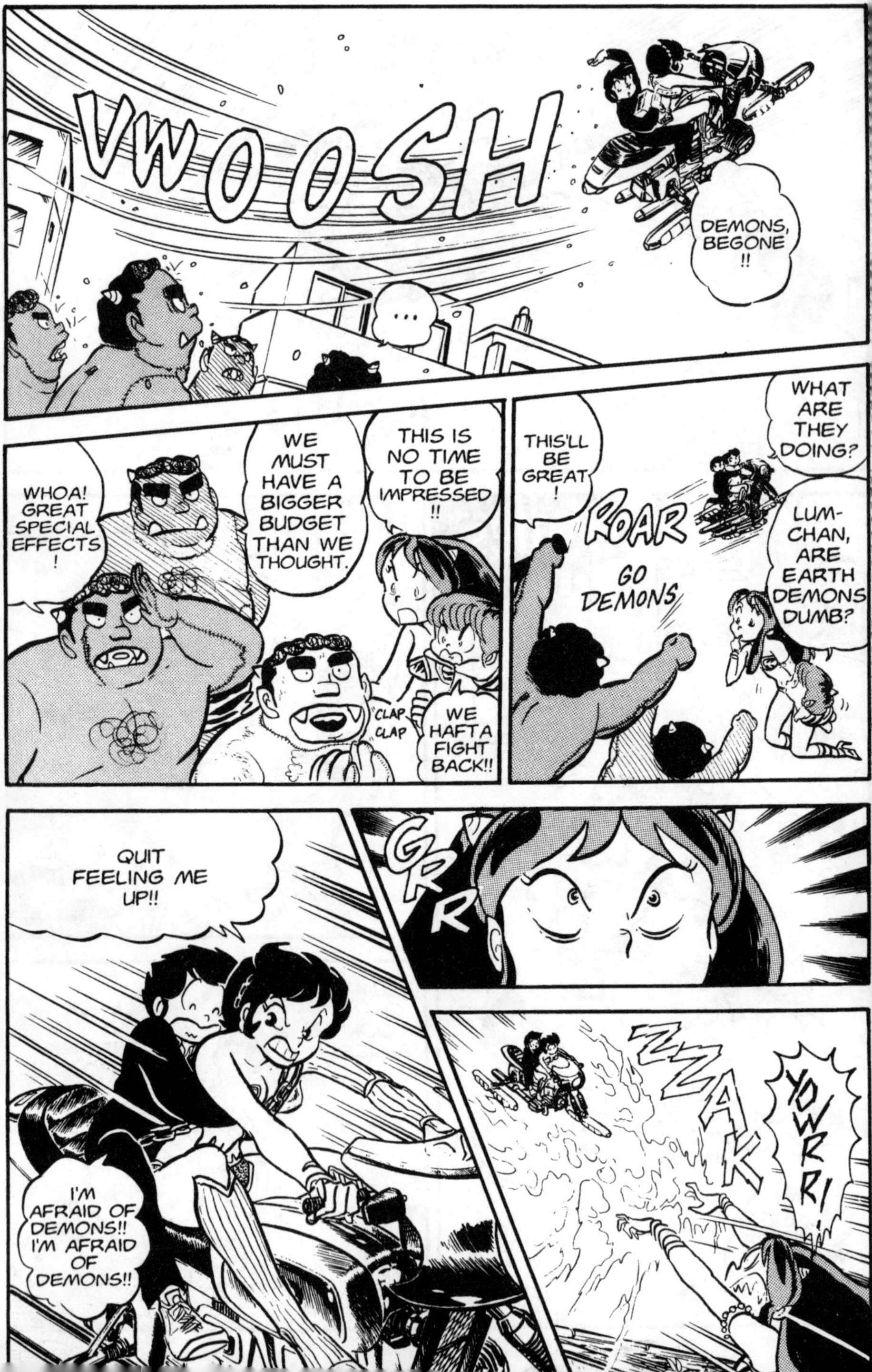
VWOOSH
DEMONS, BEGONE !!
...
WHOA! GREAT SPECIAL EFFECTS !
WE MUST HAVE A BIGGER BUDGET THAN WE THOUGHT.
THIS IS NO TIME TO BE IMPRESSED !!
CLAP CLAP
WE HAFTA FIGHT BACK!!
THIS'LL BE GREAT !
WHAT ARE THEY DOING?
ROAR
GO DEMONS
LUM-CHAN, ARE EARTH DEMONS DUMB?
QUIT FEELING ME UP!!
I'M AFRAID OF DEMONS!! I'M AFRAID OF DEMONS!!
GRR
ZZAK
YOWRRR!

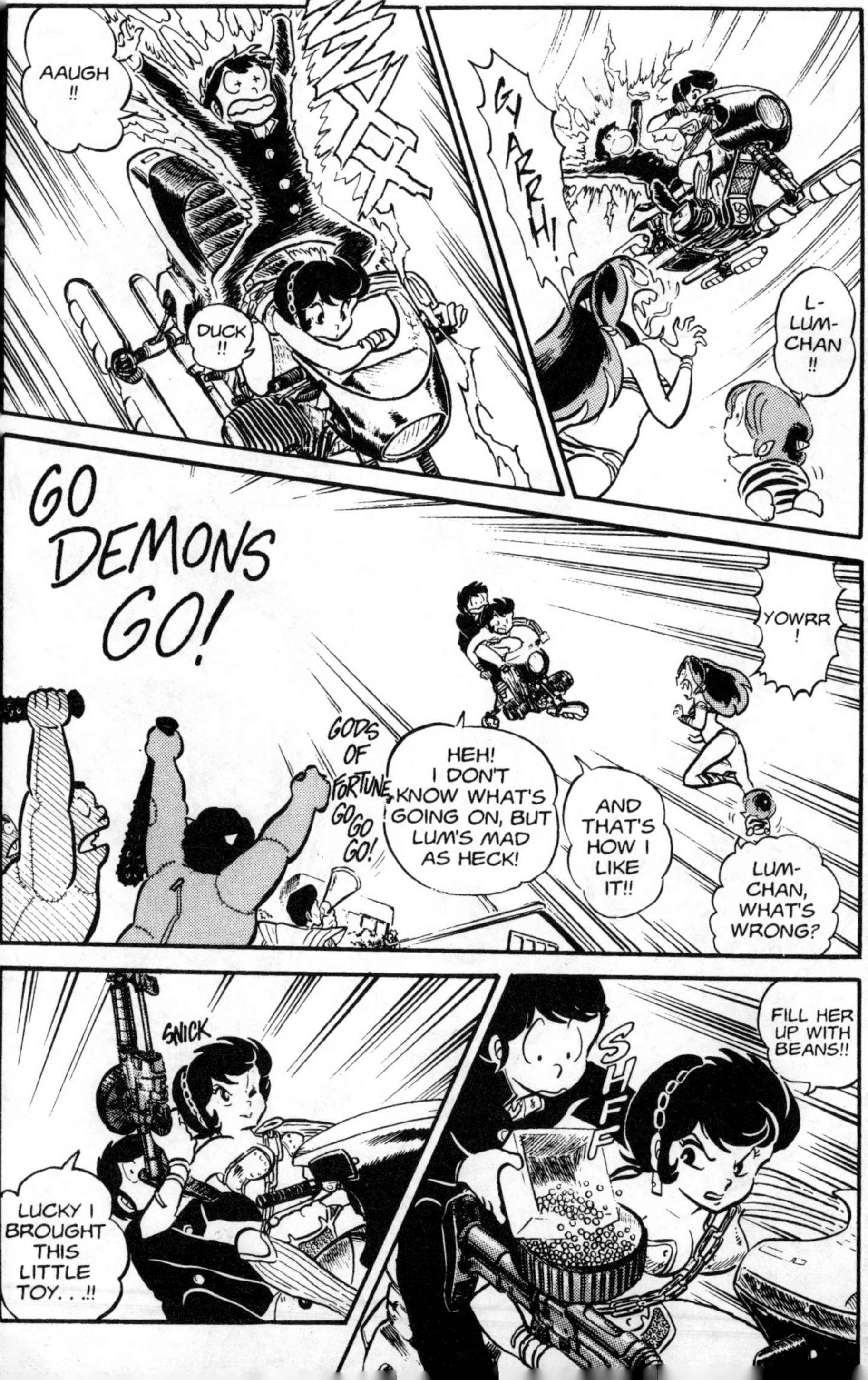
AAUGH!!
DUCK!!
GYARRH!
L-LUM-CHAN!!
GO DEMONS GO!
YOWRR!
GODS OF FORTUNE GO GO GO!
HEH! I DON'T KNOW WHAT'S GOING ON, BUT LUM'S MAD AS HECK!
AND THAT'S HOW I LIKE IT!!
LUM-CHAN, WHAT'S WRONG?
SNICK
LUCKY I BROUGHT THIS LITTLE TOY. . .!!
SHFF
FILL HER UP WITH BEANS!!

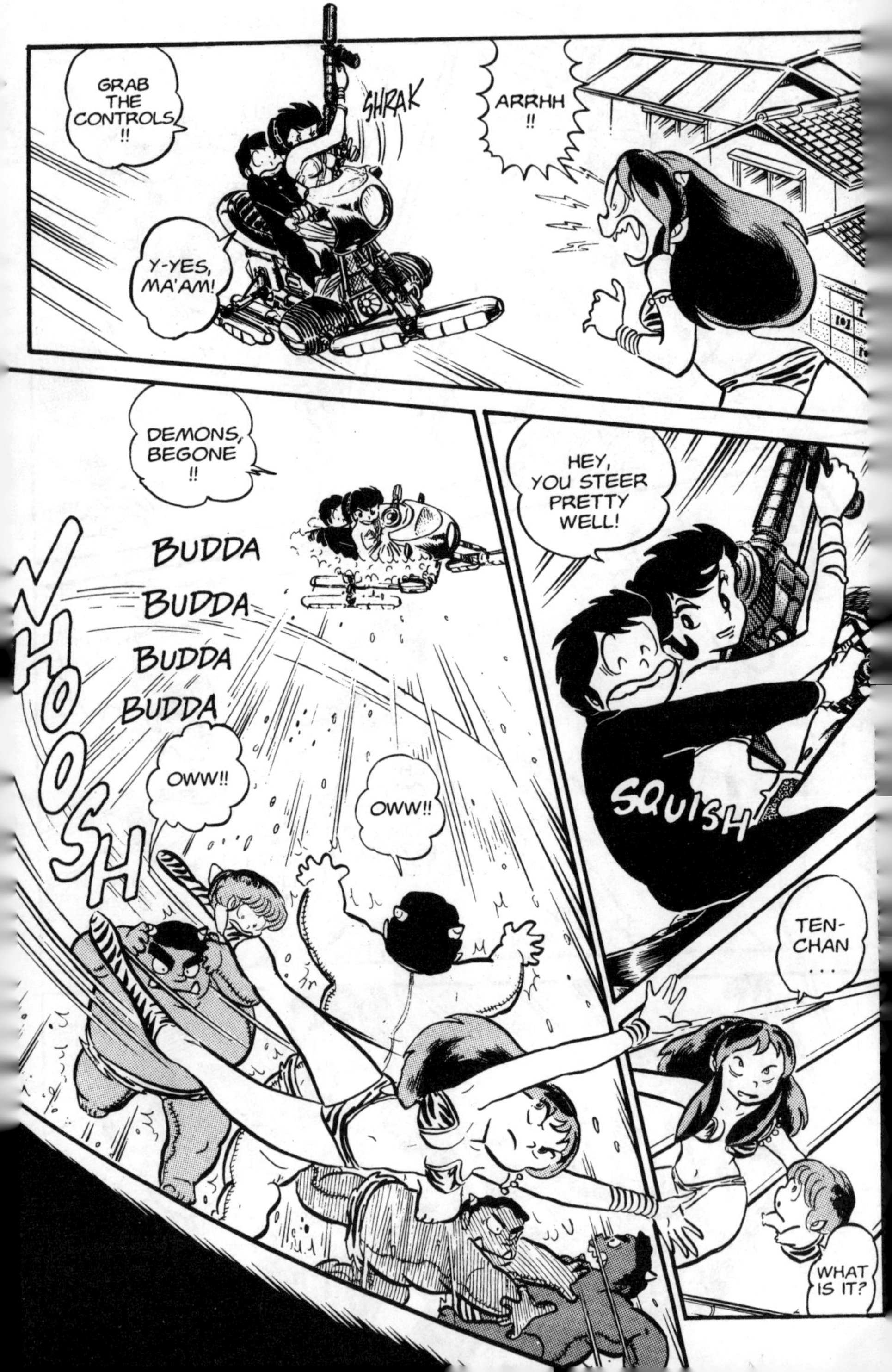
GRAB THE CONTROLS !!
SHRAK
Y-YES, MA'AM!
ARRHH !!
DEMONS, BEGONE !!
WHOOSH
BUDDA
BUDDA
BUDDA
BUDDA
OWW!!
OWW!!
HEY, YOU STEER PRETTY WELL!
SQUISH
TEN-CHAN . . .
WHAT IS IT?

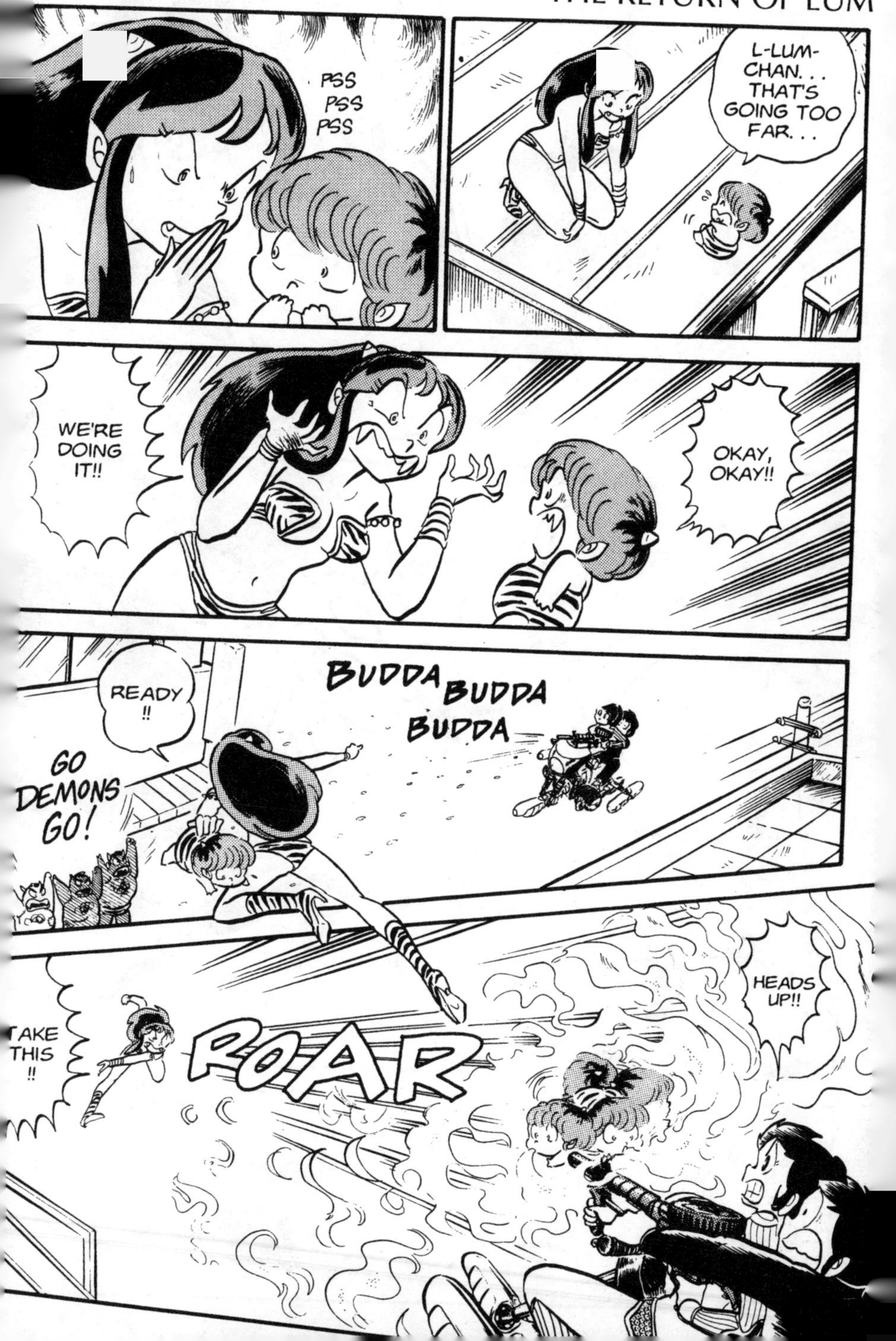
PSS
PSS
PSS
L-LUM-CHAN. . . THAT'S GOING TOO FAR. . .
WE'RE DOING IT!!
OKAY, OKAY!!
READY !!
GO DEMONS GO!
BUDDA BUDDA BUDDA
TAKE THIS !!
ROAR
HEADS UP!!

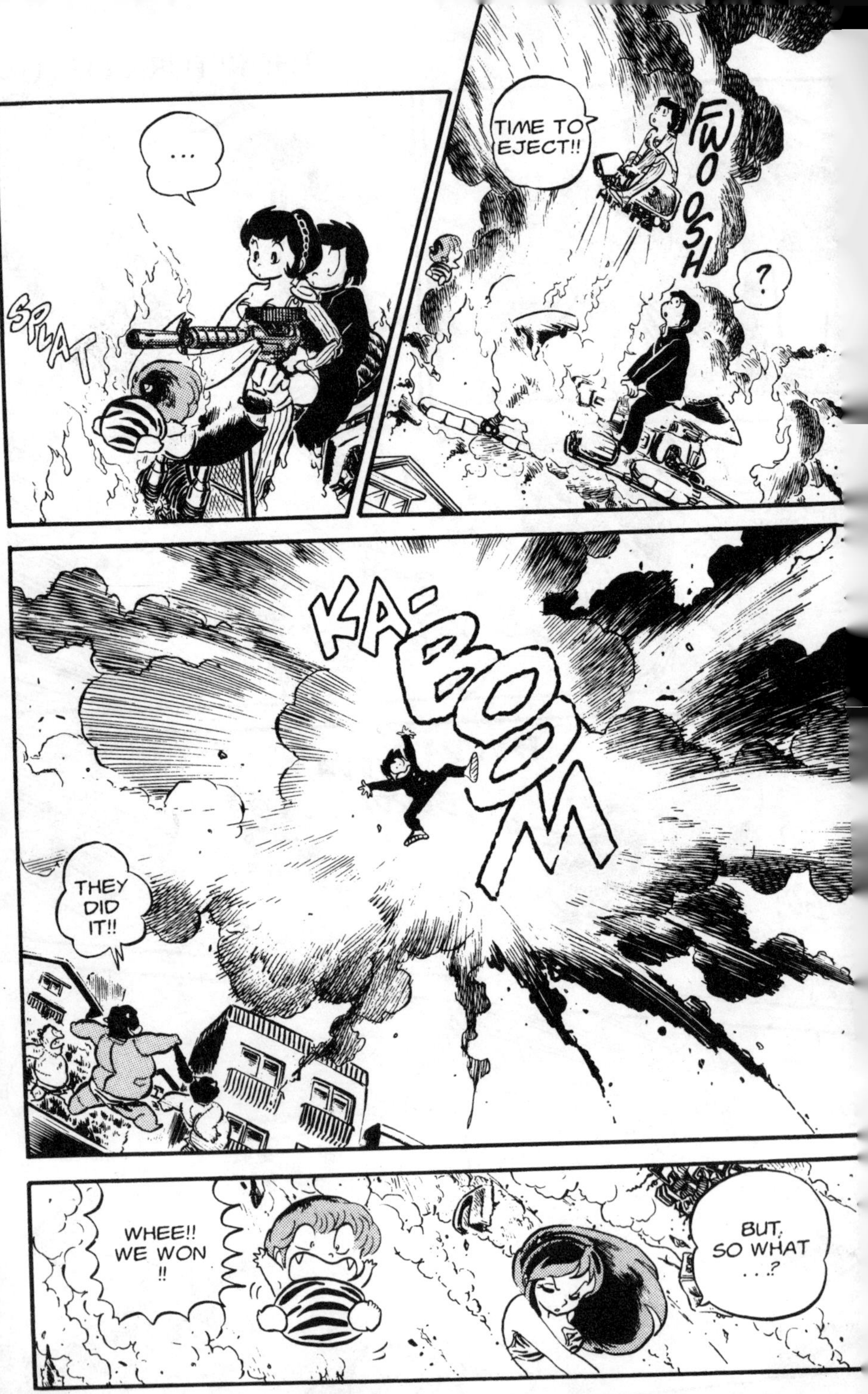
TIME TO EJECT!!
FWOOSH
?
...
SPLAT
KA-BOOM
THEY DID IT!!
BUT, SO WHAT . . .?
WHEE!! WE WON !!

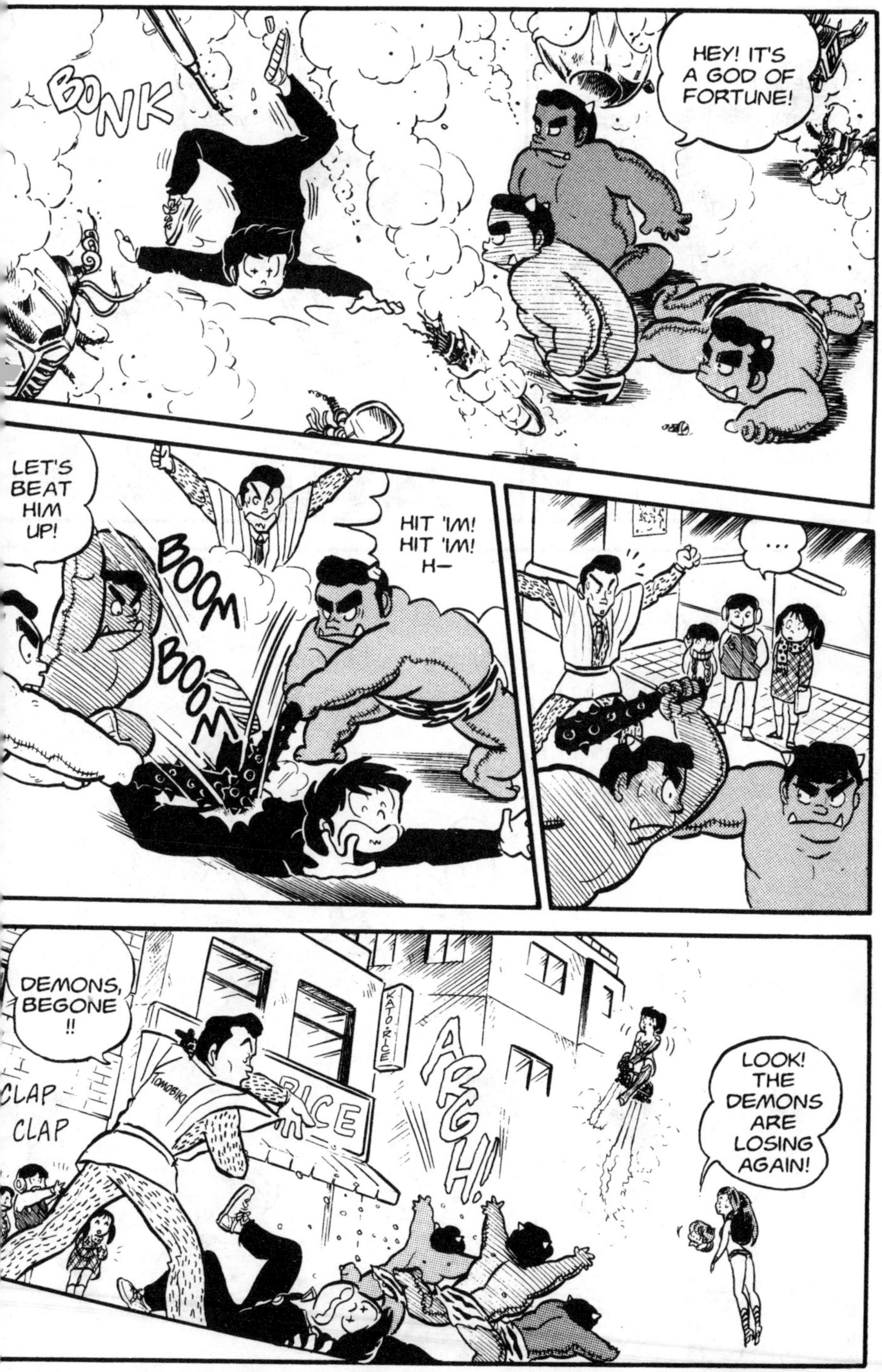
BONK
HEY! IT'S A GOD OF FORTUNE!
LET'S BEAT HIM UP!
BOOM
BOOM
HIT 'IM! HIT 'IM! H—
...
DEMONS, BEGONE !!
CLAP
CLAP
TOMOBIKI
RICE
KATO RICE
ARGH!
LOOK! THE DEMONS ARE LOSING AGAIN!

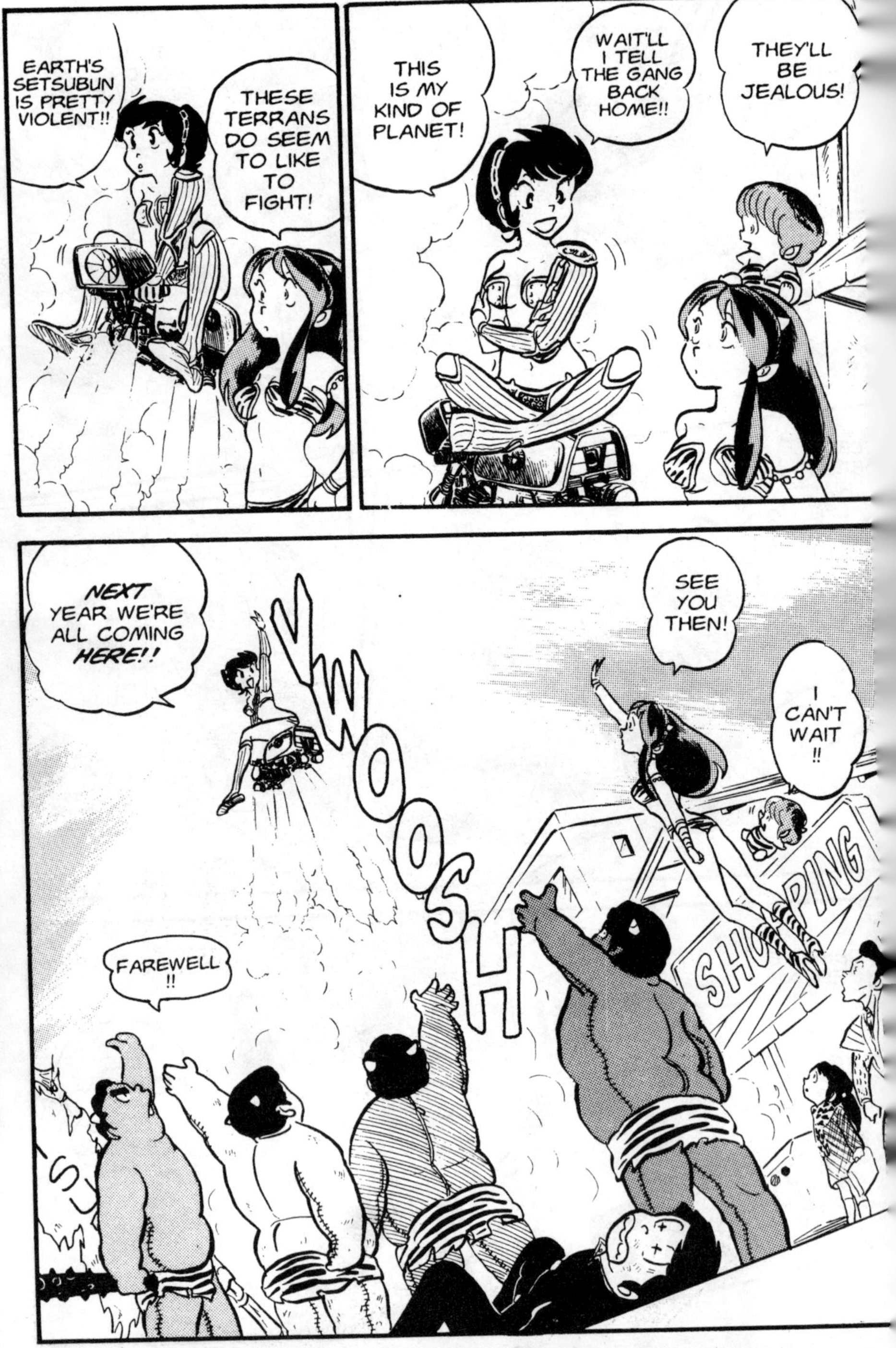
EARTH'S SETSUBUN IS PRETTY VIOLENT!!
THESE TERRANS DO SEEM TO LIKE TO FIGHT!
THIS IS MY KIND OF PLANET!
WAIT'LL I TELL THE GANG BACK HOME!!
THEY'LL BE JEALOUS!
NEXT YEAR WE'RE ALL COMING HERE!!
VWOOSH
SEE YOU THEN!
I CAN'T WAIT !!
SHOPPING
FAREWELL !!

PART EIGHT
MISS SNOW QUEEN

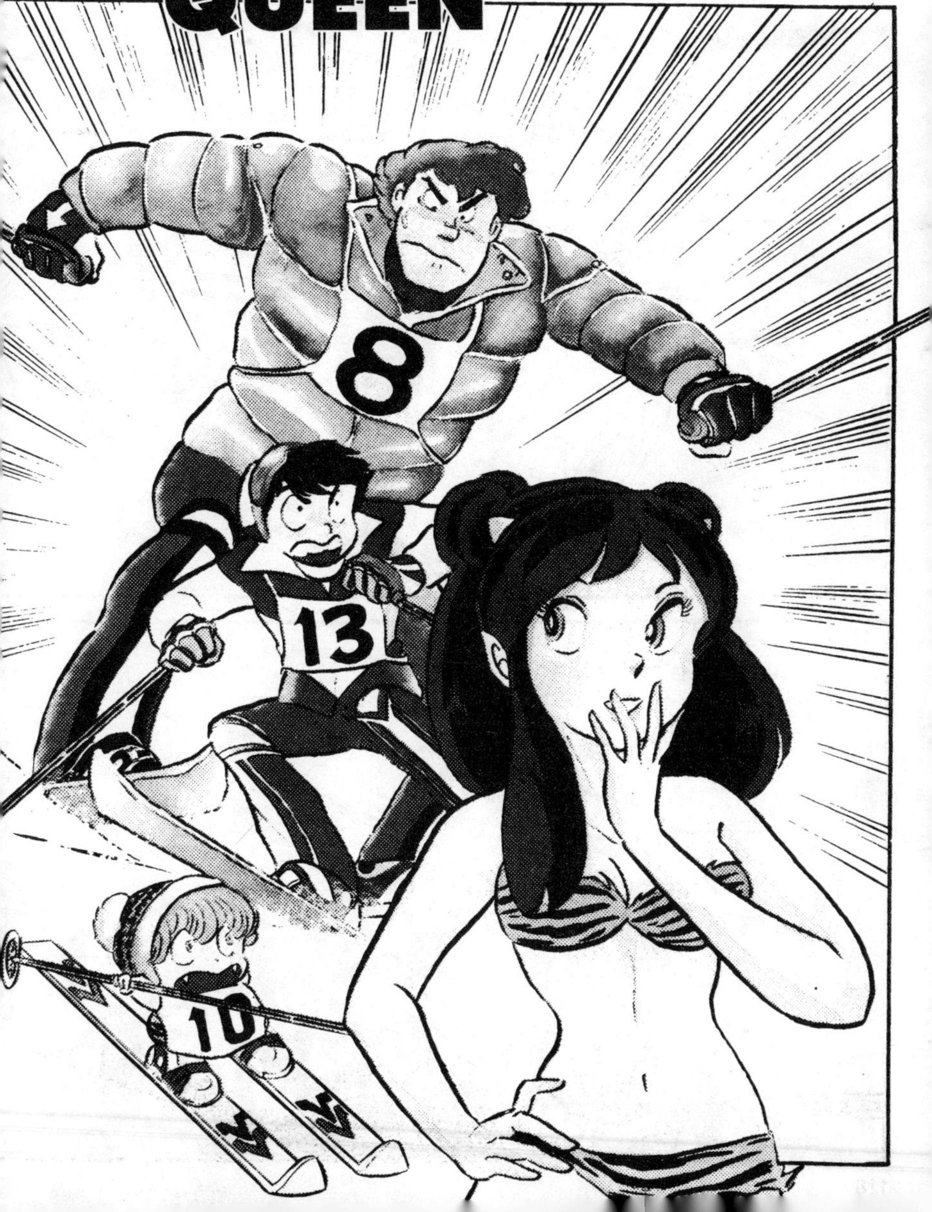
8
13
10

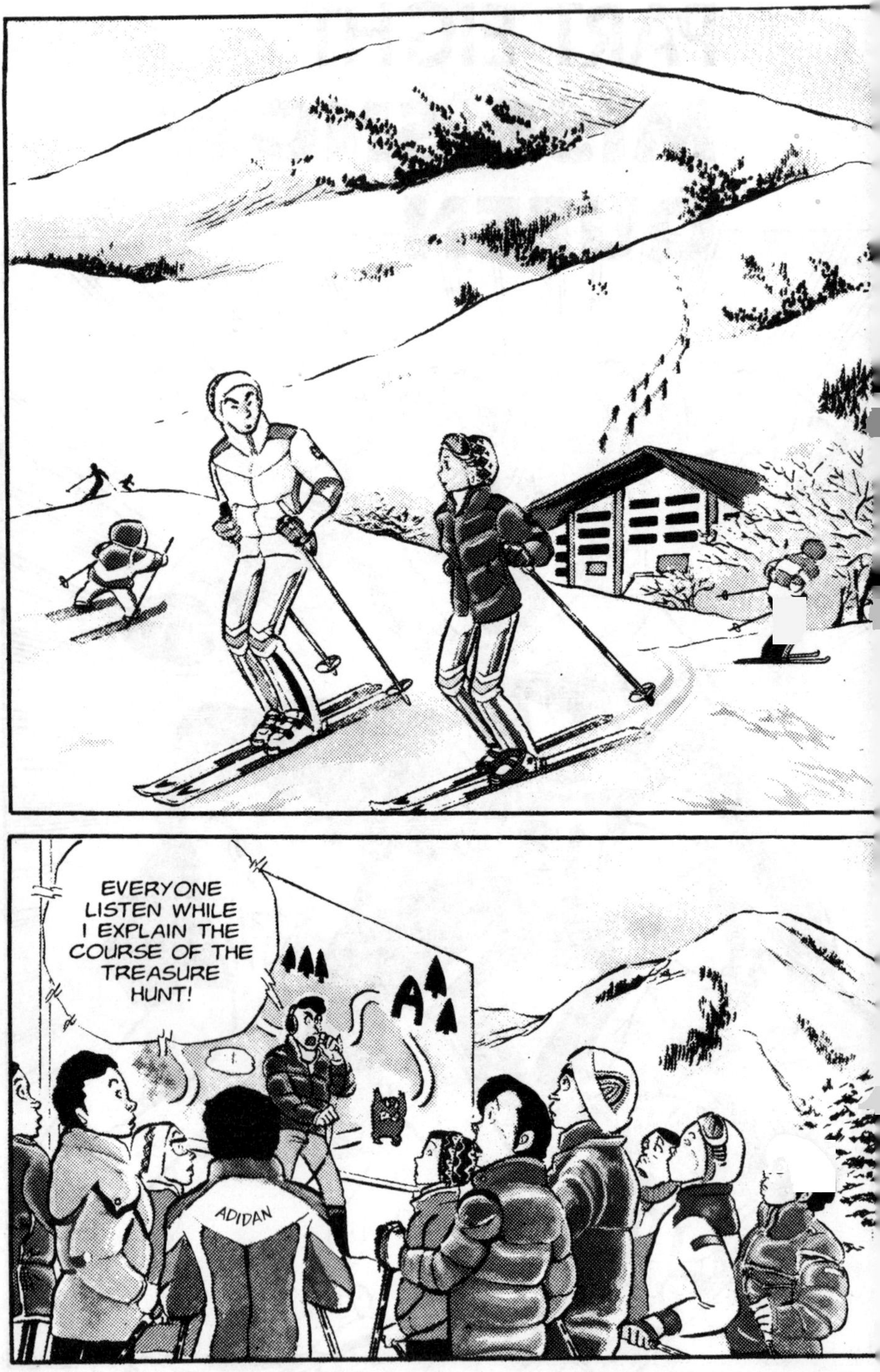
EVERYONE LISTEN WHILE I EXPLAIN THE COURSE OF THE TREASURE HUNT!
ADIDAN

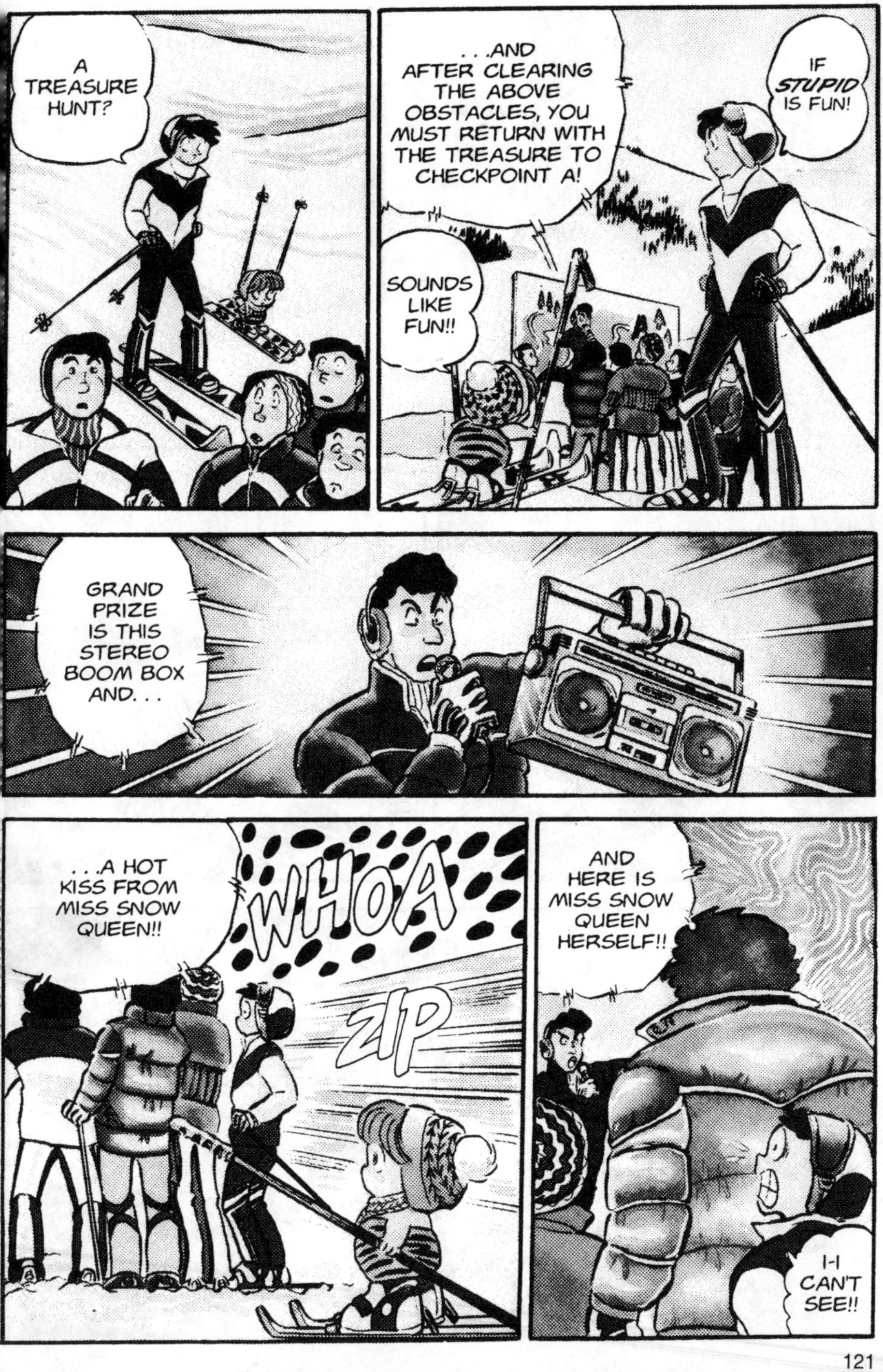
A TREASURE HUNT?
. . .AND AFTER CLEARING THE ABOVE OBSTACLES, YOU MUST RETURN WITH THE TREASURE TO CHECKPOINT A!
IF STUPID IS FUN!
SOUNDS LIKE FUN!!
GRAND PRIZE IS THIS STEREO BOOM BOX AND. . .
. . .A HOT KISS FROM MISS SNOW QUEEN!!
WHOA
ZIP
AND HERE IS MISS SNOW QUEEN HERSELF!!
I-I CAN'T SEE!!

TA-DAA

GASP!

I CAN'T SEE!!

WHAT A BABE!

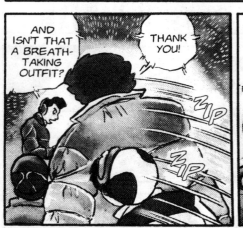

AND ISN'T THAT A BREATH-TAKING OUTFIT?

THANK YOU!

ZIP

ZIP

NOW THROW A KISS TO OUR CONTESTANTS!

SMACK

WAHOO!

MUSH

ZIP

THANK YOU, MISS SNOW QUEEN!

SEE YOU AT THE FINISH!

WOO-HOO!

FWEET

CLAP CLAP

CLAP

CLAP

RRG...

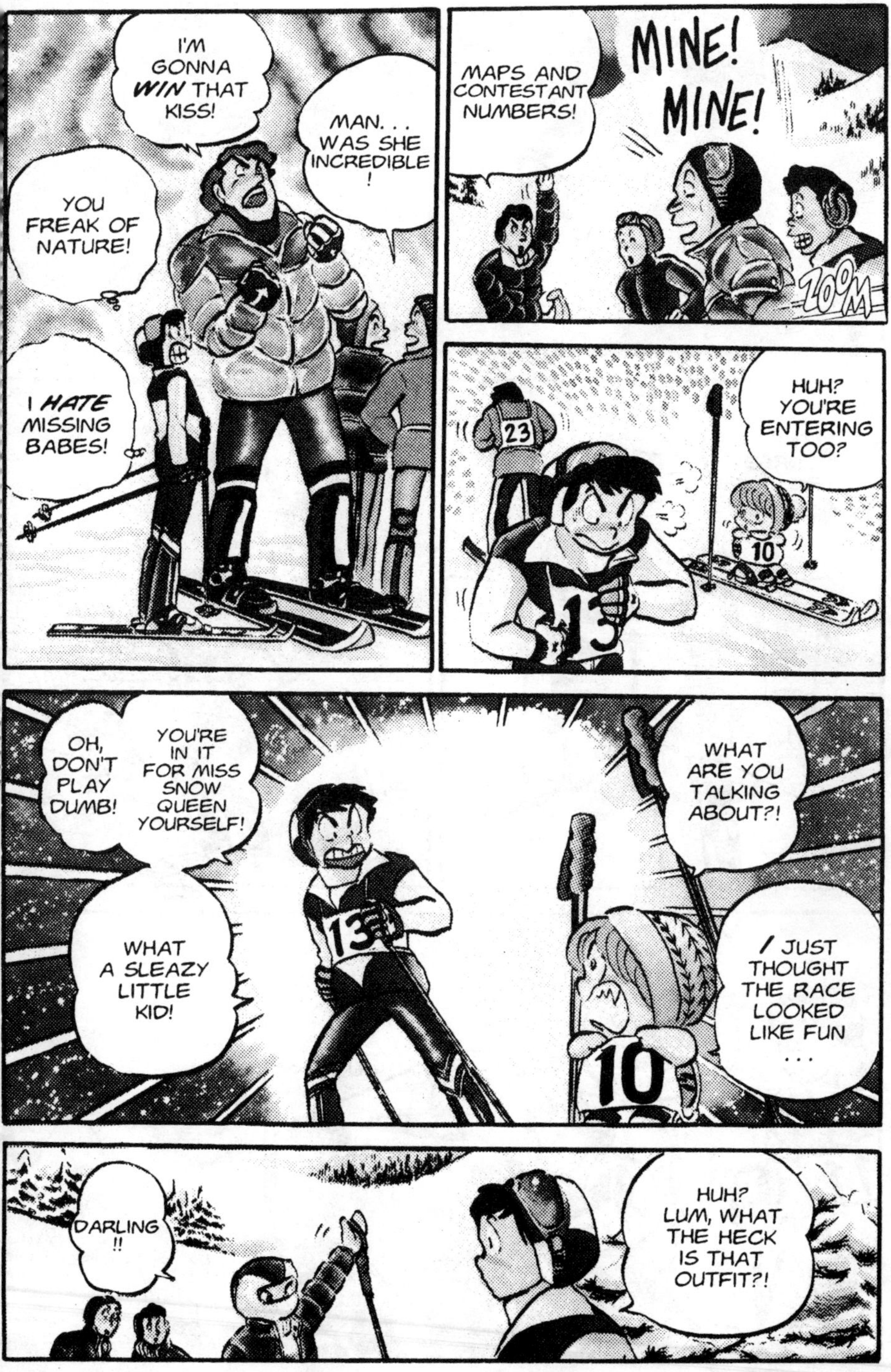
I'M GONNA WIN THAT KISS!
MAN. . . WAS SHE INCREDIBLE !
YOU FREAK OF NATURE!
I HATE MISSING BABES!
MAPS AND CONTESTANT NUMBERS!
MINE! MINE!
ZOOM
HUH? YOU'RE ENTERING TOO?
23
13
10
OH, DON'T PLAY DUMB!
YOU'RE IN IT FOR MISS SNOW QUEEN YOURSELF!
WHAT ARE YOU TALKING ABOUT?!
WHAT A SLEAZY LITTLE KID!
I JUST THOUGHT THE RACE LOOKED LIKE FUN . . .
DARLING !!
HUH? LUM, WHAT THE HECK IS THAT OUTFIT?!

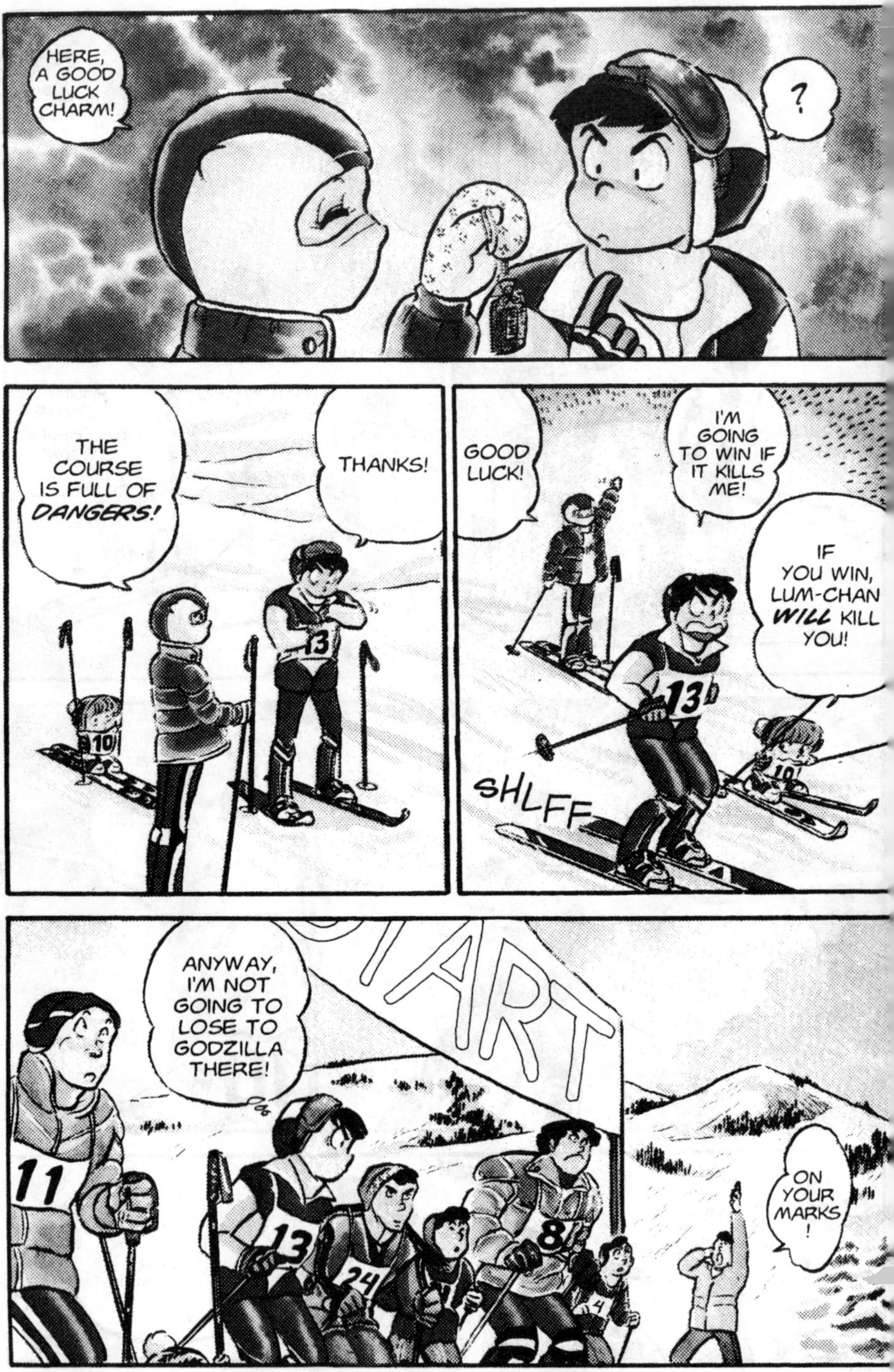
HERE, A GOOD LUCK CHARM!
?
THE COURSE IS FULL OF DANGERS!
THANKS!
GOOD LUCK!
I'M GOING TO WIN IF IT KILLS ME!
IF YOU WIN, LUM-CHAN WILL KILL YOU!
SHLFF
START
ANYWAY, I'M NOT GOING TO LOSE TO GODZILLA THERE!
ON YOUR MARKS!

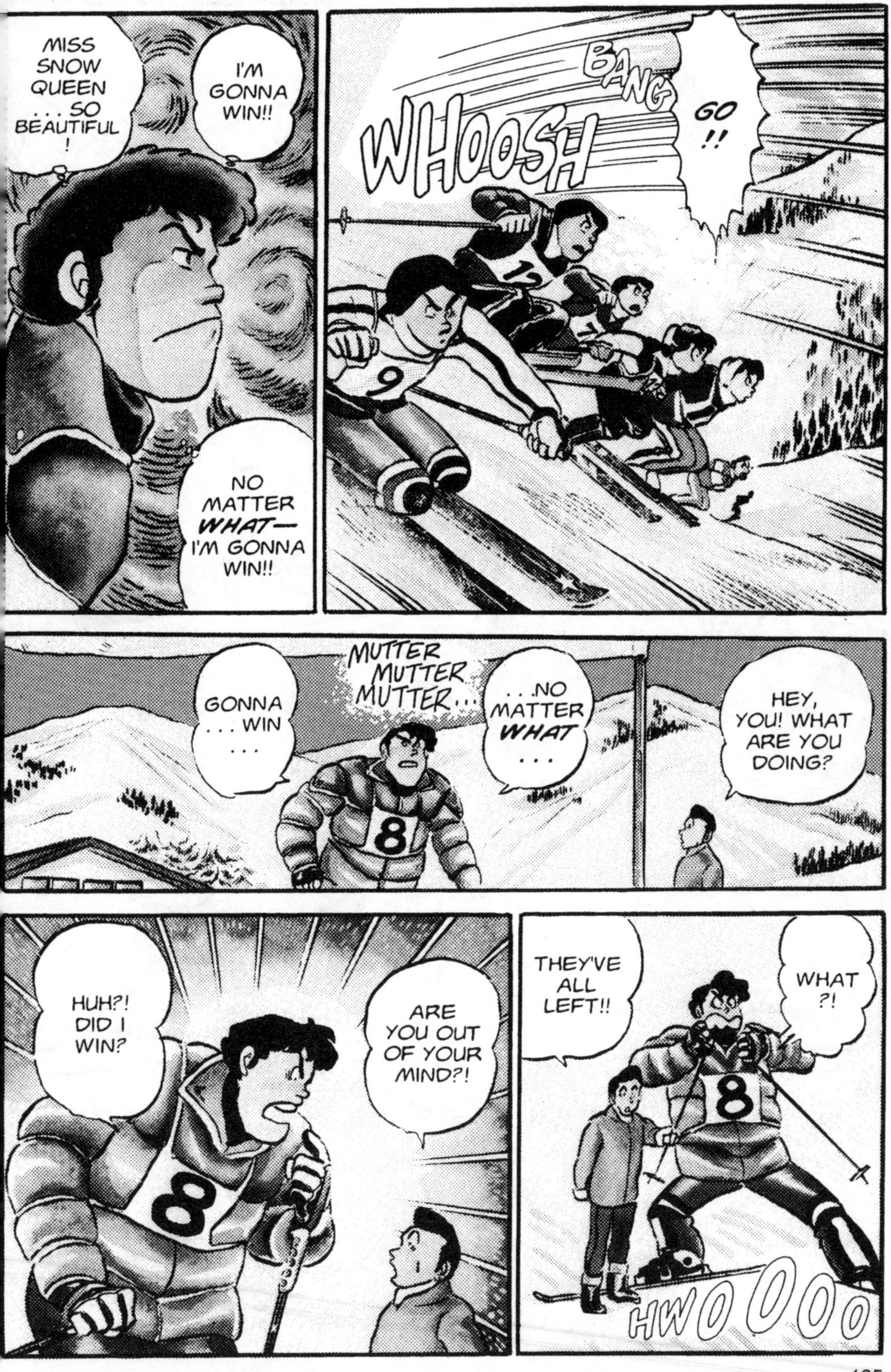
MISS SNOW QUEEN . . . SO BEAUTIFUL !
I'M GONNA WIN!!
NO MATTER WHAT— I'M GONNA WIN!!
BANG
GO !!
WHOOSH
GONNA . . . WIN . . .
MUTTER MUTTER MUTTER...
. . .NO MATTER WHAT . . .
HEY, YOU! WHAT ARE YOU DOING?
HUH?! DID I WIN?
ARE YOU OUT OF YOUR MIND?!
THEY'VE ALL LEFT!!
WHAT ?!
HWOOOO

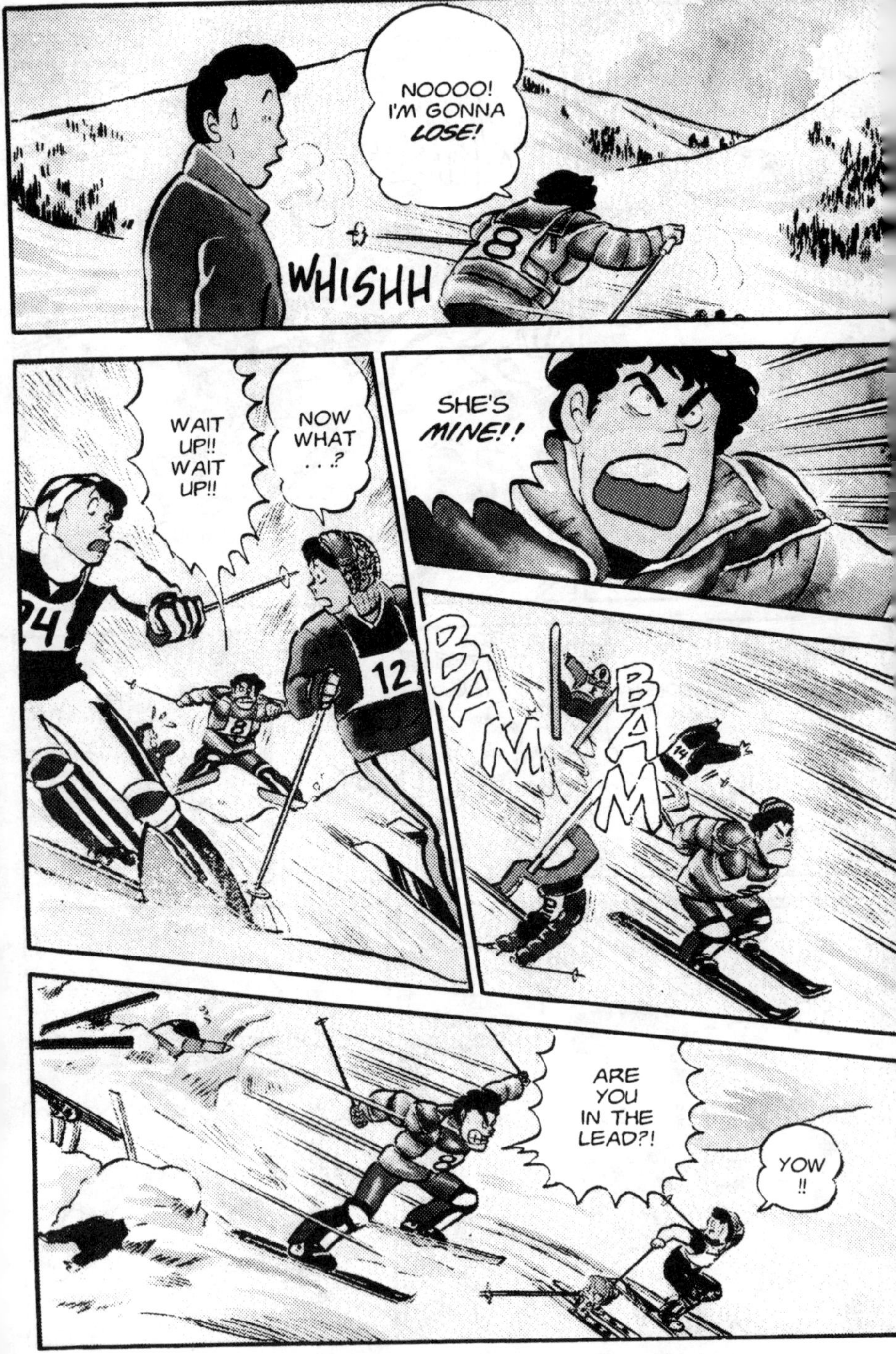
NOOOO! I'M GONNA LOSE!
WHISHH
WAIT UP!! WAIT UP!!
NOW WHAT . . .?
SHE'S MINE!!
BAM
BAM
ARE YOU IN THE LEAD?!
YOW !!

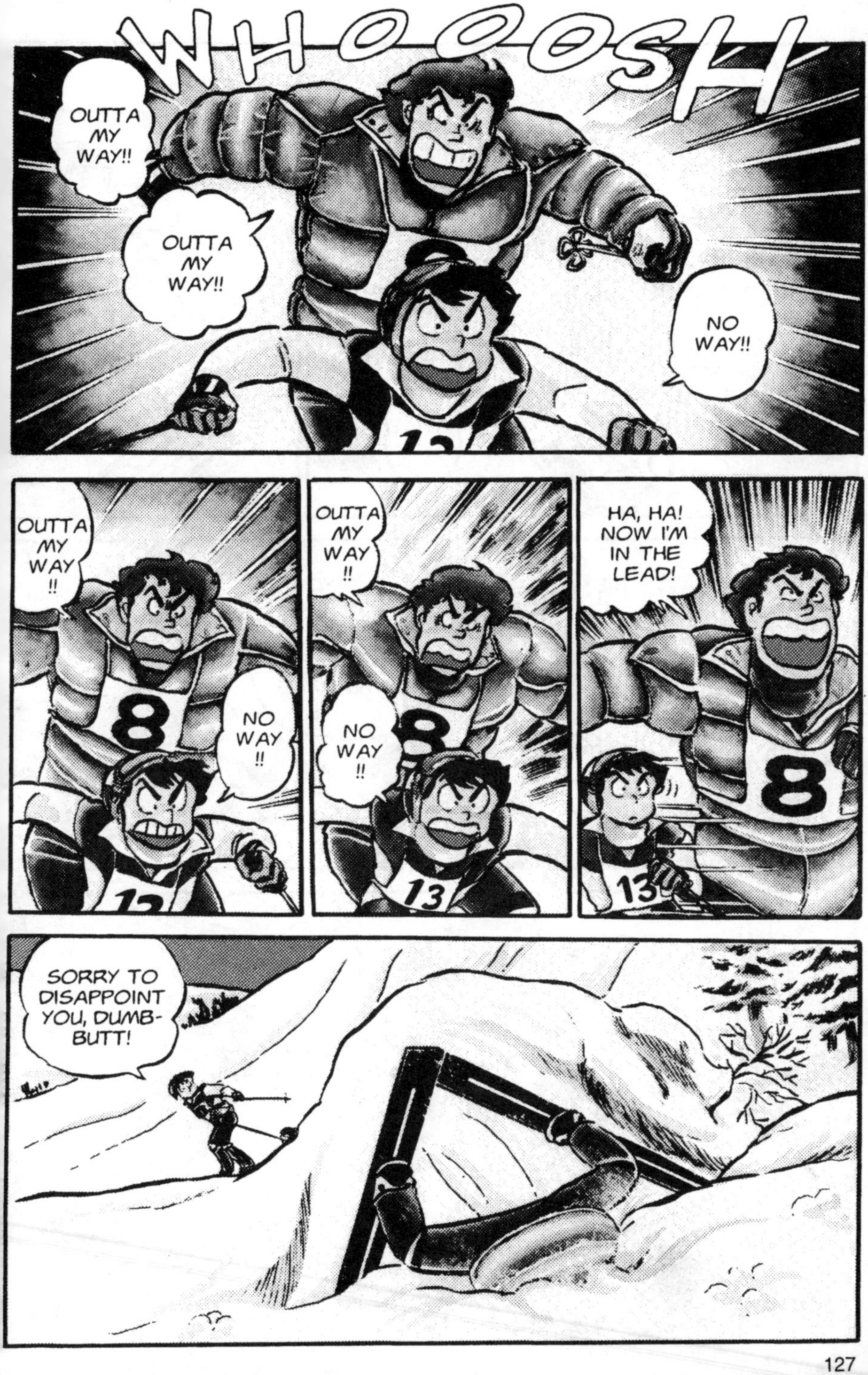
WHOOOOSH
OUTTA MY WAY!!
OUTTA MY WAY!!
NO WAY!!
OUTTA MY WAY!!
NO WAY!!
OUTTA MY WAY!!
NO WAY!!
HA, HA! NOW I'M IN THE LEAD!
SORRY TO DISAPPOINT YOU, DUMB-BUTT!

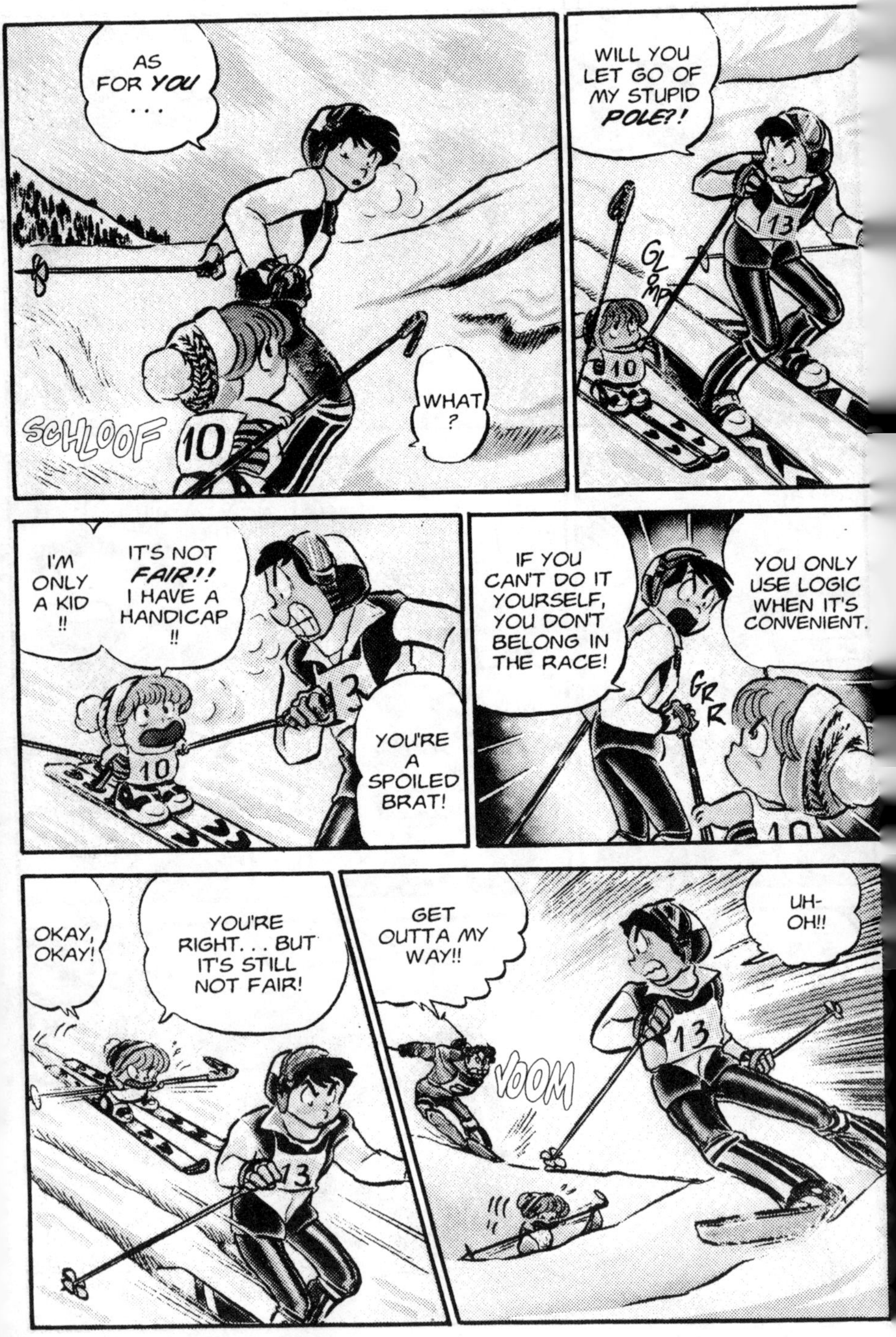

AS FOR YOU . . .
WHAT ?
SCHLOOF
WILL YOU LET GO OF MY STUPID POLE?!
GLOMP
I'M ONLY A KID !!
IT'S NOT FAIR!! I HAVE A HANDICAP !!
YOU'RE A SPOILED BRAT!
IF YOU CAN'T DO IT YOURSELF, YOU DON'T BELONG IN THE RACE!
YOU ONLY USE LOGIC WHEN IT'S CONVENIENT.
GRR
OKAY, OKAY!
YOU'RE RIGHT. . . BUT IT'S STILL NOT FAIR!
GET OUTTA MY WAY!!
UH-OH!!
VOOM

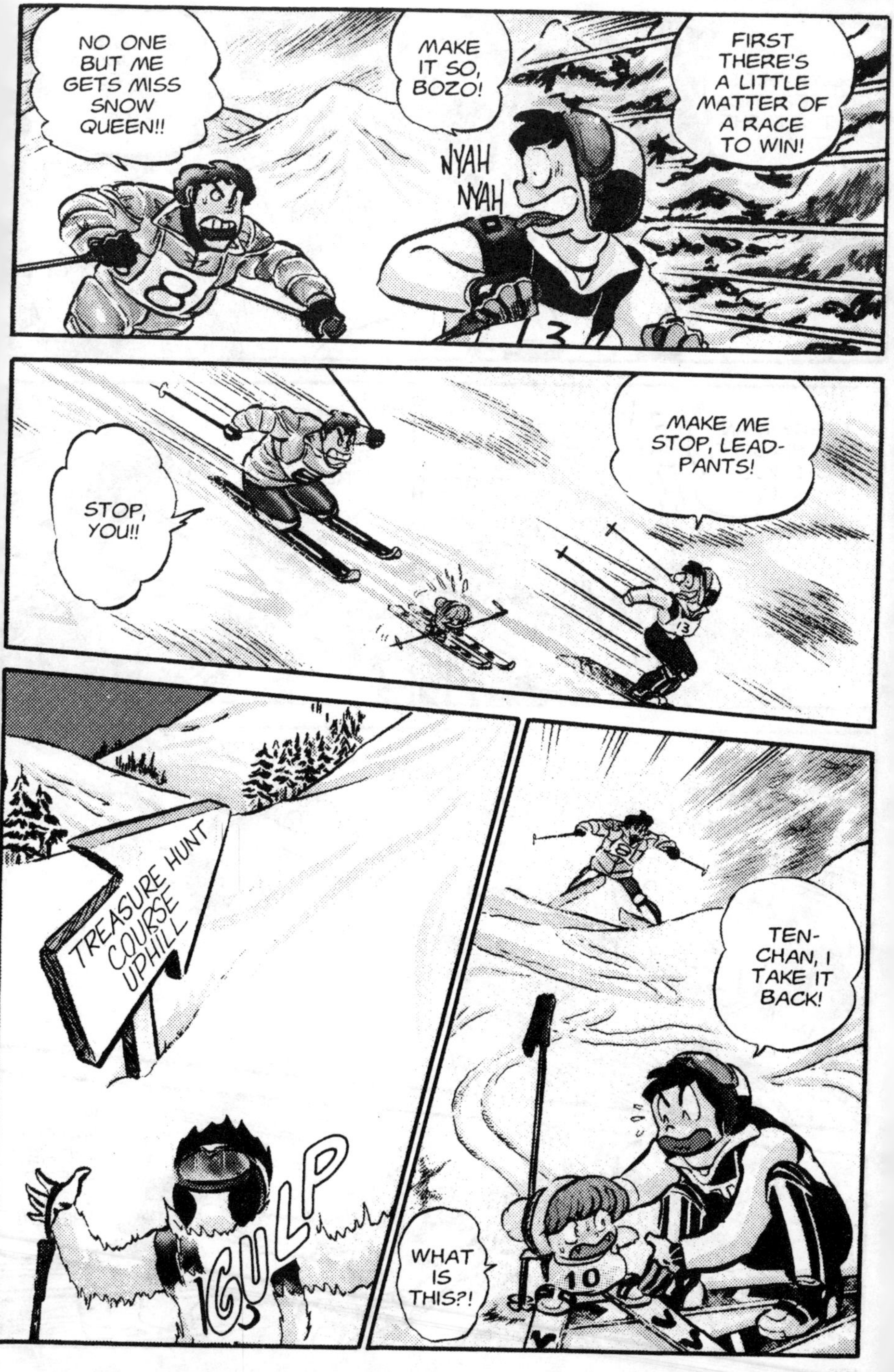
NO ONE BUT ME GETS MISS SNOW QUEEN!!
MAKE IT SO, BOZO!
NYAH NYAH
FIRST THERE'S A LITTLE MATTER OF A RACE TO WIN!
STOP, YOU!!
MAKE ME STOP, LEAD-PANTS!
TREASURE HUNT COURSE UPHILL
GULP
TEN-CHAN, I TAKE IT BACK!
WHAT IS THIS?!

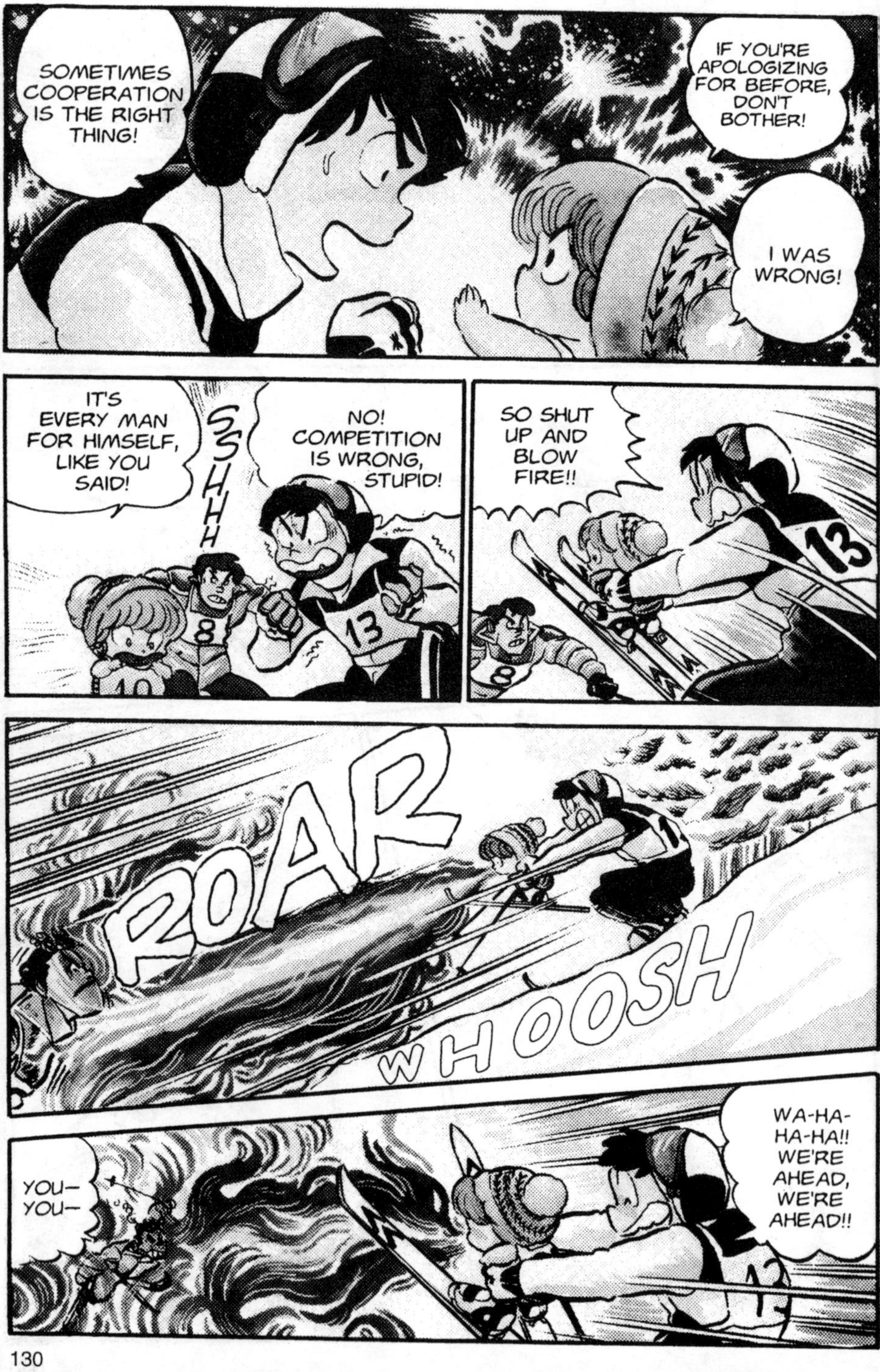
SOMETIMES COOPERATION IS THE RIGHT THING!
IF YOU'RE APOLOGIZING FOR BEFORE, DON'T BOTHER!
I WAS WRONG!
IT'S EVERY MAN FOR HIMSELF, LIKE YOU SAID!
SSHHHH
NO! COMPETITION IS WRONG, STUPID!
SO SHUT UP AND BLOW FIRE!!
ROAR
WHOOSH
YOU— YOU—
WA-HA-HA-HA!! WE'RE AHEAD, WE'RE AHEAD!!

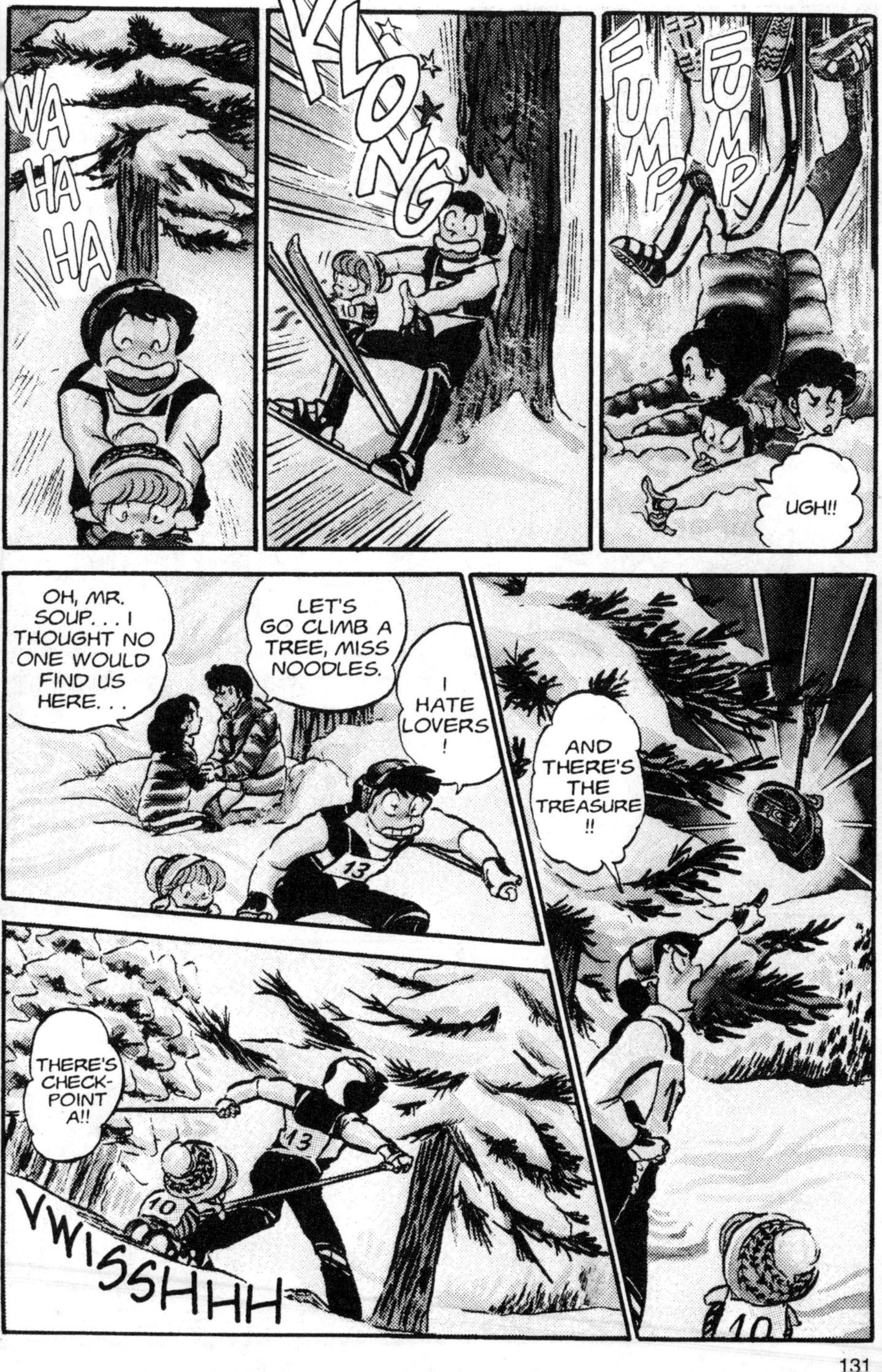
WA HA HA HA
KLONG
FUMP FUMP
UGH!!
OH, MR. SOUP. . . I THOUGHT NO ONE WOULD FIND US HERE. . .
LET'S GO CLIMB A TREE, MISS NOODLES.
I HATE LOVERS!
AND THERE'S THE TREASURE!!
THERE'S CHECK-POINT A!!
VWISSHHH

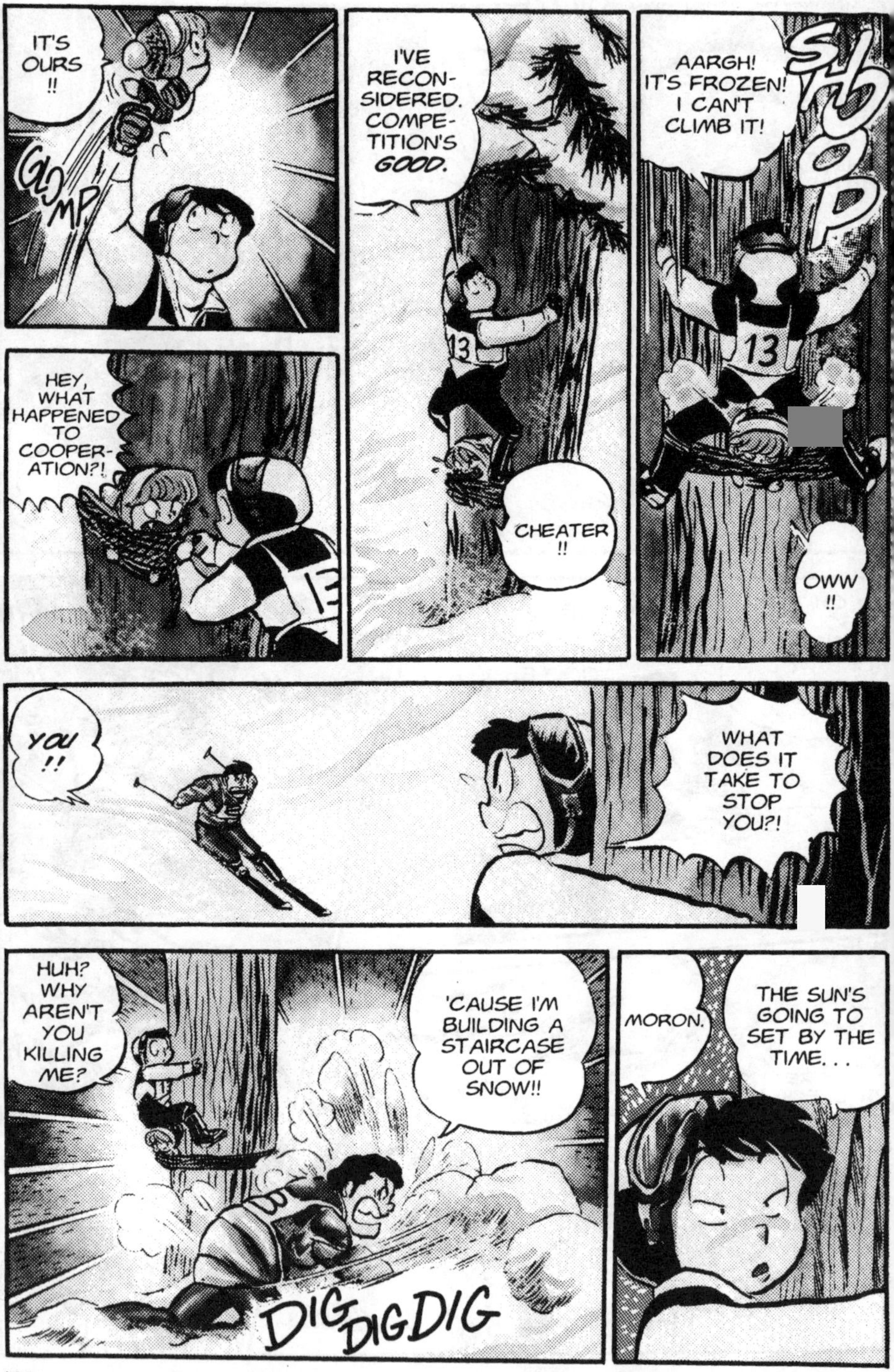

IT'S OURS !!
GLOMP
HEY, WHAT HAPPENED TO COOPERATION?!
I'VE RECONSIDERED. COMPETITION'S GOOD.
CHEATER !!
AARGH! IT'S FROZEN! I CAN'T CLIMB IT!
SHOOP
OWW !!
YOU !!
WHAT DOES IT TAKE TO STOP YOU?!
HUH? WHY AREN'T YOU KILLING ME?
'CAUSE I'M BUILDING A STAIRCASE OUT OF SNOW!!
DIG DIG DIG
MORON.
THE SUN'S GOING TO SET BY THE TIME. . .

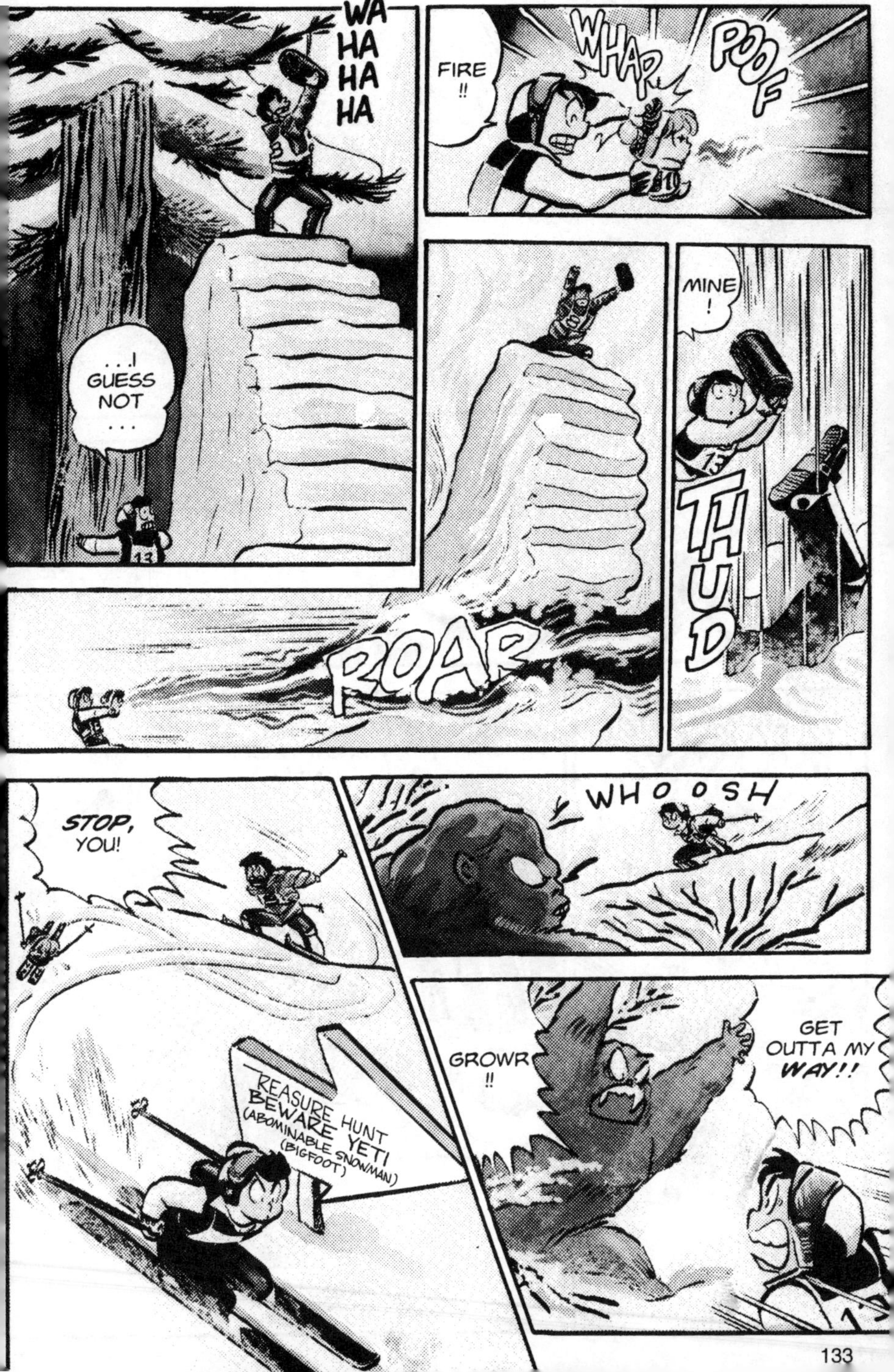
WA HA HA HA
...I GUESS NOT ...
FIRE !!
WHAP
POOF
MINE !
THUD
ROAR
STOP, YOU!
WHOOSH
TREASURE HUNT
BEWARE YETI
(ABOMINABLE SNOWMAN)
(BIGFOOT)
GROWR !!
GET OUTTA MY WAY!!

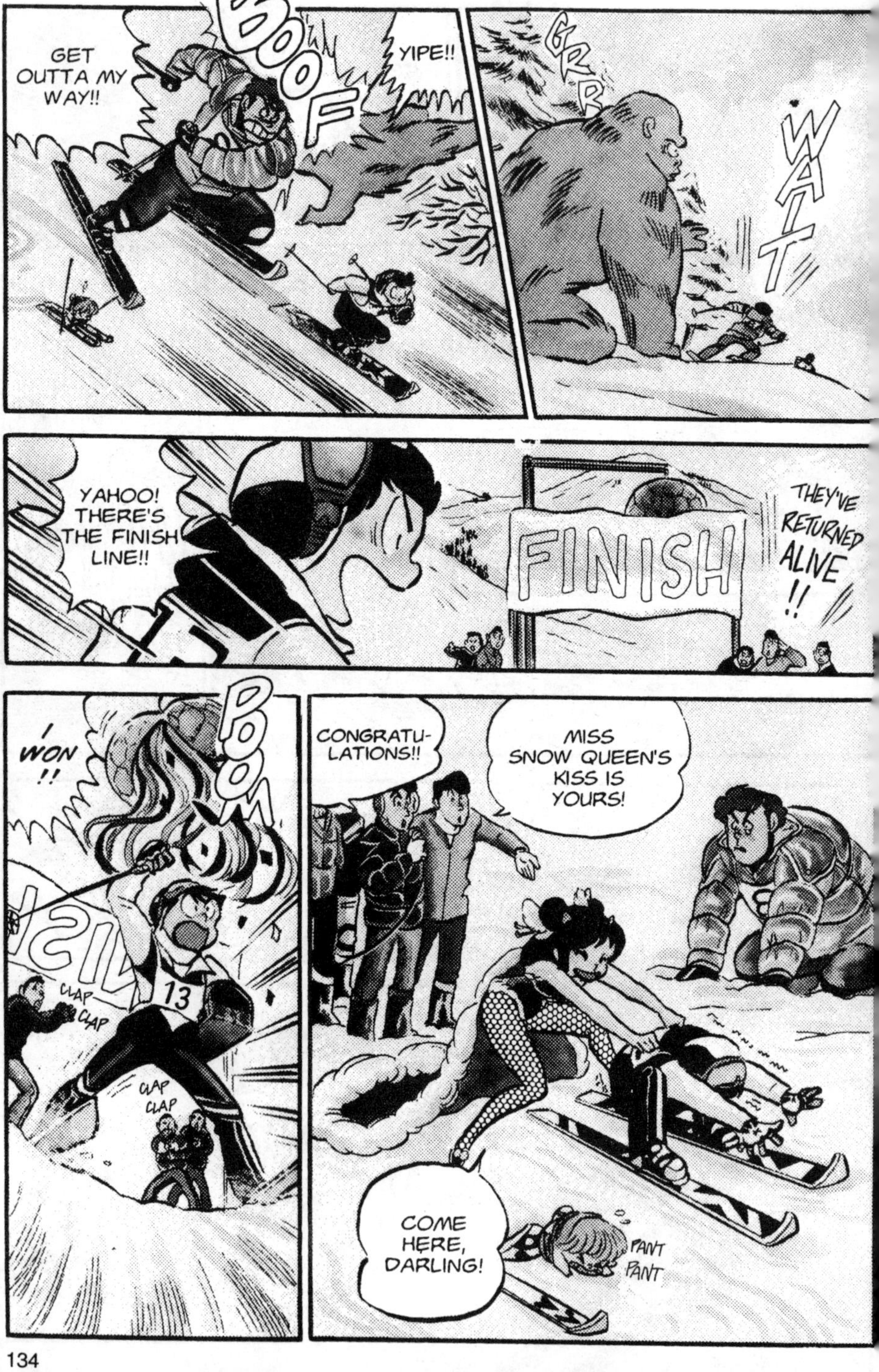
GET OUTTA MY WAY!!
BOOOF
YIPE!!
GRRR
WAIT
YAHOO! THERE'S THE FINISH LINE!!
FINISH
THEY'VE RETURNED ALIVE !!
I WON !!
POOOM
13
CLAP CLAP
CLAP CLAP
CONGRATU-LATIONS!!
MISS SNOW QUEEN'S KISS IS YOURS!
COME HERE, DARLING!
PANT PANT

PART NINE
THE ST. VALENTINE'S DAY MASSACRE

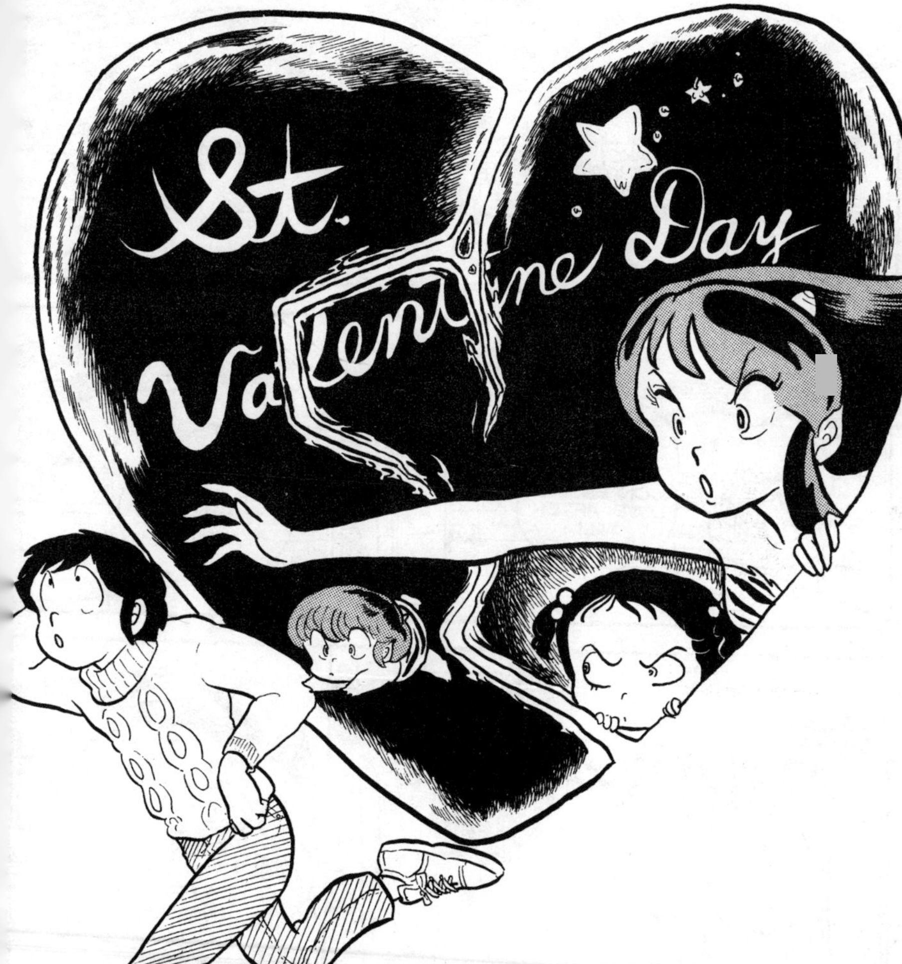
St. Valentine Day

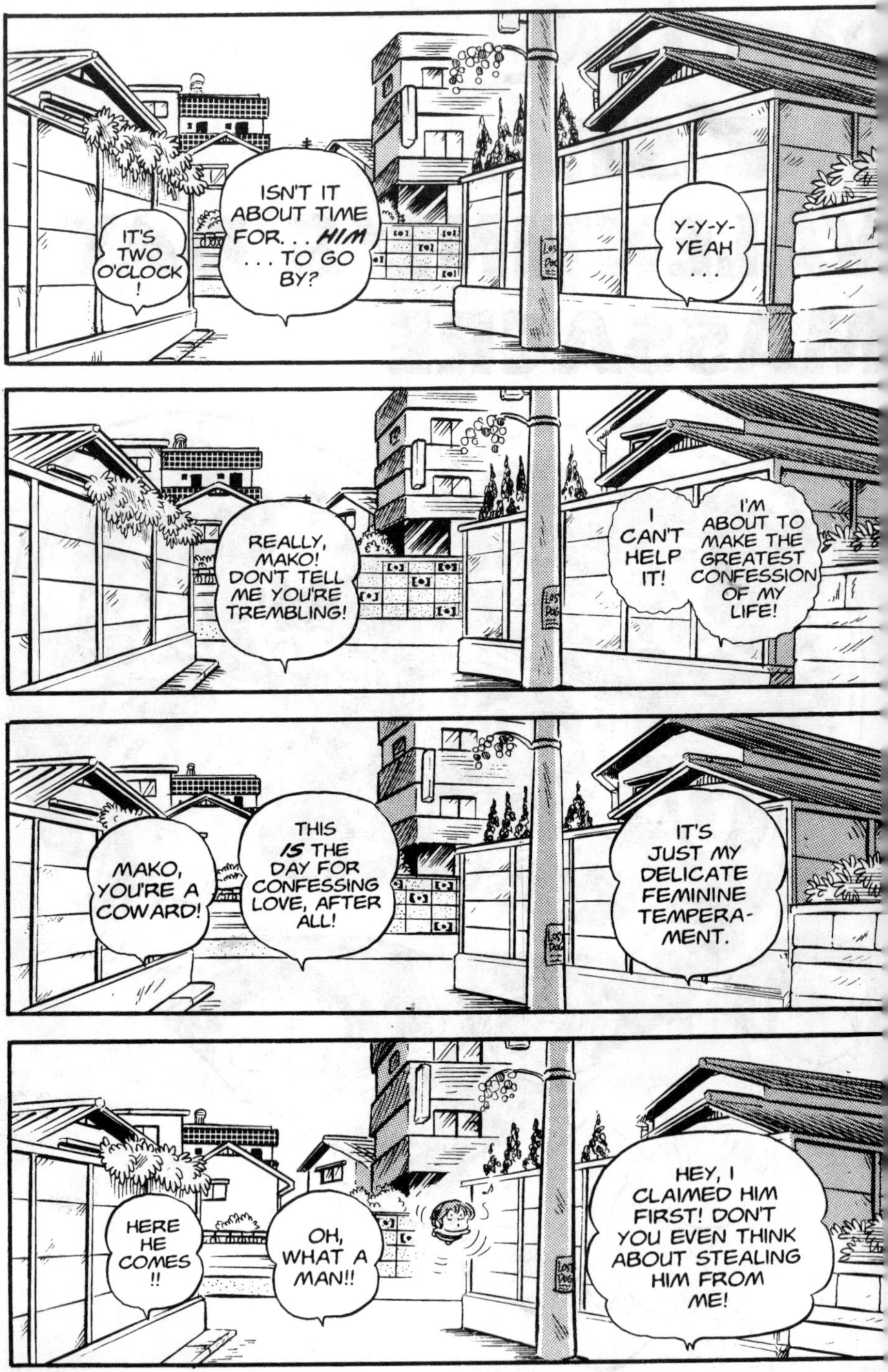
IT'S TWO O'CLOCK!
ISN'T IT ABOUT TIME FOR... HIM ... TO GO BY?
Y-Y-Y-YEAH...
REALLY, MAKO! DON'T TELL ME YOU'RE TREMBLING!
I CAN'T HELP IT!
I'M ABOUT TO MAKE THE GREATEST CONFESSION OF MY LIFE!
MAKO, YOU'RE A COWARD!
THIS IS THE DAY FOR CONFESSING LOVE, AFTER ALL!
IT'S JUST MY DELICATE FEMININE TEMPERA-MENT.
HERE HE COMES!!
OH, WHAT A MAN!!
HEY, I CLAIMED HIM FIRST! DON'T YOU EVEN THINK ABOUT STEALING HIM FROM ME!

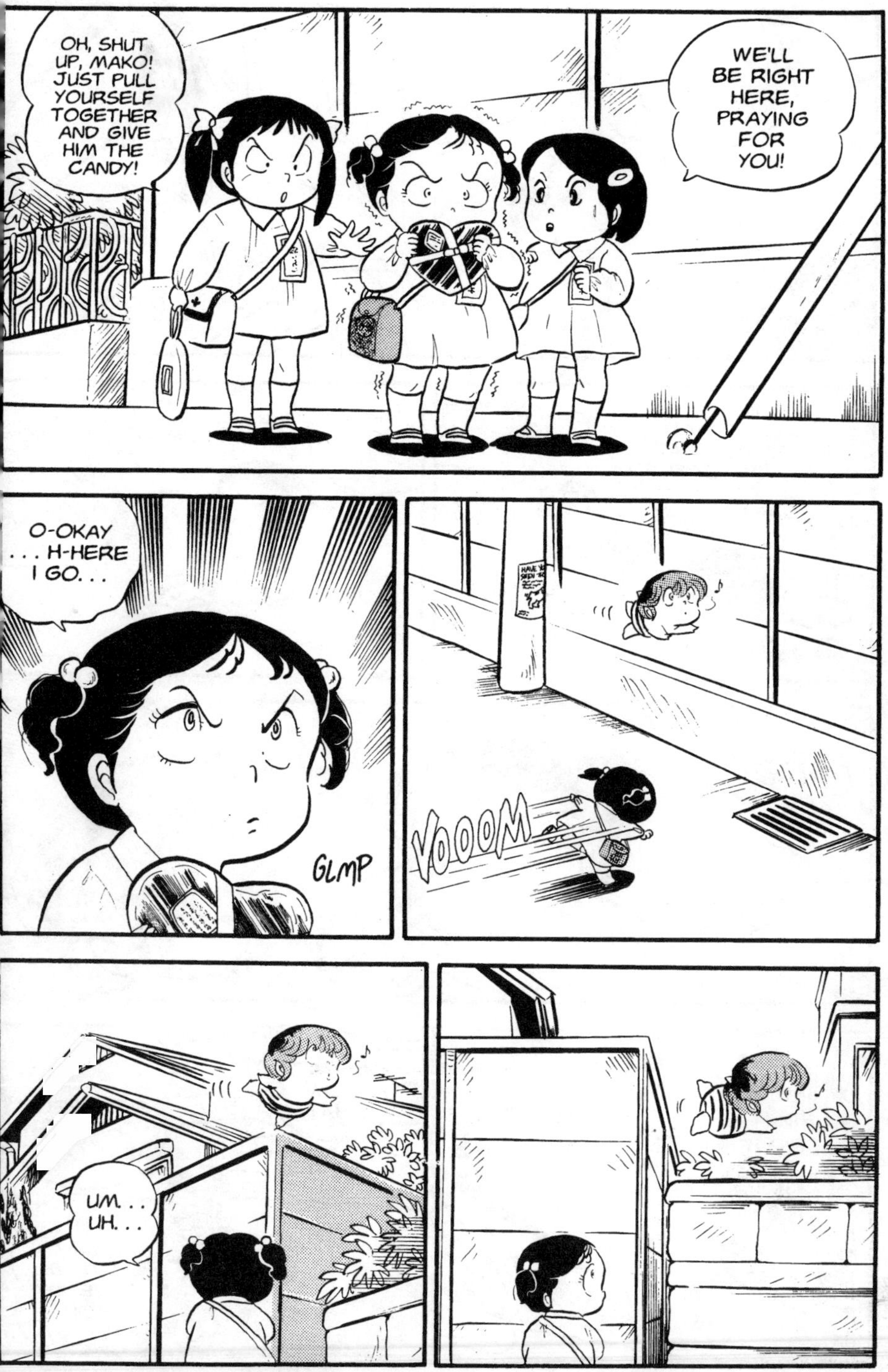
OH, SHUT UP, MAKO! JUST PULL YOURSELF TOGETHER AND GIVE HIM THE CANDY!
WE'LL BE RIGHT HERE, PRAYING FOR YOU!
O-OKAY . . . H-HERE I GO. . .
GLMP
VOOOM
UM. . UH. . .

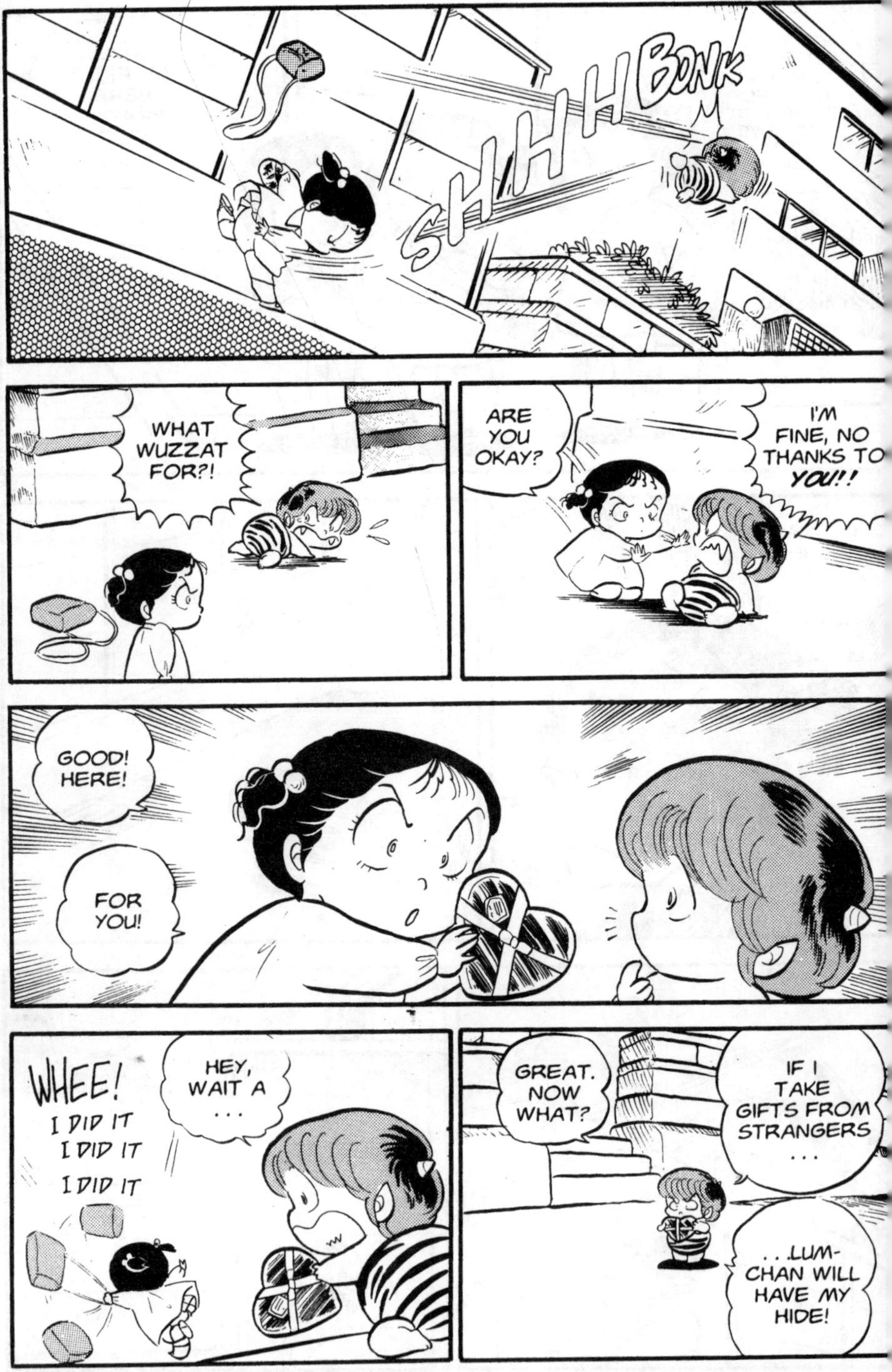

SHHHH
BONK
WHAT WUZZAT FOR?!
ARE YOU OKAY?
I'M FINE, NO THANKS TO *YOU!!*
GOOD! HERE!
FOR YOU!
WHEE!
I DID IT I DID IT I DID IT
HEY, WAIT A . . .
GREAT. NOW WHAT?
IF I TAKE GIFTS FROM STRANGERS . . .
. . LUM-CHAN WILL HAVE MY HIDE!

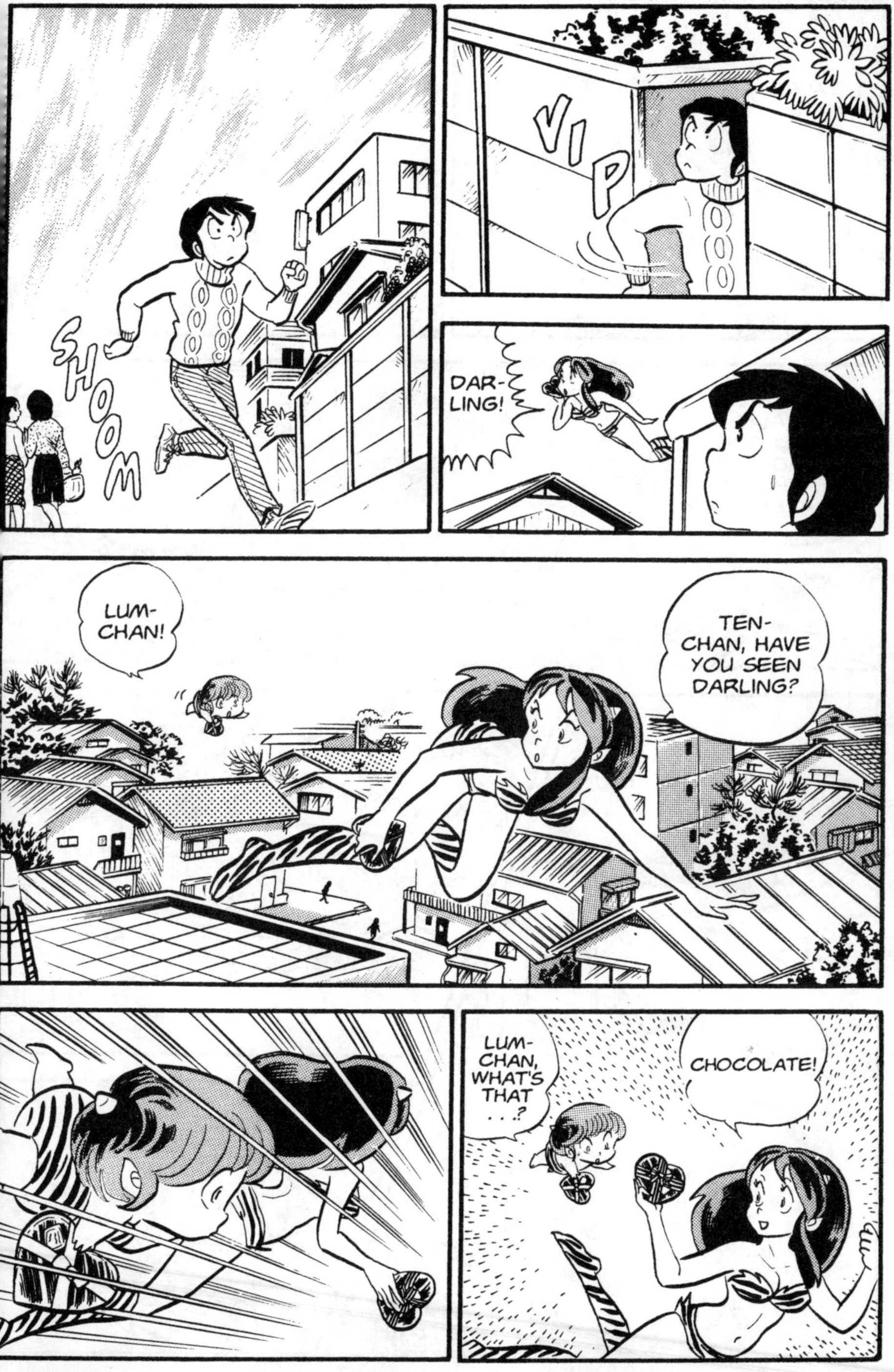
SHOOOM
VIP
DAR-LING!
LUM-CHAN!
TEN-CHAN, HAVE YOU SEEN DARLING?
LUM-CHAN, WHAT'S THAT . . .?
CHOCOLATE!

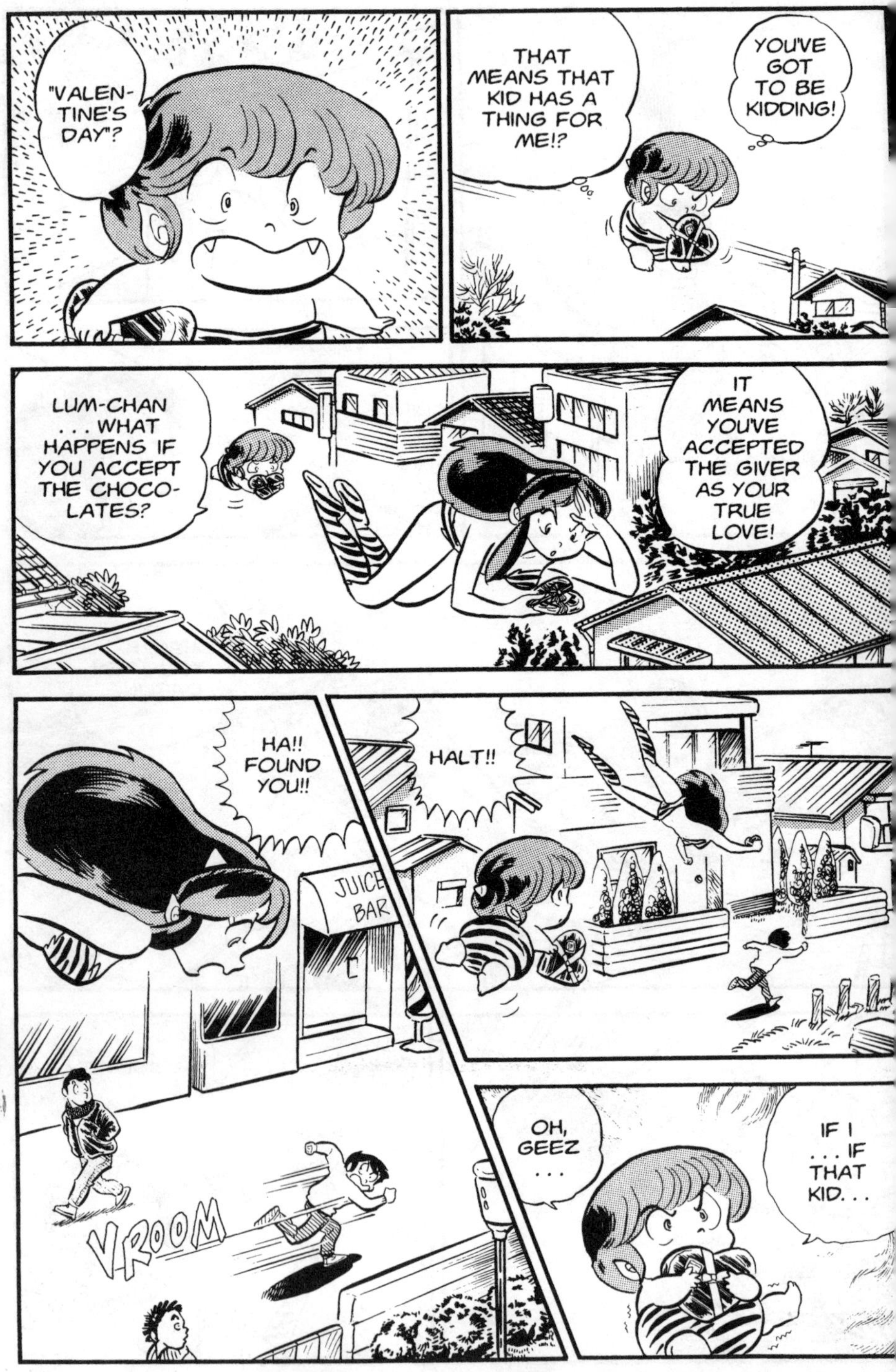
"VALEN-TINE'S DAY"?
THAT MEANS THAT KID HAS A THING FOR ME!?
YOU'VE GOT TO BE KIDDING!
LUM-CHAN . . . WHAT HAPPENS IF YOU ACCEPT THE CHOCO-LATES?
IT MEANS YOU'VE ACCEPTED THE GIVER AS YOUR TRUE LOVE!
HA!! FOUND YOU!!
JUICE BAR
VROOM
HALT!!
OH, GEEZ . . .
IF I . . . IF THAT KID. . .

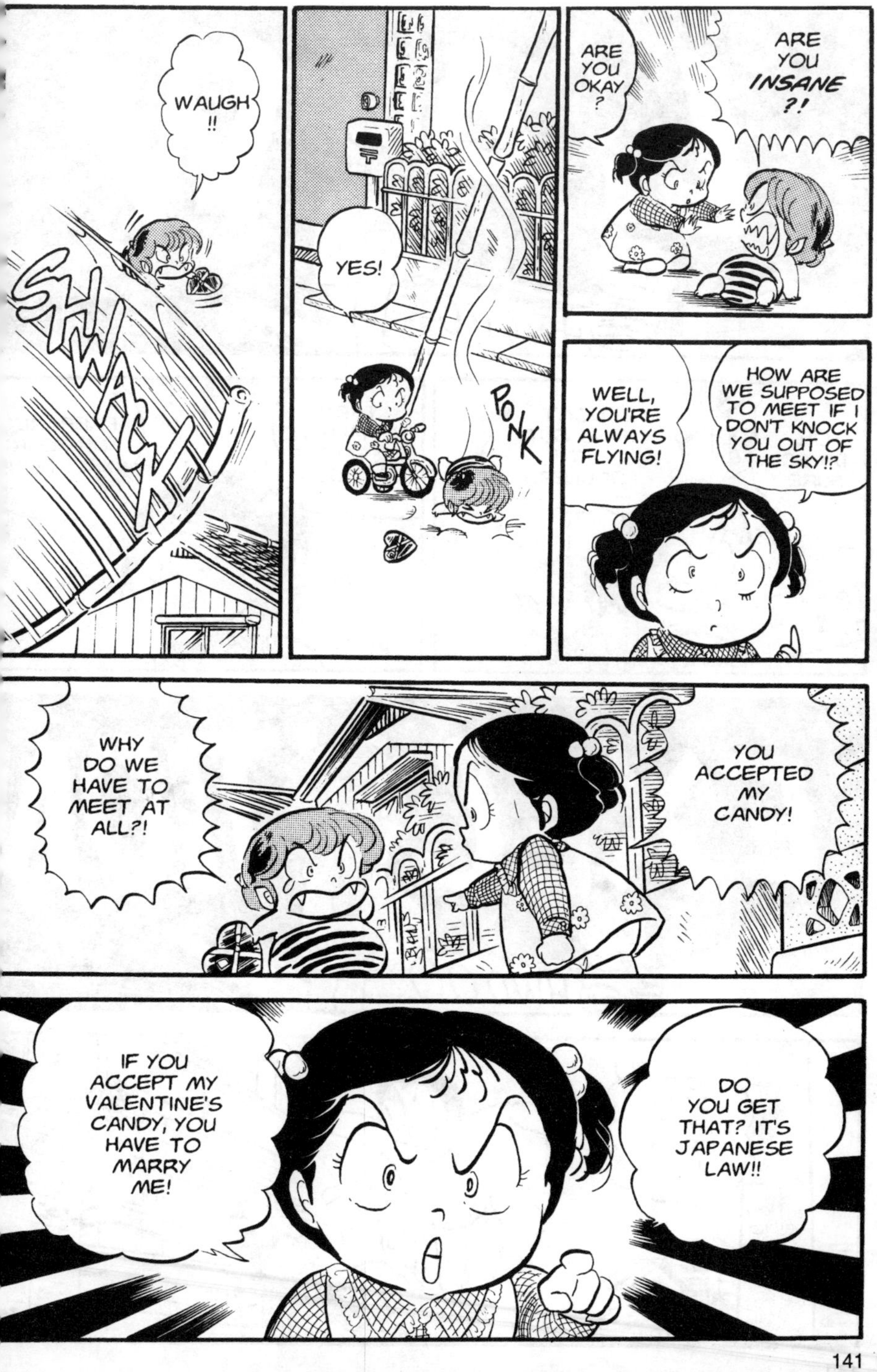
WAUGH!!
SHWACK
YES!
PONK
ARE YOU OKAY?
ARE YOU INSANE?!
WELL, YOU'RE ALWAYS FLYING!
HOW ARE WE SUPPOSED TO MEET IF I DON'T KNOCK YOU OUT OF THE SKY!?
WHY DO WE HAVE TO MEET AT ALL?!
YOU ACCEPTED MY CANDY!
IF YOU ACCEPT MY VALENTINE'S CANDY, YOU HAVE TO MARRY ME!
DO YOU GET THAT? IT'S JAPANESE LAW!!

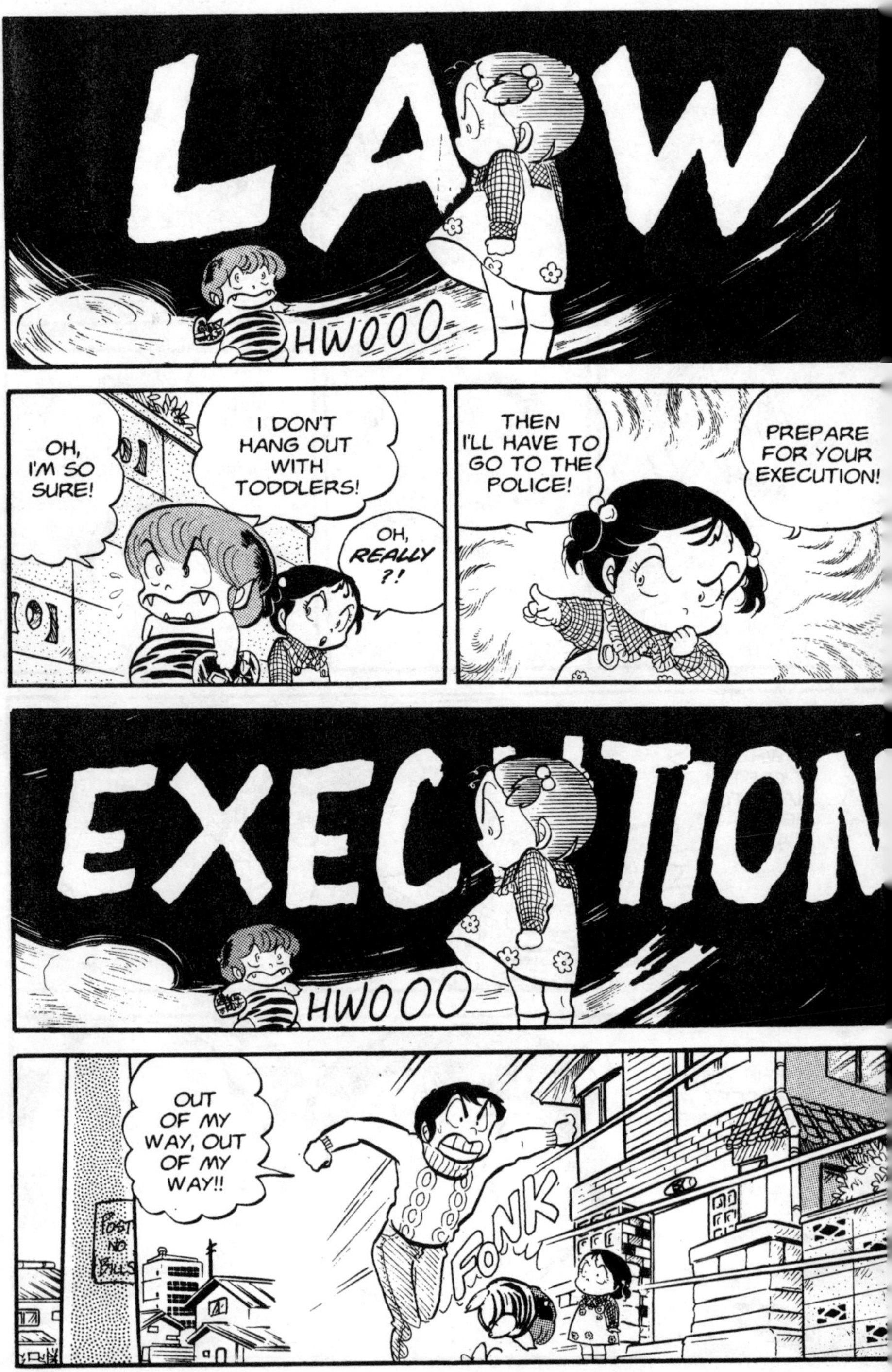
LAW
HWOOO
OH, I'M SO SURE!
I DON'T HANG OUT WITH TODDLERS!
OH, REALLY?!
THEN I'LL HAVE TO GO TO THE POLICE!
PREPARE FOR YOUR EXECUTION!
EXEC TION
HWOOO
OUT OF MY WAY, OUT OF MY WAY!!
POST NO BILLS
FONK

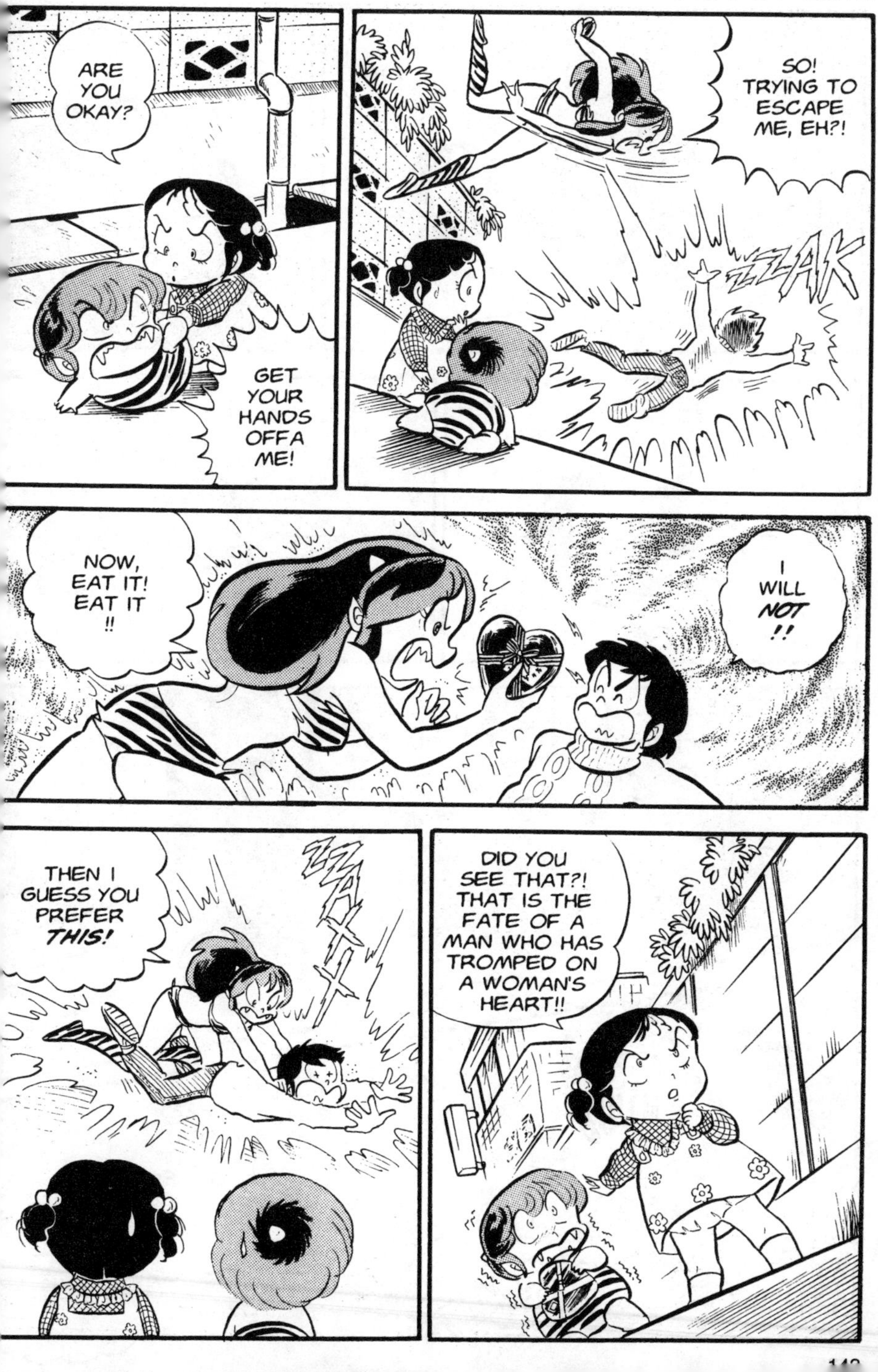
ARE YOU OKAY?
GET YOUR HANDS OFFA ME!
SO! TRYING TO ESCAPE ME, EH?!
ZZZAK
NOW, EAT IT! EAT IT !!
I WILL *NOT* !!
THEN I GUESS YOU PREFER *THIS!*
DID YOU SEE THAT?! THAT IS THE FATE OF A MAN WHO HAS TROMPED ON A WOMAN'S HEART!!

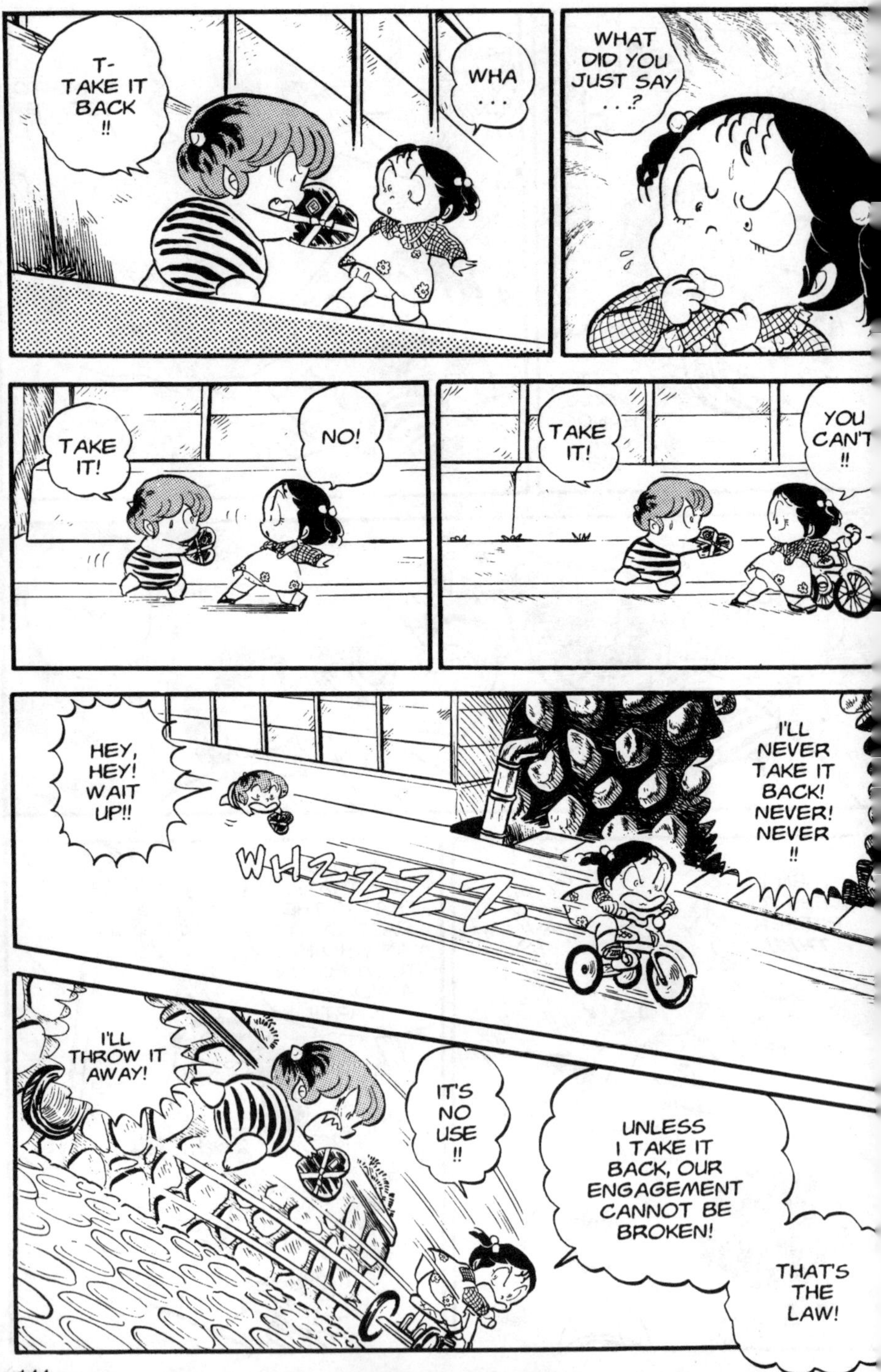
T-TAKE IT BACK!!
WHA...
WHAT DID YOU JUST SAY...?
TAKE IT!
NO!
TAKE IT!
YOU CAN'T!!
HEY, HEY! WAIT UP!!
WHIZZZZZ
I'LL NEVER TAKE IT BACK! NEVER! NEVER!!
I'LL THROW IT AWAY!
IT'S NO USE!!
UNLESS I TAKE IT BACK, OUR ENGAGEMENT CANNOT BE BROKEN!
THAT'S THE LAW!

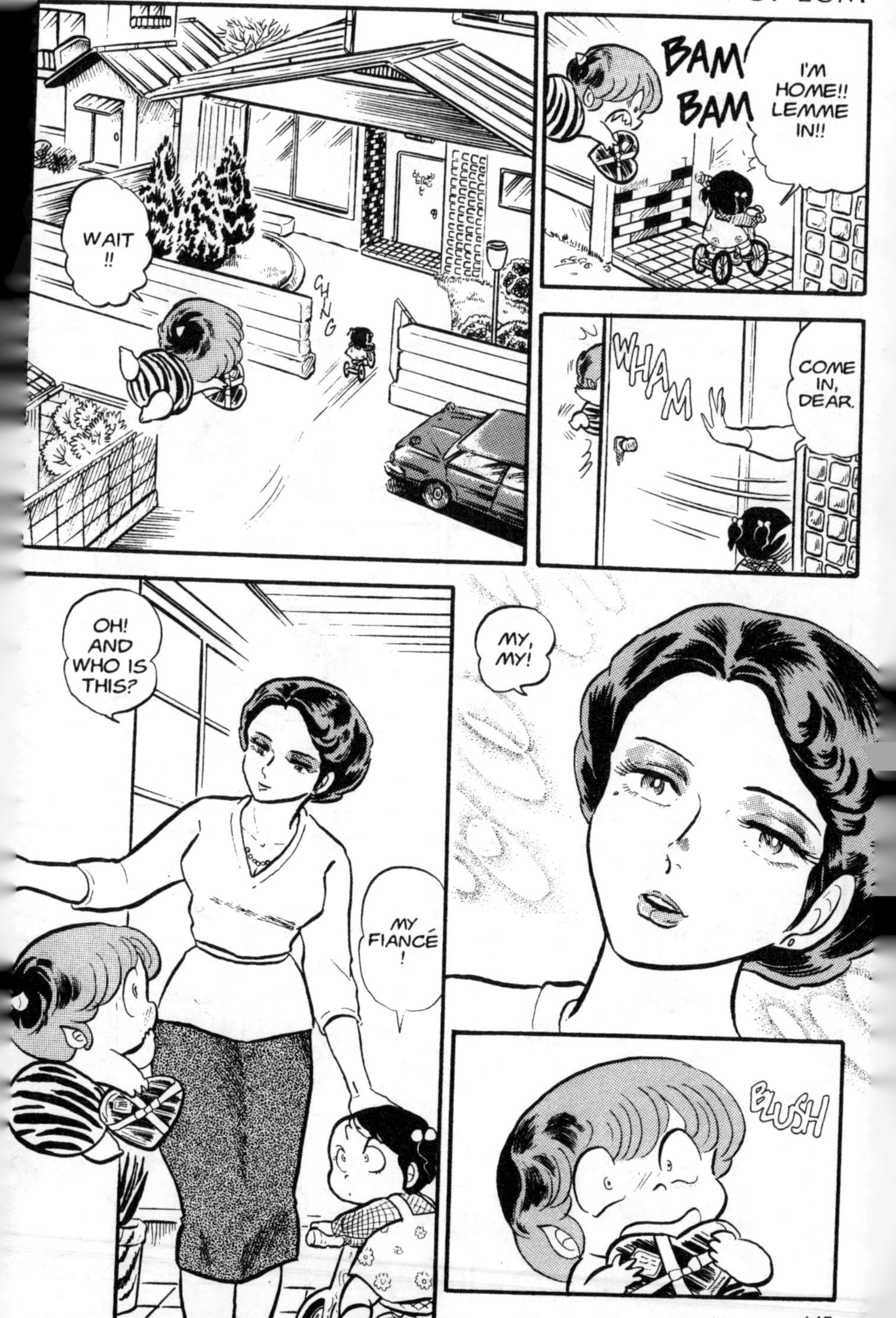
WAIT !!
CHING
BAM BAM
I'M HOME!! LEMME IN!!
WHAM
COME IN, DEAR.
OH! AND WHO IS THIS?
MY FIANCÉ !
MY, MY!
BLUSH

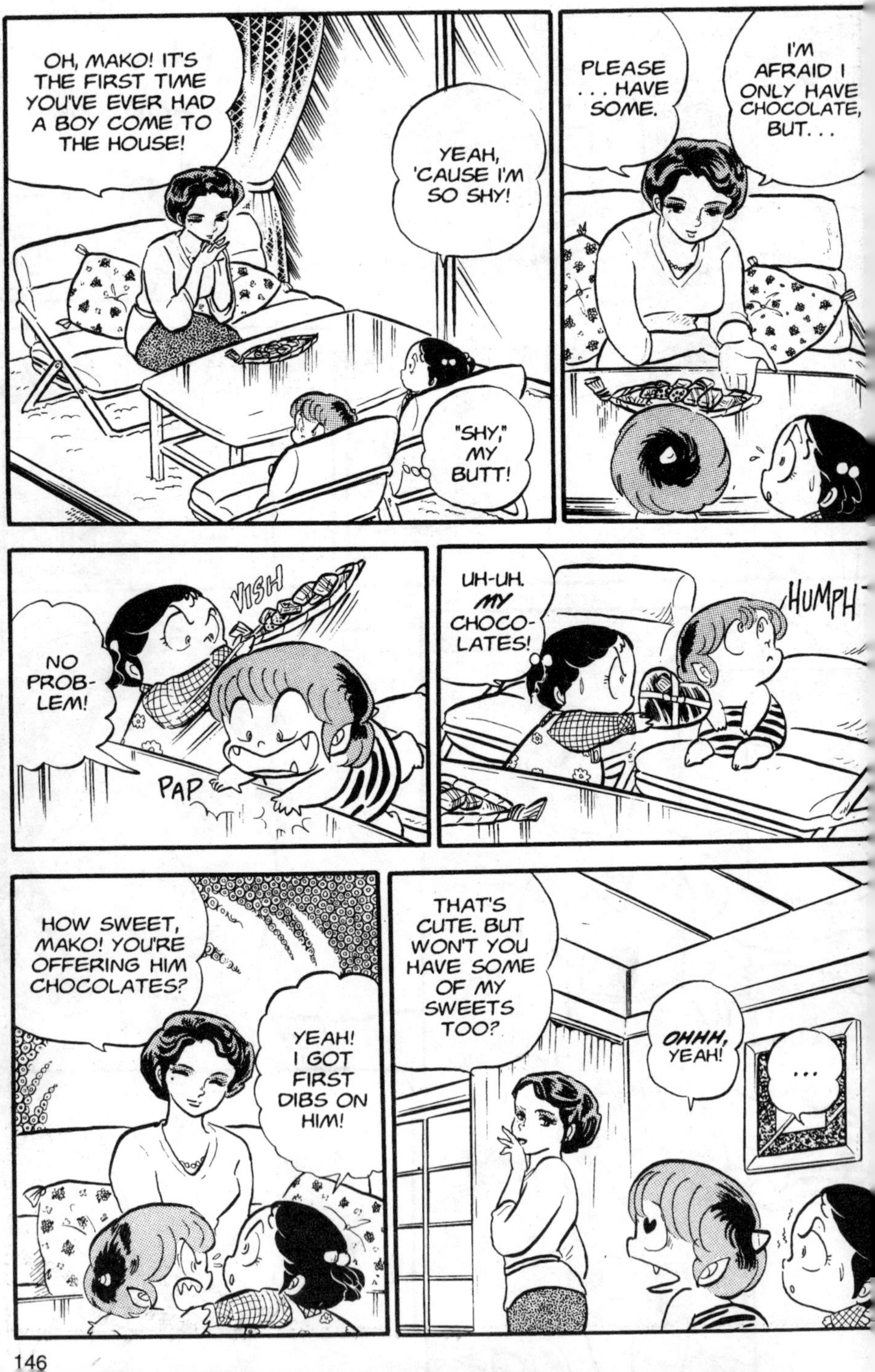
OH, MAKO! IT'S THE FIRST TIME YOU'VE EVER HAD A BOY COME TO THE HOUSE!
YEAH, 'CAUSE I'M SO SHY!
"SHY," MY BUTT!
PLEASE . . . HAVE SOME.
I'M AFRAID I ONLY HAVE CHOCOLATE, BUT. . .
VISH
NO PROB-LEM!
PAP
UH-UH. MY CHOCO-LATES!
HUMPH
HOW SWEET, MAKO! YOU'RE OFFERING HIM CHOCOLATES?
YEAH! I GOT FIRST DIBS ON HIM!
THAT'S CUTE. BUT WON'T YOU HAVE SOME OF MY SWEETS TOO?
OHHH, YEAH!
. . .

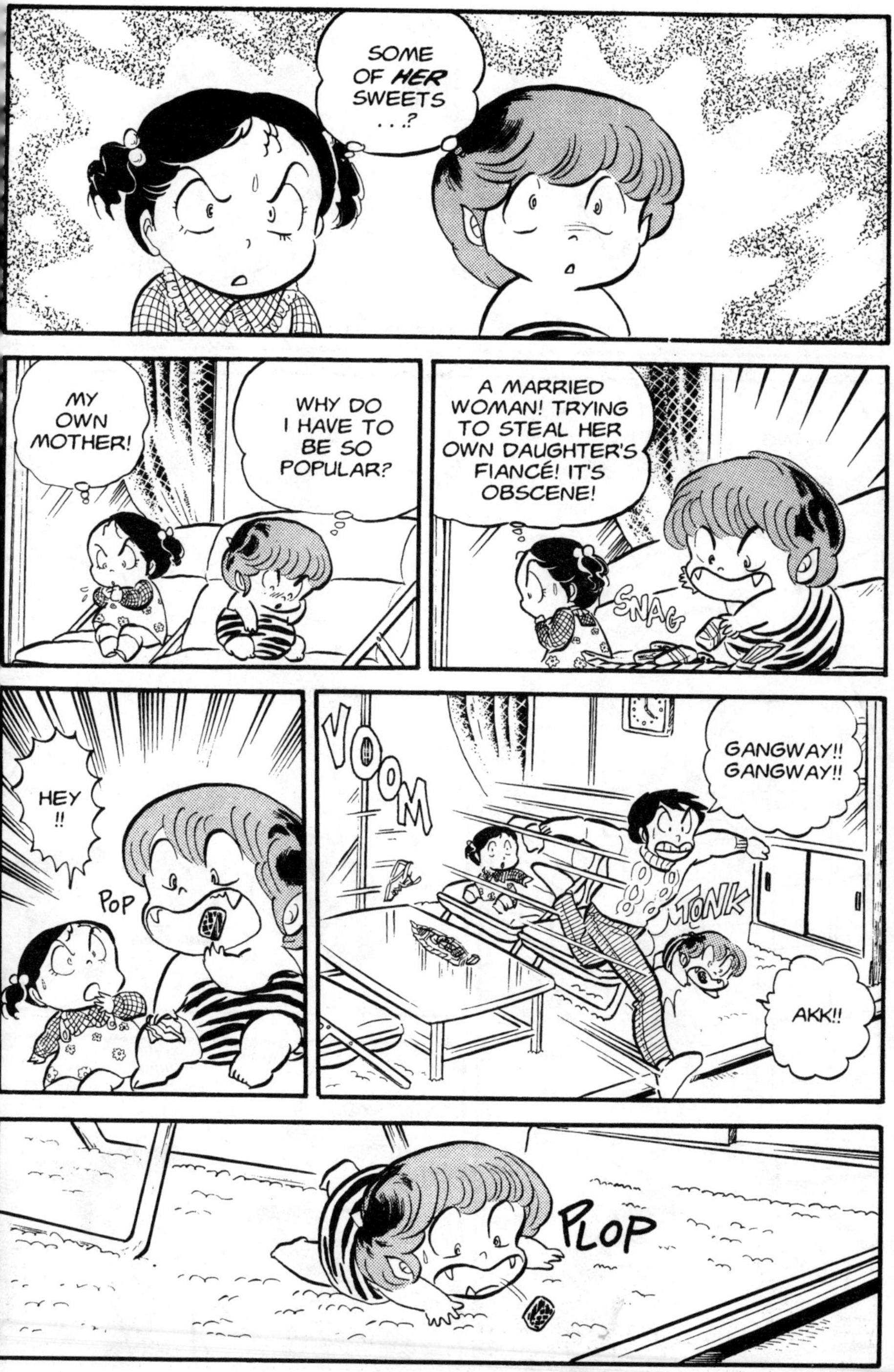
SOME OF *HER* SWEETS . . .?
MY OWN MOTHER!
WHY DO I HAVE TO BE SO POPULAR?
A MARRIED WOMAN! TRYING TO STEAL HER OWN DAUGHTER'S FIANCÉ! IT'S OBSCENE!
SNAG
HEY !!
POP
VOOM
GANGWAY!! GANGWAY!!
TONK
AKK!!
PLOP

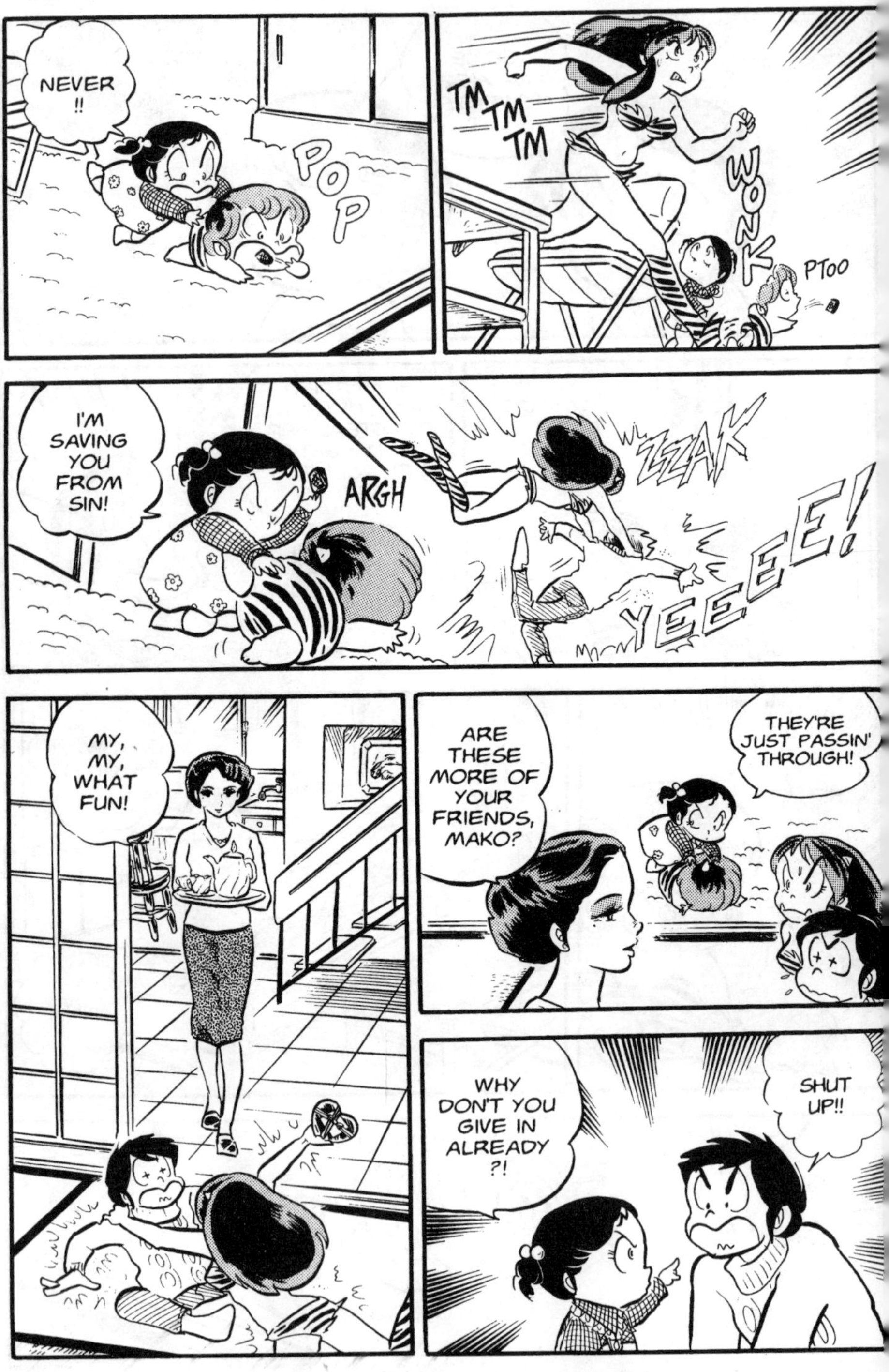
NEVER !!
POP
TM TM TM
WONK
PTOO
I'M SAVING YOU FROM SIN!
ARGH
ZZAK
YEEEEE!
MY, MY, WHAT FUN!
ARE THESE MORE OF YOUR FRIENDS, MAKO?
THEY'RE JUST PASSIN' THROUGH!
WHY DON'T YOU GIVE IN ALREADY ?!
SHUT UP!!

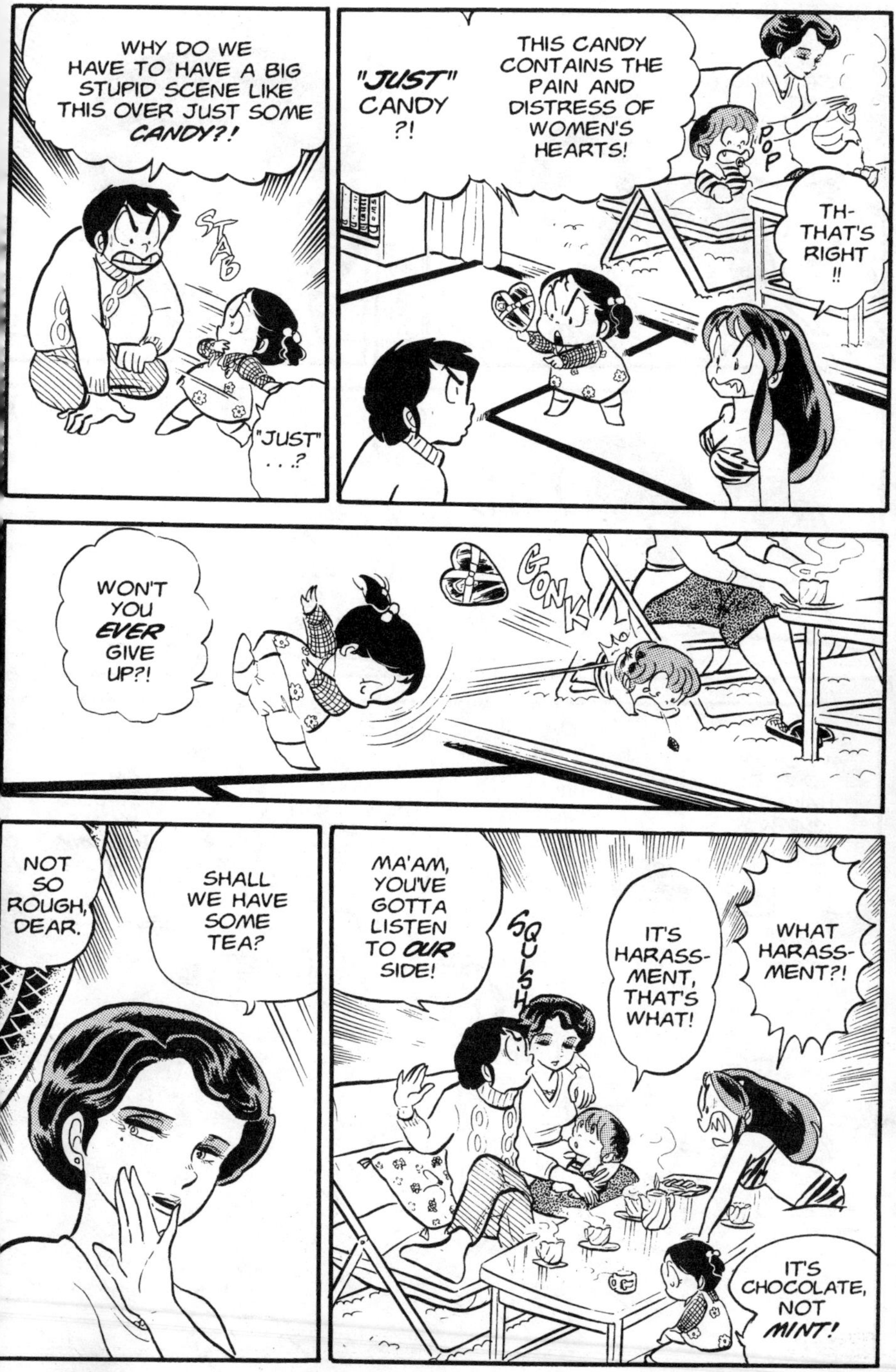
WHY DO WE HAVE TO HAVE A BIG STUPID SCENE LIKE THIS OVER JUST SOME CANDY?!
STAB
"JUST" . . .?
"JUST" CANDY ?!
THIS CANDY CONTAINS THE PAIN AND DISTRESS OF WOMEN'S HEARTS!
POP
TH- THAT'S RIGHT !!
WON'T YOU EVER GIVE UP?!
GONK
NOT SO ROUGH, DEAR.
SHALL WE HAVE SOME TEA?
MA'AM, YOU'VE GOTTA LISTEN TO OUR SIDE!
SQUISH
IT'S HARASS-MENT, THAT'S WHAT!
WHAT HARASS-MENT?!
IT'S CHOCOLATE, NOT MINT!

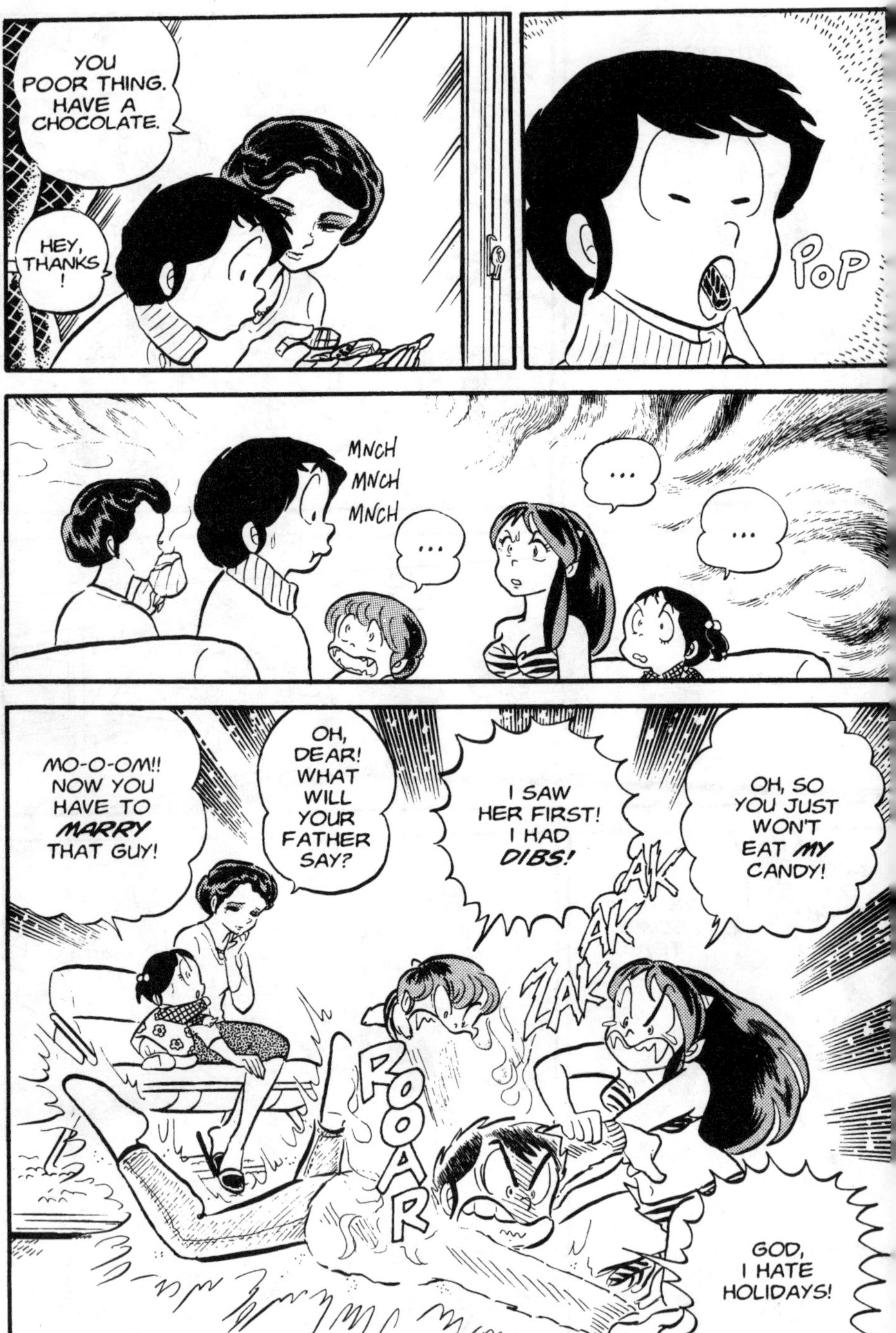
YOU POOR THING. HAVE A CHOCOLATE.
HEY, THANKS!
POP
MNCH MNCH MNCH
...
...
...
MO-O-OM!! NOW YOU HAVE TO MARRY THAT GUY!
OH, DEAR! WHAT WILL YOUR FATHER SAY?
I SAW HER FIRST! I HAD DIBS!
OH, SO YOU JUST WON'T EAT MY CANDY!
AK AK
ZAK
ROOAR
GOD, I HATE HOLIDAYS!

PART TEN
THE ANT TRAP OF LOVE

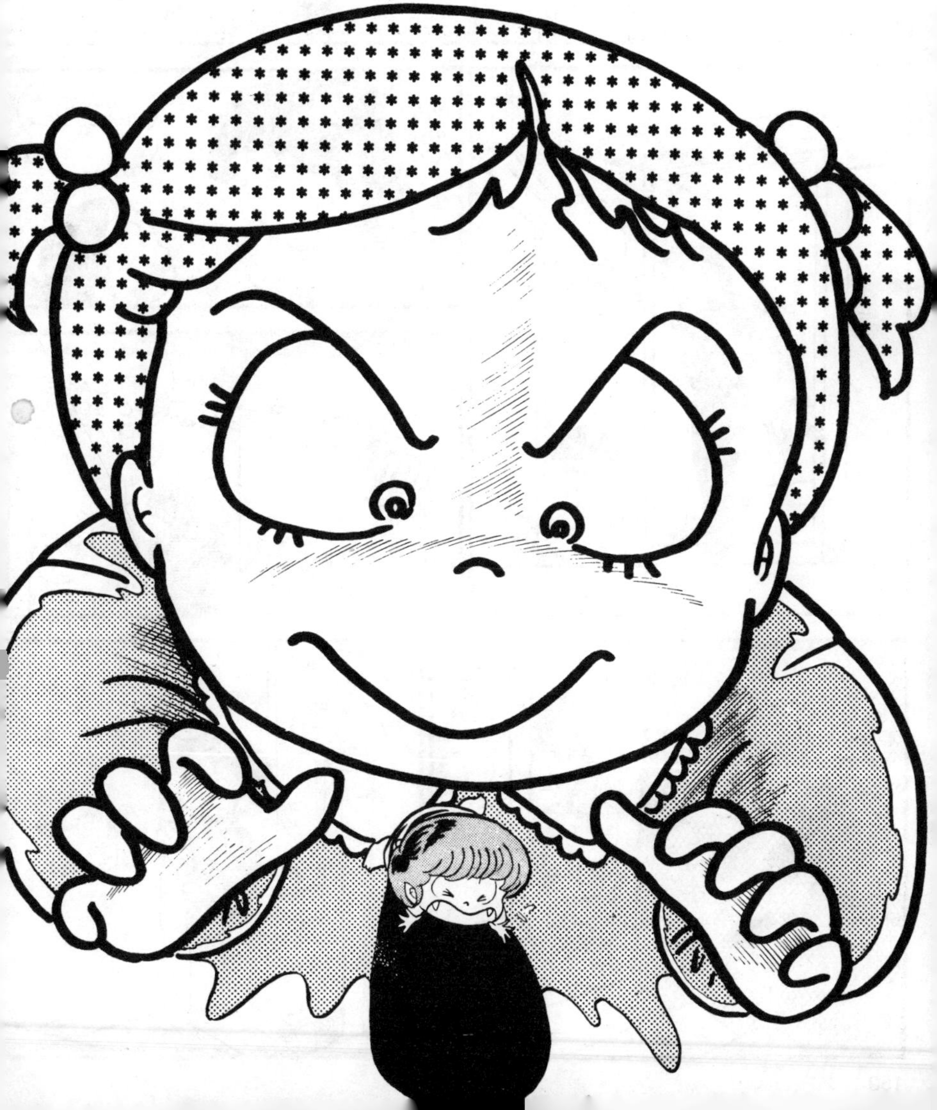

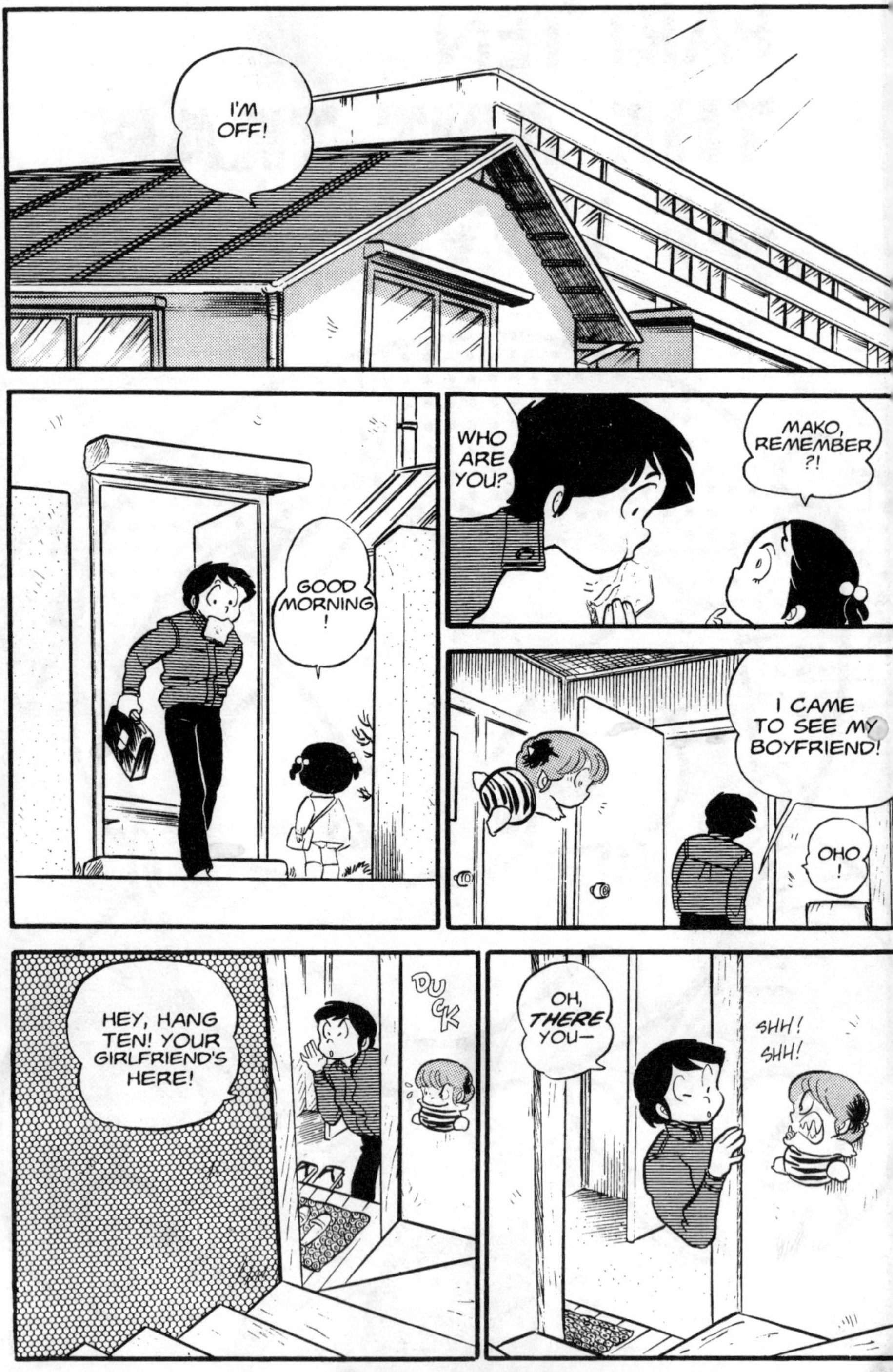
I'M OFF!
GOOD MORNING!
WHO ARE YOU?
MAKO, REMEMBER?!
I CAME TO SEE MY BOYFRIEND!
OHO!
HEY, HANG TEN! YOUR GIRLFRIEND'S HERE!
DUCK
OH, THERE YOU—
SHH! SHH!

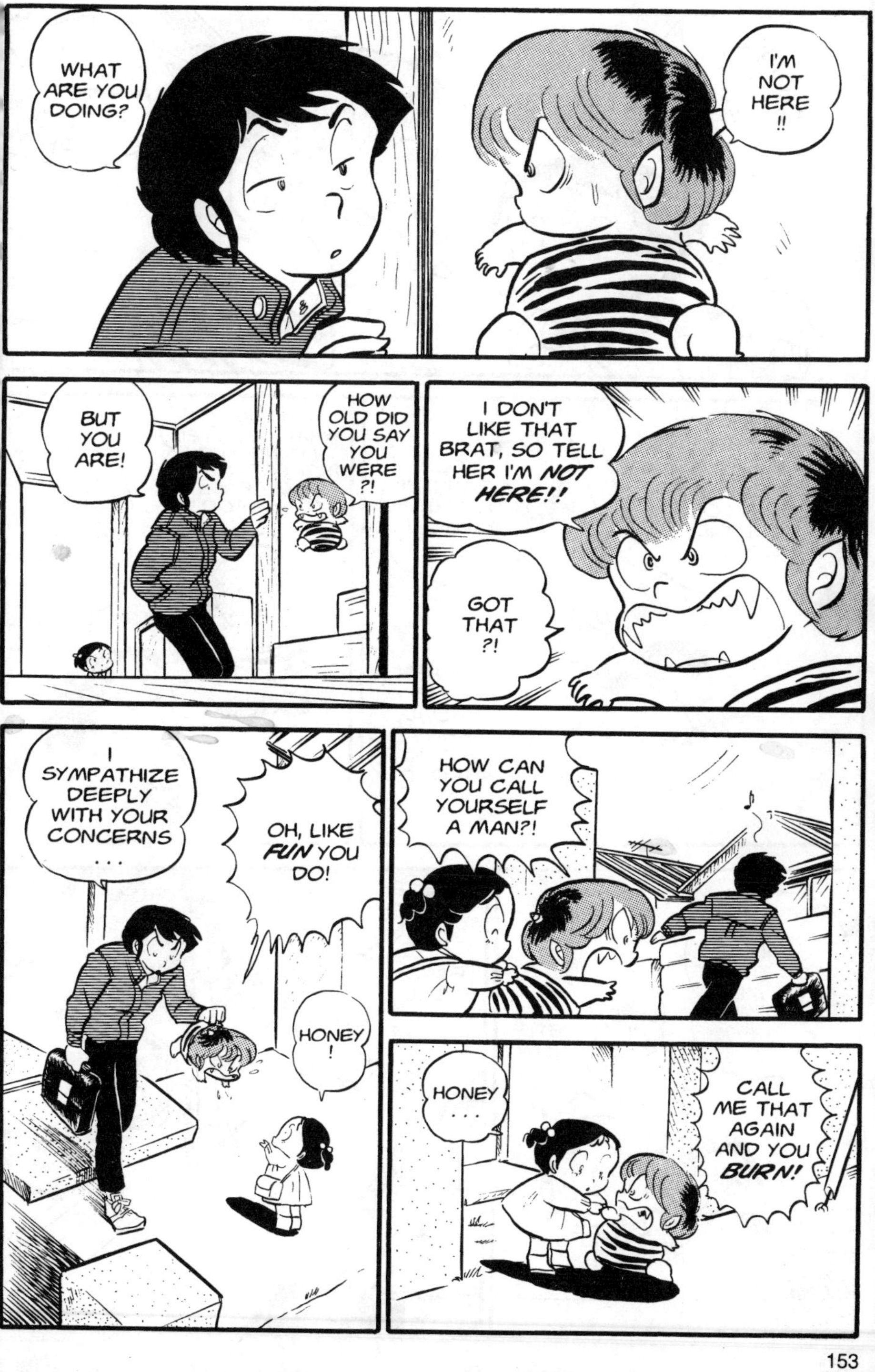
WHAT ARE YOU DOING?
I'M NOT HERE !!
BUT YOU ARE!
HOW OLD DID YOU SAY YOU WERE ?!
I DON'T LIKE THAT BRAT, SO TELL HER I'M *NOT HERE!!*
GOT THAT ?!
I SYMPATHIZE DEEPLY WITH YOUR CONCERNS . . .
OH, LIKE *FUN* YOU DO!
HONEY !
HOW CAN YOU CALL YOURSELF A MAN?!
HONEY . . .
CALL ME THAT AGAIN AND YOU *BURN!*

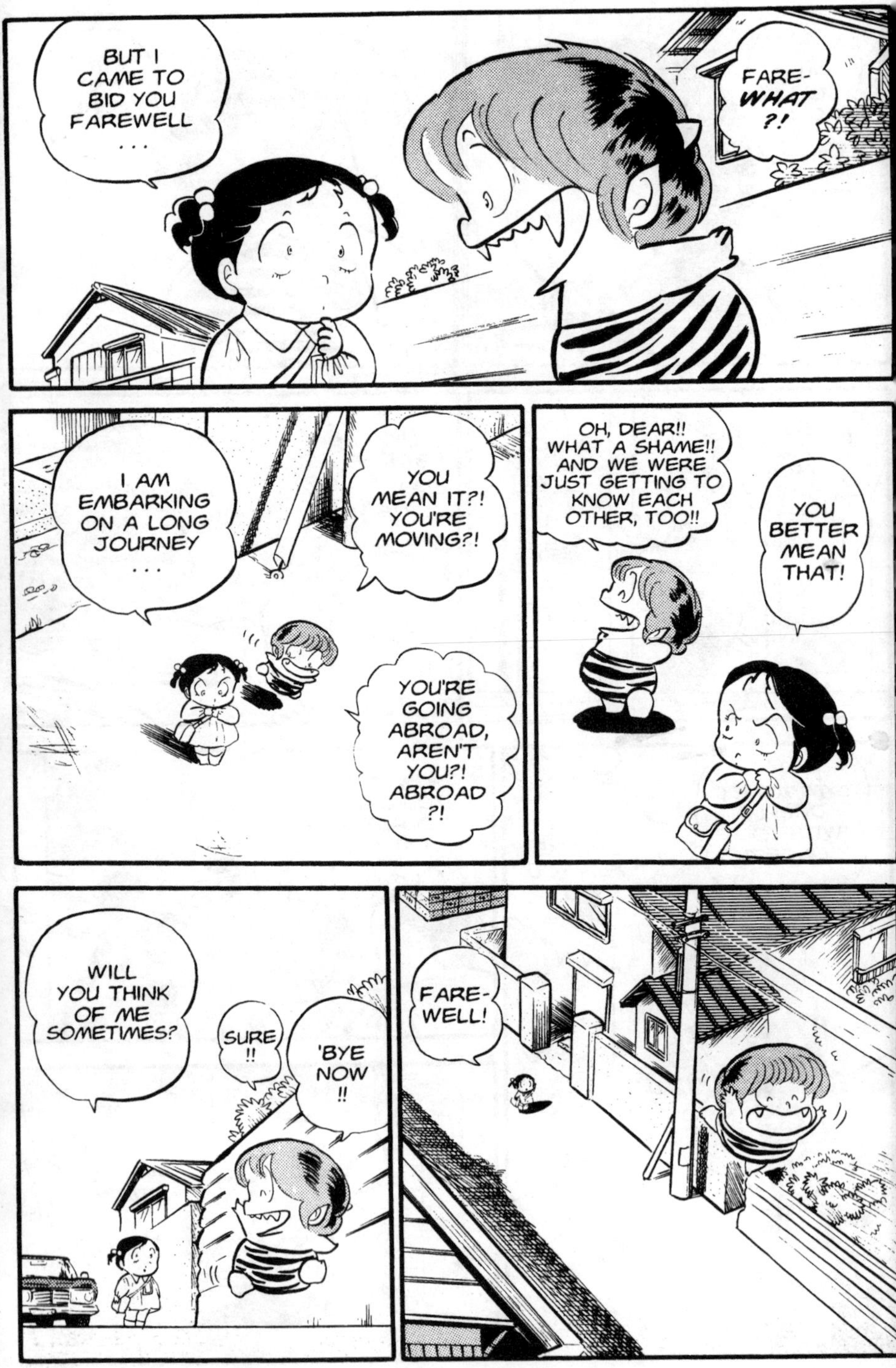
BUT I CAME TO BID YOU FAREWELL . . .
FARE-WHAT ?!
I AM EMBARKING ON A LONG JOURNEY . . .
YOU MEAN IT?! YOU'RE MOVING?!
YOU'RE GOING ABROAD, AREN'T YOU?! ABROAD ?!
OH, DEAR!! WHAT A SHAME!! AND WE WERE JUST GETTING TO KNOW EACH OTHER, TOO!!
YOU BETTER MEAN THAT!
WILL YOU THINK OF ME SOMETIMES?
SURE !!
'BYE NOW !!
FARE-WELL!

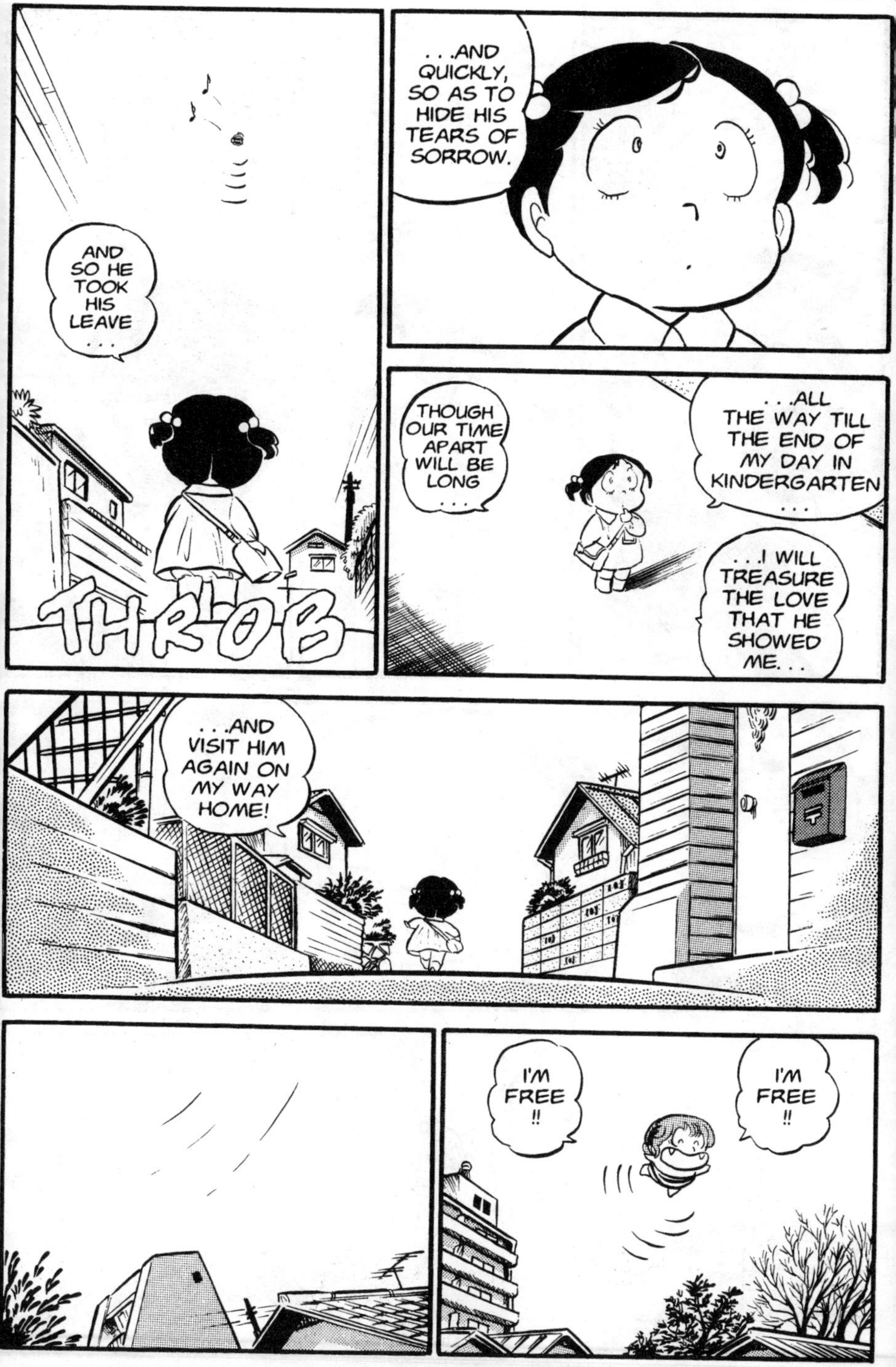
AND SO HE TOOK HIS LEAVE . . .
THROB
. . .AND QUICKLY, SO AS TO HIDE HIS TEARS OF SORROW.
THOUGH OUR TIME APART WILL BE LONG . . .
. . .ALL THE WAY TILL THE END OF MY DAY IN KINDERGARTEN . . .
. . .I WILL TREASURE THE LOVE THAT HE SHOWED ME. . .
. . .AND VISIT HIM AGAIN ON MY WAY HOME!
I'M FREE !!
I'M FREE !!

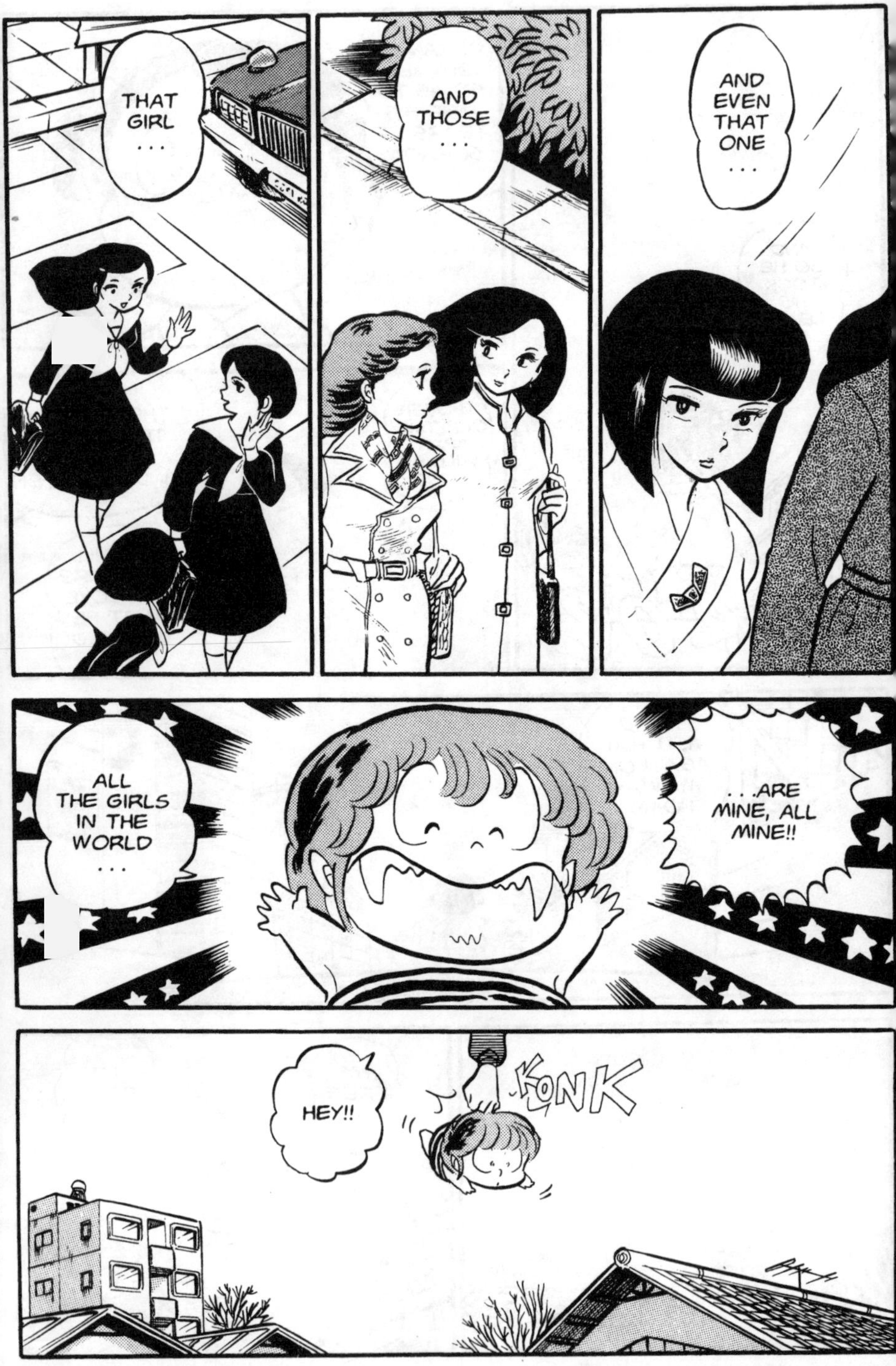
THAT GIRL . . .
AND THOSE . . .
AND EVEN THAT ONE . . .
ALL THE GIRLS IN THE WORLD . . .
. . .ARE MINE, ALL MINE!!
HEY!!
KONK

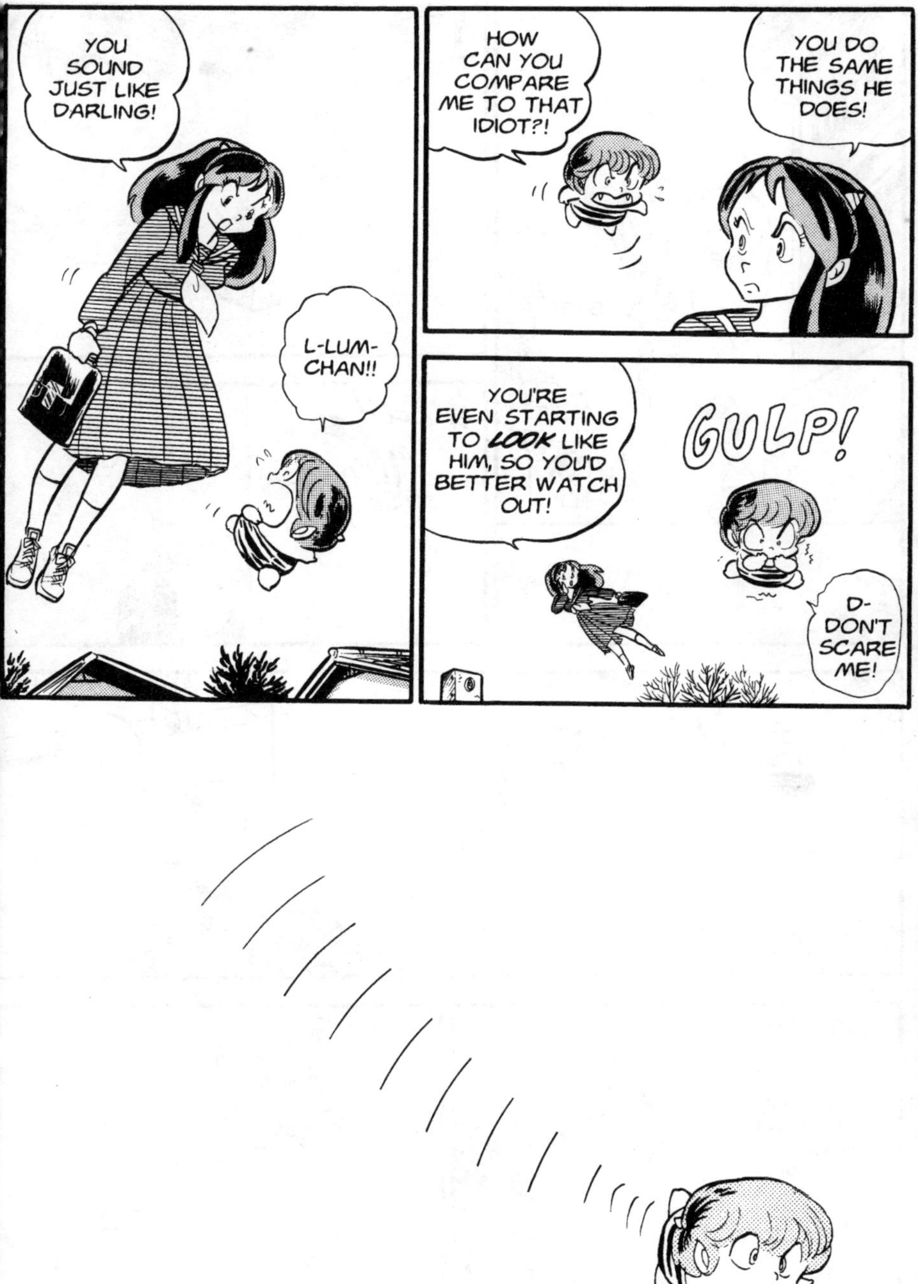
YOU SOUND JUST LIKE DARLING!
L-LUM-CHAN!!
HOW CAN YOU COMPARE ME TO THAT IDIOT?!
YOU DO THE SAME THINGS HE DOES!
YOU'RE EVEN STARTING TO LOOK LIKE HIM, SO YOU'D BETTER WATCH OUT!
GULP!
D-DON'T SCARE ME!

'BYE!

'BYE!

SCREECH

AIEE!
AIEE!
AIEE!

HONEY!

HONEY,
I'VE COME
BACK TO
YOU!

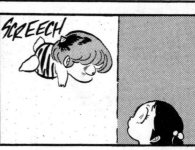

FLAP FLAP

JOG JOG

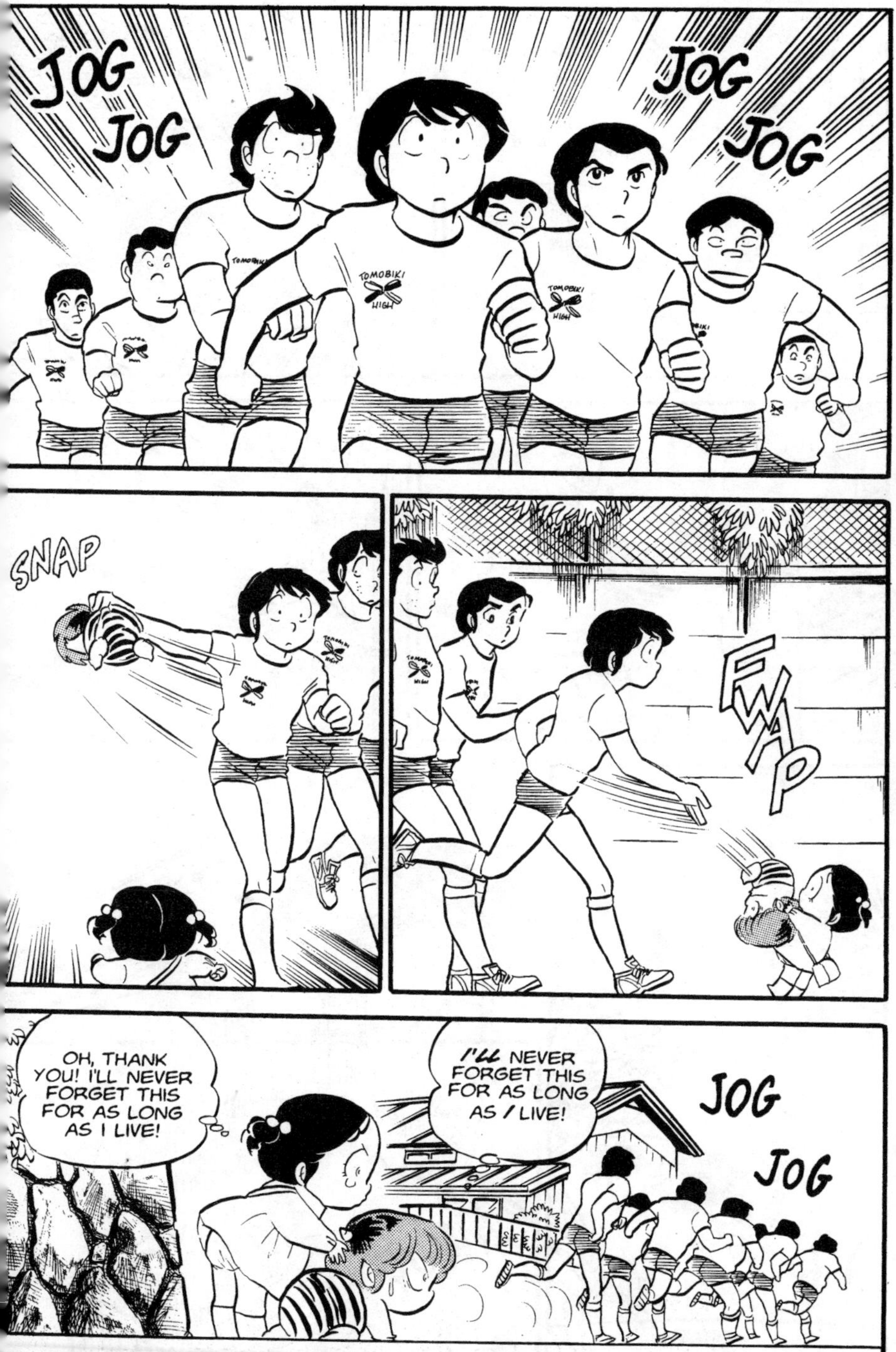
JOG
JOG
JOG
JOG
TOMOBIKI HIGH
TOMOBIKI HIGH
SNAP
TOMOBIKI HIGH
TOMOBIKI HIGH
FWAP
OH, THANK YOU! I'LL NEVER FORGET THIS FOR AS LONG AS I LIVE!
I'LL NEVER FORGET THIS FOR AS LONG AS I LIVE!
JOG
JOG

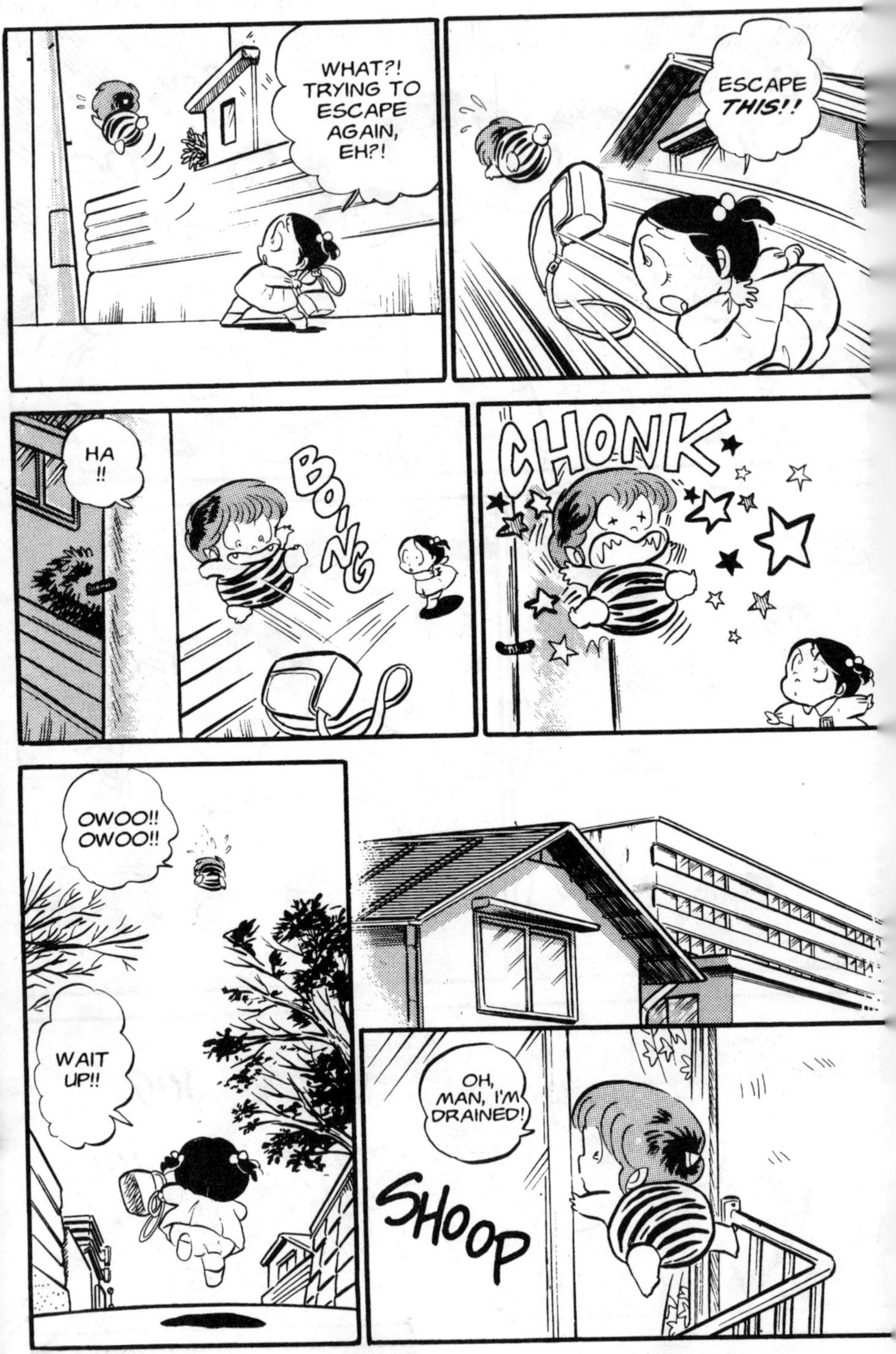
WHAT?! TRYING TO ESCAPE AGAIN, EH?!
ESCAPE THIS!!
HA !!
BOING
CHONK
OWOO!! OWOO!!
WAIT UP!!
OH, MAN, I'M DRAINED!
SHOOP

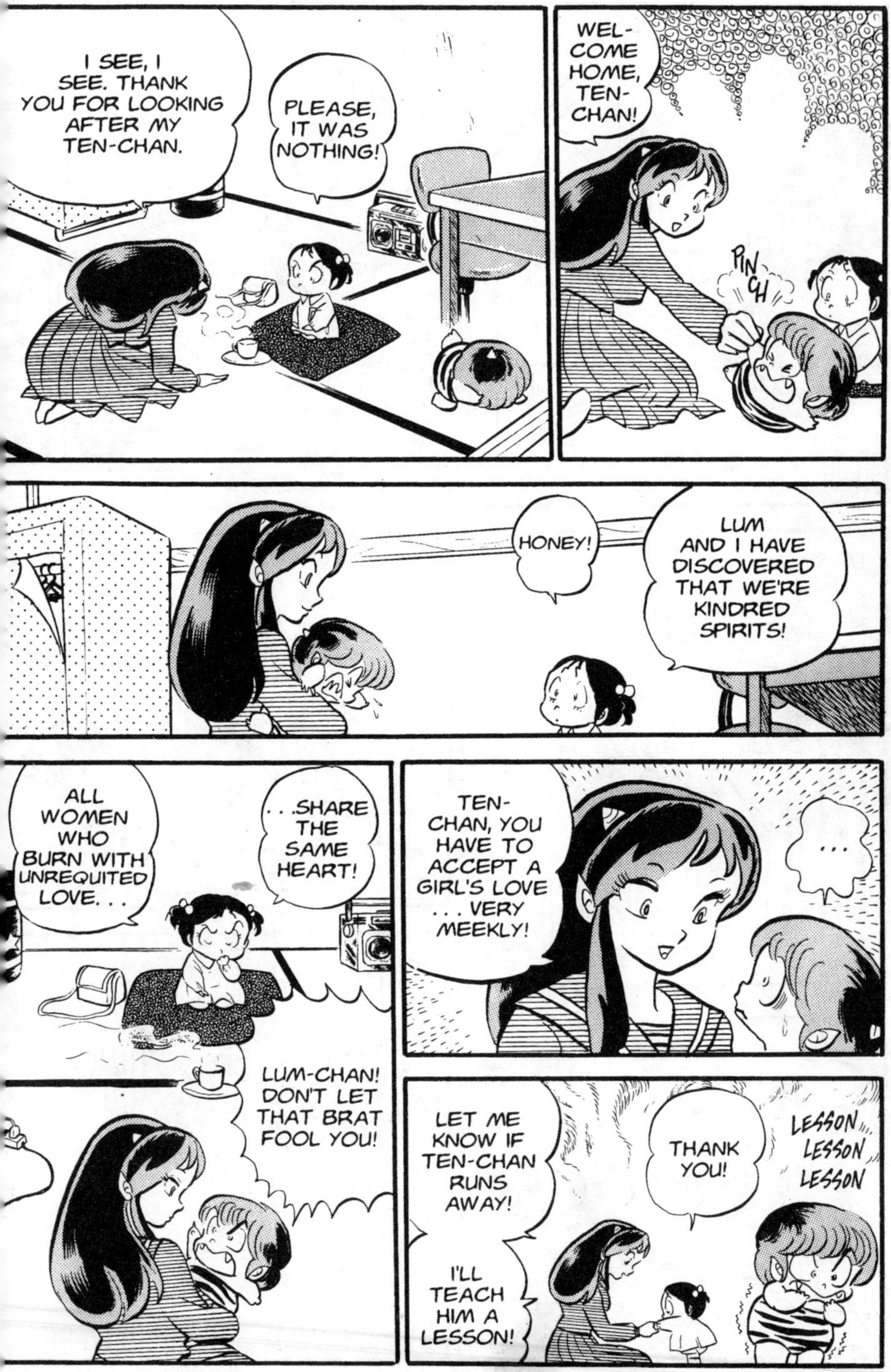
I SEE, I SEE. THANK YOU FOR LOOKING AFTER MY TEN-CHAN.
PLEASE, IT WAS NOTHING!
WEL-COME HOME, TEN-CHAN!
PINCH
HONEY!
LUM AND I HAVE DISCOVERED THAT WE'RE KINDRED SPIRITS!
ALL WOMEN WHO BURN WITH UNREQUITED LOVE. . .
. . .SHARE THE SAME HEART!
TEN-CHAN, YOU HAVE TO ACCEPT A GIRL'S LOVE . . . VERY MEEKLY!
. . .
LUM-CHAN! DON'T LET THAT BRAT FOOL YOU!
LET ME KNOW IF TEN-CHAN RUNS AWAY!
I'LL TEACH HIM A LESSON!
THANK YOU!
LESSON LESSON LESSON

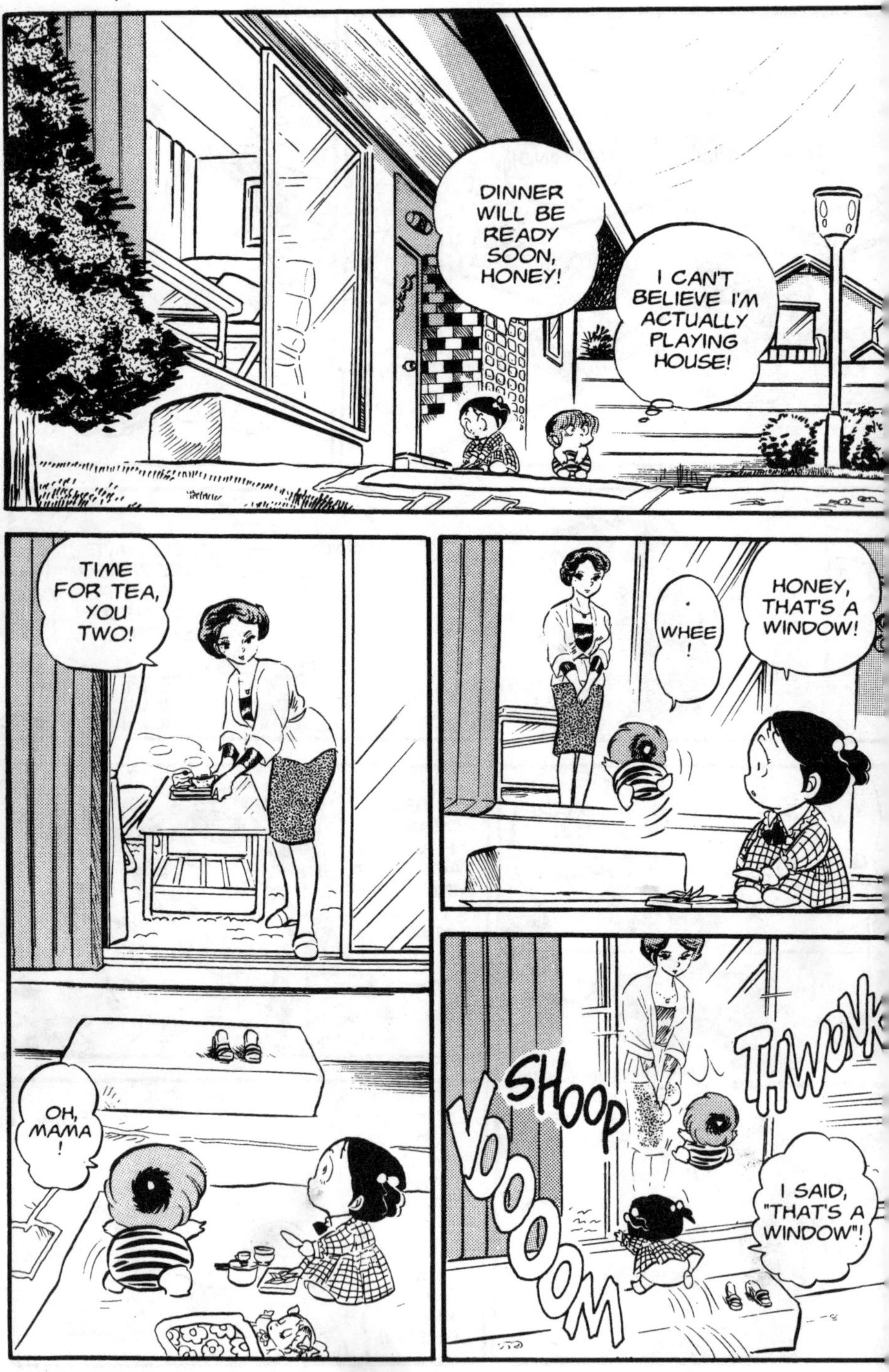
DINNER WILL BE READY SOON, HONEY!
I CAN'T BELIEVE I'M ACTUALLY PLAYING HOUSE!
TIME FOR TEA, YOU TWO!
WHEE!
HONEY, THAT'S A WINDOW!
OH, MAMA!
SHOOP
VOOOOOM
THWONK
I SAID, "THAT'S A WINDOW"!

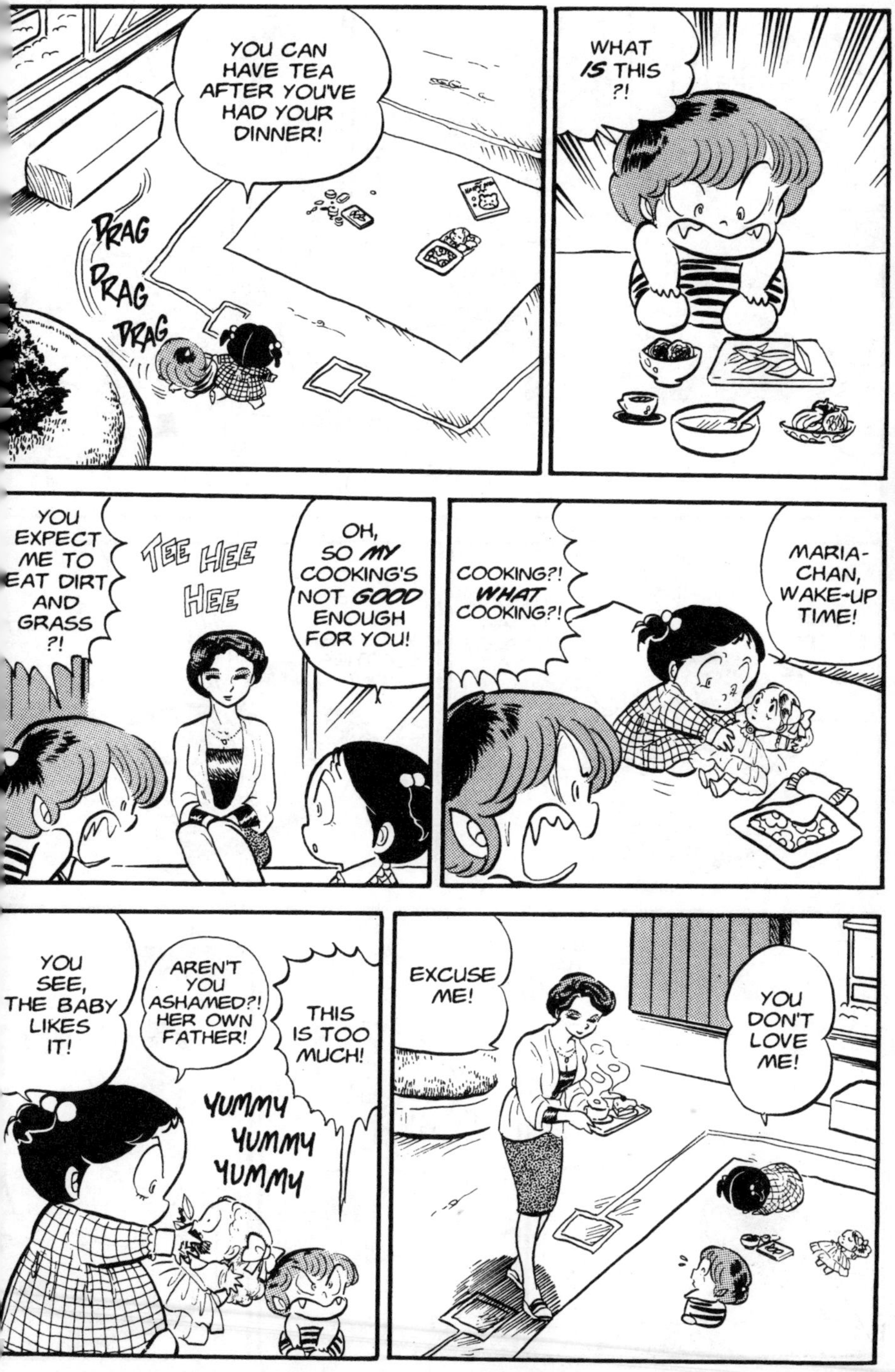
YOU CAN HAVE TEA AFTER YOU'VE HAD YOUR DINNER!
DRAG DRAG DRAG
WHAT *IS* THIS ?!
YOU EXPECT ME TO EAT DIRT AND GRASS ?!
TEE HEE HEE
OH, SO *MY* COOKING'S NOT *GOOD* ENOUGH FOR YOU!
COOKING?! *WHAT* COOKING?!
MARIA-CHAN, WAKE-UP TIME!
YOU SEE, THE BABY LIKES IT!
AREN'T YOU ASHAMED?! HER OWN FATHER!
THIS IS TOO MUCH!
YUMMY YUMMY YUMMY
EXCUSE ME!
YOU DON'T LOVE ME!

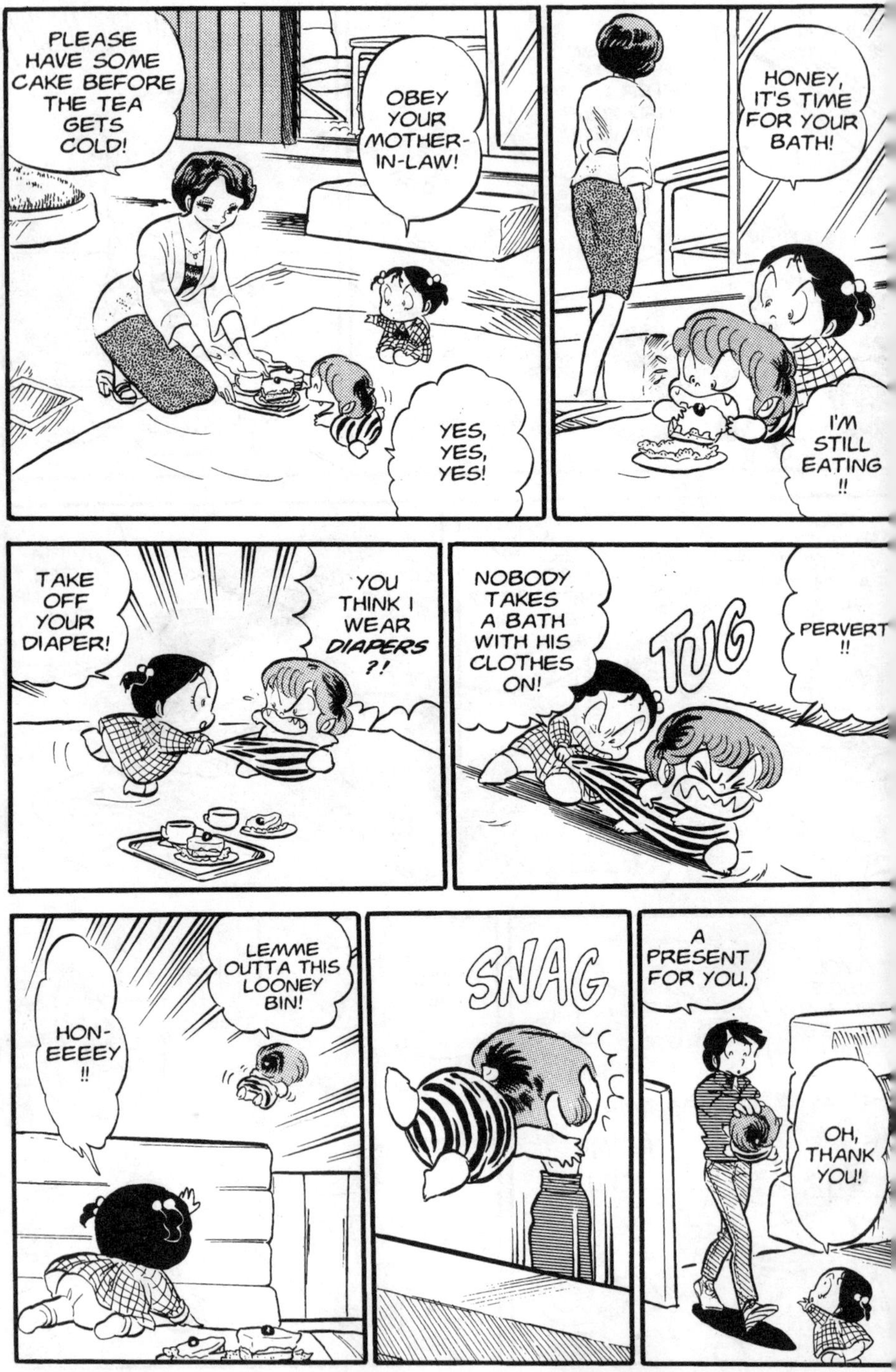
PLEASE HAVE SOME CAKE BEFORE THE TEA GETS COLD!
OBEY YOUR MOTHER-IN-LAW!
YES, YES, YES!
HONEY, IT'S TIME FOR YOUR BATH!
I'M STILL EATING !!
TAKE OFF YOUR DIAPER!
YOU THINK I WEAR DIAPERS ?!
NOBODY TAKES A BATH WITH HIS CLOTHES ON!
TUG
PERVERT !!
HON-EEEEY !!
LEMME OUTTA THIS LOONEY BIN!
SNAG
A PRESENT FOR YOU.
OH, THANK YOU!

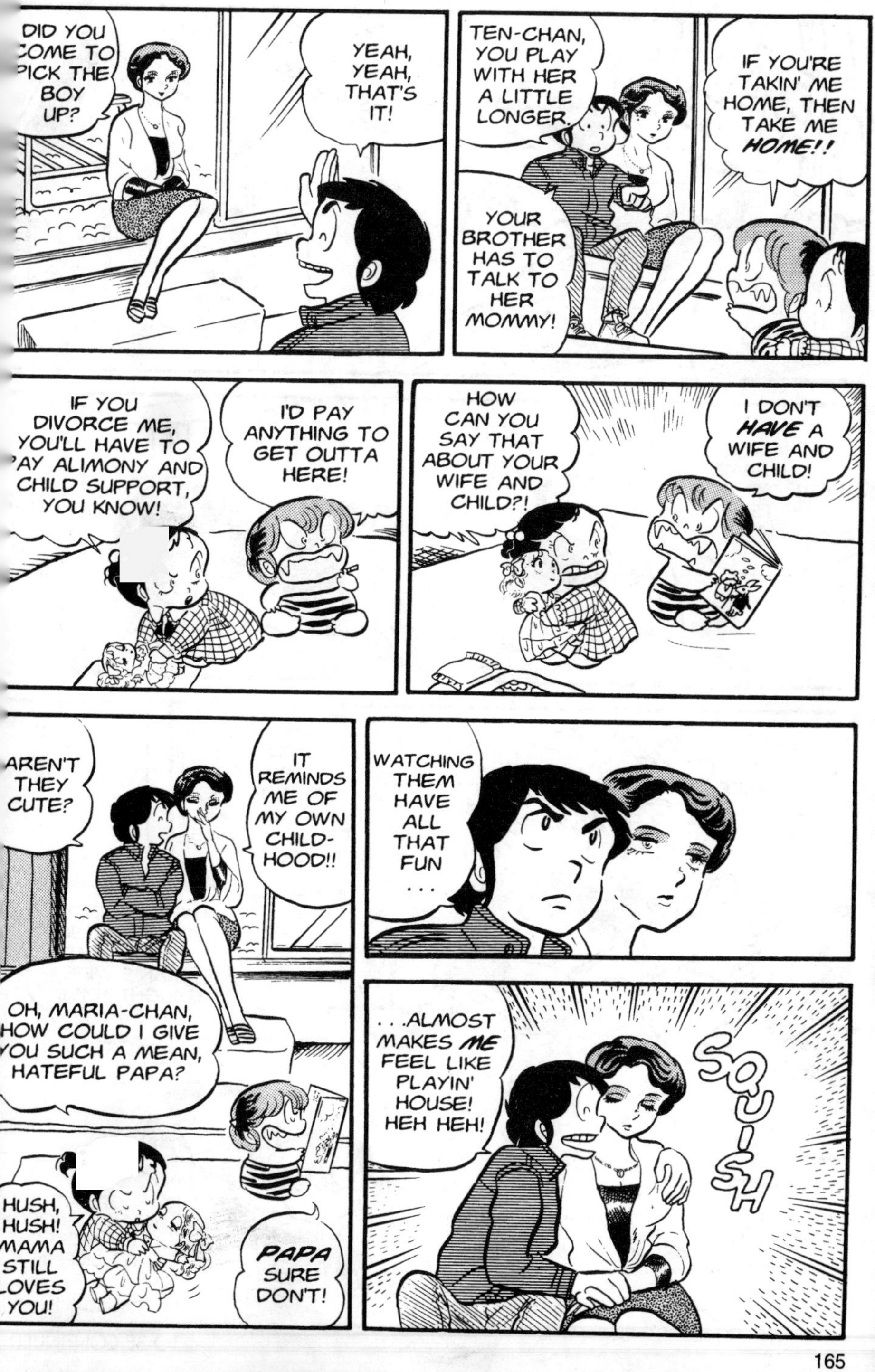
DID YOU COME TO PICK THE BOY UP?
YEAH, YEAH, THAT'S IT!
TEN-CHAN, YOU PLAY WITH HER A LITTLE LONGER.
YOUR BROTHER HAS TO TALK TO HER MOMMY!
IF YOU'RE TAKIN' ME HOME, THEN TAKE ME HOME!!
IF YOU DIVORCE ME, YOU'LL HAVE TO PAY ALIMONY AND CHILD SUPPORT, YOU KNOW!
I'D PAY ANYTHING TO GET OUTTA HERE!
HOW CAN YOU SAY THAT ABOUT YOUR WIFE AND CHILD?!
I DON'T HAVE A WIFE AND CHILD!
AREN'T THEY CUTE?
IT REMINDS ME OF MY OWN CHILD-HOOD!!
OH, MARIA-CHAN, HOW COULD I GIVE YOU SUCH A MEAN, HATEFUL PAPA?
HUSH, HUSH! MAMA STILL LOVES YOU!
PAPA SURE DON'T!
WATCHING THEM HAVE ALL THAT FUN . . .
. . .ALMOST MAKES ME FEEL LIKE PLAYIN' HOUSE! HEH HEH!
SQUISH

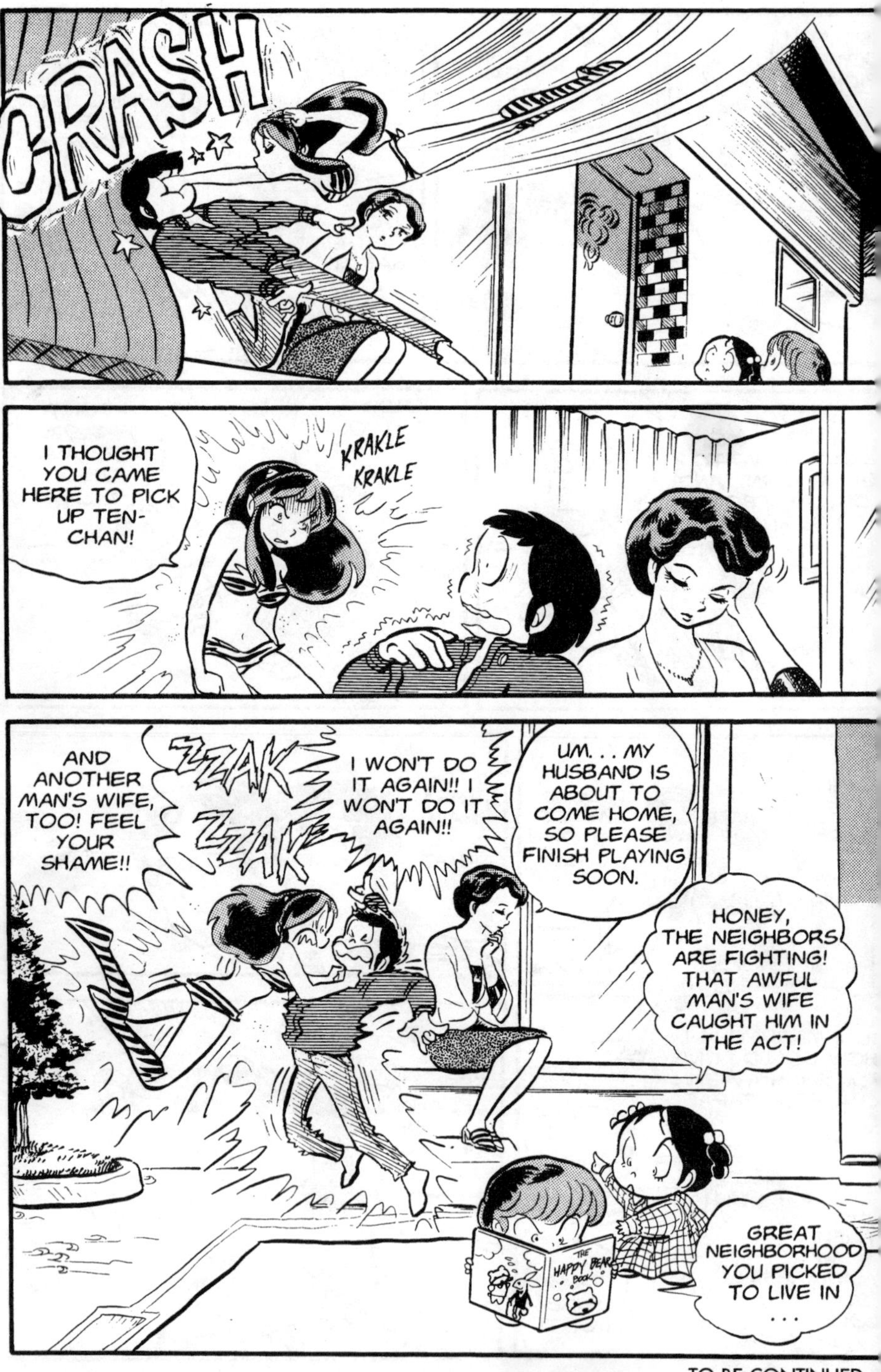
CRASH
I THOUGHT YOU CAME HERE TO PICK UP TEN-CHAN!
KRAKLE KRAKLE
AND ANOTHER MAN'S WIFE, TOO! FEEL YOUR SHAME!!
ZZAK ZZAK
I WON'T DO IT AGAIN!! I WON'T DO IT AGAIN!!
UM. . . MY HUSBAND IS ABOUT TO COME HOME, SO PLEASE FINISH PLAYING SOON.
HONEY, THE NEIGHBORS ARE FIGHTING! THAT AWFUL MAN'S WIFE CAUGHT HIM IN THE ACT!
THE HAPPY BEAR BOOK
GREAT NEIGHBORHOOD YOU PICKED TO LIVE IN . . .

TO BE CONTINUED..

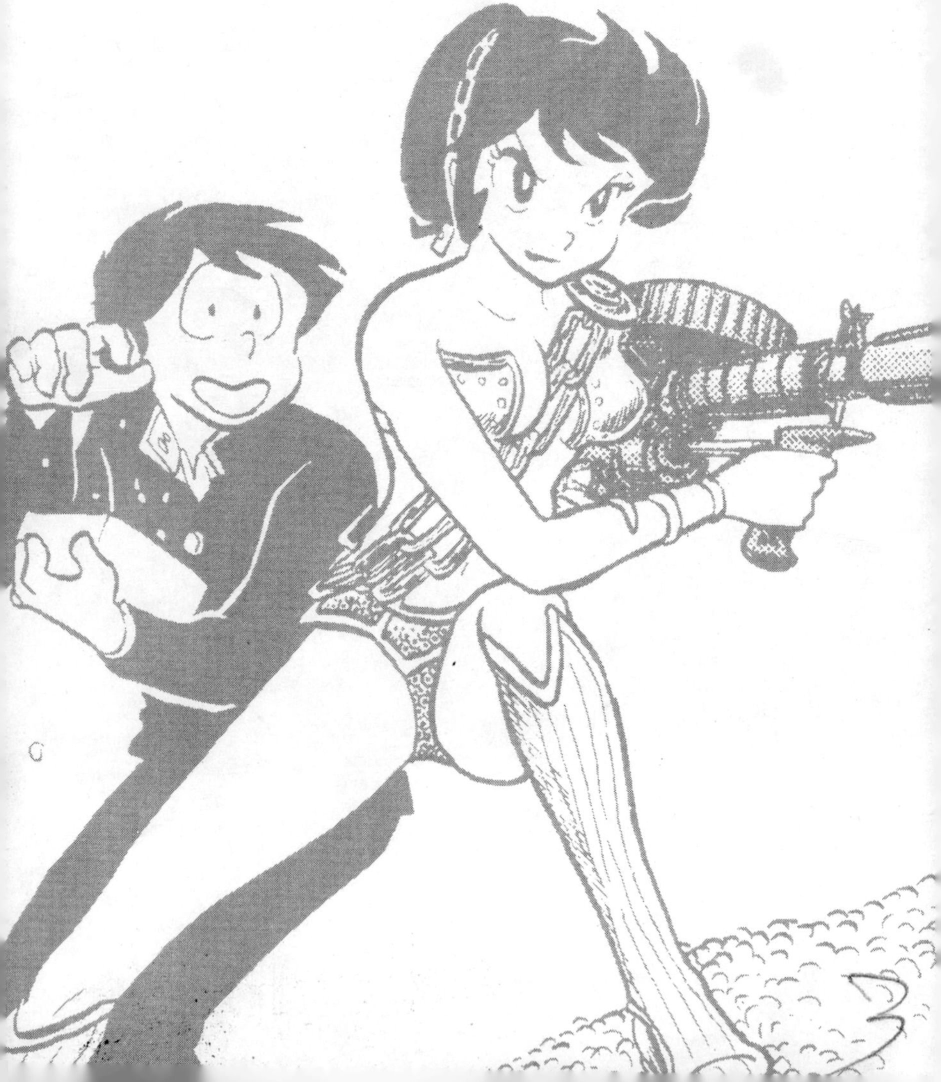